Hollywood
Under Siege

Hollywood Under Siege

Martin Scorsese, the Religious Right, and the Culture Wars

Thomas R. Lindlof

THE UNIVERSITY PRESS OF KENTUCKY

Scholarly publisher for the Commonwealth, serving Bellarmine University, Berea College, Centre College of Kentucky, Eastern Kentucky University, The Filson Historical Society, Georgetown College, Kentucky Historical Society, Kentucky State University, Morehead State University, Murray State University, Northern Kentucky University, Transylvania University, University of Kentucky, University of Louisville, and Western Kentucky University.

Editorial and Sales Offices: The University Press of Kentucky
663 South Limestone Street, Lexington, Kentucky 40508–4008
www.kentuckypress.com

12 11 10 09 08   5 4 3 2 1

Library of Congress Cataloging-in-Publication Data
Lindlof, Thomas R.
   Hollywood under siege : Martin Scorsese, the religious right, and the culture
   wars / Thomas R. Lindlof.
     p.   cm.
   Includes bibliographical references and index.
   ISBN 978-0-8131-2517-6 (hardcover : alk. paper)
   1. Last temptation of Christ (Motion picture)   2. Scorsese, Martin—Criticism
and interpretation.   I. Title.
PN1997.L3443L56   2008
791.43'72—dc22   2008015671

♾This book is printed on acid-free recycled paper meeting the requirements of the American National Standard for Permanence in Paper for Printed Library Materials.

Manufactured in the United States of America.

Member of the Association of American University Presses

To three special women in my life—
Joanne, Joanna, and Shea

Contents

Acknowledgments

Numerous institutions provided research materials that aided me in writing this book: the American Film Institute, the Louis B. Mayer Library; the Academy of Motion Picture Arts and Sciences, the Margaret Herrick Library; the UCLA Film and Television Archive; the University of Southern California, Doheny Library (Cinema-TV Collection); the University of Kentucky Libraries; the University of North Carolina at Chapel Hill Library (Special Collections); Wheaton College, Buswell Memorial Library (Special Collections); the Auburn University, Montgomery Library (Special Collections); Hillsdale College Library; the Vanderbilt Television News Archive; Asbury College Library; the Lexington Theological Seminary Library; and the Chattanooga-Hamilton County (Tennessee) Bicentennial Library (Local History and Genealogy Department). The staff of the University of Kentucky Interlibrary Loan Department, and Jason Kneipp, a library staff member at the University of Alabama, Montgomery, were particularly helpful and responsive to my requests.

A number of private companies and nonprofit organizations provided access to important documents and audiovisual materials: Journal Graphics; Cable News Network; Public Broadcasting Service; People for the American Way; LWT Productions; Cappa Productions; Sikelia Productions; Voyager Company; Institute for First Amendment Studies; Universal Pictures; Center for Visionary Activism; Mastermedia, Inc.; and, in Lexington, WTVQ-TV, WKYT-TV, WLEX-TV, and the *Lexington Herald-Leader* research services department. I owe a special debt to Nancy Lefkowitz (of Cappa Productions) and Marianne Bower (of Sikelia Productions), who graciously and efficiently answered my requests for interviews, photographs, and other materials.

Several individuals shared published and unpublished materials related to *The Last Temptation of Christ* from their private collections: the Reverend Charles Bergstrom, Rich Buhler, John Dart, the Reverend William Fore, Susan Rothbaum, Paul Schrader, Martin Scorsese, John Stewart, the Reverend Robert Thompson, and Harry Ufland. I am honored to have been entrusted with the use of these materials.

Meriting special recognition and thanks are the people whom I interviewed. The vast majority of them had no other reason to cooperate than a desire to have this story told well and accurately. I am deeply grateful for their willingness to talk with me about the events that form the core of this book. Some of them took an interest in the project and referred me to other potential sources of information; these people are Josh Baran, Perry Katz, Harley Lond, Larry Poland, Tom Pollock, Martin Scorsese, Sally Van Slyke, and Dennis Walto. Without this extra help, my research would surely have been much harder to accomplish.

My home institution, the University of Kentucky, consistently supported my work. I am grateful for two sabbatical leaves that afforded me stretches of time to make important progress on this book. Partial financial support for the project was provided through the offices of the Vice-Chancellor of Research and Graduate Studies, the Dean of the College of Communication and Information Studies, and the Director of the School of Journalism and Telecommunications. In particular, I wish to thank Dr. Beth Barnes, the current director of U.K.'s School of Journalism and Telecommunications, whose support of my endeavors is greatly valued.

Over the years, many people contributed to this project in a variety of ways—materially, intellectually, and through their friendship. I appreciate the good work of my research assistants, Chris Easterly and Autumn Grubb, and those who transcribed interview tapes for me: Anneen Boyd, Marianne Clark, Chris Easterly, Steven Jenkins, and Joanne Lindlof. I benefited from conversations about *The Last Temptation of Christ,* the film industry, historical media studies, Christianity, and other topics with many people in and out of the academy: Bruce Austin, Peter Bien, John Clark, Joe Corbitt, Chris Easterly, Monica Ganas, Jim Hertog, Stewart Hoover, Harley Lond, Gregory Ferrell Lowe, Terry Mattingly, Tim Meyer, Darren Middleton, Bob Pekurney, Tom Schatz, Greg Waller, and Justin Wyatt. I also wish to thank a circle of people who devoted time to reading drafts of chapters: Chris Easterly, the Reverend Ronald G. Luckey, Tim Meyer, Naomi Nefertari, Tom Schatz, and the anonymous readers for the University Press of Kentucky. Their appraisals of what I wrote were always useful. Two readers, in particular—my former teachers and current friends, Tom Schatz and Tim Meyer—provided comments that led to key improvements. Tom's critiques of early drafts helped guide me toward a more spacious vision for the book. Tim's evaluation of the manuscript in its final stage was timely and spot-on, and it helped resolve a couple of remaining issues. Of course, I am the only one responsible for the book's deficiencies.

I appreciate the efforts of the staff of the University Press of Kentucky in bringing the book to publication—and especially Leila Salisbury, who took an early interest in the project and shepherded it through the editorial process.

Finally, I thank Joanne Lindlof for all her love, faith, and enthusiasm on this very long and winding road. From the start she helped convince me that the book was worth writing. Along the way, she was an important sounding board and a source of great ideas of her own. And thankfully, she cheered me on as I neared the finish line. Quite simply, this book would not have been possible without her.

Prologue

August 11, 1988—Universal City, California

The news conference was winding down. The last speaker, a Southern Baptist pastor from Atlanta, leaned into the microphones sprouting from the top of the podium, ready to give his peroration to the noonday crowd gathered at the entrance to the Universal Studios Tour. He held up a petition clipped from the *Atlanta Journal.* "We have called Universal time and again. We have contacted their offices. The last conversation, last Friday, what they told us was this: 'We don't care about your petitions. Bring them and dump them with the guards, and we'll put them in a dump.' You know what they were saying? They were saying, 'We don't care about the opinions and the heartbeat of 135,000 Americans.' I want you to know, friends, *we* care about them. And I want you to know *they* can be *made* to care about them. We can't speak to their hearts." He tapped his temple with his finger. "We can't speak to their heads. We can speak to their wallets. Do it with love, but do it!"[1]

And with that, the program's speakers—Christian and Jewish religious leaders, televangelists, talk show hosts, entertainers, and moral values entrepreneurs—rose from their folding chairs. They stood for a minute, exchanging small talk with one another, then walked away as news crews backpedaled in front of them, probing their air space with boom microphones. Suddenly someone with a bullhorn revved up the crowd with chants of "Boycott MCA!"—each time louder and more strident. After the last chorus, the people let loose a hearty burst of cheers and started emptying out of the plaza. Late arrivers came streaming in from parking lots and side streets, joining the crowd that jostled and flowed along toward Lankershim Boulevard. At the bottom of the hill they came up against a row of sawhorses, patrolled by police on horseback.

For a few long minutes they waited. Finally the signal came. The barriers were moved away and the marchers set themselves in motion—"Kind of like the Dodgers had let out at the stadium and [the fans] all were coming down Lankershim Boulevard," a police captain told the *Orange County Register.*[2] Carrying Bibles, placards, and crosses, pushing baby strollers, holding hands, and singing hymns, the thousands of Christians who had driven or ridden church buses from places like Tustin, Long Beach, Pomona, Santa Ana, Azusa, and West Covina strolled the northbound lanes under a blazing sun.

Local TV news helicopters pivoted hundreds of feet overhead. From that vantage, the effect on the city's traffic was dramatically visible from north to south. The Hollywood Freeway was gridlocked for miles from the Universal City off-ramp, and police controlled access to Lankershim all the way to the 134 Freeway a mile to the north. Though the organizers had failed to apply for a permit from the city of Los Angeles, this legality no longer mattered. "There was a momentum there that took on its own mass and nothing could stop it," said John Stewart, a KKLA-FM talk show host and one of the chief organizers, "because we controlled that day."[3]

This was indeed their day, their day to stop traffic and force all of Los Angeles to see the power of their numbers and witness the raw emotion of their complaints. They had heard the tribal drumbeat of southern California's Christian radio stations—KKLA's signal reaching deep into the heart of Los Angeles and the San Fernando Valley, KBRT-AM blanketing Orange County and south all the way to San Diego. Listeners were told, Stewart recalled, to "find one person in their congregation, if they could, who would be willing to put the word out, organize it, and make sure everybody could get there in plenty of time."[4] Reinforced by broadcasts from the PTL television network and the Santa Ana–based Trinity Broadcasting Network, the message roused Californians by the busload and delivered them to Universal City on a hot August weekday, because they believed—in the words of the Reverend Donald Wildmon, the defiant leader of the American Family Association—"M.C.A./Universal planned, the very next day, to release a movie which portrays the Lord Jesus Christ as a liar, a fornicator and a weak, confused, fearful individual unsure of who he is."[5]

Surely no less serious an offense would have brought them to the doorstep of MCA, Inc., the parent company of Universal Pictures. For these Christians in their polo shirts, jeans, ball caps, and sundresses, the act of protesting didn't come naturally.

"The reason I am here is I believe [Universal is motivated by] the almighty dollar," said a Catholic from San Clemente. "We have to step up as Christians. There's too much apathy."[6]

"There comes a time when you have to stand up," said the wife of a retired contractor from San Bernardino. "It seems unreal they can do a film like this."[7]

Asked what she planned to do after that day, an African American women said, "I plan to tell everybody I see, 'Don't see the film.' My school, my church, my acquaintances, my associates. Because it's blasphemous to my Lord and Savior, Jesus Christ."[8]

A bearded, bare-chested young man, white cloth wrapped around his hips, strands of grapevine on his brow, stood with a big wooden cross leaning on his shoulder. Asked how he was going to protest the film, he replied, "Just by bearing witness that Christ died for all men."[9]

The multitude bore witness with their bodies, their hymns and hallelujahs, and the signs they had crafted in recent days and nights in living rooms, kitchens, and church basements. What they displayed to the world was nothing short of a riot of bare-knuckled sloganeering: "Don't Show the Movie!" "Stop This Attack on Christianity." "Faith Not Filth." "Dios No, Sera Burlado." "Universal Is the Devil's Advocate."

Many of the signs showed a flair for phrasemaking: "The Greatest Story Ever Distorted." "Scriptures Not Scripts." "Holy Word Not Hollywood." "The Lie Is $6.50, The Truth Is Free."

One marcher found in Psalms 53:1 the words she needed to channel her fury against the infidel: "The Fool has said, 'There is No God.'"

Another had tacked a bill of particulars to the top of a one-by-four:

> The HISTORICAL DISTORTION *and*
> DEFAMATION *of the* CHARACTER
> *of* Jesus Christ *in this film is* MORALLY
> OFFENSIVE!

Other signs warned of a final justice trumping anything that Hollywood's artisans of screen magic could produce—"Coming Soon: Judgment Day at Universal"; "Get Right or Get Left."

Inscriptions of anti-Semitism also rose darkly out of the maelstrom. One placard reading "Jews II"—alluding simultaneously to Universal's famed shark movie and the Holocaust—floated conspicuously above the crowd at the news conference. Another sign showed a cartoon figure of Adolf Hitler lighting a match to a building called "Universal Studios Gas Chamber." Questioned by a *Chicago Tribune* reporter, the artist said of his work, "I mean no personal attack. . . . But they are rubbing Christians the wrong way, and they know it. So I'm rubbing them back. This sign is fiction, just as their film is."[10]

Inside the Universal Studios complex, security officers approached the heads of departments and offered to evacuate their quarters. Fred Mound, senior vice president of distribution, waved them away from his office suite. "These people aren't going to hurt anybody," he said. "This is a peaceful demonstration."[11] For Universal's production president, Sean Daniel, the reference point for all of this was the civil rights and peace marches of an earlier era, in which he had participated as a student. The irony of now being subjected to an uprising of Christian suburbanites was not lost on him.[12] For others, however, the sight of thousands of agitated people moving past the studio's front door was something new and ominous. "The fact is those folks protesting were within a stone's throw away," one publicity executive said, "and any one of them could have rushed the building. . . . There were moments when I felt if somebody knew what they were doing, and they were fanatical about it, they could really cause some concern."[13]

Set back about fifty yards from Lankershim was Universal's "producer's building," a ziggurat of white terraces and lush foliage that housed the marketing and sales departments. The fourth floor office of Sally Van Slyke, vice president of national publicity, opened onto a balcony that offered a panoramic view of Lankershim Boulevard. With nearly all work at the studio on hold, colleagues from the production, marketing, and distribution departments were coming into her office for a catered lunch of deli sandwiches, potato salad, soft drinks, and bottled water.

The *New York Times* reporter Aljean Harmetz was the only member of the press invited inside the studio that day. During the next week, her stories in the *Times* would disclose how Universal's executives viewed the controversy and what their plans were for opening the film. At Van Slyke's suggestion, Harmetz called Joan Bullard, the spokeswoman for the Universal Studio Tour. Harmetz learned that Universal would probably earn about $4,500 in parking charges from the demonstrators. The congregants on the balcony joked that though receipts from the tour would probably be lower than usual that day, they might make up for it with parking fees.[14]

Possibly thinking about her lead in the next day's *Times* article about the march, Harmetz turned to the person standing next to her, Josh Baran, and asked, "How many people do you think are out there?"[15]

To Baran the question was more than a chance to help a reporter with her story. It was also an unwitting invitation to help his client, Universal Pictures. The president of a Venice Beach public relations firm, Josh Baran had been hired eight months earlier to assess the sensitive religious issues raised by the film and reach out to liberal religious organizations and allied groups. As the controversy stalked the cultural landscape like a tropical storm system, filling newspapers, television news programs, and talk shows with conjectures and debates about the unfinished film, Baran found himself moving into crisis mode—"media-training" Universal's executives, steering reporters toward "friendly" clergy, defending the studio in an unprecedented full-page ad placed in the nation's major newspapers.

Now, with the film's opening just one day away, the media storm seemed to be on the verge of breaking up into potentially dozens of localized disturbances. There were real threats to deal with, and it was Baran's job to make sure the studio had its defenses well organized and its contingency plans in place. At each of the nine theaters showing the film, patrons would pass through metal detectors, off-duty police would search purses and bags, and angry Christians would gather in designated protest areas. For the first time in memory—perhaps for the first time since 1915, when thousands of angry African Americans marched against *The Birth of a Nation*[16]—moviegoing was an act loaded with political significance and fraught with physical danger.

Baran concentrated on how the march at Universal City was going to play in that night's network news programs and the next morning's papers. If the crowd took on the appearance of an immense and unstoppable force, how would it affect the theater owners who had not yet decided whether to book the film and were under intense pressure in their communities not to show it? Would it inflame virulent protests across the American heartland?

A large protest—or even a "larger-than-expected" turnout—is often critical to the news media's story hook. Reports of impressive crowd sizes lend credence to the organizers' claims that their cause has broad-based support; they also reverberate within a movement itself, stirring strong feelings of community among members and helping attract others to the cause. An extraordinary crowd can even make history, persisting in the collective memory for decades: the twenty-five thousand who crossed the Potomac to encircle the Pentagon in the first major Vietnam War protest in 1965; the half million who trekked to Woodstock in 1969; the Million Man March that thrust the Nation of Islam onto the national stage in 1995.

A smaller crowd, on the other hand, is usually all it takes to consign stories of protest to the back pages or push them off the media agenda altogether. It can also signal a setback—if not an abject failure—of the group's message, deflating the spirits of organizers and foot soldiers alike.

"I don't know, Aljean," Josh Baran finally said. "Seven thousand?"

Baran himself did not necessarily trust the number he gave her, but the public's perception of the attack on Universal was at stake.

"Nobody knows how to count crowds," Baran said later. "It's all lies, it's all nonsense. . . . So, when I said seven, she just wrote the damn thing down. I would have guessed there were twenty or thirty thousand people or more, but who knows? Who knows?"[17]

The next morning, the headline above Harmetz's byline read, "7,500 Picket Universal over Movie about Jesus." Not only did she not source the number, it turned out to be the lowest estimate reported by the nation's major media outlets. The *Philadelphia Inquirer* described a crowd of 10,000—a number echoed by ABC's Peter Jennings—and the *Chicago Tribune* reported "a crowd estimated by police at 10,000 to 15,000 people." But CBS's Dan Rather, the *Atlanta Journal,* and the *Los Angeles Times,* all put the crowd at 25,000, also citing police sources. John Dart, the religion reporter for the *Los Angeles Times,* saw his colleague Russell Chandler's number before the story was filed and thought that "he took a high figure that wasn't warranted. . . . The journalist's temptation is to go with the higher figure, because if you go with the lower figure, you're going to look silly if somebody else has the higher figure."[18]

Crucially, the Associated Press took the highest figure of 25,000 in the story it moved to hundreds of newspapers that day. This number has since been replicated in nearly every account of those occurrences of August 11, 1988. Whatever the reality of that day, the event at Universal City had secured its place as the largest public protest of a media company in U.S. history.[19]

Their lunch finished, the executives settled back to watch, as if they were viewing a Fourth of July parade. Many of the executives had only the slightest familiarity with the evangelical Christian culture. They laughed when a convoy of leather-jacketed Christ's Sons, a motorcycle club from Orange County, rumbled by on their choppers. They were surprised to see people of African, Asian, and Hispanic heritage walking among the mainly white crowd. One of them recalled, "We'd wave to them, and they waved back, but they didn't realize those were the key people they were probably targeting."[20] Some of the studio's own employees joined the march and waved good-naturedly to their bosses on Sally Van Slyke's balcony.

The overwhelming majority of the marchers were peaceful and meant no harm. But during the previous two months, a number of disturbing incidents had prompted the studio to take special precautions. The death threats received by MCA's senior executives were met with a solution familiar to this high-profile world: round-the-clock bodyguards. Their families were frightened, but Lew Wasserman; MCA's president, Sidney J. Sheinberg; and Tom

Pollock, Universal's motion picture division chairman, understood that the top officials of media companies—particularly Jewish officials who approve the release of controversial pictures—would always be targeted by the rabid fringe of the Christian right. "They've been killing me for years," Wasserman said wearily to Pollock at one point during the crisis.[21]

Even Sally Van Slyke, publicly visible as the studio's spokesperson, had become the target of vicious threats. With her staff she managed to keep her composure and resolve intact. As one colleague put it, "She was our lieutenant, in many cases our general, in getting through this whole thing."[22]

No one on the balcony that day knew better than Tom Pollock how they had reached this pass. When Pollock sat down in February 1987 with Martin Scorsese and his wife, the producer Barbara De Fina, to discuss a film based on the novel, he was aware of its brief, troubled life at Paramount years earlier. Paramount's president, Michael Eisner, and the studio's production chief, Jeffrey Katzenberg, were attracted to the concept of a fresh take on the Christ

Sally Van Slyke and Tom Pollock at Universal Studios, August 11, 1988, with marchers on Lankershim Boulevard in the background. (Author's collection)

story, especially one that America's most brilliant filmmaker was passionate to make. Through the summer of 1983 and into the fall, budget concerns, casting difficulties, and a sudden change of producers plagued the project. But it was the Christian outrage boiling up seemingly out of nowhere that most seriously worried Paramount's management, and rumors of the movie's death spiral spread across the film community. Finally, after enduring torrents of mail at Gulf + Western's Manhattan offices, Chief Executive Officer Martin Davis placed the call to Barry Diller, Paramount's chairman, to stop the project just weeks before production was to begin.

Trepidations from the Paramount debacle shadowed the project's arrival at Universal. Soon after the meeting with Scorsese, when he was told that the project was going to be approved, Sid Sheinberg warned Pollock about the possible consequences for the company. As Sheinberg remembered it, "I expressed to him my concern that he was entering into an area where frankly we would have a lot of potential aggravation, and I'm not sure I really knew the ultimate commercial reason for this aggravation because I never thought that [this film] was a subject matter that would become very successful."[23] But there was a difference between Pollock's informing Sheinberg or Wasserman of his intent to green-light a film and asking for either's approval. "The decision was not theirs," Pollock was to say later. "And unless they had been radically opposed to it, I would have gone ahead and made it anyway. Because you don't ask permission unless you're prepared to follow what someone else says."[24]

Then there was the reaction months earlier of Josh Baran, who told Pollock, after reading the script and enduring a couple of sleepless nights, that this was going to be the most controversial film ever released by any studio in the history of the movie business. He said to Pollock, "Tom, this is certain. This film is going to shake the studio. This is going to be like a nuclear bomb." Pollock asked him how he could be sure. Wasn't he exaggerating? "I don't think so," said Baran.[25]

But Tom Pollock was still at a place where he could not understand *why* people were incensed. Taking off his necktie and suit coat, he left Van Slyke's office and walked alone through the marketing department—the bunker, it had been called during these crisis-filled weeks—through the studio gate and out to Lankershim Boulevard. Pollock didn't tell the marchers who he was. Still, he felt nervous. He had been named in newsletters, petitions, and fact sheets distributed by the American Family Association and Focus on the Family and other groups as one of the "non-Christian" MCA executives responsible for this reviled film. The frequent misspellings of his name—"Tom Pollack"—were annoying enough, but what truly bewildered him were the blatant misrepresentations of the film and Universal's motives that he read about in this literature and saw on the religious cable channels.

He moved among the marchers, wanting to find out why they came, what they were saying, what they knew about the film. He began by asking, "Why are you here?"

'Cause last Sunday in church, my minister told me to come.

"Well, what do you think is going on here?"

Well, they have Jesus having sex. They have Jesus in a homosexual affair. They're desecrating my Lord. They can't do that.

"And of course nobody had seen the movie," Pollock recalled. "They were all misinformed. . . . By then, logic and rationality were gone."

After a certain point, it was not enough simply to absorb what they were saying about a movie they had not seen. He felt compelled to tell one of them, "Well, I have seen the movie, and in fact, Jesus is not portrayed as a homosexual."[26] It is not known what the interlocutor thought of this information from the Universal chairman.

After spending a half hour questioning the people who hated his organization and the movie it was now introducing to the nation, Tom Pollock reentered the studio gate. He had a few hours left to attend to the afternoon's other business before getting ready for the next day's premiere, when *The Last Temptation of Christ* would open in New York, Los Angeles, Chicago, San Francisco, and five other cities at theaters owned by the Cineplex Odeon chain. Audiences would finally be able to judge for themselves Martin Scorsese's effort to "push the concept of Jesus into the twenty-first century,"[27] as the director put it.

Taking a last look at the crowd before walking back to his office, Pollock asked a question that, Aljean Harmetz noted in the next day's *New York Times,* was not in the least rhetorical: "Do you think anyone will come tomorrow?"[28]

BY ALMOST any standard, the firestorm accompanying the release of *The Last Temptation of Christ* was beyond the pale of media controversies before or since. No film since *Last Temptation*—not *Do the Right Thing, Natural Born Killers, Basic Instinct, Dogma, The Passion of the Christ, Farenheit 911, Brokeback Mountain,* or *The Da Vinci Code*—aroused the passions of a wider spectrum of the public, involved the country's religious, political, and media communities to a greater degree, or resulted in more worldwide actions against distributors, theaters, and theater owners. By the day of the massive rally at MCA

headquarters, the film had already borne an unreasonable, maybe even irratio-
nal, burden of expectations. Large numbers of religious conservatives were
fully invested in the belief that Hollywood would run roughshod over their
values and way of life if Martin Scorsese's film was allowed to open unchal-
lenged, while many of the film community's decision makers and artists
believed their free speech rights and economic prerogatives would be put in
jeopardy if they did not act aggressively to turn back the challenge.

Ironically, this crisis swirled around what some considered an "art film,"
a film that—according to statements by its director, screenwriter, and actors—
was never intended to foist a tabloid version of Jesus on America. *The Last
Temptation of Christ* boasted no A-list stars. It certainly did not appeal to the
cherished moviegoer demographic of twelve- to twenty-four-year-olds. It had
a running time of 164 minutes and a pace that often slowed for disquisitions
on faith, God, and love. Clearly unfit as a vehicle for contributing to any of
the revenue streams that large, diversified media corporations have come to
expect from their motion picture divisions—such as licensed merchandise,
theme park exploitation, and sequels—the film's only promotional hooks were
its distinctions as a Martin Scorsese picture and as an alternative, "what-if"
version of the Christ story. And the latter was arguably more of a liability than
a benefit, given the weak performance of other religious-themed films of the
eighties, such as Monty Python's supremely irreverent satire, *The Life of Brian,*
and Jean-Luc Godard's modern allegory, *Hail Mary.* At the end of its North
American theatrical run, *The Last Temptation of Christ* had played in only 140
theaters and grossed $8,373,000, which put it in the bottom ten of 1988's top
one hundred releases.[29]

How did this austere, commercially unpromising film arouse the ire of so
many Americans? Why was it seen as such a moral and spiritual calamity that
the mere possibility of its release was attacked at every turn?

One answer, of course, is that it wasn't the size or the popularity of the
film, but its subject matter and the way it was realized artistically, that caused
the provocation. But this answer is not only inadequate, it begs still other
questions. Whose story of Christ was it? What was the vision, the artistic
argument, that animated this work of fiction, and how did it persevere through
one obstacle after another? How did two major motion picture companies
arrive at the decision of making a film so far afield from the types they normally produce, a film that was practically radioactive in its implications—and
why did one of them back out of its commitment? How did the movie become
captive to the social and political forces at play in the late twentieth century,

as well as a force of its own, shaping the battlegrounds of future culture war struggles? And what does this episode reveal about the dramatic arc of media-inspired controversies, about the logics, strategies, and tactics that keep a culture war dispute alive until it is of no further use to those who created it?

This book is the story of a work of the imagination—and ultimately, of Hollywood itself—under siege. Drawing on interviews with many of the principals and previously unused historical materials, the book tells how a singularly provocative film became entangled in Hollywood's priorities; the motives, miscalculations, and courage of those who brought it to the screen; the dialogue it engendered about the parallel cultures in the United States that have grown further apart in the years since; and the lasting effect the film and its conflicted reception had on the entertainment industry.

All controversies are supernovae of popular discourse. And at least one measure of the success of works like *The Last Temptation of Christ* is their ability to energize people's voices about the things that matter most to them. As the controversy peaked in the summer of 1988, *Last Temptation* stimulated conversations at all levels of the public sphere about freedom of speech and access to art in a pluralistic society; the putative power of religious leaders and their constituencies; the secular media industry's obligations to the public, particularly when it intervenes in the spiritual arena; and, in a more reflexive vein, what it means for this or any other issue to blow up into highly polarized forms of opinionated talk. This book explores how *The Last Temptation of Christ*—or, more accurately, people's ideas of what the film represented—triggered debates about a range of issues concerning art, religion, and cultural politics that were latent in the national consciousness and are still being debated today.

The Christian right's efforts to bring a media conglomerate to its knees was also a highly visible part of the summer's spectacle. The beleaguered studio saw its normally secure grip on exhibition melt away; boycotts against MCA were first threatened, then announced; and the company's senior management team was vilified as latter-day crucifiers, which revived fears of Jewish dominance among the Hollywood elite, and of interfaith antipathy more generally. MCA, and the motion picture industry as a whole, responded with one of the toughest defenses ever mounted on behalf of any film, company, or individual. These unfolding events, so "real" as they undoubtedly appeared to most Americans, belied the extent of their construction by publicity specialists, the mainstream news and entertainment press, and other cultural players.

The Last Temptation of Christ was in fact one of the first instances—and is, in many respects, still the prototype—of the strategic employment of certain practices for calibrating (or manipulating) a culture war drama. Today many of these practices have become routine. Indeed, the notion that controversies are triggered solely by the transgressive actions of an artist is largely a myth. Creative projects now usually come from writers, directors, and performers who have proven themselves capable of skillfully probing the boundaries of social conventions, moral codes, and good taste. For their part, studios study the risks and benefits of edgy, envelope-pushing films early in the development process. As soon as such films are ready to roll out, sophisticated publicity campaigns engage with audiences through the ever-proliferating apparatus of talk shows, entertainment news magazines, op-ed columns, Web sites, blogs, and so forth. And if moral panics erupt, crisis managers stand ready to frame the terms of the debates and, if necessary, limit the collateral damage suffered by their clients.

Advocacy groups also depend on a steady flow of provocative content to advance their causes. They run a well-tuned machinery of their own, pushing their views and mobilizing their troops on cable TV channels, talk radio, and direct-mail and Internet operations. Even if such groups do not actually foment culture war flare-ups, many of them are ever on the lookout for media products that can be vilified for violating the transcendent values they hold dear.

Simply put, professional accomplices are required at least as much as true believers for a crisis to go to full incandescence. Through all their efforts, a film transcends its status as a commodity and becomes a highly charged token of moral drift, artistic integrity, or any number of other imputed qualities. The danger of this path, however, lies in its essential unpredictability. For all those who are tempted to exploit the prevailing tensions in the public sphere, there is always the chance of misplaying (or misunderstanding) their roles in the drama. This book reveals the logic and tactical maneuvering of a media company—behavior that was often skillful, but also sometimes less than perfectly executed—when it was required to shift abruptly from business-as-usual to uneasy, sometimes hostile encounters with the public, news media, and theater owners. This side of the film's journey—the boiler-room dynamics of crisis control at full bore—is, in the words of one of the key figures, "the greatest story never told."

The trajectory of this tempest would surely have been different—indeed, it might not even have happened—were it not for the extraordinary vision of the novelist who wrote this work more than fifty years ago and the sheer ambition and tenacity of the film's director. The penultimate work of Nikos Kazantzakis' most productive period of writing, and his second-biggest seller, after *Zorba the Greek, The Last Temptation* was the first major novel to explore the humanity of Jesus and the struggles forced by his dual nature as God and man. Under attack almost as soon as it left its author's hand, the novel moved indomitably ahead. From the furor aroused by the novel's European publication, to censorship attempts in the United States in the 1960s, to the worldwide battles against the film and its video release, critics and defenders have clashed repeatedly over the story's speculative thesis and its Nietzschean hero.

Last Temptation's long march to the screen was marked by a willful pursuit of the improbable, even by the standards of an industry inured to grandiose ambition. Indeed, few other motion pictures faced such formidable obstacles just getting to production. A passion of Martin Scorsese's for more than fifteen years, Nikos Kazantzakis' version of the Christ story was never easily digestible material in the context of Hollywood's commercial imperatives. Just when it was widely thought to be unmakeable, the project was shepherded into production through the concerted efforts of two of the most powerful players of the 1980s: Michael Ovitz, president of Creative Artists Agency, and Tom Pollock, Universal Pictures chairman. The deal they engineered played a large role in reestablishing Scorsese as a sought-after director with the prestige to have his films financed by major studios.

Although critics disagree about where *The Last Temptation of Christ* ranks with the rest of Scorsese's work, almost all agree that the film's startling imagery and unusual interpretations of Christ's life broke decisively with the biblical epic tradition. For the first time, a film coming out of the Hollywood system dealt seriously with Christ's relevance in the post-Enlightenment age. The importance of the film for Scorsese himself is also undeniable. *The Last Temptation of Christ* articulated with disarming frankness many of the themes that had always been implicit in his work. It spoke in the most elemental way to his lifelong concerns with personal redemption and the possibility of living heroically in a corrupted world.

As Scorsese said in our conversation: "I was very zealous about making a film about Jesus, ultimately to engage the spectator and make it accessible to a modern viewer. More accessible than the things of the past. And the first thing, in order to do that, was to do the film unlike any of the films that had been done about Jesus. And to make Jesus's character according to the Kazantzakis book, which is fully divine and human—but the fully human side, *so* human that those in the audience who were despairing and saying, 'Oh, I'm no good, I've done this, I've done that, and I pray to Jesus but that's not going to help me'—And no, he feels the same way in the film. So *he* knows, you know. He knows."

This is where the tale begins, with two artists—separated by thirty-five years, both of them functioning at the highest levels of their respective fields—striving to say something daringly original about the most important spiritual figure in the Western world and the greatest inspiration of their own lives. And oblivious to the consequences.

1

Dying Dangerously

FOR ALMOST AS LONG as Christianity has existed, authors have
retold the life of Jesus Christ. The vast majority of these plays,
poems, stories, and novels are unabashedly devotional. Their purpose, wrote
Theodore Ziolkowski in *Fictional Transfigurations of Jesus,* "is to produce a
Poor Man's Jesus, as it were, a Gospel reduced to the lowest common denomi-
nator of the times and put into terms that require no effort of the imagination."[1] Making far greater demands on readers' imaginations are works that
conjure entirely new mythologies of his life. The impulse to say something
daringly original about the Christ figure has erupted in novels as diverse as
D. H. Lawrence's *The Man Who Died* (1930), Robert Graves's *King Jesus* (1946),
José Saramago's *The Gospel according to Jesus Christ* (1994), Norman Mailer's
The Gospel according to the Son (1997), Jim Crace's *Quarantine* (1999), and
Nino Ricci's *Testament: A Novel* (2003).

There is no one template or formula for these literary experiments. Some
authors draw on archaeological evidence, historical theory, and other scholarly
sources to re-create the world of two thousand years ago. Others try to deconstruct Jesus psychologically, using today's metaphors or modes of analysis. Still
others use the Christ story as a canvas for projecting their own concerns or
conflicts. Whatever their motives, writers typically set anchor just far enough
into the Scriptures to ground their fiction in a commonly recognizable Jesus,
before going on to confront readers with new voices, new themes, and new
questions about his identity. What actually happened at critical junctures of
his life? What are the alternative ways of interpreting his relationships with
the disciples, Mary Magdalene, his family, God? What could have been the
nature of his psyche, his emotions and aspirations? Who was he, *really?* Was
he a great ethical teacher? An unusually powerful healer and exorcist? Was he
a political revolutionary, a Jewish prophet with an apocalyptic message? Or
was he what the Gospels say he was: a singular man both human and divine
who was bodily resurrected?

Inevitably, writers take enormous artistic risks when they enter this territory. As Salman Rushdie suggested in his essay "Is Nothing Sacred?" it is in the nature of novels to go where a sacred text cannot: "Whereas religion seeks to privilege one language above all others, one set of values above all others, one text above all others, the novel has always been about the way in which different languages, values and narratives quarrel, and about the shifting relations between them, which are relations of power."[2]

Few writers brought more quarreling values and narratives to bear on the authority of the Gospels than the Greek poet and novelist Nikos Kazantzakis. His 1955 novel, *The Last Temptation of Christ,* was in many ways the capstone of a lifetime trying to reclaim the values of early Christianity, "such as love, brotherhood, humility, and self-renunciation," as Lewis A. Richards observed about Kazantzakis' ideals.[3] A philosophical expeditionary, Kazantzakis was at one time or another a disciple of Henri Bergson, Frederick Nietzsche, Karl Marx, Buddha, St. Francis, and a mine worker named George Zorbas—the model for his most popular book, *Zorba the Greek.* He especially admired the fearless attitude of Nietzsche, who wrote, in *Thus Spoke Zarathustra,* "Mankind is a rope fastened between animal and superman—a rope over an abyss." One crosses over this existential abyss, Kazantzakis believed, only by acting creatively and fearlessly. And to be able to do that, one must cast off society's petty illusions—chief among them the institutional Church. In Kazantzakis' jaundiced opinion, the Church has kept a grip on its earthly protectorate of power and privilege by holding out the promise of eternal life to its flock.

But Kazantzakis was a religious man in his own fashion. "It is not God who will save us," he famously wrote in *The Saviors of God,* "it is we who will save God, battling, by creating, and by transmuting matter into spirit."[4] In this view, God is an unfinished project and we are all potentially saviors-in-the-making. But the greatest, most honorable savior was Christ, who gave humankind the best example of how to give oneself over to the creative, vital action of love. The novel Kazantzakis decided to write in the early 1940s would tell how this supremely heroic life could have unfolded—a Christ who battles the old, bankrupt orders of materialism, family, and tradition, and whose every step toward the cross is a step toward union with God. He wanted readers to feel the reality of Christ's radical intervention in the world and rediscover the liberating power of belief in him. At first, while living in Greece under German occupation, he was going to give it the title *Christ's Memoirs.*[5] Eight years later, in 1950, he took up residence in Antibes on the French Côte d'Azur and again started working on this novel.

Though Kazantzakis had a rich knowledge of the New Testament, he spent a year in research for the project. According to the Kazantzakis scholar Peter Bien, he was most inspired by the nineteenth-century French philosopher Ernest Renan, especially his magisterial biography, *Vie de Jésus* (*The Life of Jesus*). Kazantzakis was taken by Renan's idea that Jesus might have hesitated on his way to the cross. Of course, Christians "know" that Jesus was tempted in every way that we are, but the Gospels are discreetly silent on the exact nature of these temptations. Was it possible, at this decisive moment, that Jesus felt a pang of regret about all the worldly pleasures he had denied himself? Renan thought so, and this gave Kazantzakis an idea he could extrapolate in dramatic form. In November 1950, a month after he reread *Vie de Jésus,* Kazantzakis' notebook indicates that he chose *The Last Temptation* as the "probable title" of the novel.

The opening pages of *The Last Temptation* reveal a character much like us—someone with desires, ambitions, and moral and psychological vulnerabilities. But he is also much unlike us. Early on, we see that Jesus is torn between accepting his divine calling and escaping to a life of mundane happiness. He feels attracted to the girls in his village, but he does not act on these impulses. He castigates himself for being a coward, for refusing to marry his cousin and childhood sweetheart, Mary Magdalene. When he is tempted to give in to these desires, invisible claws dig under the skin of his head, causing him to buckle to the ground in painful convulsions. He tries to make himself unworthy in God's eyes by turning against the commandments, by refusing to go to synagogue, even by using his carpentry skills to build crosses for the Romans' crucifixions. In spite of it all, he has premonitions of a destiny beyond his control or understanding. When he witnesses an execution on a cross he has built, stigmata break out on his body. "All his blood massed in the very center of each of his hands; the veins swelled and throbbed violently— they seemed about to burst. In his palms he felt a painful spot, round like the head of a nail."[6]

The key to understanding Jesus' psychology in *The Last Temptation,* according to Peter Bien, is the idea that every person, Jesus included, "is evil by nature as well as good, violent and hateful as well as loving. . . . For Kazantzakis, the psychologically sound individual does not ignore or bury the evil within him; he channels it into the service of the good."[7] In Jesus this ability is magnified, and at times—particularly in his dealings with Judas, the Zealot disciple who has proven himself loyal and steadfast enough to carry out the act that sets Jesus' death in motion—he draws the dark side closer.[8] In instances like these we gain the clearest view of how Kazantzakis envisioned the tormented, uncertain qualities of Jesus' dual nature.

Throughout the novel, Kazantzakis follows the order of events laid out in the Gospels. But for the last fifty-two pages, in the "last temptation" sequence, he forces readers out of their comfort zone. As he hangs on the cross, close to death, Jesus is visited by a guardian angel who tells him that the Passion is just a dream. All his life he suffered and now, at the hour of his deepest need, abandoned by his mother, brothers, and disciples, God has taken pity on him and returned him to earth to enjoy what he denied himself for thirty-three years.

The guardian angel shows him a glorious wedding procession winding through verdant hills; it is Jesus' own marriage to Mary Magdalene. Later, after the Magdalene's death at the hands of soldiers sent by Caiaphas, Jesus goes to live with Mary and Martha, the daughters of Lazarus, who bear him sons and daughters. In a series of brilliant set pieces, Kazantzakis describes the ordinary joys of Jesus' time on earth—and the profoundly bitter loss of hope for mankind—that follow from putting down the mantle of a martyr. In one memorable scene he crosses paths with St. Paul, who is preaching about the resurrected Christ. Jesus heatedly denies that he was ever crucified and resurrected; instead, he has been living "under another name and with another body."[9] Paul is unswayed. He replies that it does not really matter if the story of the resurrected Christ is true or false, as long as people have something to believe in. People have so great a thirst for salvation that he, Paul, will invent the Son of God, if he must.

Fittingly, it is Judas who brings Jesus back to self-awareness. In the last scene, Judas exposes the guardian angel's true satanic identity and turns angrily on Jesus, calling him a traitor and cursing the day they met. The disciples join in, and as the chorus of denunciation reaches a crescendo, Jesus awakens on the cross. "A wild, indomitable joy took possession of him. No, no, he was not a coward, a deserter, a traitor. No, he was nailed to the cross. He had stood his ground honorably to the very end; he had kept his word." In his final moments of life, he sees that his disciples did not succumb to despair after all; they are already on their way across the world, proclaiming the Good News. Jesus' heroic cry is the novel's finale: "IT IS ACCOMPLISHED! And it was as though he had said: Everything has begun."[10]

Without question, *The Last Temptation* took liberties with the Gospels that orthodox believers would find audacious, if not truly blasphemous. And soon enough, the ecclesiastical authorities passed judgment on what this resolutely nonconformist author had written. On April 28, 1954, without divulging any rationale for its action, the Vatican issued a decree that put *The Last Temptation* on its Index of Forbidden Books—a list of authors and works that the Church deemed theologically false or morally unfit, which dated from the Roman inquisition of the sixteenth century.[11] Although its placement on the Index did not actually ban *The Last Temptation* from any venue, the novel would always bear this mark of official displeasure.

Only Roman Catholics were duty-bound to obey the dictates of the Index, but the Greek Orthodox Church had its own issues with Kazantzakis. Just two years earlier he had narrowly avoided being excommunicated by the Orthodox Church for the alleged sacrilege of his novel *The Greek Passion.* With plans afoot in Athens to publish *The Last Temptation,* Church officials did not hesitate to seek harsher measures than the wrist slap of a forbidden books list. In February 1955 the Holy Synod moved to block not only the novel's publication, but also its translation to the Greek language. (It had originally been published in German.) Most of the country's leftist newspapers defended Kazantzakis and chastised the Church for presuming to pass judgment on what should be published in a liberal democracy. Within weeks of blasphemy charges being filed, the Church was losing ground in the court of public opinion. Finally, in late May, the Greek parliament voted to oppose any motion that would curtail Kazantzakis' speech rights.[12] Later that year *The Last Temptation* went on sale in Greek bookstores and became the year's biggest publishing success.

In 1960 the novel, renamed *The Last Temptation of Christ* by its publisher, Simon and Schuster, arrived in U.S. bookstores to mostly enthusiastic reviews. The book's defiance of Christian dogma resonated with the ferment of the sixties.[13] *The Last Temptation* became a favorite text at seminaries for challenging students' ideas of Christ, and for those seeking a different, "authentic" Jesus—a Jesus more in tune with the tumultuous times of the twentieth century—it was the hip book to read. By the second half of the 1960s, baby boomers were dropping out of organized religion at a higher rate than any previous generation. But far from rejecting spirituality out of hand, the counterculture sought enlightenment in Eastern religions and Native American wisdom traditions, and in books with mystical themes, such as Herman Hesse's *Siddhartha,* J. R. R. Tolkien's Lord of the Rings trilogy, Aldous Huxley's *The Doors of Perception,* and Carlos Castaneda's pop anthropology books about the Yaqui sorcerer Don Juan. With its portrait of a self-questioning and often misunderstood Christ, *The Last Temptation of Christ* moved into the slipstream of this spiritual adventurousness.

Elsewhere in the land, the book sparked very different reactions. In July 1962, in Arcadia, California, a satellite of Los Angeles nestled in the west end of the San Gabriel Valley, a "middle-aged spinster, a member of the John Birch Society," as one account characterized her, walked into the city's library bearing a list of forty-one quotations from a book she referred to as "that salacious Jesus thing."[14] The woman asked that *The Last Temptation of Christ,* which had been sitting quietly on the library's shelves for two years, be removed from circulation.[15] Not long afterward, the Arcadia Council of Protestant Churches voted 14–7, with 10 abstentions, to recommend to the city council that it order the library to ban the Kazantzakis novel.[16] With that vote, these clergymen, in league with a group calling itself the Citizens Committee for Clean Books, began waging a pitched battle over the book's alleged blasphemy.

Arcadia was the first shot fired in one of the fiercest attacks ever launched on California's public libraries.[17] With virtually no warning, censorship drives against *The Last Temptation of Christ* swept like a prairie fire for nearly two years through the towns of Chula Vista, Anaheim, Monrovia, Fullerton, Newport Beach, Santa Ana, Long Beach, and Pomona, the cities of San Diego and Los Angeles, and a number of communities in the East and Midwest.[18] Although religious objections were at the heart of efforts to oust the novel from libraries, the book-banning contagion was also fueled by a zeitgeist of reactionary politics. During the early 1960s the ultraconservative John Birch Society gained grassroots strength among southern Californians who worried about the agitation of blacks for their civil rights, the expansion of the liberal welfare state, and other signs of imputed socialist influence.[19] Groups sprang up that operated as fronts for the Birch Society or shared tenets of its strident anticommunism: in Los Angeles County, the Watchdogs for Freedom and the California Christian Citizens' Association; in Long Beach, the Education Society; and in San Diego, the San Diego Patriotic Society.[20] The members of these groups focused on what they saw as a rising tide of cultural pollution. There was already a sense that the common culture had changed for the worse, that the courts were creating legal havens for decadent behavior under the guise of "personal freedom." Obscenity was the overriding concern.[21] But that concern bled into other areas—especially of the perceived spread of atheism, sexual licentiousness, and leftist tendencies in the arts. *The Last Temptation of Christ* acted as a lightning rod for these fears.

At first, the libraries responded timidly to the threat. The Chula Vista library board split 2–2 on a motion to replace a stolen copy of *The Last Temptation*. The tie vote stymied the library until a patron came forth to donate a copy.[22] When Newport Beach's copy was found to be "missing," the head librarian told the press, "We haven't had money to replace it. As it is a controversial book, we aren't going to replace it yet."[23] The trustees of the Fullerton library defused a tense situation by restricting the book to readers older than eighteen, an action that was emulated in Santa Ana.

Resistance to the spreading attempts to suppress the novel finally began to stiffen in Long Beach—the city where the children's fable *Little Red Riding Hood* was once criticized for the bottle of wine tucked in the wolf's basket, and *The Little Mermaid* labeled satanic for the title character's transformation from sea creature to a female human.[24] Leaflets, petitions, letters, and phone calls, some of which seemed to be orchestrated from outside the city, rained down on Long Beach city officials. In a meeting in November 1962, the city council recommended that only adult readers be allowed access to the book, and it remanded the issue of permanently removing the book to the city manager. Later, at another packed meeting of the city council, ministers stood up and denounced the novel as "the most despicable thing" ever published, and Blanche Collins of the library gave a spirited defense of her institution's mission to offer the public access to varied viewpoints. This time the council and city manager sided with Collins and ruled that the book should stay in the library. Although the city weathered the storm over the Kazantzakis novel, the Education Society of Long Beach pressured the library for several more months about balancing its collection of "left-wing" material—such as Jessica Mitford's *The American Way of Death*, Langston Hughes's poetry, and Pete Seeger's songs—with "conservative" books and magazines.[25]

It was in Arcadia that the struggle over *The Last Temptation of Christ* turned overtly political. For weeks Arcadia's librarians and trustees were "the object of a bitter hate campaign," as one reporter characterized the confrontation.[26] The forty-one quotations that the John Birch Society member lifted from the novel were mimeographed and passed around by children. A similar list was circulated by the "Americanism Committee" of the Watchdogs of Freedom.[27] The Citizens Committee for Clean Books collected thousands of signatures on petitions, mostly from church congregations. The committee was so confident of the legitimacy of the action it proposed that it took out a full-page advertisement in the *Arcadia Tribune* a week before Christmas. The ad declared, in part, "The Library Board has, by its own admission, kept books out of the Library which were offensive to some, and by this fact they have exercised censorship. Our position is that we wish to remove ONE book that is blasphemous to the Son of the living God, Jesus Christ, whose birthday we are celebrating."[28]

At the end of a rancorous three-hour meeting in January 1963, the library trustees voted unanimously to ignore the church council's demand. But the opponents were not done. "That was only a little skirmish," said one of them. "We will go to the city council and we will take it to the people if necessary."[29] *The Last Temptation of Christ* soon became the pretext for a months-long effort to redraw the distribution of power over Arcadia's culture. The protest leaders proposed changing the city's charter so that the library board's decisions on book policy would be merely "advisory" and nonbinding. In 1964 the issue came to a head when the Arcadia City Council voted 3–2 not to approve the change. That fall's election results brought the matter to a conclusion. Of the two city council candidates who pledged to remove *The Last Temptation* from the library if they were returned to office, only one was reelected.[30]

The victories for *The Last Temptation of Christ* came at a price: some librarians lost their jobs; some library boards found themselves bitterly split; and relations among library boards, city councils, and citizen groups in several localities were damaged for months or years. The fact that the book emerged vindicated from the controversies did little to change polarized attitudes about the book. Hailed by its admirers as one of the greatest works of the literary imagination about the struggle for spiritual meaning, the book was roundly damned by others as a blasphemy. The defenders of traditional values lost all their legal and political battles, but the heirs to their cause would stage a mighty resurgence twenty-five years later. And if some of them forgot why they had fought to block the public's access to *The Last Temptation,* or forgot that the battles had even happened, they proved themselves more than willing to use their newfound power to revisit many of the same issues.

IN FEBRUARY 1971 Sidney Lumet, the director of such dramas as *Fail-Safe* and *The Pawnbroker,* announced to the press that he had quietly optioned the rights for *The Last Temptation of Christ.* Lumet told the *New York Times* that he had been thinking for nearly a decade about adapting it to the screen. "I suppose you could say it's a dramatization of how a man pushes himself to extremes he never knew he was capable of," he said.[31] According to reports in the *Times* and *Variety,* a September start date for shooting in Israel was in the works.[32] But as it turned out, shooting never started, the film wasn't cast, and no studio approved the project. "I never could lick it in terms of a screenplay," Lumet later admitted.[33] "I just couldn't pull it off."

In the summer of 1971, as Lumet struggled with adapting *The Last Temptation,* the novel landed in the life of another director at a very different place in his career. Working long, humid days in the woods and fields outside the Arkansas town of Camden, Martin Scorsese, an intense, twenty-eight-year-old New Yorker who had just moved to California, was trying to make the most of an opportunity to break into feature films. Months earlier, the producer Roger Corman had hired him to direct the low-budget "exploitation" picture *Boxcar Bertha* for American International Pictures (AIP). Based loosely on the memoirs of the female hobo Bertha Thompson, *Boxcar Bertha* was a story of Depression-era outlaws cast in the mold of Arthur Penn's 1967 critical and box-office success, *Bonnie and Clyde.* Corman had mined this territory the year before with *Bloody Mama,* starring Shelley Winters as a machine gun–wielding gang leader, and he calculated that the genre had some commercial life left in it.

A refined, soft-spoken Stanford graduate, Roger Corman was known for giving young filmmakers such as Francis Ford Coppola (*Dementia 13*), Peter Bogdanovich (*Targets*), and Jonathan Demme (*Caged Heat*) a shot at directing the films he produced. They came out of these apprenticeships armed with the directing credits they needed for moving up to projects at the major studios. Martin Scorsese also saw *Boxcar Bertha* as his path to Hollywood. Unlike his first feature, *Who's That Knocking at My Door?* which he struggled for three years through a disintegrating marriage and cobbled-together financing to make, shooting on weekends with a student crew whenever actors, equipment, and locations were available, *Boxcar Bertha* afforded him a union crew and a comparatively expansive $600,000 budget. Nevertheless, Corman's system demanded of young directors that they follow the AIP exploitation formula, and *Boxcar Bertha* was no exception. Corman asked for a nude scene about every fifteen pages of script. He wanted to see violent action punctuating the movie at regular intervals. He also wanted Scorsese to shoot the sort of wild, bullets-flying car chase scene that was de rigueur for period gangster movies.[34] In terms of casting, Scorsese recalled that Corman simply told him, "'Your star will be Barbara Hershey and her friend David Carradine.' And he also included [the actor] Barry Primus in that, too. In other words, I had no choice in casting."[35] As long as Scorsese clearly understood what they were making—a quick, cheap, sensationalistic picture for the drive-in and second-run circuits—Corman was agreeable to giving him the freedom to do it his way.

Scorsese did manage to design a number of unusual camera angles and visual effects. He also supervised a music score made up of hillbilly, delta blues, and jazz tracks, which foreshadowed his later innovative uses of popular music. But freedom meant more to Scorsese than visual pyrotechnics or a great score. It meant personalizing the story. It meant insinuating his own interests, conflicts, and fixations into the material so that the movie becomes a simulacrum of his inner world. It meant creating a way of seeing the world and impressing this vision on every stage of filmmaking, from what goes into a frame of film to the master themes that impose order on a lifetime's body of work. This auteurist conceit can be fully realized only when the director is in control of the entire production apparatus. Very few directors operate at that level of artistic power—in 1971 Scorsese himself was a few years away from exercising full control of his films—but he was already learning that in a by-the-numbers genre picture like *Boxcar Bertha,* story and characters can be subtly subordinated to his own artistic purpose, provided that in the end he gives the audience the kind of moral closure it expects.

As the weeks of shooting went by, Barbara Hershey, who played the title role, began to notice religious themes and symbols cropping up in *Boxcar Bertha.* Class conflict was the film's thematic axis, as it had been for *Bonnie and Clyde,* but Scorsese shifted the drama toward the compassionate, Christ-like qualities of the union organizer Big Bill Shelley, played by David Carradine, and the Magdalene figure of Bertha.[36] At times the parallels are too obvious. When the outlaws are on the lam, for example, they find refuge in a country church. On a wall of the church sanctuary, dominating the background of the shot, is a large mural depicting a white-robed Jesus gazing lovingly at Mary Magdalene. Elsewhere, the New Testament allusions are used with a surer feel. In one of the early scenes, Bertha wanders into an impromptu speech that Bill Shelley is delivering to some workers. Like a charismatic messiah, he preaches solidarity and imparts a brief parable about fighting the railroad bosses. Later Shelley goes to the local union hall to donate his share from the gang's first train robbery. But the union official shows disgust with Shelley's lawbreaking and scolds him for consorting with "whores and niggers."

The climax of the gang's running battles with the railroad company is Bill Shelley's death at the hands of hired goons. The script called for Shelley to be nailed to the side of a freight car, the crucifixion-style murder signifying his martyrdom for the cause of working people. The first shot shows a nail exploding through the back of the boxcar door, followed by quick cuts of the killers remorselessly finishing their grim work while Hershey, as Bertha, is sprawled helplessly on the ground. After the killers are all slaughtered by a member of Shelley's gang, and the train begins to pull Shelley's lifeless body down the tracks, Bertha runs alongside the boxcar and tries, unsuccessfully, to keep up—the entire sequence recalling the Gospel accounts of Mary Magdalene's witness at the Crucifixion and Jesus' ascension to heaven.

One night before shooting wrapped, Scorsese held a screening of *Who's That Knocking at My Door?* for the cast. As Barbara Hershey watched the frankly personal film—much of the Catholic iconography was shot in St. Patrick's Old Church, his neighborhood church, and the principal character's confused feelings about women mirrored Scorsese's emotional turmoil earlier in life—she thought about a novel she read as a nineteen-year-old. Hershey was profoundly moved by the book's core idea that Christ was tempted by desires to lead a normal life but gave them up to finish his mission on the cross. "I had always been fascinated by the Christ story, but I never really got it until that book," she told Mary Pat Kelly, a friend of Scorsese's, in *Martin Scorsese: A Journey.*[37]

When the screening was over, she asked Scorsese if he had ever thought about making a film about Jesus. "Oh, I'd love to make a film on the Gospels, or on Jesus," he replied.

"I have this book for you, then. Have you ever read *The Last Temptation of Christ?*"

He said that he hadn't.[38] Then she apparently said—only Scorsese remembers her saying this—"You should, and when it becomes a movie, you'll direct and I'll play Mary Magdalene."[39]

Weeks later, when they were back in Los Angeles, Hershey and David Carradine went to Scorsese's apartment on Franklin Avenue one evening for dinner and to watch the annual network broadcast of *The Wizard of Oz* on his twelve-inch Sony set. They talked about other films they could do together. Hershey had brought along a paperback copy of *The Last Temptation of Christ* for him to read.

Neither Kazantzakis nor the book was unknown to Scorsese. Ten years earlier, a Greek émigré and fellow NYU student, John Mavros, urged him to read a novel that had just been published in English translation. *The Last Temptation of Christ,* he asserted, revealed the humanity of Jesus like no other book. "This is the *right* way to do a film about Christ, this is the *right* story,"

Mavros kept saying excitedly.[40] Though the humanity angle fascinated Scorsese, he was just getting his bearings in film studies and had no time to investigate the novel. But when Hershey brought him the novel in 1971, he was ready for it.

Certainly anyone who originates a project based on the life of Jesus Christ must feel something for the story. For Scorsese the feelings went very deep, all the way back to the Lower East Side of Manhattan. With the possible exception of Federico Fellini, no filmmaker has so persistently and vividly invoked the influence of his early years—whether in interviews, on talk shows, in the books he's written, in his own movies—and no work occupies a more privileged place in that mythology than *The Last Temptation of Christ*. The key biographical vectors were always movies and religion, and they converged in Little Italy around 1950. At the age of seven, Marty Scorsese moved with his family from suburban Queens to his grandmother's second-story apartment on Elizabeth Street. The trauma of the move, compounded by chronic asthma, kept him indoors after school. His isolation was relieved by regular trips downtown to movie theaters with his father, Charles Scorsese, or occasionally his mother, Catherine, and older brother Frank. For hours he sat in the dark transfixed by Westerns, gangster movies, mysteries, costume dramas, comedies, adventure pictures. Judging from the stories told about these excursions, Marty Scorsese might well have seen more movies than any kid his age in New York City. But he took special delight in the religious spectacles coming into vogue in the early 1950s—movies like *Demetrius and the Gladiators, The Silver Chalice, Samson and Delilah,* and *Quo Vadis.* He loved nearly everything about them: the classicism of the architecture; the grandiloquent speech and manners of the actors; the ancient rites and ceremonies; and, most of all, the thrill of seeing great Bible stories brought to life. He has spoken of taking notepad and pencil with him, for sketching what he saw on the screen. Even the most pedestrian of these movies yielded some detail of interest that he filed away in his prodigious memory for later use. One afternoon a parish priest took Marty to the Roxy Theatre to see *The Robe*. It was the first movie to employ the new Cinemascope format. But more than that, it had Christ in it. The experience of seeing *The Robe* nudged the needle of Scorsese's ambitions to magnetic north. More than once he has said, "I'd always wanted to make a film of the life of Christ ever since I first saw him portrayed on the screen in *The Robe* when I was eleven years old."[41]

Movies took the boy out of his surroundings for brief periods, but for help dealing with the streets day to day, Marty Scorsese turned to God. Unsurprisingly, his fascination with religion is traced to memories of images. He told Richard Corliss in 1988: "My grandmother was the one who had the portrait of the Sacred Heart. Also the niche with the statue of the Virgin Mary grinding the snake under her foot. Also the beautiful, gigantic crucifix over the bed, with Jesus in brass and the palms from Palm Sunday draped over the crossbar."[42] Catherine Scorsese also kept Madonna and Child statuary in her bedroom. On the living room wall she arranged a "museum" of reproductions of the Mona Lisa and Michelangelo's Sistine Chapel frescoes and images of saints, in addition to family photos.[43] As for the Church, his parents apparently did not take it too seriously. Marty, however, found something there that he needed. "It was a tough area," he said about the Elizabeth Street neighborhood, "so I guess the acceptance I went for was in the Church."[44]

Occupying a full block on Mott Street and surrounded by high brick walls, St. Patrick's Old Church is a vestige of old New York dating from the first great wave of Irish immigration of the early nineteenth century. A travelogue to Little Italy written in 1924 observed that St. Pat's "leave[s] one with the feeling that this church was built within a fortress, as though in inimical territory, though the few trees within the fortress are the only ones in the neighborhood."[45] In the early 1950s, the cathedral was still an oasis of peace and good works. There he learned the Catholic catechism, the eternal truth that Christ lived and died so that we could be more like him, forgiving and loving our enemies. He became an altar boy, helping out in the Saturday morning funeral Masses. The miracle of transubstantiation, in particular, made a deep impression. The offering of blood, he told Richard Corliss, was "the life force, the essence, the sacrifice."[46]

The nuns told their young charges stories about the saints and their incomparable acts of devotion. They also told cautionary tales of people who were shamed or struck dead because they ran afoul of this or that rule of God. The blood of Jesus' Passion flowed freely in many of them, a nightmare instrument for inspiring fear and atonement in the sinner. In his spiritual memoir, "In the Streets," Scorsese recalls one such story about a woman who desecrated the Eucharist wafer by taking it home instead of swallowing it whole at church. "She got it in her mouth, she took it back to the pew, and she took it out and put it in her handkerchief, went home, and put it in a trunk. And that night while she was sleeping, the trunk began to glow. Then blood started coming out of the trunk. . . . And then she was terrified, and she had a priest come in, and the priest took the host and put it back where it should be."[47]

Church was full of these moments of clarity for Marty Scorsese. But outside St. Pat's, compassion was not an easy code to live by. He tried to make sense of the day-and-night difference between the love preached by the priests and nuns and the rough justice he saw every day on the streets. Writing in "In the Streets," he recalled the questions that he had asked himself: "So how do you practice these basic, daily Christian—not even specifically Catholic, but Christian—concepts of love and the major commandments? How do you do that in the world? I figured that maybe wearing the cloth you might be able to find a better way to do that. The final payoff will be salvation, therefore you'll be happy. That's when I started getting the idea of really wanting that vocation, selfishly, so that I'd be saved."[48]

Intending at the age of thirteen to become a cleric, Marty enrolled in the preparatory seminary at Cathedral College on the Upper East Side. But it ended sooner than anyone had expected. After just a year, he was expelled for failing grades. Marty worked hard to raise his grades at Cardinal Hayes High School in the Bronx; still hoping to study for the priesthood, he knuckled under to the no-nonsense regimen of the school's Marist Brother teachers. Increasingly, though, he looked skeptically at the church's doctrines and the rules it set for governing parishioners' lives. On Sunday mornings he sometimes heard the priest speak from the pulpit about films that had been condemned by the Legion of Decency, the infamous agency whose judgments about movies Roman Catholics pledged to follow. The Legion's ratings were even posted in the halls of many of the city's cathedrals. Often as not, it was not violence that was disapproved most, but sexually suggestive scenes or themes that ran counter to Catholic positions on divorce or other lifestyle issues.[49]

The Church's apoplexy over morally suspect movies hit new heights when Roberto Rosselini's *The Miracle*—a short film starring Anna Magnani as a peasant girl who imagines she is the Virgin Mary—opened at New York's Paris Theatre in December 1950. In a statement read at all the Masses at St. Patrick's Cathedral on January 7, 1951, Cardinal Spellman branded the film "a despicable affront to every Christian," "a vicious insult to Italian womanhood," and a communist plot to "divide and demoralize Americans."[50] Catholics picketed the theater and the Church backed the New York Board of Regents' decision to revoke the film's license on grounds of sacrilege. A year later, the U.S. Supreme Court overturned the state appellate court's decision to uphold the ban of *The Miracle*. The high court's ruling established, for the first time, full First Amendment protection for motion pictures. Marty Scorsese was too young to see *The Miracle* or understand what the fuss was about, but as he grew older, the battle royals over Otto Preminger's *The Moon Is Blue* and Elia Kazan's *Baby Doll* and the Legion of Decency's ongoing exertions to censure movies perplexed him.

It wasn't until he turned twenty, when he took his first film class at NYU, that Scorsese finally let go of "the vocation." By then he knew that sex was not inherently sinful. Yet he found it hard to rid himself of the guilt that the Church attached to unsanctified relations with a woman.[51] He also became acutely aware of the Church's tendency to turn a blind eye to hypocrisy as long as one accepted its authority unquestioningly. The last straw came one Sunday in 1965. Married and with his first daughter on the way, he went to Mass at a church near his apartment in New Jersey. The priest used the pulpit that morning to tell the parishioners of his support for U.S. involvement in the Vietnam War. He recalled in "In the Streets" why the sermon dismayed him: "Their sons were probably going to go off and get killed. And here was this guy—an old man, too—who got up and told them it was right. I never went again. I had no political commitment, I just knew that there was something wrong."[52]

The questions he had asked from an early age were ones he still asked: How do you live this life of compassion? How do you practice the concepts of Christianity outside the Church? How do you go about the act of forgiving people when so many consider it a weakness? But he no longer had the Church to organize the answers for him. The proscriptions against what he could think, feel, and do were gone; the bright line between the sacred and the profane was erased. His questions about difficult moral choices now went into his screenplays and camera shots, into the lines and behaviors of his actors— all of it a cinematic sacrament.[53] Inevitably, this highly personal approach to God influenced the kind of movie about Christ he wanted to make. If most churches treated Christ as the Chosen One who knew his mission from day one—basically, Christ as the ultimate insider—Scorsese searched for a version that spoke to his own quest. He had in mind a Jesus with a dangerous, demanding message of love to preach; an exceptional human being who struggles fiercely to know what God wants of him; a Jesus who, like himself, often feels like an outsider, but, unlike him, finds the strength to transcend the vicissitudes of life.

Nothing remotely like this had been attempted before. The movie Christs he saw in theaters were narrowly conceived, banal, predictable. In the biblical pictures of the 1950s, Christ's presence hovered just off-screen, a hallowed backdrop to some other human melodrama. During the 1960s, Nicholas Ray's *The King of Kings* and George Stevens's *The Greatest Story Ever Told* were released about five years apart. Scorsese found elements to like in both films, especially their epic visual style, but ultimately they disappointed. When he saw *King of Kings* Scorsese was taken aback by the young, blue-eyed Jeffrey Hunter, who looked in close-ups more like an air-brushed pinup than the suffering Jesus.[54] He dismissed the George Stevens picture as having "an antiseptic quality about it, a hermetically sealed holiness that didn't teach us anything new about Jesus."[55] They were just the latest in the long line of glow-in-the-dark Christs, as Scorsese often characterized the type—chaste, otherworldly Messiahs designed to be *safe* for viewing. And by taking no risks, these portrayals were also, in Scorsese's eyes, fake. He became convinced that nothing less than a radical overhaul of the cinematic Jesus was required. Only a more human, approachable Redeemer—the primitive Jesus of history, not the deified Christ of the church—would challenge audiences to reappraise who he was and to think in a fresh way about the relevance of his personal example to their own situations.

Sometime around 1965, Scorsese began sketching out an idea for a film about Jesus in the style of the cinema-verité documentary, shooting it in black and white, "almost like a newsreel of the ancient world"—except that it would be set in the contemporary Lower East Side, with the apostles living in tenements and the Crucifixion taking place on the docks.[56] This surreal fable would put in play Scorsese's ideas of the supernatural and the mundane cohabiting on the same plane. But his plans suddenly derailed when he saw Pier Paolo Pasolini's *The Gospel according to St. Matthew* at the Bleecker Street Cinema. A committed Marxist and atheist, Pasolini was inspired by a chance encounter with the Gospel of Matthew to direct a modestly budgeted film based on that book's version of the Christ story.[57] Pasolini emphasized Jesus as a revolutionary figure whose miracles and strong, unflinching sermons got him in trouble with the Jewish high priests. *The Gospel according to St. Matthew* owed much of its understated power to the way Pasolini visualized the story. Filming on location in the dry, hilly landscape of Calabria, Pasolini chose a Spanish student, Enrique Irazoqui, to play Jesus and cast local townspeople in supporting parts. The naturalism of the acting, combined with Tonino Delli Colli's beautifully composed black-and-white images, lent *The Gospel according to St. Matthew* the sort of intimate, gritty realism that Scorsese had envisioned for his Lower East Side Jesus film.

Scorsese had mixed feelings about the film. On the one hand, it was the most moving depiction of Jesus to come from a Gospel source—"But it was the film I wanted to make. I almost felt that something had been taken from me."[58] Pasolini's achievement convinced him, as he said later, that "there was no point in going back to the Gospels . . . that a film would have to do something new, something different."[59]

By 1972 Scorsese's fortunes—and the world of American cinema he was entering—had shifted decisively. In that momentous year, spanning *Boxcar Bertha*'s release and the making of his landmark film, *Mean Streets,* his dream of establishing a career as a feature film director was rapidly materializing. He could not have timed it better, as the successes of films such as *The Godfather, The Last Picture Show,* and *Five Easy Pieces* prompted Hollywood to begin recruiting visionary young filmmakers. Coincidentally, the Age of Aquarius "rock operas," *Godspell* and *Jesus Christ Superstar,* then in production, would soon break new stylistic ground for religious-themed films. The idea of revitalizing the substance of the Christ story remained a driving ambition, but until he got back to Los Angeles from shooting *Boxcar Bertha,* he had no sense of how to bring this inchoate idea into being. He toyed with the idea of adapting Robert Graves's *King Jesus,* a speculative biography based on the poet's mythological ideas. But Scorsese kept returning to *The Last Temptation of Christ.* The novel's "battle between the spirit and the flesh" provided the strikingly fresh approach he had been looking for; it was also a theme that resonated with the filmmaker's own fascination—going back to his youth in Little Italy—with the possibility of practicing selfless love in a world ruled by violence, greed, and evil.[60]

Though the novel was long, dense, and by turns philosophical and earthy, it had the makings of a powerful film. It would be the first film to examine Jesus' interior life, even to the extent of showing him mired in psychological crisis. It would turn the popular idea of Judas on its head, positing him as the only apostle who truly understood and cared about Jesus. The last temptation itself functioned as an ingenious story device. If done as skillfully as Robert Enrico's stunning Oscar-winning short film, *An Occurrence at Owl Creek*

Bridge,[61] it would keep viewers in suspense to the very end about whether Jesus did in fact escape death on the cross.

Above all, the novel stripped Jesus of the iconic trappings that kept him under glass. *Last Temptation,* Scorsese believed, could give moviegoers the most empathetic, intimate Jesus they had ever seen—a Jesus so human that even those in the audience who are in despair and think their lives are worthless could see that he knows what they are going through. "Where would Jesus be?" Scorsese said years later. "I always said this—where would he be? He would be on Eighth Avenue. At that time [in the early 1970s], Eighth Avenue between 42nd and 57th Streets was one of the worst areas. . . . He would be with the pimps and the whores and the druggies and the lost, the dispossessed."[62] This, he thought, was the Jesus that all of us really wanted to believe in. And this was the story he wanted to tell.

The copy of the novel that Hershey had given him took root in Scorsese's life. The book became his constant companion, all through the making of *Mean Streets, Alice Doesn't Live Here Anymore,* and *Taxi Driver.* He stole whatever time he could for the book, absorbing and savoring the passages he read. He made notes in the margins of the pages. At times he put it away just to make it last longer. The luxuriant prose so captivated Scorsese, slowing him down to a crawl, that he realized he "couldn't shoot the language."[63]

Another reason he moved slowly through the book was that he was underdeveloped as a reader. His parents had never particularly encouraged reading outside school, and the only literature at home he could recall was his father's newspapers, the *Daily News* and *Daily Mirror.* "It took me a long time to learn how to read a book," he remembered. "I *tried* and tried and tried, and I found it very difficult."[64]

In late September 1978 Scorsese had the book with him when he arrived in San Gimignano, the Tuscan City of the Towers, to visit the set of Paolo and Vittorio Taviani's *Il Prato* (The Meadow). While the film was being shot outside the village walls, he passed the time by reading his way to the end of *The Last Temptation of Christ.* But getting to that point was merely a postscript to a decision he had made two years earlier. After finishing the sound mix for *Taxi Driver*—and satisfied that he knew what the rest of the book entailed, including the last temptation, even before reading it—Scorsese instructed his agent Harry Ufland to start the process of optioning the film rights.

Ufland's first order of business in March 1976 was to establish contact with Helen Kazantzakis, who had survived her husband's death nearly twenty years earlier and now acted as administrator of his literary estate. This would prove to be no easy task. The widow traveled often and unpredictably, and even her associates were sometimes in the dark about her whereabouts. Ufland's letter of inquiry went first to Oslo, Norway, and two months later it caught up with her in Geneva, Switzerland. Despite the delay, she was eager to get discussions going.[65]

Following phone conversations with the literary agent Howard Hausman of the William Morris Agency, who was representing Helen Kazantzakis, Ufland and an attorney, Peter Grossman, put together an offer for the motion picture rights to *The Last Temptation of Christ*. They proposed a fee of $15,000 for a two-year option period, which would be applied against the purchase price of $150,000, plus 5 percent of the net profits, should Scorsese exercise the option to produce the film. Importantly, they agreed to Hausman's suggestion that "Scorcese Productions [*sic*] will have caused a first draft screenplay to be written prior to the expiration of the first option period," and only then could the option be renewed for another two years.[66] Ufland and Grossman also asked for a fifth-year extension, in case Scorsese's schedule did not allow him to make the film by the end of the second two-year period.

Meanwhile, the producer team of Robert Chartoff and Irwin Winkler joined the nascent project, supplying funds for the option payment. *Last Temptation* happened to come along just as the fortunes of Chartoff-Winkler Productions had decisively turned a corner. The company's latest film, *Rocky*—the riskiest picture the two men had ever put into production, budgeted so tightly that they were forced to mortgage their homes to finance the completion bond—was at that moment opening across America to blockbuster business. *Rocky* established an incredibly lucrative franchise for United Artists in the years that followed and cemented Chartoff's and Winkler's reputations as dedicated producers who would go the last mile for a director. Winkler, in particular, was known for taking a hands-on approach to producing—from formulating the story idea or finding the material to going on location and involving himself in every aspect of its realization. In an interview with Julia Cameron for *American Film*, Winkler summarized his producer's code: "A producer has to *live* with his movie. Unless he's willing to do that, he has *no rights*." He was no less emphatic about what he expected from a director: "'You take a gun, and you hold it in your right hand, if you're right-handed. You cock that gun and point it right at the director's head. You hold it there all during preproduction. On the first day of shooting, you take that gun—still cocked, still loaded—and you hand it to the director. He points it directly at your own head.'"[67] Roughly translated: Winkler expected a director to stay on-task and true to his passion; in return, Winkler pledged to watch his back. Only a strong director would ally himself with this equally focused, impassioned producer; but if he did, the rewards could be substantial.

Hausman received the Scorsese team's offer and immediately raised a concern about the fifth-year option. "I am reluctant to open this question now," he wrote to Ufland, "partly because Mrs. Kazantzaki is in her seventies and because it could appear as if Marty planned to merely stockpile this with no intention to move with reasonable diligence." Ufland, however, argued that they needed the flexibility of a fifth year, given his client's escalating value as a director.[68]

Other sticking points came up: the question of who ultimately had the rights to the English translation of *The Last Temptation*—the translator Peter Bien or the book's U.S. publisher, Simon and Schuster—and how long the holdbacks on sequels, remakes, and television or live theatrical versions would last. (A holdback is a period of time in which the license holder of a literary property has the exclusive rights to its commercial use.) The lawyers quickly resolved the first question (Simon and Schuster controlled the translation rights), but the issue of holdbacks was less tractable. Scorsese's team wanted a holdback of seven years from the date of release so that all the film's revenue potential could be exploited. But Hausman stood firm at a four-year holdback, and there the deal stalled for three months.

Finally, Peter Grossman advised Winkler that it would be unwise to prolong the negotiations. "Mrs. Kazantzakis," he wrote, "lives in Europe and travels extensively, and I am afraid that making an issue out of the holdback could delay by a further two or three months the date on which the documents would be signed—and without any guarantee that we would succeed in extending the holdbacks."[69] They also agreed to drop the fifth-year option. Though Ufland and Winkler chafed under these concessions, it was now evident that Helen Kazantzakis would not approve the deal without them.

An agreement between Scorsese Productions and Helen Kazantzakis was drawn up, the start date being April 1, 1977. All business and legal issues were settled, and the ability to film *The Last Temptation of Christ* seemed to be securely in Scorsese's grasp. But as April turned to May, and May into summer, a new problem arose: Helen Kazantzakis could not be found. The peripatetic widow had left Geneva without telling her business associates of her itinerary. By late July Peter Grossman grew frustrated that the execution copies of the option agreement had not been returned—and, indeed, that Helen

Kazantzakis might be having second thoughts about the deal. Writing to Hausman, Grossman urged him to use every means at his disposal to find her and "make sure that if she does not already have the agreements, they are transmitted to her without a further day's delay. . . . Just for the record, I want to reiterate that there is in effect a binding agreement. I do not know what exactly has caused the delays, but if your client is entertaining offers from any other parties, she does so at her peril."[70]

Hausman eventually tracked her down through his European sources. "Mrs. Kazantzakis," he explained to Grossman, "was traveling extensively from spring to mid-summer and is now, I am informed, in Athens or in Cyprus. Some of her travels were in mainland China, and other inaccessable [*sic*] places."[71] He confirmed that she had the option papers in hand and was going through them with her English translator.

Unwelcome though the delay was, it gave Scorsese's representatives some leverage to extract a better deal. A revised agreement was sent back with the fifth year of the option reinstated. Despite her qualms, Helen Kazantzakis agreed to the extension. She also reacted uneasily to the standard clause giving Scorsese the unlimited right to make changes in such areas as characters, story events, and dialogue. Her concerns were relayed through her advisor, Patroclos Stavrou, who pointed out that "cineasts, with whom we cooperated in the past, gave us assurances . . . that they would respect the spirit of the work and the stature of the author, Nikos Kazantzakis."[72] Grossman, in reply, told Stavrou that financing would be difficult to secure if Scorsese did not have the normal creative license. He urged them to trust Scorsese's intentions, "as reflected in the films he has already created. Based on that prior body of work, it seems obvious to me that Mr. Scorsese is not going to abuse the spirit of this book."[73]

Helen Kazantzakis—who had lived with the author for nearly thirty turbulent years; who had brought him books from the library at Cannes that summer of 1950 as he prepared to write *The Last Temptation of Christ;* who had typed the manuscript and always thought it her husband's most superlative work—was finally ready to sign the film rights over to Martin Scorsese.[74] In late November 1977 she went to the American embassy in Bern and signed the option agreement. Two fully executed copies arrived in Peter Grossman's Beverly Hills office the next month.

"If my English were not so dreadfully poor," she wrote to Grossman, "I would have dared to write directly to Mr. Scorsese and tell him how excited I feel when thinking that one day—I still hope for it—I'll be able to applaud the two names Kazantzaki-Scorsese, united in one masterpiece."[75]

AFTER SCORSESE ACQUIRED the rights to *The Last Temptation of Christ* in late 1977, the project went to United Artists (UA) under the terms of Chartoff-Winkler's first-look deal. Only a couple of months later, in January 1978, UA's executive triumvirate of Arthur Krim, Eric Pleskow, and Mike Medavoy—under whose aegis Scorsese made *The Last Waltz* and *New York, New York*—resigned all at once after clashing publicly with UA's parent company, TransAmerica Corporation.[76] The studio's new management, headed by Andy Albeck, "had a different philosophy about making films," as Scorsese delicately put it,[77] and *Last Temptation* languished on a list of other projects that UA declined to develop.

In April 1980, Howard Hausman wrote to Harry Ufland to tell him that his client Helen Kazantzakis was asking about the status of *Last Temptation*.[78] Scorsese was finishing *Raging Bull* at the time and no closer to making *Last Temptation* than he'd been the previous spring, when the option was renewed for two more years. One of the conditions for the renewal was that a first draft script be completed, or at least a writer engaged to write it. This never happened. Now, with Helen Kazantzakis plainly frustrated by the lack of progress, and thus the renewal of the film rights possibly in jeopardy, it was time to convert the sprawling novel into the more compact, action-oriented form of a screenplay.

As early as 1976, Scorsese had talked with Paul Schrader about adapting *The Last Temptation*. There were certainly tantalizing indications in Schrader's screenplay for *Taxi Driver* of what he could do with the Kazantzakis novel. His unforgettable creation for that film was Travis Bickle, the self-confessing God's lonely man, who, like an avenging angel from the Old Testament, takes it upon himself to cleanse the streets of Manhattan with bloody violence. Sin and salvation were not just abstract ideas for Scorsese and Schrader; they were themes that saturated the moral horizons of their lives and the stories they chose to tell as filmmakers. Inevitably, each man traveled this terrain differently. Many of the characters in Scorsese's films—from *Mean Streets*' Charlie and *GoodFellas*' Henry Hill to *The King of Comedy*'s Rupert Pupkin, *Casino*'s Sam Rothstein, and *The Aviator*'s Howard Hughes—suffer from self-destructive (or self-denying) tendencies that they are helpless to stop. They finally come to terms with who they are, but only after fully indulging in the pursuance of those tendencies. As Father Principe, the priest whom he idolized as a youth, drolly observed, Scorsese's movies are often "too much Good Friday, not enough Easter Sunday."

Schrader also made a specialty of spiritually wounded heroes, writing (or directing) films that revolve around themes of sin and guilt. But whereas Scorsese's characters emerge in the end as saved souls, touched even by a kind of nobility, Schrader's characters in films such as *Hardcore, Patty Hearst, Mishima, Light Sleeper, Affliction,* and *Auto Focus* find themselves caught in the grip of obsessions that invade their lives from outside, such as pornography, sex, drugs, and revolutionary politics. Try as they might to rescue themselves, they often don't succeed. In fact, death is often the end point of his protagonists' agony. If redemption is the Catholic dream that Scorsese replays over and over in his films, the fall from grace is Schrader's repetitive Calvinist nightmare.

Whatever their differences when left to their own devices, their work on projects in which they collaborated as writer and director—*Taxi Driver, Raging Bull, The Last Temptation of Christ, Bringing Out the Dead*—fit like joints in a piece of furniture. "We approached a shared core from different directions," Schrader wrote in the *New Yorker.* "We are both quite moral. We believe decisions have consequences. There is right, there is wrong, and, in the end, there is a price to pay. His background is urban, New York, Italian, Roman Catholic; mine is rural, Midwest, Dutch, Protestant. We were just enough similar, just enough different to be good for each other. The friction created more light than heat."[79]

Undoubtedly a big part of the attraction of *Last Temptation* was its counterpoint to nearly everything Paul Schrader had learned as a boy growing up steeped in the doctrines and lifestyle of the Dutch Reformed Church. He recalled his early years in Grand Rapids, Michigan, as a near-total indoctrination in the moral universe of Calvinism. He went to church three times a week, chapel every day, catechism twice a week, youth society twice a week.[80] The family read the Bible aloud daily. On Sundays his relatives gathered after dinner for theological discussions. He came to know the stories and heroes of the Bible the way other children his age knew the legend of Davy Crockett. The young Schrader reacted strongly to the lavish references to blood in the passages he read. Reflecting on these wellsprings, Schrader has remarked: "Christianity really is a blood cult and a death cult; as much as they say otherwise and talk about the God of Love, it really does focus on the Passion and the bleeding, and those are the images that hit a child."[81]

Martin Scorsese and Paul Schrader, 1988. (Courtesy of Paul Schrader)

Calvinists were taught that they had a fateful choice to make. They could put the gift of grace to righteous purposes, or they could allow themselves to be defiled in satanically inspired pursuits. This Manichaean outlook led most of them to steer clear of worldly amusements like music, dancing, and, above all, the movies. No one from a Calvinist family could in good conscience enter a movie theater, and employment in any of the film trades was totally out of the question. There was no point even in trying to tell the good movies from those less worthy. They were all products of an evil, unregenerate system. From the pulpit and in Calvinist publications the Church issued a steady stream of invective against movies—the film industry was called a "bubonic plague," a "maelstrom of iniquity," the world "where Satan has his throne"—to fortify the faithful as they tried to carry out this lifestyle of cultural separation.[82]

Eventually, television pierced the church's protective shield. Paul and his brother Leonard discovered the lure of *Howdy Doody* and other kids' shows at neighbors' homes. It took a while longer to cross the line against moviegoing. (Schrader was in his late teens before he set foot in a theater.) He left the pious life behind in his early twenties, but his roots in Calvinism equipped him with lasting insights into the nature of human weakness. It also served to remind him of how odious a film like *Last Temptation* could seem to the millions of Americans who hold onto absolutist, biblically based beliefs. For a man of Schrader's background and tastes, a film that entertained the possibility of Jesus' surrender to earthly pleasures was just too enticing to pass up.

During a lull in his schedule following the production of his erotic thriller *Cat People,* he managed to shoehorn in *Last Temptation.* The agreement Schrader signed with Chartoff-Winkler stipulated a first draft due no later than ten weeks after the formal start of his writer's services—November 15, 1981—followed by an eight-week period in which Scorsese and the producers would advise him of any revisions they wanted. Importantly, Schrader insisted on including a special clause: "In the event that Scorsese voluntarily elects not to direct the Photoplay, then, prior to our employing or engaging another director to direct the Photoplay, we will first offer you [Schrader] the opportunity to have Writer direct the Photoplay on terms to be negotiated in good faith."[83] As both Scorsese and Irwin Winkler knew, Schrader was as passionate about the film as Scorsese. With this clause, he was laying down his marker for the next shot at directing *Last Temptation* should Scorsese decide to drop out or the project fall into limbo.[84]

The screenplay gave Schrader the perfect excuse to take a tour of Christianity's origins. Hiring a young scholar from Claremont College as his personal biblical consultant and guide, Schrader set out on a ten-day trip to Israel in the summer of 1981. They did much of their traveling on foot, walking as best they could the very steps that Jesus walked. For a man who spent his coming-of-age years immersed in literature glorifying these holy sites, it was a breathtaking experience. Schrader learned about the polyglot nature of the ancient world, the trading communities where East met West, and realized that Jesus was but one of many roving prophets of the time. He learned that the land around Capernaum was quite verdant in the first century, not the desert tableau of today. Schrader regretted that the film did not place Jesus and his disciples in a greener environment, "but once you went to Morocco or Tunisia," he said of Scorsese's early 1980s location scouting, "that was the end of that."[85]

Back in Los Angeles, he consulted a body of theological and historical studies. Much of this research could not be added to the script proper; otherwise, it would impose an onerous burden on the reader.[86] So he footnoted the sources in a backup document that ran thirty pages. The most influential of these sources was the two-volume set *Jesus* and *Christ,* published in English in 1979 and 1980, respectively, by the controversial Belgian theologian Edward Schillebeeckx. The first volume, subtitled *An Experiment in Christology,* so disturbed the Vatican that Schillebeeckx was hauled up before the Sacred Congregation for the Doctrine of the Faith. In a secret four-day hearing on charges filed by the Holy Office, the theologian was questioned about whether he believed the Council of Chalcedon's formulation in A.D. 451 that the man Jesus is "consubstantial" with the divine Father.[87] Many of Schillebeeckx's colleagues came to his aid, including 144 American Catholic theologians who signed a petition appealing to the Vatican to conduct a dialogue instead of an interrogation.[88] He was not disciplined on that occasion, but for at least another decade Rome continued to watch his writings for evidence of heresy. In brief, Schillebeeckx's thesis is that the New Testament's texts about salvation and Jesus' works should be read as reports of experiential (rather than metaphysical) meaning. He doesn't deny Jesus' dual nature, but rather sees the need for a new formulation based in sacramental reality. Otherwise, the human-divine amalgam is just an exotic hybrid to today's believers—"a kind of mermaid," as a journalist quoted Schillebeeckx.[89]

Schrader then listed everything of any import that happened in the book. He noted nearly four hundred incidents: character comings and goings; conflicts and deaths; miracles, speeches, and journeys; scenes of prophecy and decision. Next he drew up a grid. He checked off an incident wherever it intersected with one of the novel's themes. The main theme was the revelation of God to Jesus, captured in the question "What does God want of him, and how?"[90] This theme would unfold throughout, as Jesus wrestles with the occupying force of God. Character relationships formed the other thematic armatures of the script. One theme was the antagonism between Jesus and Judas about whether the Kingdom of God or the insurgent war against the Romans should carry Jesus' ministry forward. The other theme was the heavily coded relationship between Jesus and the Magdalene. (In his first draft Schrader wrote a brief flashback of Jesus' refusal to marry her when they were young; Scorsese took it out, and the missing backstory arguably had the effect of obscuring their relationship in the film.)[91] Finally, Schrader checked off incidents that are featured in the Gospels or that help to move the narrative along—"Is it a critical scene vis-à-vis the biblical story? Is it a theme you can't get around—the Garden of Gethsemane, you know? Does it have comic relief?"[92]

At the end of this process, he threw out the incidents that had no checkmarks and kept the ones with the most checks. With only forty-six scenes left to form the outline of *The Last Temptation of Christ,* Schrader had found the spine of the film.[93] "When Marty had the outline," he told Mary Pat Kelly, "he had the movie. Everything was laid out. There wasn't any room for him to interfere with my writing process."[94] Schrader felt it was the best thing he had ever written, and Scorsese agreed. Schrader, he said, "[cut] to the heart of many scenes like a laser in a precise and brilliant restructuring of the material."[95] Even after he knit the narrative together, adding scenes for exposition and transition, the screenplay came in at a lean ninety-nine pages and eighty-two scenes—a blueprint for a film that Schrader thought would run ninety or a hundred minutes.

Though the screenplay hewed closely to the novel's dramatic contours, Schrader left his own imprint on it. He wrote two scenes that he thought were borderline unplayable, just in case the actor playing Jesus could pull them off. "One was the Garden of Gethsemane, simply because the audience is so far ahead of you. You know exactly what he's going to say. And he's got to say that. [The actor] can't get around that. . . . And then the other thing that I thought was almost impossible to do was for the aged Christ, in 70 A.D., to ask God to forgive him and to be returned to the cross. Now that is a really tough scene."[96]

Schrader smuggled in ideas that had personal meaning for him. In one startling scene, Jesus pulls his bloody heart out of his chest and holds it before the disciples. In part a nod to his alma mater, Calvin College, whose emblem is a heart in a hand, the scene also expressed his belief that the everyday lives of ancient people were so suffused with the spiritual that they probably would have seen, and accepted as reality, extraordinary events.

He also tried to shape the script around his understanding of who Jesus was, and what he meant to say and do. Schrader always thought of Jesus as a true subversive. By turning social hierarchies upside down, by challenging the way people clung to material things and the pride of self, and by preaching God's love to everyone—especially the poor, oppressed, and impure—Jesus called on his followers to do the unthinkable. At the time of his death, he must have seemed the least likely person to have history on his side. So, how did the disciples react to Jesus' miracles? Schrader guessed that they probably would have been seized by a wild, visceral fear—or, in the case of the Last Supper, by revulsion.

> Jesus breaks the bread loaves and passes them around. He pours wine for the others:
>
> JESUS: Take and eat; this is my body.
> Drink, this is my blood.
>
> As they do, the bread and the wine transubstantiate into flesh and blood in their mouths. Peter is the first to cough up the bloody flesh. The others, sickened, follow. They wipe their bloody mouths.

Nearly equal in shock value, but in a different way, was Schrader's treatment of Jesus and Mary Magdalene's wedding night. The scene was written with great tenderness, but its erotic charge is unmistakable.

> INT. JUDEAN HOUSE—NIGHT
> Jesus and Magdalene make love on blankets spread over straw. He kisses her breasts, her lips.
>
> MAGDALENE: I feel like I've just been born. That this is the first day of my life.
>
> JESUS: I never knew the world was so beautiful. I was blind. (kisses her breasts again) I didn't know that the body was so holy. But now I understand.

MAGDALENE: Understand what?

JESUS: That this is the road.

MAGDALENE: What road?

JESUS: The road on which the mortal becomes immortal. God becomes human. I was so stupid: I tried to find a way outside my own flesh. I wanted clouds, great ideas, death. But now I know: a woman is God's greatest work. And I worship you. God sleeps between your legs.

MAGDALENE: I want to have a child with you.

JESUS: Me too.

Magdalene hears a noise at the door.

MAGDALENE: What's that?

The Guardian Angel steps into the darkened room.

GUARDIAN ANGEL: It's me. I wondered if I could watch. I'm lonely too.

JESUS (laughs): Yes, yes. Watch.

Jesus resumes lovemaking.

That Jesus was tempted in every way is an article of Christian doctrine.[97] Still, the detailed visual description of it could be jarring, even for liberal-minded believers. In writing these and other scenes, Schrader played the part of the provocateur to the hilt. He had used this strategy before, notably in *Raging Bull,* to force Scorsese to rethink his assumptions about the material, and to ensure that at least some of his own ideas survived the production process.

Another of Schrader's goals for the screenplay—which he pursued with Scorsese's blessing—was to rough up the lyricism of the book's language. In the view of Peter Bien, the novel's English translator, the screenplay robbed the novel of its linguistic achievement, which was "its integration of New Testament *koine* Greek into the demotic idiom of contemporary Greece."[98] But films are born with cultural references different from the literary works from which they derive. In this case, Schrader and Scorsese were determined to get the dialogue as far from the legacy of the biblical epic as they could. If *Last Temptation* was going to succeed on the screen, they had to radically reduce the distance between Jesus' world and the twentieth-century world of movie audiences—and for this to happen, the characters would have to speak more plainly than in any previous film about Jesus, in a vernacular familiar to contemporary Americans.

Schrader wrote the most down-to-earth dialogue for the disciples, whom he and Scorsese agreed would have been illiterate, working-class men.[99] In one scene, the disciples sit idly in a tavern, waiting for Jesus to return. "Now they say they're going to kill everyone who was baptized," says James. "Nobody told you to get baptized. Serves you right," answers Philip. "You were baptized, too, asshole," says Peter. "Begged for it. So, shut up."

"People are going to recoil at that," said Schrader about the dialogue, "because it violates all they've read and heard over the years, but that's just unfortunate—there's no other solution."[100]

Bob Chartoff and Irwin Winkler received Schrader's first draft in March 1982. *The Last Temptation of Christ* was finally in screenplay form and the director signaled that he was prepared to clear his schedule to make it. Martin Scorsese stood at the threshold of realizing his lifelong passion of making a film about Christ; now he just needed to find a studio willing to underwrite the rest of his journey.

2

Paramount

IN MAY 1982 Paramount Pictures announced that it was promoting a thirty-one-year-old production executive to the post of president of worldwide production. With the abrupt departure of Don Simpson from the position, the studio president, Michael Eisner, decided that he had to fill it with someone whose efficiency, aggressiveness, and implacable dedication to controlling production costs matched his own.

If anything, Jeffrey Katzenberg exceeded that rigorous standard. In the seven years since he was hired as an assistant to Paramount's chairman, Barry Diller, Katzenberg had demonstrated that he would work as many hours as it took and clear any obstacle in his way, with as little wasted motion as possible, to get a task done. Katzenberg was known in the film community as Paramount's "golden retriever" (a nickname he detested); his new job entailed seeking out the best creative material and bringing it back to the studio. It was a job he relished and carried out with a preternatural intensity. Before there was such a thing as speed dial, Katzenberg made more than a hundred calls a day. Most of them took less than sixty seconds.[1] Dawn Steel, then a young vice president, recalled that he rotated through "the top two hundred people in his sphere" at least once every two weeks, vacuuming up information about story ideas, literary properties, deals, and would-be deals.[2]

Then there were the calls to people he didn't know, some of them higher in stature and power. Whereas some people might hesitate to make these calls—or give up after coming up against the avoidance tactic known in the industry as the "slow no"—Katzenberg never gave up. Under his tutelage, Steel learned what she called the Jeffrey Katzenberg Theory of Getting Things Done: "*If they throw you out the front door you go in the back door, and if they throw you out the back door you go in the window, and if they throw you out the window you go in the basement. And you don't ever take it personally.*"[3] It was actually less a theory than a survival imperative. The only thing that mattered was getting the best information—or gaining access to the best information holders—and in a subculture built on interlocking relationships, the way to increase the yield of development deals is to plug into those circuits and keep expanding the universe of people who might have something to offer.

So it happened one morning in his first summer as production chief that Katzenberg dialed up a producer who wasn't yet on his list. According to Irwin Winkler, he said, "You don't know me, and I don't know you, but I'm interested in doing business with you. Could I take you to lunch?" Winkler said he would be delighted and the next day the two men met at West Hollywood's Ma Maison. Chartoff-Winkler's adaptation of Tom Wolfe's book about the early space program, *The Right Stuff,* was then in production; but by the end of their lunch it was evident that Winkler had nothing to sell.

As they were about to leave, Katzenberg asked one more time if he was sure he didn't have anything. Winkler hesitated. After all, Katzenberg was buying him lunch and he should at least throw him a bone. The producer conceded that there was this one screenplay, but warned that it would not be right for Paramount.

"What is that?" asked Katzenberg.

"You know, there's no sense in really even talking about it because I just don't think you'll be interested."

"Well, what is it?"

"It's *The Last Temptation of Christ.*"

Katzenberg rolled his eyes. "Well, let me read it anyway."

"I really don't think you would be interested in it."

Katzenberg waved off his protestations and told him to send Paul Schrader's script over. Several days later, Katzenberg called back to say that Paramount was interested. Winkler was elated at the news, but also perplexed.[4] He could not discern any obvious reason for Paramount to get involved with *Last Temptation.* Throughout the preproduction phase, Winkler said, "I was always scratching my head, saying, 'Why in the world do they want to make this movie?' Because it was so far away from the kind of films that they had a reputation for making."[5]

Irwin Winkler was under no illusion about the film's painfully poor fit with the direction of the movie business. The glory years of the 1970s, when talented young directors were courted by studio presidents and allowed to call the shots, were long gone. By the early 1980s, a confluence of onrushing developments was reshaping the entertainment industry—from the dimming influence of the 1960s counterculture; to the acquisition of previously independent studios by publicly traded conglomerates; to the growth of multiplex cinemas; to the exploding home-video market and the rapid build-out of cable systems in the nation's urban areas. A new model for making money from creative product was being hastily assembled. But not just any kind of creative product. The way of the future had been adumbrated with the astounding successes of Steven Spielberg's *Jaws* and George Lucas's *Star Wars*. The studios now focused on developing concepts that could easily be marketed to an audience of teens and young adults—especially ideas with the potential to become pop-culture franchises, capable of throwing off massive ancillary revenues in merchandising tie-ins and soundtrack sales before moving on to the lucrative home-video and pay cable windows. In short, the era of *high concept* was ascendent.[6]

The essence of high concept, in Steven Spielberg's words, is a story "you can hold in your hand."[7] Or, as the journalist Tony Schwartz wrote in a 1984 *New York* profile of Paramount's top executives, "A concept—or high concept, as it's come to be known—refers to an idea that can be summarized in a sentence. And then sold to anyone over the age of seven."[8] True high concept, however, is more than an idea writ small. The classic examples, such as *Jaws, E.T.: The Extraterrestrial,* and the Indiana Jones series, tap a deep vein of the mythic imagination—the misfit's redemption; the triumph of the pure of heart; and of course, David-versus-Goliath underdog narratives—with a few deft storytelling strokes. All the studios adopted it to some degree, but high concept reached its apotheosis at Paramount in the late 1970s and early 1980s, when the studio delivered to America's theaters the likes of *Saturday Night Fever, Grease, Heaven Can Wait, Meatballs, Star Trek, Urban Cowboy, Friday the 13th, Raiders of the Lost Ark, An Officer and a Gentleman,* and *Airplane!* Paramount inherited its DNA of high concept from the down-market medium of network television in the person of Michael Eisner. As ABC's head of feature films and program development, Eisner sat in on countless pitches from agents and producers. He trained himself to listen past all the elements that get thrown into a pitch and home in on the mainspring of a story. He described his reaction to a good story as a palpable sensation: "When I heard a good idea it had an effect on my mind and my body. Sometimes I felt it in my stomach, other times in my throat, still others on my skin—a kind of instant truth detector."[9]

When Eisner joined Barry Diller at Paramount in 1976, they applied this television-bred sensibility to the high-risk proposition of picking the twelve to fifteen pictures per year to put into production. Not all of them could be hits. But by emphasizing story over star power, by favoring studio-developed material over the packages offered by agencies, and by drumming Eisner's cost-curbing mantra into the mind of every production executive, Paramount didn't need a hit every time; even below-average grossing pictures could be profitable.

Irwin Winkler's confusion was understandable. *Last Temptation* was hardly cut from the same cloth as *Star Trek II: The Wrath of Khan*. The interest in it apparently came from another side of the studio's agenda, the side that annually green-lit a handful of "prestige" films. By most accounts, the push for serious drama more often came from Barry Diller, but even the populist-minded Eisner championed projects like *The Elephant Man* and *Ordinary People*.[10] About *Last Temptation*, Harry Ufland remembered that "Michael Eisner and Jeffrey Katzenberg were big proponents of the film and they really thought that it was not only going to be a very important film"—indeed, a potential Oscar nominee—"but they thought it would be successful commercially."[11] Katzenberg recalled only that he and Eisner were drawn to the idea of a brilliant filmmaker pursuing his passion. He said, "I don't think any of us thought that it was going to have the level of controversy that it did have. It was not meant to undermine or take a negative interpretation of people's faith. . . . It wasn't made as a piece of propaganda."[12]

According to David Kirkpatrick, the Paramount production executive who supervised *Last Temptation,* it was a combination of elements—including the potential upside of the novel's controversial history—that swayed the studio's thinking. "[The approval] had a lot to do with the fact that there had been a certain level of success at the company, that this was a highly original viewpoint on Christian mythology, that it had a world-class director involved, and it had a bit of controversy behind it. Michael Eisner was always looking for that sort of special project. He always would say, 'A project sometimes can have so many negatives to it that it's a positive.' And we were developing classic material. We were developing *Ethan Frome* and we were trying to decide if we should do something with *Scarlet Letter* or *Moby Dick*. And I think [*The Last Temptation of Christ*] was the kind of thing that Michael felt was different from the other material. . . . Anything that is unique and not referential to all the other sort of high concepts is something to make because it's easy to sell. Because it sells different and unusual. So it was really a combination of the artistry and also the fact that in part it really *was* a high concept. It was really being skewed as a high concept coming from a sort of intelligent, artistic point of view. And it was really driven by Michael."[13]

Several weeks after the Ma Maison meeting, Diller, Eisner, and Katzenberg joined Scorsese and Winkler for lunch at New York's Regency Hotel to hear their plans in more detail. Katzenberg talked at first about another religious film about a legendary Israelite that was in line for final approval. A Richard Gere vehicle, *King David* was conceived as a "down-the-center epic-adventure movie," as Katzenberg put it—apparently not something that would compete with Scorsese's project.[14] The conversation circled back to *Last Temptation*. Barry Diller looked across the table at Scorsese and asked him why he wanted to make it. "Because I want to get to know Christ better," Scorsese replied in utter seriousness.[15] Diller blushed, Scorsese said later, because "he didn't expect that answer. Neither did I, in a way. What I was thinking of is that I make a film that is not just a movie, but the act of making the film has to do with religion itself—*self-knowledge*. Which is not exactly what a Hollywood studio has in mind."[16]

If his motive was beyond their ken, Diller and Eisner recognized—indeed, they had the utmost respect for—Scorsese's pure passion for the story. Concluding lunch with the understanding that *Last Temptation* would be subject to certain budget restrictions, Diller said, "Let's make the movie."[17]

ON SUNDAY, JANUARY 16, 1983, Scorsese, Winkler, Chartoff, and their assistants boarded a flight for Israel to conduct the first location scout for *The Last Temptation of Christ*. Twenty years earlier, Pier Paolo Pasolini had taken a similar trip in preparation for *The Gospel according to St. Matthew*. According to his biographer Barth David Schwartz, within hours of his caravan's leaving Tel Aviv, Pasolini was already expressing disappointment about the modern look of Israel, the "reforestation works, modern agriculture, light industry."[18] Scorsese, however, was intoxicated with the idea of shooting in the Holy Land, and Arnon Milchan, his producer for *The King of Comedy* and an Israeli closely connected to the Knesset and the country's military complex, promised the group an entrée to the highest levels of government.

Upon their arrival in Tel Aviv, Scorsese and his party were whisked to Jerusalem, where they were introduced to President Yitzhak Navon, Yitzhak Rabin (then a member of the Knesset), and Jerusalem's mayor Teddy Kollek—meetings whose purposes were equal parts social and political. Throughout the rest of the scout, *Variety* reported, the group received "the 'A' treatment."[19] Kollek showed Scorsese the Valley of Hinnon southwest of Jerusalem, where the apostate King Ahaz sacrificed his sons in fire, and escorted the group to potential sites for the Crucifixion scene. In the City of David, Scorsese visited shrines such as the Church of the Holy Sepulcher, said to house the tomb of Christ, and he inquired about shooting under the Al-Aqsa Mosque in the Marwani Musallah. (The elders declined his request.) The rest of the trip was spent surveying the countryside. They chartered airplanes and an army helicopter was put at the party's disposal, enabling them to quickly cover a wide swath of the nation.

Location scout trips are normally low-profile affairs, but by the time Scorsese flew back for the opening of *The King of Comedy,* notices about the Israel trip had already appeared in *Variety, Hollywood Reporter,* and the *Los Angeles Herald-Examiner.* Most of the stories claimed that Robert De Niro was already attached to the film in the role of Jesus. Speculation about De Niro had first surfaced a year earlier, in *Rolling Stone*'s "Random Notes" column, where Paul Schrader opined about *Last Temptation:* "This is like another Scorsese–De Niro thing. . . . But this one deals with a real sufferer. A heavyweight sufferer instead of a middleweight."[20]

Asked by *Hollywood Reporter*'s correspondent in Tel Aviv whether De Niro had been offered the part, Scorsese denied that he had seen the script.[21] But the year before, Scorsese had in fact given him Schrader's adaptation. De Niro reportedly took off a hat to reveal his skull—shaved for his role in *Once upon a Time in America*—and said to Scorsese, "Do I look like Christ?"[22] Irwin Winkler also met with De Niro in New York and discussed, among other things, how the Crucifixion would be done, how a nail could be driven through his hand. De Niro apparently resisted getting involved in the project. He did not share Scorsese's affection for biblical material, nor did he warm to the idea of playing Kazantzakis' Christ, whose indecisiveness he likened to Hamlet's.[23] Paramount, however, thought the reteaming of Scorsese and De Niro would help to "presell" the film; the studio even announced De Niro's participation in *Last Temptation* at its annual presentation to exhibitors at the ShoWest trade show in Las Vegas. The next day Jeffrey Katzenberg caught up with Scorsese and apologized, explaining that the De Niro billing was a mistake. But before ShoWest ended, Winkler convinced him to talk to De Niro about it just one more time.[24]

On February 26 Scorsese took the Concorde to Paris for a one-day visit with the actor. During their years of working together they had explored subjects of mutual interest in a process that evolved, in Scorsese's words, as a "gravitation to each other."[25] For example, *Raging Bull* originated with De

Martin Scorsese and Boris Leven on location scout in Israel, 1983. (Courtesy of the Martin Scorsese collection)

Niro; only when Scorsese was able to find a personal connection to the material did he commit to direct. *GoodFellas* came first from Scorsese, but it moved forward at Warner Bros. when De Niro agreed to play the role of Jimmy "the Gent" Conway. With *Last Temptation*, there was no such gravitation. Their meeting that night, Scorsese recalled, "was a slightly awkward situation because I hadn't really planned to ask him, but I think the studio was expecting that."[26] The next morning, De Niro told Scorsese that he would do it if there was no other way for the film to be made, but Scorsese resolved not to ask his friend to get up on the cross if he didn't feel something for the part. With *The King of Comedy* suffering dismal box office results in its first week of release, it was a precarious time for Scorsese to be starting an ambitious project without a star. The issue of casting Jesus would grow more problematic as *The Last Temptation of Christ* moved further into preproduction.

To help him visualize *Last Temptation,* Scorsese turned to the legendary Hollywood art director Boris Leven, who had also worked with him on *New York, New York* and *The Last Waltz.* Together, Leven and Scorsese searched art books for reproductions of Gospel scenes that might suggest looks for *Last Temptation.* Some paintings of Georges de la Tour, Rembrandt, and Caravaggio yielded lighting and compositional ideas for the Last Supper sequence.[27] Giotto's fourteenth-century fresco *The Betrayal of Christ* served as a model for Jesus' betrayal in Gethsemane.[28] A Hieronymus Bosch painting, *The Bearing of the Cross,* inspired the film's ultra-slow-motion shot of Jesus carrying the beam of the cross on the Via Dolorosa.

Later that spring, Leven went with Scorsese on a second scout, first to Israel, then to Tunisia and Morocco. Though the archaeological sites of the Holy Land were impressive, they were essentially protected ruins hemmed in by the people, buildings, and highways of a developed society. The primitive quality that Scorsese and Leven were after, the look of a living first-century scene, was found in Morocco. A few miles outside Marrakech, they came into a desert village called Oumnast that had no electricity or television antennas. "There was nothing," Scorsese recalled. "People are still walking with donkeys, and it looks like something three, four thousand years old."[29] It was a community built to a human scale, the type that would have existed in antiquity—one that could pass as Nazareth or the Capernaum of Jesus' early ministry. Scorsese briefly flirted with the idea of filming in Morocco for three weeks before going on to Israel, but the cost of operating in both countries was deemed too high.

By May Scorsese was ready to revise the script. Paul Schrader was preoccupied with a screenplay on the life of the novelist Yukio Mishima and unavailable for further work on *Last Temptation.* After trying a couple of revisions himself, with less than satisfactory results, Scorsese called on his friend and sometime collaborator Jay Cocks. First they had to get out of the company town atmosphere of Los Angeles. They retreated to a rented house set on a hill in the desert above Palm Springs. But for a bad fuse that blew out the electricity one day, there was nothing in the isolated area to distract them. "We had two copies of the book on the table in front of us," recalled Cocks. "We had an assistant of Marty's who would retype and do things for us. We were able to work that intensely because we had a very good structure from Paul. I would rough out a scene. He'd read it, make suggestions. I'd rewrite, read it again, more suggestions, rewrite again, and then maybe move on."[30]

One morning they began reading the script and realized that the dialogue had to sound grittier, more like *On the Waterfront,* because the disciples were fishermen, "tough guys who worked with their hands," said Cocks.[31] They went through the script, "arguing over every word," Scorsese recalled, and eventually rewrote about 80 percent of the dialogue.[32]

The new dialogue worked best in some of the least likely scenes. The Sermon on the Mount, which is depicted in the Gospels of Luke and Matthew as a formal speech delivered to a multitude of rapt listeners, was changed into a loose, call-and-response-style sermon. Jesus starts out tentatively:

JESUS (V.O.[VOICE-OVER]) This is what I've always been afraid of. There's so much to say. What if I say the wrong thing? What if I say the right thing?

A pause. The words start to come.

JESUS: Come closer everybody. "My brothers, my sisters." I'm calling you that because we're all a family. A little closer. My voice isn't very strong, and I've got something to tell you.

The crowd gets closer, still more curious than anything else.

JESUS: I'm sorry if I have to tell you stories. But it seems to be the only way I can talk to you.

They read the lines of this scene back and forth, Cocks recalled, "as a kind of pep rally or political speech, with that kind of rhythm, because he's trying to get the crowd excited. And maybe that kind of looseness came through in the writing."[33]

Jesus takes a step forward, going with the momentum of his strong feelings.

JESUS: Listen, I used to think God was angry too. But not anymore. He used to jump on me like a wild bird and dig his claws into my head.

But then one morning he came to me. He blew over me like a cool breeze and said "Stand up." And here I am.

ZEBEDEE: Go to hell!

MAN IN CROWD: These are all stories for children. They can't help us.

Jesus starts into the crowd, confronting them directly.

JESUS: What are you hungry for? And you, you're thirsty? What are you thirsty for? For justice. Justice.

ANDREW: And bread.

JESUS: Bread too, bread too. I'm telling you, whoever's hungry for justice, whoever's thirsty for justice . . . they're the ones who'll be blessed. They'll be filled with bread. They'll never be thirsty again.

What Cocks and Scorsese were after in this critical scene was the sense of exhilaration that Jesus feels at finding his preaching voice. Jesus, Scorsese said, is "getting the beat, he's getting the language and the rhythm of it. . . . It's like watching a guy get himself together and it's great. When he gets it he feels terrific about it. He says, 'Here I am.'"[34]

They also tried to magnify the significance of certain scenes, such as the raising of Lazarus. In Schrader's version, Lazarus merely emerges from the tomb of his own accord. Cocks and Scorsese injected a brief struggle in the effort to get Lazarus out of the tomb, thereby dramatizing Jesus' fear of facing death and foreshadowing what would be asked of him later.

Jesus stands at the entrance of the tomb and yells. His voice echoes: a wild, strange cry, like something from another world.

JESUS: Lazarus! In the name of the prophets, in the name of Jeremiah and my Father, in the name of the most Holy God, I call you here!

At first, nothing. Then we begin to hear a soft rustling inside the tomb. Jesus is apprehensive. He stares at the tomb's entrance. Suddenly a decomposed skeletal human hand reaches out. The crowd gasps. Jesus, startled, jumps. Slowly, Jesus reaches out, moves a bit closer and clasps the corpse's hand. He is terrified. Suddenly, the corpse pulls back as if to yank Jesus into the tomb. Jesus is more frightened. He stands his ground. Then, Jesus decides to pull and the corpse comes out. The disciples and the crowd are stunned. The desicated [sic] figure, Lazarus, is covered head to toe in white burial cloth. His free hand slowly unwraps the cloth from his face. Strips of rotting flesh hang loose. Lazarus embraces Jesus.

Some of the more provocative parts of Schrader's screenplay were excised, including the brief flashback featuring a younger Mary Magdalene and Jesus betrothed in the village of Magdala, as well as a scene in the last temptation sequence in which the pregnant Mary Magdalene is stoned to death by Saul and some guards. Schrader's line, "God sleeps between your legs," uttered during the fantasized lovemaking, and the shots of disciples coughing up flesh during the Last Supper stayed in until the last revision in November. The theme of Jesus' rejection of his mother, however, was not only kept but expanded.

Mary comes out of the crowd near him and grabs Jesus' arm.

MARY (MOTHER OF JESUS): Son. Please. Come back with me.

JESUS: Who are you?

MARY (MOTHER OF JESUS): Who I am. What's the matter with you? I'm your mother.

JESUS: I don't know who you are. I don't have any mother, I don't have any family. All I have is a father, and he's in heaven.

MARY (MOTHER OF JESUS): I don't care who you think you are, don't talk to me that way.

JESUS: Who are you? I mean really. Who are you?

He shakes off her arm and keeps walking, the disciples close behind him. She stands still, quietly crying.[35]

By the end of their second trip to Palm Springs, Cocks and Scorsese's emendations had increased the length of the screenplay to 89 scenes and 111 pages. When Scorsese worried aloud about the extra pages, Paul Schrader replied sardonically, "Well, just remember that on those days when you have to shoot them."[36] All together, Cocks and Scorsese revised the screenplay seven times that year, and it effectively made the crossing from Schrader's poetic work to a script ready to be shot to Scorsese's dramatic and stylistic specifications.

Coordinating the casting sessions in Los Angeles was Cis Corman, who had performed the same duty on *Raging Bull* and *The King of Comedy*. Well acquainted with Scorsese's instincts, Corman did not always cast apposite to character description; it was often more interesting to go in other, less conventional directions. But she wasn't sure if this methodology would work for *The Last Temptation of Christ.* Kazantzakis' novel hardly comported with the sanctified images of Jesus she saw as a girl when she went to Mass with her Catholic friends, and her own upbringing in a Reformed Jewish family in Brookline, Massachusetts, was no help, either. She began to think it might be better to cast safely, to stay well within known types. "I then realized I have to approach this and look for actors like I look for actors on everything, and not get bogged down by the idea that this is holier than holy."[37]

The auditions followed a protocol similar to that of the other Scorsese films Corman had worked on: "First of all, when an actor finds out that they're going to meet Marty Scorsese, it is like—well, they're beside themselves. Marty would say to me, 'Come to my house. Come at two-thirty.' I'd say, okay. And I would call the agent and say, 'Tell the actor to get there at about three-thirty, quarter of four. And to bring a book.' And maybe by four-thirty we would start seeing people." Corman would brief Scorsese on the actor's work and then he talked alone with the actor. "He was absolutely wonderful with actors. I would have to open the door and say, 'Marty, I'm sorry—' He would never say to an actor, time is up. I had to rescue him all the time. I would give them as much time as I could. The actors, of course, would walk out of that room and couldn't believe that they had met with Marty Scorsese. And when he hired somebody and they were working together, he did that by himself."[38]

Barbara Hershey was put through three months of screen tests for the part of Mary Magdalene because Scorsese, Winkler, and Robert Chartoff felt they had to prove—to themselves and to Hershey—that acting ability and her suitability for the part were the only considerations, and not because she had given the novel to Scorsese.[39] Scorsese called on his longtime friend Harvey Keitel to play Judas because, Scorsese argued, he is the character who stands in for the audience: "He is the audience: Judas. And that's why for me the audience is a person who lives in New York, on the East Coast, and has that kind of accent. It's me, in that respect."[40] Harry Dean Stanton, who grew up a Southern Baptist in Kentucky, was chosen to lend a televangelist fervor to Saint Paul in the last temptation sequence.[41] For the brief but critical role of Pontius Pilate, Scorsese cribbed an idea from William Wyler's *Ben Hur:* using British actors for the Romans, in contrast to Americans for the Jews. The idea was to convey differences of social caste and political authority by this very precise change in accents.[42] Cis Corman met first with David Bowie in her office, but the part of Pilate—envisioned by Scorsese as a young, charismatic prefect—was offered to another British pop star, Sting.

The second tier of actors came together by early fall: Verna Bloom (Jay Cocks's wife) as Mary, mother of Jesus; Irvin Kershner as Zebedee; Andre Gregory as John the Baptist; Kathy Baker as Martha, the sister of Lazarus; and Michael Been, Paul Herman, Paul Sorvino, Victor Argo, and John Lurie as apostles. Schrader's first draft of the screenplay described the guardian angel as an Arab boy. But to avoid criticism for identifying Satan as Arabic, Cocks and Scorsese rewrote the character to be an old man, a father figure. Hume Cronyn and Lew Ayres both read for the part, and Ayres—an MGM contract player from the 1930s and 1940s—was eventually chosen, owing in part to concerns about Cronyn's health.[43]

The most important casting decision, of course, was that of the Messiah. There is not a single reference to Jesus' physical appearance in the New Testament. As a Palestinian Jew of that period, Jesus could well have been a dark-skinned man with Semitic features and a close-cropped beard.[44] But because of Hebrew proscriptions against religious art, the first frescoes and mosaics of Jesus dating from the third century were created by Gentiles. These images typically depicted him as Greco-Roman, sometimes with a beard, but often without one.[45] From the Medieval period onward, wrote Jaroslav Pelikan in *Jesus through the Centuries,* "the humanity of Jesus depicted in the icons was a humanity suffused with the presence of divinity; it was, in this sense, the 'deified' body of Christ that was being portrayed."[46]

Movie portrayals deviated little from this visual orthodoxy of the Europeanized Christ. By one count, fifty-seven actors played Jesus Christ in feature films between 1897's *The Passion Play of Oberammergau,* in which Frank Russell first inhabited the role, and 2004's *The Passion of the Christ.*[47] All but three of these actors were bearded, and all but one identifiably Caucasian. A more Semitic-looking Jesus might have been historically accurate, but Scorsese rationalized that audiences were more likely to accept a fully human Jesus if they didn't also have to deal with a radically different appearance. "The Jesus in the film," he was to say later, "is the Jesus that *we* 'know' from calendars and from the statues. Light, auburn hair. Long hair. Blue-eyed. And a slight beard. And that's the Jesus that we as Westerners and Americans 'know,' so to speak."[48]

As the summer dragged on, the process of casting Jesus consumed more of Scorsese's time than he had expected. Among others, John Malkovich, Christopher Walken, Jonathan Pryce, and Eric Roberts came to the Bel Air

Hotel for auditions, as Harvey Keitel played Judas to their Jesus.[49] Scorsese was impressed with Roberts's performance, but the actor took himself out of contention.[50] Finally, in early September, Scorsese settled on Chris Walken, and the actor's screen test was shown to Paramount executives. They reacted negatively, said David Kirkpatrick, because Walken had played too many odd-ball characters to be sympathetic as Jesus.[51] In long, stressful conversations with the studio, it became clear to Scorsese that his choice of Walken was getting entangled with concerns about the film's escalating costs. At one juncture, Katzenberg asked Scorsese if he would go to the mat for this—What if Walken was suddenly, inexplicably, unavailable to do the picture? What would he do? Scorsese said that, of course, he would have to get another actor. Katzenberg's clever line of questioning produced the desired answer: Chris Walken was not indispensable; the movie could go on without him.[52]

Later, Walken's agent, Sue Mengers, told Scorsese that Paramount was using Walken's unsuitability as an excuse to back out of the film.[53] Whether or not Mengers was right, Scorsese had to bury his bitterness and find a replacement.

Earlier that summer Scorsese had compiled footage of a twenty-four-year-old actor, Aidan Quinn, whose rebellious, motorcycle-riding Johnny Rourke in the yet-to-be released *Reckless* was creating a buzz. He was intrigued with Quinn's resemblance to the James Dean of *Rebel without a Cause*. In Scorsese's mind, Dean had always been a model for the fusing of alienation, yearning, and willful contrariness in Kazantzakis' Jesus—especially in the scene where Jesus tries to displease God by making crosses for the Romans' executions. Quinn came in to audition with Barbara Hershey and gave "an amazing screen test," according to one of Scorsese's associates.[54] Scorsese and Cis Corman saw a vulnerability in his face that they believed would work for Jesus. The studio quickly agreed and Quinn proceeded to immerse himself in the part.

The conflict over casting used up some of Scorsese's political capital with the studio. But that was only a prelude to a much graver situation: the production budget, which had been inching up all summer, suddenly exploded. Boris Leven, recalled Scorsese, "kept talking to me about opening the production up a little bit and making it breathe in a sense in terms of size."[55] This meant bigger, more elaborate sets and expensive set decorations, props, and costumes that incorporated the historical detail they were finding in their research. One set of Jean-Pierre Delifer's costumes—those intended for Jesus, Mary Magdalene, the disciples, and ordinary Palestinians—were being created in Marrakech workshops by local craftsmen using traditional Moroccan fabrics.[56] The

clothes worn by the Romans and the Jewish religious hierarchy were constructed at even greater expense at Bermans and Nathans in London. The toga
for Pontius Pilate was sewn from an eight-meter length of natural deerskin so
supple, recalled Delifer, "it might look like silk." When the invoices for the
costumes came in, Irwin Winkler realized for the first time that the film's costs
were spiraling out of control.[57]

Another factor propelling the budget higher was the cost of working in
Israel. An early warning had come that spring when Chartoff-Winkler received
a bill from the Israeli government for the use of an army helicopter during the
January location scout. Instead of the original estimate of four to five hundred
dollars an hour, they were shocked to see helicopter charges of nearly four
thousand dollars per hour. After several attempts to get the bill corrected, Hal
Polaire, the executive producer, wrote to the Israeli minister of commerce and
industry: "Our concerns, now, are whether we can afford to expose ourselves
to an operation in Israel and find the same situation occurring, and whether
we can afford to have this film made in Israel at all."[58]

The helicopter contretemps was patched up, but almost every location cost,
from hotel rooms to the rates for an Israeli crew, seemed to come tagged with
exorbitant surcharges. Paramount's cost-averse management was accustomed
to making films no farther away than one short flight from Los Angeles,[59] and
now Chartoff and Winkler, whose *The Right Stuff* had gone substantially over
budget, were proposing to shoot *The Last Temptation of Christ* on the other
side of the globe, in a nation constantly on the brink of war. By late August
Winkler had already twice gone back to the well. The studio grudgingly
approved both requests and the budget swelled to $14 million for a ninety-day
shooting schedule.

The numbers were about to go up again. *Last Temptation* was going to be
shot all over Israel—from Timna for the raising of Lazarus, to the Roman
amphitheater in Beit Shear for the scene with Pontius Pilate, to the Negev
Desert for the monastery and wilderness and village scenes, to Jerusalem for
various scenes involving that venerated city. The location changes required at
least one down day for the company to move, which spread out the shooting
schedule.[60] And each location had its own unique issues. To shoot at the historic ruins, for example, they would have to approach the Israeli antiquities
authorities and obtain a permit; Chartoff-Winkler would then put up a bond
to guarantee that the site was returned to its original condition when the
company finished.[61] Winkler ran the numbers and came up with a hundred
days of principal photography and a new budget of $16 million. They needed

to ask for more money, he told Scorsese: it would be better to ask at that point than to shoot for four or five weeks and then say they needed more.[62]

The timing for another budget hike was not propitious for Winkler himself. *The Right Stuff* had been a strenuous shoot in the Mojave Desert, and the idea of working thousands of miles away from his family on another desert production was distinctly unappealing. Winkler had also begun the dissolution of his partnership with Chartoff, with whom he had been teamed since 1962.[63] "So I was starting to have one foot out the door by then," he recalled.[64]

On Tuesday, September 27, 1983, Scorsese and Winkler went in to see Michael Eisner and David Kirkpatrick. Winkler carried a copy of the October 3 issue of *Newsweek*, featuring a cover story about *The Right Stuff*. The movie was opening to positive critical notices, and with the coincident entry of the former Mercury astronaut John Glenn into the race for the Democratic presidential nomination, all signs pointed toward a buoyant theatrical run. After accepting the congratulations of his peers, Winkler turned to *Last Temptation*. He reviewed the casting, Leven's set design enhancements, the logistics of shooting in Israel. More money was needed to ensure a first-rate production, he concluded. About $2 million more. The executives' faces went blank. In that instant, Scorsese recalled, "something happened in the room."[65]

"Every time you come back, you ask for more money," Eisner complained. "And we're getting all this difficulty for the film, you know, and we're not sure about your casting."

Not only did Eisner demur on the budget request, but Scorsese saw in his reaction the bottom suddenly falling out of the studio's support for the project.

As if to put an emphatic caption on Scorsese's reading of the situation, Eisner fixed them with a glare and said, "When you walked in this room, you had a green light. You are now at a blinking yellow."

They retreated down the hall to an empty office. Winkler, disturbed at what had just transpired, said that the film was shaping up to be something that had all the earmarks of a difficult production. "They're going to fight us every inch of the way."[66]

"Irwin, I'm going to make this film if I have to take a camera into the desert and do it myself."

"I don't know if I'm prepared to do that," Winkler answered.[67]

A few days later, Winkler notified Scorsese and Paramount that he was withdrawing from *Last Temptation*. Ultimately, he could not abandon his code—*A producer has to live with his movie. Unless he's willing to do that, he has no rights.*[68] Winkler's exit was a significant loss for both; Paramount respected his production acumen and relationship with Scorsese, and Scorsese valued him as the kind of producer who could protect him from external pressures and distractions. He never forgot the first difficult weeks of shooting *Raging Bull*, when Winkler ran interference for him and took the brunt of United Artists' objections. Then, during the film's long months of editing, Winkler shielded Scorsese from the information that United Artists "was, sight unseen, selling the picture."[69] Winkler had the combination of judgment, finesse, and toughness that Scorsese sorely needed at this moment, as Paramount reevaluated nearly everything about the film. But Scorsese couldn't blame the producer for putting his personal affairs first.

The first week of October, Katzenberg introduced Scorsese to his new producer, Jon Avnet, a partner in the Tisch-Avnet Company, who had just come off the breakout success of *Risky Business* for Warner Bros. Avnet immediately set to work devising a more measured production; the alternative, it was now understood by all parties, would be for Paramount to pull out. Katzenberg called Harry Ufland on October 14 to tell him that *Last Temptation* had been given the go-ahead again.[70] The budget was rolled back to $11.4 million, and Katzenberg made it clear that he preferred that Scorsese come in between $9 and 10 million; he told Ufland, parenthetically, that Scorsese would probably find out that he wouldn't need a hundred shooting days. Several days later, a story in the *Los Angeles Times* reported that a new accord between Paramount and the *Last Temptation* production team had been struck "after months of rumors that the studio had given up on the project."[71]

MONTHS LATER, Michael Eisner said of the Christian opponents of *Last Temptation*, "It's obviously an organized campaign but we've never been able to figure out what group was behind it."[72] The attack on the film flew low under the media radar—and even under Paramount's radar. The opponents thought that if they spread the word quickly, if they could persuade Americans to express outrage in no uncertain terms, they stood a chance of hitting Gulf + Western's soft spot: its aversion to risking reputation and corporate profitability on one highly controversial movie. But even if they did these things, they still needed a great deal of help—help beyond their control—to convince the conglomerate to back away from its commitment to Martin Scorsese.

The first portent of this stealth attack came in the March 1983 issue of the *N.F.D. Informer,* the newsletter of a media watchdog group run by the Reverend Donald Wildmon. A balding, folksy Methodist minister, Wildmon had come a long way since the night in December 1976 when he had had a life-changing epiphany.[73] Relaxing with his family for an evening of television viewing at their home in Southaven, Mississippi, the thirty-eight-year-old Wildmon suddenly realized that no matter which of the three network channels he tuned to, he could not avoid exposing his children to shows filled with sex, violence, or profanity. Previously he had always taken the attitude that television's "mind-poisoning junk food" was just one of the unpleasant realities of living in a pluralistic society. By his own admission, he had fallen into the habit of ignoring the issue, of looking the other way. But in the weeks following that evening, as he read dozens of articles citing television's harmful effects, Donald Wildmon decided that looking the other way was no longer an option. Not only was it within his power as an individual to effect change in the culture, he believed it was a mission that God was calling him to follow. In his first foray as an activist in early March 1977, he promoted "Turn the TV Off Week" among the members of his own congregation. Despite the dubious results of the stunt, the national press attention it garnered suggested that a homegrown moral values outfit could play on a bigger stage than the Bible Belt. That summer he resigned as pastor and moved his family to Tupelo, in northeast Mississippi. There he founded a nonprofit organization, the National Federation of Decency (NFD), its unofficial goal the remaking of the face of the multibillion-dollar television industry.

In a crowded field of media reformers and advocacy groups, all vying for the same limited pool of donor support, Wildmon needed a modus operandi that would set the NFD apart. It took years of trying various techniques, but he eventually discovered the model for achieving his goals. He found that if the networks were impervious to pressures from outside groups, the advertisers weren't. By turning a spotlight on every company advertising in shows saturated in violence, sex, profanity, or anti-Christian bias (as determined by coders trained by the NFD), the networks would come under enormous pressure from their own clients to change programming policy. There was really no carrot in this approach, only a stick: the outrage of Christians, articulated in waves of letters and phone calls to the offending advertisers. It was a shrewd strategy, but Wildmon lacked a broad constituent base for making the threat credible.

Wildmon won this much-needed credibility in 1981, when the NFD allied with the Moral Majority and other religious right groups to create the Coalition for Better Television (CBTV). The deal was clinched when he showed Jerry Falwell a dollar bill and said, "The networks don't care about your moral

values, but they do care about this."[74] Overnight, the coalition delivered to
Wildmon the support of two hundred organizations and a membership base
of three million. CBTV's breakthrough victory came that June. Television's
largest advertiser, Procter and Gamble, shocked the industry when it voluntarily pulled out of several prime-time shows identified by CBTV as excessively
violent, sexual, or profane.[75] The coalition disbanded the next year, but by
then Wildmon had increased his constituency and established his bona fides
as a leading media "watchdog."

Of all the groups opposing Paramount's *Last Temptation,* only the NFD
was skilled in the art of corporate intimidation (or extortion, as some critics
regarded its methods). As always, Wildmon's weapon of choice was the rhetorical threat of a boycott. But this case was different from the others. He was
going after a film that did not even exist. The modest item in the March 1983
issue of the *N.F.D. Informer* was headlined, "Film to Have Jesus Fighting
against Being Accepted as the Messiah." It spoke of a "recent splash of anti-
Christian films from Hollywood and the networks" and told readers of a
planned October start date for *Last Temptation.* The article closed with a list
of the parent company's retail products: "Gulf & Western makes Backwoods
Smoker, Big A auto parts, Cameron fragrance, Comfort Stride hosiery, Easy
To Be Me bra, Jordache clothing, No-Nonsense pantyhose, Pascalle fragrance,
Supp-Hose stockings, and Ultra Sense pantyhose. If you care to write, the
address is: Pres. David N. Judelson, Gulf & Western Industries, 1 Gulf & Western Plaza, New York, NY 10023."[76]

The point of the product list didn't have to be explained to the *Informer's*
readers. These were products that each reader could refuse to buy if this repre-
hensible news from Hollywood became reality—a consumer's decision that
Gulf + Western should, of course, be apprised of. By summer of 1983, the
NFD was blasting bulletins about *Last Temptation* to its affiliate chapters and
the hundreds of other names (mostly evangelical Christians) on its mailing
list.

At roughly the same time, a group of Lutheran nuns—the Evangelical Sisterhood of Mary—independently took notice of *The Last Temptation of Christ.*
The Sisters of Mary had arrived from Germany in 1966 and established a
convent named Canaan in the Desert on ten acres north of the Phoenix Mountain Preserve in Arizona. In time they built a media production center at the
convent for distributing newsletters and devotional videos to thousands of
people on their mailing list. The Sisters had a combative side, too. Clad in

khaki habits and white veils, they were known locally for protesting "blasphe-mous" plays like *Godspell.* When they thought their Savior was grossly misrep-resented, the Sisters felt compelled to show up on a theater's sidewalk on opening night and picket. As one of them explained, "Jesus is Lord, he's sover-eign, he's almighty. We are never on the same level as our Lord Jesus, and to even imply that we are on the same level is very heartbreaking both to our-selves and to our Lord."[77]

It must have been with the same sense of heartbreak that Mother Basilea Schlink wrote a letter in the summer of 1983: "It has been brought to our attention that a book, THE LAST TEMPTATION OF CHRIST by Nikos Kazantzakis is being made into a film of the same name with shooting to begin on location in JERUSALEM in mid-January 1984. We were able to locate a copy of this book at our public library and now make this urgent appeal for your help that this film might be stopped. In this book of 500 pages the reader follows a gross distortion of the actual Biblical account of Jesus' life up to the Crucifixion."[78]

Mother Schlink went on to tell her readers of some of these distortions—Jesus' resistance to God's call; Jesus' visit to the Magdalene's brothel door; Jesus' admission of sin and his fear of insanity. "Unspeakable things are put into Jesus' mouth," she hinted darkly. Near the end of the novel, she noted, Jesus' delirium on the cross becomes a pretext for an "immoral relationship" with Mary Magdalene, followed by a disgracefully polygamous marriage to the sisters Martha and Mary. It is only in the last lines of the book that one learns that said delirium was orchestrated by the Devil. By then, she wrote, "the viewer will already have had his mind filled with such fabrications and blas-phemies that are not easily forgotten."

She closed by asking the readers of her newsletter to pray against the film. She suggested that their concerns be put in writing and mailed to the New York office of Gulf + Western's chairman, Martin Davis, and the Los Angeles offices of Paramount Pictures.

Suddenly, letters objecting to the film began arriving at Paramount. "We tried to answer each one of them with a thoughtful note," said David Kirkpat-rick.[79] A clerical worker was put in a temporary office and given the job of replying to everyone who wrote—to send them mailing addresses, to let them know that they were being heard and that the studio would not knowingly make a picture that was inappropriate, to assure them that *The Last Tempta-tion of Christ* was a work of artistic achievement and that the studio was mov-ing ahead on it.[80] Some of the more poignant letters—such as one from a mother who feared that the film might put her daughter's belief in God at risk—were sent along to Scorsese, who responded personally.[81]

In September the negative reaction stepped up. Churches became force multipliers for the protest, circulating petitions, Mother Schlink's letter, and other information about the film in their congregations. (They did this job so well that it was difficult to turn it off months later, after the need had passed.)[82] The same phrases and passages turned up in batches of letters bearing the same postmarks. Many of the writers cited the same "facts" about the novel, and some charged inexplicably that Jesus was portrayed in the movie as a homosexual. The stream of letters and cards turned into a deluge, delivered in large quantities at Gulf + Western corporate headquarters in New York. By October the protesting mail was cresting at more than five thousand pieces a week, and full-time workers were hired to help regain control of the mailroom.[83] The hundreds of letters, cards, and petitions delivered every day spoke as one voice against *The Last Temptation of Christ* and advised one path to follow: kill the project immediately.[84]

Some of the writers said their pieces bluntly on a single piece of stationery or on the back of a postcard: "Dear sir: How could you sponsor such trash as 'The Last Temptation of Christ'? I ask that you disassociate yourself from this film of lies!" But most went on for one, two, three, or more pages. The idea for the movie was "the product of a very sick mind," and the book on which it was based was "vile and filthy," "pornographic," "a false calumny," "a most abhorrent form of pollution," "full of unspeakable blasphemies and sordid fabrications." They beseeched Gulf + Western's Martin Davis not to surrender to "the almighty dollar" or be party to a film that "brings reproach, discredit, and disgrace to our Lord and Savior, Jesus Christ." Others pledged to throw their support behind a consumer revolt against Gulf + Western. "Such a blasphemous movie would stir a vast number of people to boycott your products," predicted one of these writers. "I would personally do everything in my power to inform others of your involvement in such a movie if it were to materialize."

But for every letter that fulminated against the film or damned everyone associated with it, there was a letter that entreated the executives to obey a higher ethos, to cease and desist the film's production out of respect for believers, the Christian faith, and Jesus Christ himself. A Texas woman wrote, "You have such a wonderful opportunity at your disposal of spreading the Good News about Jesus Christ." A twelve-year-old girl in Arizona asked Gulf + Western not to make *Last Temptation* "because it shows false teachings of

Christ. Non-Christians would believe that and it isn't true. Then they would think we have a terrible God and that is not true. We have a great God." The reasonableness and sincerity of these letters suggested that feelings of offense could rise up from a broader cross-section of Christians, not just religious fanatics.

The escalating response was undoubtedly fueled by an article written by Art Levine, under the title "Raging Messiah," for the August issue of the politically progressive magazine *Mother Jones*. Billed as a "sneak preview of Scorsese's new bio-pic," most of the article was fashioned as a screenplay of *The Last Temptation of Christ*, although it did not resemble either Kazantzakis' novel or Schrader's own screenplay. Instead, Levine ruthlessly parodied Scorsese's artistic conceits by grafting the narrative template of *Raging Bull* onto Gospel personages and events. Jesus, for example, is portrayed as a Jake La Motta–like boxer getting himself in shape for the title bout that would make him the Messiah. The rest follows suit. A foul-tempered Joseph abuses Mary for the indiscretion of giving birth to Jesus; Vito and Peter are disciples who try to psych up a nervous Jesus for his entrance into Jerusalem; Caiaphas and Pontius Pilate are transformed into mobster figures; and the Devil tempts Jesus with gastronomic visions of spaghetti, veal parmigiana, and "other Italian dishes."[85]

Unbeknown to *Mother Jones*'s editors, this odd, profanity-filled "humor" piece was about to reach a very different audience. Donald Wildmon's staff at the NFD routinely combed news magazines, liberal periodicals, and the entertainment trade journals in search of news they could cite as evidence of the media industries' depravity. Reacting quickly to the *Mother Jones* piece, the *N.F.D. Informer* put together a two-page spread for its September issue, under the headline "CBS, Time Help Promote Vicious, Sick Anti-Christian Article." The opening pages from "Raging Messiah" (with the profanity omitted) were reprinted, "because we felt you needed to see the depth of degradation of the article which Time and CBS felt worthy of their financial support."[86] If "Raging Messiah" was *Mother Jones*'s way of lampooning Scorsese's oeuvre, the point was probably lost on the *N.F.D. Informer*'s more literal-minded readers.

Word of an anti-*Temptation* campaign began seeping into the exhibitor community. One executive who was riveted by what was happening was Salah Hassanein, an executive vice president of United Artists Communications. Born in Egypt to a Catholic mother and a Muslim father, Hassanein immigrated to New York City as a young man after World War II. Salah Hassanein joined United Artists Theaters, where he built a nearly forty-year career running the East Coast circuit for Marshall and Robert Naify, UA's major shareholders. Described by colleagues as "gregarious, hard-driving, and mercurial,"[87] Hassanein carved out an unusual degree of influence over the entire United Artists chain. "He was polite, but only polite, to the Naifys," said a film distributor. "Really, you would think he owned the company."[88]

The alarming tone of the letters and calls protesting *Last Temptation* reminded Hassanein of other religious films in his decades of experience that had stirred passionate feelings—*Martin Luther, The Greatest Story Ever Told, The Life of Brian,* and particularly the 1976 historical epic, *Mohammed: Messenger of God.* That film endured a series of difficulties during production, including a stormy walkout by the Islamic scholars hired as technical advisors. When *Messenger of God* was finally set to premiere in the United States, an extremist Muslim group seized a B'nai B'rith chapter in Washington, D.C., and threatened to kill hostages and bomb the building they were occupying unless all the film's American showings were canceled.

The standoff ended without injury, but the incident confirmed Salah Hassanein's worst fears about provocative movie portrayals of gods and prophets. He became convinced that local multiplexes—United Artists' multiplexes— would be ground zero for any explosive reactions set off by *The Last Temptation of Christ.* Accordingly, in October Hassanein wrote to Paramount's head of marketing and distribution, Frank Mancuso, to inform him that the film would not play at any of United Artists' 3,200 screens. The loss of United Artists, the largest chain in the country at the time, would seriously hurt *Last Temptation*'s box office prospects, but UA's decision also suggested that it might be the first big domino in a tumbling cascade of other exhibitors passing on the movie. It was Mancuso's duty to tell Barry Diller that if Paramount continued with its plans to make *Last Temptation,* it might not be able to show the picture in most of the theaters in America. "And that sent a real tremor through the studio," said Avnet.[89]

Hassanein's missive seemed to reopen and even widen fractures in the studio's support of the film. *The Last Temptation of Christ,* David Kirkpatrick recalled, "was sort of a maelstrom of activity largely political in relationship to the material, and so consequently we were always being sort of dragged into not only dealing with the president of production, but the president of the studio and the chairman of the studio. . . . Michael and Barry were at odds over it because, I think, on the one hand, Michael really wanted to make it . . . and Barry was sort of a little less convinced."[90] The fate of the film also became entwined in the Paramount executives' worsening relations with Martin Davis of Gulf + Western, who imposed a tough management style on the company after the death of the previous chairman, Charles Bluhdorn, in February.[91] A self-confessed control freak, Davis was prone to undercutting the authority of his division heads by weakening, or trying to force the ouster of, their lieutenants. With Paramount, this tactic took the specific form of attempting to turn Diller against his own senior management, Michael Eisner in particular.[92] Now, as letters attacking *Last Temptation* poured in, Davis for the first time took an active interest in Paramount's content decisions. He asked pointed questions about why the film was being made—whether it was a socially responsible thing to do, and whether, as so many letters claimed, it really was blasphemous.[93]

Barry Diller, Michael Eisner, and Jeffrey Katzenberg were hardly qualified to answer these questions. Not only were all three men raised as Jews, they were secularists in sensibility and lifestyle. They concluded that some sort of consultation with Christian theologians would help equip them with arguments to defend the project as well as pinpoint those parts of the screenplay that would draw fire if they were filmed as written. But they couldn't afford the time for the issues to be thoroughly studied; Martin Davis's concerns had to be answered *now*. Alternatively, several theologians could be brought to the studio, where, under the probing questions of Jeffrey Katzenberg, their collective erudition could be tapped in a single session. Out of this give-and-take would, it was hoped, emerge insights into any transgressive tendencies lying in the script and who would be most offended if the filmmakers were to go there.

Taking his cue from Katzenberg, David Kirkpatrick engaged Scorsese's friend Mary Pat Kelly to organize a theological "seminar."[94] Kelly was already on Paramount's payroll, doing research for Scorsese and prepping the actors on the scriptural foundations of their characters—a position Kirkpatrick jokingly called "theologian to the stars."[95] More than a year after approving *The Last Temptation of Christ,* with the project now on life support, the studio was finally going to discover what manner of film it had on its hands.

THE SEMINAR PROJECT afforded Mary Pat Kelly the chance to convene "four of the top theologians in the world,"[96] as she put it. John McKenzie, a Jesuit priest who was retired from De Paul University's theology department, was a leading Catholic intellectual and proponent of the biblical theology

movement, which sought to recover the original meanings of biblical literature.[97] Rosemary Radford Reuther was a Catholic feminist and prolific author
whose latest book, *Sexism and God-Talk,* conceived Jesus as an itinerant libera-
tor struggling against social inequality.[98] Rounding out the group were John
Cobb, a Protestant theologian from the Claremont College School of Theology, and Jack Elliott, a Methodist teacher and scholar from San Francisco
State University. All of them had read the Kazantzakis novel years before;
nevertheless, Kelly mailed them new copies along with the latest version of the
screenplay.

The morning of November 4 was brilliantly sunny as Katzenberg, Kelly,
Kirkpatrick, and the four scholars walked into an executive dining room for
what was surely the first meeting of theologians ever held at a Hollywood
studio. They sat at a large round table set with microphones, water pitchers
and glasses, and a floral centerpiece. After introductions around the table,
Jeffrey Katzenberg led off the discussion. Was the book still a controversial
work? What was its reputation then? Everyone agreed that the novel was controversial in the 1960s, when reactionary groups tried to remove it from libraries, but their views of its influence veered off in sharply different directions.
Last Temptation, said Mary Pat Kelly, was an ingredient of the new theology
of the early 1960s—"the door opening into a different way of seeing Christ."
Rosemary Reuther disagreed, saying the novel merely reflected Kazantzakis'
point of view. Both John Cobb and Jack Elliott thought that the book appealed
to "extreme orthodox" people. Surprised at hearing this, Katzenberg asked
them to clarify what they meant. Kazantzakis played up the supernaturalistic
powers of Jesus, said Cobb; further, the novel's attribution of messianic claims
to Jesus ran counter to the liberal tradition in which Cobb grew up.

Just as it looked as though dissent would overtake the proceedings, Elliott
brought them together on a key point. "The whole Christian community," he
began, "has always looked at Christ on the one hand as human and, on the
other hand, he has wings and there is an aura about him and he is always in
the clouds. So people are reading and they are going to movies looking for
both of those things. For humanity on the one hand, but not too much.
Because if you give him too much, then somehow he is less divine. [In Kazantzakis' book] there is a wonderful tension between this being a human being
with lots of problems and wrestling with anguish and doubt, and on the other
hand, having illusions of grandeur."

Reuther took Elliott's observation a step further. The traditional statement
regarding Jesus' humanity, derived from the book of Hebrews, is that he was

like us in all things except that he never sinned. This caveat, she said, had profound implications: How could Jesus empathize with us, and us with him, if the temptation he faced was abstract, easily shrugged off?

"What Kazantzakis essentially does," said Reuther, "is throw out that concept and have Jesus Christ really tempted in all kinds of directions. Tempted in the flesh, but also tempted in the spirit. It is that kind of interiorization perception of his temptation that is essentially controversial." Even more controversial for anyone interested in Jesus were the precise ways that Kazantzakis chose to portray him as a man whipsawed between human impulses and God's relentless demands:

ELLIOTT: One of the things that fascinated me about Kazantzakis' book is the idea that Jesus might be crazy. That is going to be as offensive as hell. That he is suffering from migraines with big birds on his back and that he is making crosses. Nobody has ever suggested that before.

MCKENZIE: That is not plausible. Jesus was not a neurotic.

COBB, ELLIOTT, REUTHER: No, he was not a neurotic.

KATZENBERG: This is very much a part of the book and very much a part of the screenplay. The fact that it is a fabrication and a new added dimension that Kazantzakis theorized about makes me wonder how the people will react to someone taking what is a fairly radical departure from the historical theology. I guess what we are struggling with is, do we have the right to do that? Do we have the right, does Marty Scorsese have the right, to interpret the story and create another point of view about Christ? Hundreds and hundreds of millions of people throughout this world have a strong belief. Do we have a right to tamper with that? Does anybody have the right to tamper with that?

REUTHER: It has been tampered with for two thousand years!

COBB: There's no problem about that!

ELLIOTT: And furthermore, there is such a tradition of Jesus being tempted and, in a way, what Kazantzakis is doing is spelling that out in very conceivable terms. He was tempted to worship wealth, he was tempted to feed himself because he was starving to death, and that is part of the pious tradition. Kazantzakis just goes further and talks about the other aspects of temptation.

Reuther seconded the notion. If the film was to be true to the novel, it must show Jesus trying to reject a mission that he feels is just too overwhelming. The scenes of sexual and familial temptations, and especially of Jesus making crosses for the Romans—"the worst possible thing he can do to make God hate him," she noted—must be understood in the context of this struggle. She warned, however, that the more effective Scorsese was in filming the images of temptation, the more criticism the film would draw from conservative Catholics and Protestants.

Katzenberg continued to press them: Was the studio treading on spiritual territory where it had no right to go? As far as Jack Elliott was concerned, just because most people do not want to deal with questions about Jesus' doubts and temptations doesn't mean the questions should not be asked. "You should ignore the lunatics," John McKenzie interjected. But then he asked, "How big are the lunatics? Awfully big."

"That is really the question," said Katzenberg. "Part of why we are sitting here today is that within about three days of us announcing that we were moving with this story, we received an overwhelming amount of letters throughout the United States, not from one particular group. . . . They simply said that doing an interpretation of the story of Christ that is not true to tradition is in itself an act of blasphemy, is in itself heretical, and you do not have the right to tamper with it." McKenzie answered that Jesus had always been treated badly by motion pictures, and if he were Jesus, he would write a letter, too. He put the issue bluntly to Katzenberg:

MCKENZIE: I reviewed a novel recently and it really wasn't very good. I said the characters in this novel are moral pygmys. . . . It is almost like the artist who couldn't ever draw feet but he was great at drawing the sexual organs. So are you big enough to handle the whole Jesus, or should you, like *The King of Kings*, take the easy way out and just show his feet?

KATZENBERG: The dialogue is helping. No resolution will come of this.

MCKENZIE: This is a dangerous job. Anything about Jesus is dangerous.

The discussion shifted to the screenplay. David Kirkpatrick asked their opinions of the depiction of Jesus' relationship with his mother, Mary. McKenzie remarked that it was an aspect of the film that he did not like, but he also admitted that little is known of the relationship. Reuther acknowledged that the Gospel texts were contradictory on this point. On the one hand, she noted, there was a clear pattern of rejection by his family; on the other hand, there was another pattern of Mary's showing her support of Christ. Jack Elliott also found the relationship puzzling, but John Cobb said he had no problem with it.

On the subject of the last temptation—the novel's penultimate event and its most original story device—the participants' responses were hearty and unanimous.

ELLIOTT: [The business of the last temptation] is the thing I liked about the whole book, and I think it's done well in the script also. I would just hope that when that is filmed it remains very unclear to the audience that this is not the way the story really ends. The sense I got out of the book was, "Oh, my God, you mean Kazantzakis is telling us that he didn't die on the cross and he ended up getting married?" He left me hanging till the very last page of the book. I think that if this thing is going to come across, it will have to do exactly the same thing.

REUTHER: You are going to have to feel that he really does escape.

KELLY: Yeah.

MCKENZIE: You have got to make this clear to the viewers who are, by that time, walking out of the theater!

ELLIOTT: I think that has got to be the winner in this thing because [otherwise] it is going to look absolutely sacrilegious and heretical.

MCKENZIE: Blasphemous.

ELLIOTT: And then what happens is that it is a dream, or it is an anxiety.

REUTHER: It is a temptation.

KATZENBERG: Again, I say to you, very much in Marty's defense: he sees Jesus as an extraordinarily heroic character and a man, in the end, who makes the right choice. The right choice as the world wants him to make the right choice.

REUTHER: But only after having really canvassed the alternatives!

Kazantzakis' concept of the last temptation was essentially a familial temptation, and if Scorsese's film was to be true to this theme, sexuality would have to play a role. How large a role and exactly how it would be shown were the salient questions. Jesus' encounter with Mary Magdalene in her brothel, they agreed, was a highly charged scene. Jack Elliott argued, however, that the point of the scene was not Jesus' search for sexual pleasure, but rather the anxiety and indecision he was trying to resolve in himself.

Katzenberg and Kirkpatrick were keenly interested in knowing how much of the fantasized marital rapture between Jesus and the Magdalene should be shown on the screen. Rosemary Reuther voiced caution about showing their wedding night as a sex romp. At the same time, she said, it was important to put their sexual relationship "in the context of marriage and family so that becomes the predominant matter. . . . That is the choice he is making."

COBB: But if there is a scene of Jesus and Magdalene on the bed, which really is sexually stimulating, that will just create tensions and upset people.

MCKENZIE: It will never go!

KATZENBERG: So what you are saying, I want to be real specific, you believe that having the two of them on the bed naked is a red flag that is inviting a reaction that doesn't give the whole affair a fair hearing.

MCKENZIE: It will block out everything else.

During the last half hour, Katzenberg asked his guests if they saw problems with other aspects of the screenplay. They again expressed unease with the focus on Jesus' struggles with his vision—what one called "an emotionally wavering and intellectually uncertain man." The scholars noted that portraying Judas as Jesus' close ally was clearly not the orthodox interpretation, but it wasn't a liability either. Then their reactions to a key scene—the Last Supper—erupted in one unequivocal opinion:

ELLIOTT: That is gross. That was the most offensive thing in the script.

KELLY: Yes.

MCKENZIE: That's gross to the max! [*laughter*]

KATZENBERG: Gross in a religious heretical sense, or because it is just a physically gross act? It was gross to me when I read it, and I am not looking at it from a religious or historical standpoint. I would find it gross in a stab-them-in-the-back "Friday the 13th" way.

ELLIOTT: A stereotypical critique of Christians for two thousand years is that they engage in cannibalism. They actually eat flesh, and that is underwriting that stereotype. When we talk about the Lord's Supper we are talking about people eating flesh and drinking real blood. Now that is a mystery that is going on there. We don't truly know what is taking place during the supper, and the script demystifies the moment.

REUTHER: I think one has to examine one's theology of communion. I would certainly understand eating Jesus' body and drinking his blood as entering into a common spirit with the whole community to come to the body of Christ. I would like to portray that in another way.

COBB: What the problem is here is that we are talking about our vision and not Kazantzakis' vision. I don't think that we have to offend so grossly, but you shouldn't expect this script to reflect our view of communion. This is very Kazantzakis, he wants this to be gross. He wants to make the flesh fleshy, all the dripping blood and gore.

Despite their disagreements with the book and each other on a number of issues, the scholars agreed that the subject of Jesus' temptations was legitimate, even long overdue, for artistic exploration. John Cobb told Katzenberg, "I will be troubled if this kind of criticism would stop you. When you ask certain types of questions, we try to answer them. . . . I think that this [film] is a very powerful statement about Jesus."

Mary Pat Kelly briefed Scorsese by phone. She later met with him and Harry Ufland, presenting them with a transcript of the seminar tapes and the finding that the theologians did not consider the material blasphemous.[99] The good feelings about the seminar reverberated up to the studio's front office. Upon receiving his copy of the transcript, Michael Eisner wrote on the front cover in bold strokes: "I'm now convinced more than ever that we should be making this movie, and I will personally go up and accept the Academy Award."[100]

JEFFREY KATZENBERG was less sanguine about the results of the seminar. Certain issues had been put to rest—for example, that it did not violate accepted doctrine to show Jesus as having been seriously tempted. But the seminar transcript was rife with cautions and warnings about how conservative Christians would react. On November 16 Scorsese and Katzenberg met to discuss the questions arising from the seminar. How would Scorsese show the last temptation? How much detail would go into the lovemaking between Mary Magdalene and Jesus? How would Scorsese treat the scenes in which Jesus rejects his mother? A note from the meeting betrayed Katzenberg's concerns: "Marty realizes the incredible negative reaction the film has gotten on all fronts. . . . At this point [when Jesus rejects his mother] Jesus doesn't believe anyone understands him. He is trapped, emotionally blinded by his torment. Because of the way it is played, the scene could be violently off-putting. Because of such adverse reactions, pay special attention to not make Jesus unlikable in this scene."[101]

Katzenberg also worried about whether the film would look strange. One of Boris Leven's sketches depicted a fateful meeting between Jesus and his apostles in a cave filled with blue light. As Jesus pulls his heart from his chest, drops of blood fall into a pool. The moonlight picks up the color of the blood and turns the whole cave red. Katzenberg thought the use of red, blue, and green gels would be too garish, distancing the audience from the film. He worried that the Lazarus and Last Supper scenes were too reminiscent of a horror film. Combined with the script's emphasis on a psychologically over-wrought Jesus, were these elements making the film seem too dark? Would audiences embrace this Jesus as an extraordinarily heroic character?

If the film's green light had turned to blinking yellow at the September 27 meeting, it now seemed to Scorsese that several traffic lights were flashing in a code he couldn't comprehend. A sense of paranoia began to descend on the production. Scorsese would later tell a *Washington Post* reporter: "Living in Hollywood at the time was like living in a Kafka world. In the movie of 'The Trial,' they tell the hero, 'I had lunch with the judge the other day, and he's very interested in your case.' And he said, 'Really?' 'I might be able to have a hearing with him in the next three or four weeks. He's very interested in your case.' 'Really? But when does it come up?' 'We don't know. You have to wait.' That's the way it was trying to make this film. Katzenberg would tell me, 'Listen, Marty, I just want you to know, Michael Eisner really wants this film made.' And then a week later, Eisner would say, 'Katzenberg is the one who's really behind this picture.' And then I'd hear, 'Barry Diller is really behind you on this point. He wants this picture finished, he wants it done.' And then I'd hear, 'The only friend you have here is Michael Eisner.' Every day, every half-hour, it would change."

On Thanksgiving morning, Barry Diller called Scorsese and said he wanted to see him and Harry Ufland at eleven o'clock.[102] At the appointed hour Scorsese and Ufland were shown into a small office where the Paramount chairman was getting ready to go on a skiing vacation. He chose his words carefully. The picture was going to be canceled, he told them. It wasn't just one reason, it was a whole series of problems. There were the financial risks of shooting in Israel, but the parent company was also frustrated with the onslaught of letters. The picture had become too difficult for him to champion.[103]

Scorsese was devastated. Diller apologized for not telling him this two months into the project rather than making him spend a year of his life on it.

"I understand that you really have to feel for this subject matter," Scorsese said to Diller.

"That's right. I don't feel the same way you do. I don't feel enthusiastic enough to undergo all the problems I would have to undergo."

Scorsese admitted that the production had gotten out of control. "We should have done this the European way, with a $7 million dollars budget."

"Well, that's different."

Sensing an opening in Diller's remark, Ufland asked whether he would reconsider if Scorsese trimmed four weeks off the shooting schedule and took no salary.

Reluctantly, Diller agreed to look at a restructured *Last Temptation*. They seemed to have their foot in the door again. It was difficult to tell from the company's murky politics, however, whether the budget was the decisive issue, or if Diller was trying to deflect their attention from the situation he faced with Martin Davis.[104] One thing was certain: with the protesters now intent on jamming Gulf + Western's New York switchboard, Davis was tiring of the delay in canceling the film.[105] Diller later said, "It appeared that we'd have to defend this movie from the moment filming started to the moment of release. It just didn't seem worth it. Marty [Davis] made it known that he didn't want the aggravation."

That evening, Scorsese went to Brian de Palma's home for Thanksgiving dinner. De Palma, who would tease Scorsese about Paramount always putting projects in turnaround, greeted him jovially at the door: "Well, have they put your picture in turnaround yet?"[106] Scorsese, unwilling to say what happened that morning in Diller's office, replied that it wasn't.[107] But the rumors broke publicly on December 7, in Frank Swertlow's *Los Angeles Herald-Examiner* column: "How about this for razzle-dazzle? It looks as if Martin Scorsese's 'The Last Temptation of Christ' is going into turnaround at Paramount. . . . Word has it from several high-level sources that the controversial portrait of an earthy Jesus Christ is not going to be given the go-ahead for a January shoot. The official word hasn't even hit the production staff yet, one of whom assured Page 2, 'The picture is definitely not in turnaround.'"[108]

For the next month Scorsese worked alone at a friend's house, storyboarding and designing shots. Jay Cocks came to town in late November and the two of them checked into the Westwood Marquis Hotel to give the script a final polish. Scorsese also met regularly with Jon Avnet, who faced the unenviable task of bringing the budget down by 30 percent. Avnet recalled: "I had to basically gut everything that hadn't already been gutted. . . . What I tried to do was get control of the production, which was, first, find out what Marty wanted to do and then make sure that it was being done. See if there were more economical ways of accomplishing what he wanted to accomplish."[109] One of the economizing concepts he came up with was that of a simultaneous second unit; under this plan, Scorsese would, in effect, supervise the first unit crew and a nearby second unit at the same time.[110] Adding a second unit schedule of thirty-five days would enable all the principal photography to be finished in just fifty-five days, which, by Avnet's estimates, would achieve deep cuts in locations and extras, as well as in set construction and redressing costs, all without sacrificing any quality in the shots that Scorsese wanted.

The simultaneous unit idea worked brilliantly on paper. For the first time the budget fell below $10 million, but it was not enough. Avnet and Hal Polaire scoured every line of the budget for more savings. Nothing was exempt, no item too small or too sacred. The cast budget was slashed by $400,000, some of it achieved in the reduced shooting period, the rest of it premised on rene-gotiating "poverty deals" with Quinn, Keitel, and Hershey. Avnet even planned to try to have the actors fly coach class to Israel. Postproduction was cut to thirty-two weeks, and the editing staff and salaries were reduced as well. "If necessary," Avnet wrote to Katzenberg, "I will throw in my KEM and facilities at no charge, and if absolutely necessary, Marty will edit."[111]

The film's principals absorbed some of the pain, too. Scorsese would work only for the director's fee he had already been paid, and Avnet estimated that he and Scorsese could save $100,000 in budgeted expenses while in Israel. Paul Schrader had $150,000 coming to him in the back end, which Avnet hoped could be deferred—like the front-end sacrifices being made by the actors, editors, Scorsese, and himself—until the picture became profitable. Avnet also proposed that Chartoff and Winkler's exit settlement be renegotiated.

"In conclusion," Avnet told Katzenberg in his December 19 letter, "I feel that Marty is clearly committed to this schedule emotionally as well as finan-cially. We have twice gone over the new shooting schedule and I now have in my possession the majority of shots Marty has designed. This unprecedented preparation will pay off."[112]

The new budget came to rest at what seemed to be an absolute floor—approximately $7.5 million. They had done what they told Diller they would do. They demonstrated, said Avnet, "that Marty was capable of doing an incredibly ambitious film in a completely controlled and unbelievably eco-nomical manner."[113] With the budget stabilized, Hal Polaire flew ahead to Israel, where a crew was already building village sets under the supervision of the production manager, Charlie Maguire. More than a hundred rooms were reserved for the cast and crew at the Laguna Dan Hotel in the Red Sea resort of Eilat.[114] Scorsese, awaiting Paramount's approval, was daily booking morning and evening flights to New York and Tel Aviv.

On December 23, Scorsese, Avnet, and Ufland were summoned to Jeffrey Katzenberg's office. Diller and Eisner entered a few minutes later. Coming quickly to the point, Diller said simply, without going into any of the reasons, that the movie would not be made at Paramount.[115]

Undaunted, Scorsese launched into his gung-ho speech.[116] He showed them the new budget and shooting schedule, the storyboards, shot lists, the sacrifices the actors and others had bought into. Even as they spoke, Aidan Quinn was flying to Israel. Everything was speeding toward the January 23 start date. It was all set to go. It just needed a yes.

And if they wanted, he would even direct the sequel to Paramount's new teen hit, *Flashdance.*

Diller listened politely, but repeated that they were not going to make the picture. The executives, Avnet remembered, took no satisfaction in the decision. They were just as upset as the filmmakers that the ability to make the picture at Paramount was finally and irrevocably turned off.[117]

Scorsese turned to Harry Ufland and said, "Does this mean it's a no?" Everyone in the room laughed in a sudden release of tension.[118]

He slumped back in his chair, trying to collect himself. Scorsese recalled, "I don't know how many times I could have been told no. How many different ways I could have been told no. It was just cathartic for everyone, but I really meant it. 'Does this *really* mean I can't make the film?'"[119]

Said Avnet: "Subsequently I've seen other people be disappointed, but I've never seen anybody as upset as Marty. . . . It was very rough to see Marty like that. Obviously everybody there had been trying to support him, and here they are, basically right before Christmas, saying, No, you can't go."[120]

Normally the studio puts a project in turnaround before "hard costs" (wardrobe, sets, set decorations, props, and so forth) are assessed. But in *Last Temptation*'s case, the trigger was pulled at the last moment. Just over $2 million, including $650,000 in location costs, had already been spent.[121] Jon Avnet urged Eisner and Katzenberg not to shut down the production. "If you stop funding it right now," he said, "even if we set it up a week from now or two weeks from now, once you pull the plug, you can't unplug it. If you release people from their commitments or you tear down the sets or you lose the crew, it's tantamount to stopping it."[122]

Eisner assured him that Paramount would continue to fund the production for at least two more weeks and absorb some of the costs so that they would not be tallied against the film.[123] This beneficence, however, was a calculated move, aimed at increasing Paramount's chances of recovering its investment.[124]

At that moment, however, the first priority was holding the actors in place. That morning, Mary Pat Kelly had flown out of Chicago in a blizzard to rendezvous with Aidan Quinn—who was flying to London from Dublin—for their El Al flight to Israel. Soon after her British Airways plane lifted off, Quinn's agent tried to reach Kelly at her sister's home in Chicago to tell her that she shouldn't go to Israel because the project had been canceled. Meanwhile, Quinn was detained upon his arrival at London's Heathrow Airport. In the wake of the previous week's Irish Republican Army bombing of Harrod's department store, which killed nine people (including four police officers), the actor aroused suspicion with his explanation that he was on his way to Israel to play Jesus. The questioning by police caused him to miss the El Al flight. Kelly, still unaware that the film had just been scuttled, flew on to Tel Aviv. She was met by a driver from the *Last Temptation* production office who also knew nothing of the cancellation. They waited at the airport for more than four hours. Finally they saw Aidan Quinn coming through customs, his exercise equipment in tow. "We're delighted to see him," said Kelly, "but he's making a sign—like, 'cut,' it's over, it's off. It was canceled!"[125]

The crisis could not have come at a worse time, during the holiday season, when many studio officials were on vacation with their families. Nevertheless, Avnet and Ufland hastily set up meetings and made dozens of phone calls. Warner Bros. and Universal quickly passed on it,[126] as did Twentieth Century Fox, although Jean-Louis Rubin, Fox's head of international distribution, said he would front them $3.3 million for the foreign rights.[127]

"The scramble to find a new home for 'Last Temptation' is especially awkward because no one wants to say no to Scorsese," reported Michael London on January 6 in the *Los Angeles Times*.[128] Ufland acknowledged the difficulty of reading people's reactions: "Most of them would not really put their feelings in writing, other than to say, Marty is brilliant, everybody's brilliant, the world is brilliant, but we're not going to make it."[129] But in off-the-record comments, studio officials said they were wary of the film's purported high price as well as the religious opposition then being reported in newspaper stories.[130]

Their studio contacts exhausted, Avnet and Ufland began talking to independent companies. David Puttnam, who received the script in late December, telexed Ufland to say that his company, Goldcrest Films, could not make any commitments until new funding was received in March.[131] Scripts were sent to Bob Rehme, who had just settled at New World Pictures after a stint as head of Universal, and Douglas Rae of Handmade Films; neither of them could move on it as quickly as the situation demanded. Reports bubbled up that Cannon Films, known for its hard-action and ninja movies, was offered *Last Temptation,* but Ufland told the *Los Angeles Times* that the stories were a "plant" intended to boost Cannon's reputation.[132]

Day by day the reprieve played out to its endgame. Paramount continued to fund the production office in Tel Aviv through the second week of January (the film's accumulated costs now topped $3 million). Aidan Quinn and Mary Pat Kelly spent Christmas Eve in Bethlehem and then drove in a rented car to the Lebanese border, passing burnt-out tanks left behind from the 1982 invasion. They traveled to all the locations that were to be used in the movie. They visited the Mount of the Beatitudes and waded in the Sea of Galilee, picking up tiles that seemed to have ancient symbols engraved in them. Finally, Quinn came down with food poisoning and flew back to the United States.[133] It was time for Paramount to unplug.

The evening of January 12, Avnet called Hal Polaire and instructed him to shutter *The Last Temptation of Christ.*[134] Over the next several days the sets were struck. Eventually, most of the costumes, set dressings, and props were routed to Paramount's other religious picture, *King David,* which was due to start shooting in Italy that spring.[135]

For Martin Scorsese, the shutdown was an aftershock of a trauma that had been months in the making. All along he'd felt he was being guided by God to make *The Last Temptation of Christ.*[136] The film, Scorsese wrote in "In the Streets," was his attempt to use the movie screen as a pulpit, "to get the message out about practicing the basic concepts of Christianity: to love God and to love your neighbor as yourself."[137] The hubris of this mission was ultimately as insupportable as it was magnificent. He refused to blame Katzenberg, Eisner, or even Diller for denying him the pulpit. Instead, he inspected his own actions to see if he had a hand in what happened. Maybe he had been too stubborn, maybe he'd taken when he should have given— because, he said, "there's a fine line between arrogance and sticking to your guns on certain things."[138]

Above all, Scorsese vowed that he could never again let the film be encumbered by the machine of Hollywood. As he looked back on the months of preparation, he realized that the time had not been wasted. He had in fact found the way to make *The Last Temptation of Christ.*[139] It would have to be done more simply, the way the Italian neorealist films were made, with the freedom of action that only a low budget can provide.

To outside observers, *Last Temptation*'s collapse was a minor perturbation at the end of Paramount Pictures' highest-performing year under the Diller-Eisner regime. The studio scored big hits in each of the first three quarters of 1983—*48 Hours, Flashdance,* and *Trading Places,* respectively—and another unexpectedly high-grossing movie, *Terms of Endearment,* emerged as the leading contender for major Academy Awards.[140] This level of success seemed due, at least in part, to the uncommon stability of its top management. We now know, of course, that this appearance was deceptive. The turmoil that set in soon after Martin Davis assumed the job of Gulf + Western chairman broke dramatically to the surface in September 1984 when, in a span of three weeks, Barry Diller left to become chairman and chief executive at Twentieth Century Fox; then Michael Eisner departed to become chairman and CEO of the Walt Disney Company; and finally Jeffrey Katzenberg also moved to Disney to head its motion picture division.

The events that led to this realignment constitute one of the most familiar tales of executive intrigue in entertainment history. What has gone unwritten—though not undiscussed—is *Last Temptation*'s role in the deteriorating relationships between Martin Davis and Paramount's senior executives. The picture's budget, casting, and script problems—and most of all, the protests and the effect they had on its exhibition prospects—were indisputably major factors in the cancellation. But many insiders believe the last straw came when Davis inserted himself in the decision-making loop.[141] Jon Avnet, who joined the project near the apogee of its troubles, put it this way: "Not many people say no to Michael Eisner, Barry Diller, Jeff Katzenberg in their own studio very often. This is not something that they wanted to do. This is something that, from where I sat, appeared to be foisted upon them."[142] Within a year of the cancellation, Paul Schrader encountered Eisner on a cross-country flight. At first, Eisner told Schrader, the new management at Gulf + Western had given him carte blanche to pick and develop pictures. Even though Eisner had been wooed by a number of studios, he never took the opportunities seriously—not, that is, until he was overridden on the Scorsese project. "That's when I started thinking about these other offers," Eisner said.[143]

In David Kirkpatrick's view of the matter, *Last Temptation* "changed the face of Hollywood because Martin Davis ultimately got his way. . . . Within six months, Barry Diller and Michael Eisner and Jeff Katzenberg had all left the studio. Michael went and regenerated Disney, which has become one of the largest media giants in the world, in no small part due to Mr. Katzenberg. And Mr. Diller went and ran Fox. So in that sense, had *Last Temptation* not have happened, or not happened at Paramount, Michael Eisner may have never gotten into the kinds of issues with Marty Davis that chose Frank Mancuso to be the successor to Paramount as opposed to Michael Eisner. You know, it's never one thing. It's always the weave of things that defines anybody's life, but I think from the standpoint of the corporate life of Disney, it may not actually exist in the way we know it today had it not been for *The Last Temptation of Christ.*"[144]

If the decision staggered Scorsese and Paramount's executive corps, it was cause for relief and jubilation among the film's opponents. The Sisters of Mary were apparently content to stay quiet about their role. The National Federation of Decency, however, was not shy about taking credit for tripping up *Last Temptation.* An NFD spokesman told *Christianity Today* in early 1984 that he was pleased with the outcome, adding that the Kazantzakis book was "blasphemous from beginning to end."[145] Donald Wildmon himself boasted in his autobiography that the NFD's organizing efforts produced a "massive outcry of protest—phone calls, postcards, letters and more," that led Paramount to abandon the film.[146]

During the 1970s and early 1980s, the motion picture industry had largely managed to escape the gun sights of the cultural conservatives' campaigns against the media. Network television and pornography were considered far more serious threats to the nation's moral fiber. But after only a few months of intensive petitioning by tens of thousands of Americans, Paramount's executives found themselves stumbling into coils of ideological razor wire. With the right film—a film unlike any other in the significance of its subject matter and the extremity of its depiction—and with the right political climate, activists found they could create a protest so fevered it could bend, or break, the will of top management. The rules of engagement had changed almost overnight. Until the studios figured out how to defend themselves, high-risk projects would be subjected to special scrutiny, and Scorsese's film would be out in the cold.

3

Universal

"THE TRICK was to survive," Martin Scorsese said of the situation he faced in January 1984.[1] Two of his last three films had failed to turn a profit—the latest, *The King of Comedy*, generated only $2.5 million in domestic gross receipts[2]—and with *The Last Temptation of Christ* canceled, his future as a director seemed to be at the point of hemorrhaging. The last time he'd felt under threat of losing it all, in the late 1970s, after his experimental musical *New York, New York* stumbled at the box office, he'd reacted by making his most aggressive film ever. Robert De Niro's portrayal of the boxer Jake La Motta was a study in self-inflicted brutality unlike any other in American cinema. "It was like a punch in the face," said Scorsese about *Raging Bull*, "a violent movie that would shake them and make them feel something."[3] Scorsese saw *Raging Bull* as his parting shot, the savage bookend to a brief career in major studio filmmaking. By the time it came out, he just assumed that he would be exiled from Hollywood. He would make New York or Rome his base of operations, busying himself with "documentaries and educational films on the saints. I was going to make films for television, that sort of thing."[4]

There was nothing out of character about this remark; in those years Scorsese was given to bouts of fatalism after suffering real or perceived setbacks. But this time was different. *Last Temptation*'s cancellation forced him to confront the issue of his survival once and for all. The choice couldn't have been clearer. He could devolve further in the direction he was heading, becoming one of those directors, like Orson Welles or John Cassavetes, whose uncompromising attitudes ejected them into some lonely, erratic orbit far beyond the sun of Hollywood. Or he could start over and learn to be a "pro" in the established system. In going this route, he would have to submit himself to a degree of humility he had not experienced since *Boxcar Bertha*. He would have to prove himself all over again, but at least there was the possibility of bootstrapping his way back into major studio filmmaking. Though in artistic temperament he was an outsider, Scorsese wanted the respect and financial patronage of insiders because, deep down, he wanted a place at the industry's big table, the same table where John Ford and Howard Hawks once sat. And if that was truly what he wanted, he could not afford to let his career slide back to where it started, saddled with *Boxcar Bertha*–sized budgets and forever excluded from working at the highest levels of film production. As he told *Playboy* in 1991, in one of his clearest statements of how he sees himself professionally: "I don't want to be considered an adjunct to the business, or some sort of strange punctuation that's on the margins. . . . I've *always* tried to blend 'personal' movies with being inside the industry."[5]

The first thing he had to do those initial weeks of 1984 was put aside his bitter feelings about *Last Temptation*. Next he had to get back on the horse. He had to find a picture to direct—the kind of project that would show the skeptics that he wasn't one of those profligate auteurs who could not (or would not) adapt to the new realities of the entertainment business. By reinventing himself as a disciplined filmmaker, he could get through the current tribulation and accrue the credit he needed for getting his own films made again.

The first scripts he saw while he was still in Los Angeles came from Katzenberg and Eisner. There was one that had Sylvester Stallone attached, *Beverly Hills Cop*. They told him it was a "fish out of water" story; to Scorsese, it sounded like the Don Siegel film *Coogan's Bluff*.[6] He passed on it. Another script, *Witness,* was set in the Pennsylvania Amish country, a milieu he neither understood nor wanted to understand.[7] Returning to New York empty-handed, he was shown a script by his lawyer, Jay Julien. "Now my lawyer is giving me scripts," Scorsese thought warily.[8] But the first few pages pulled him in. Written by a Columbia University student, Joseph Minion, and titled "A Night in Soho," the story follows Paul Hackett, a young computer programmer, on a harrowing all-night journey through lower Manhattan. The protagonist's psychic confusion, his encounters with bizarre women and hostile residents, his deliverance at a place of calm—it was all familiar territory for Scorsese. He also liked the script's wickedly black comedy, so fittingly like what he had just been through with *Last Temptation*.[9]

The script had been optioned at the Sundance Film Festival by an independent outfit, Double Play Company, headed by the actors Griffin Dunne and Amy Robinson (who played Charlie's girlfriend in *Mean Streets*). With Scorsese committing to direct, Geffen Films put up $3.5 million to produce the project, retitled *After Hours.* Dunne was cast in the role of Paul Hackett, and Scorsese and crew got ready for a superefficient eight-week shoot in Manhattan's TriBeCa district. "The director made a shrewd choice," noted *Esquire*—"a low-budget success [like *After Hours*] might be the only way to counter the notion that he's in the business of making critically acclaimed flops."[10]

Though the Paramount cancellation almost broke the back of Scorsese's career, *The Last Temptation of Christ* was still his perennial next film. (Scorsese even added a clause to subsequent directing contracts, giving him the ability to put any new project on hold if *Last Temptation* suddenly got a green light.)[11] At first Paramount gave the turnaround rights solely to Martin Scorsese Productions, commencing on February 8, 1984. Shortly thereafter, Scorsese agreed to include the Jon Avnet Company and Ufland-Roth Productions on a share basis in the turnaround. It fell to Scorsese's agent and loyal friend, Harry Ufland, to find backing for the orphaned project. Rejections by all the major studios left Ufland no choice but to pursue less auspicious avenues to getting the film on track—independent companies, venture capital, foreign subsidies. Moreover, with the liquidation of the Paramount production, *Last Temptation* became much harder to make. Now anyone interested in backing the film would have to pay Paramount for its investment—$3.9 million, plus accrued interest (which, by July 1986, stood at $1.4 million)[12]—or try to negotiate a lower figure, before even starting to mount a new production.

The cancellation also tarnished *Last Temptation* with a notoriety that was hard to shake. People were saying no very quickly, often before Ufland had a chance to talk with them about the script. Sensing that "whatever move we made, something was ahead of us,"[13] Ufland discovered that the redoubtable Salah Hassanein, who had earlier warned Paramount that *Last Temptation* wouldn't play in any United Artists theater, was announcing the same to other studio heads and financiers.[14] Scorsese told Ufland that he wanted to speak with Hassanein personally. He pinned his hopes on a passionate pitch that would change Hassanein's mind, or, at the very least, persuade him not to obstruct their efforts further.

Initially, the UA theaters head rebuffed Ufland's attempts to set up a meeting. As it happened, Ufland's partner, Joe Roth, was married to the daughter of the legendary producer Sam Arkoff, and through the intercession of Arkoff himself, who was friendly with Hassanein, they were granted an audience.[15] On a snowy morning in early February, Scorsese, Ufland, and Roth climbed into an unmarked white van sent by Hassanein to take them to his estate in

Glen Cove, Long Island. "If we're not back by 5 o'clock," Roth told his staff, "definitely call the police."[16]

The meeting began amicably. Though he hadn't read the script, Hassanein said his children liked the Kazantzakis novel and told him he was wrong to object to it.[17] He asked Scorsese why he wanted to make this film. As he had explained so many times, Scorsese said that he was making it so that even people who felt alienated from the institutional Church could commune with the Lord. "I have had three divorces. Does this mean I can't speak to God because the church says I can't?"[18]

These words resonated with Hassanein, who—like Scorsese—had been taught in Catholic schools. There even came a point, recalled Scorsese, when Hassanein mused about investing in *Last Temptation* himself.[19] Still, Hassanein reminded them of the dangers of speaking too directly of religious matters. He cited the litany of movies that provoked incendiary situations; the worst one, of course, was *Mohammed, Messenger of God.*

"You don't understand," he lectured the group. "You make the movies. They don't come to your theater and destroy the theater. . . . Religious films are too much trouble."[20]

"I don't care if you hate the movie, but let us get it made," Harry Ufland pleaded. "Please don't follow us around and tell people not to do it. Then do what you want when the movie is made."[21]

By the end of the three-hour meeting, Hassanein agreed to refrain from speaking ill of the project. He would see the film when it was finished and then decide.[22]

It was a small victory in an otherwise barren season. Ufland's inquiries were yielding few signs of interest. One encouraging lead came from New World Entertainment, a company founded by Roger Corman and, with its large output of exploitation fare, a profitable bottom dweller in the Hollywood food chain. On January 6, exactly a year after Corman had sold the company, Bob Rehme was appointed chief executive and cochairman of New World. One of the first projects Rehme pursued was *The Last Temptation of Christ,* a move viewed by industry insiders as signaling the company's bid for respectability.[23] Despite rumors that Rehme was interested in buying only the Schrader screenplay (reportedly for a low-ball offer of ten cents on the dollar), he and New World's president, Jonathan Axelrod, flew to New York on January 20 to confer with Scorsese.[24] Negotiations stalled over the terms for reimbursing Paramount, and without a co-investor, Rehme was unwilling to take the leap.

More refusals came rolling in as the year progressed. Denis O'Brien of Handmade Films wired Ufland with disappointing news: "As you may recall, we ventured a long way from the edge of the cliff with *The Life of Brian* . . . and do not think we would be prepared to enter the territory again, either with regard to subject matter or cost production. We admire your bravery."[25]

"It is a very, very well written script," wrote the veteran producer Ray Stark. "I do respect Mr. Scorsese and all of you gentlemen for trying to bring this to the screen, but in no way is it the kind of picture that could draw any benefits from my association with it."[26]

A New York distributor had these comments for Harry Ufland: "As promised I read *The Last Temptation of Christ* quickly. It is of course a terribly well written screenplay. . . . However, it is impossible to separate the quality of the script from the content, and I am afraid that the content offended me. . . . I feel that the film clearly undermines so many beautiful, treasured beliefs which will cause infinite pain to people on whom such pain should not be inflicted. With regrets therefore I cannot involve myself."[27]

But for those who were neither personally offended nor afraid to accept the brunt of a religious conflict, there was still the disincentive posed by having to repay Paramount. Ufland urged Paramount to restructure the terms of reimbursement if the studio expected ever to get any of its money back. Katzenberg suggested an up-front payment of $1.5 million plus a "first-dollar position" on theatrical rentals, thus treating the $3.9 million as an investment in the picture. Ufland countered by saying it was unfair to expect to recoup the whole amount, since so little of it could be used should *Last Temptation* be produced.[28] By the time Katzenberg moved to Disney in late September, they were still at loggerheads. Then, with the arrival of the Frank Mancuso regime in October, an agreement was quickly struck: the holders of the turnaround agreed to pay $1 million to Paramount upon receipt of new financing for *Last Temptation,* as well as 5 percent of the total gross receipts once the film's revenues broke even with costs.[29]

Though the deal made it unlikely that Paramount would ever be repaid in full, it did lower the barrier for new investors. Earlier that year, one of Scorsese's many meetings about reviving *Last Temptation* was with Humbert Balsan, a producer with Paris-based Lyric International.[30] They talked about mounting a "European-scale" production on the Continent or in North Africa. The cost would be in the range of $5 million and the film would be made without any stars.[31] It might be possible, Balsan said, to obtain seed money from the Culture Ministry of France—from its *aide directe* fund for special projects. Joined by his business partner, the Lebanese filmmaker Maroun Baghdadi, Balsan arranged an October meeting in Paris between Scorsese and Jack Lang, the French minister of culture. Lang greeted the director warmly and offered a subsidy of $300,000 to help get the project off the ground, payable when financing for the entire film was locked in.

As soon as this news broke in *Variety*, waves of letters began washing up on Lang's desk, attacking Scorsese as a maker of perverted movies and denouncing the government's support of the project. According to one observer, the letters were sent "from small and hitherto quiet communities of evangelists and charismatics. The wording of these letters and the common misconceptions about the script (most of the writers were convinced that Scorsese wanted to turn Jesus into a homosexual), suggest that the campaign worked on a tip-off from across the Atlantic." Conservative Catholic groups appealed directly to the archbishop of Paris, Cardinal Jean-Marie Lustiger, to give his blessing to their goal of blocking the project. Earlier the archbishop had been criticized for remaining silent while Jean-Luc Godard's *Je vous salue Marie* (Hail Mary)—a film portraying the Virgin Mary in modern-day France as a cabdriver's girlfriend—was released amid nationwide protests. This time Cardinal Lustiger felt obliged to act. He wrote a personal letter to President François Mitterand, advising against the use of public funds for a film that would undermine the Gospels. Lustiger's "harshly worded intervention"[32] at the Elysées Palace apparently had its desired effect. On March 19, Jack Lang assured the country's religious leaders that none of the Culture Ministry's money would be invested in *The Last Temptation of Christ*.[33]

Both Lang and the producers put a brave face on the episode. Lang held out the possibility that Scorsese's film could receive money from a production review board, whereas Humbert Balsan claimed that the decision not to go ahead with *Last Temptation* was only temporary, owing to the director's other commitments, and had nothing to do with religious issues.[34] But the political climate engendered by the still-brewing controversy over the Godard film—in May Pope John Paul II had issued the first-ever papal denunciation of a film, saying *Hail Mary* "distorts and insults the spiritual significance" of Christian beliefs—dampened the interest of potential European investors for months to come.[35]

The French imbroglio had just happened when Scorsese was shocked to find the project endangered from an unexpected quarter. While he was in Cannes showing his new film *Mishima*, Paul Schrader learned not only that

Scorsese's option on *Last Temptation* had lapsed, but also that he had just signed to direct *The Color of Money* for Disney's Touchstone division. To Schrader, this could only mean that Scorsese was losing his will to go on trying to make *Last Temptation*. Invoking the clause in his contract giving him the right to direct the film if Scorsese was unsuccessful, Schrader wrote to Scorsese: "I hear that your enthusiasm is waning, and there are some people in Egypt and France that might have some money. If you ever slacken I will walk over your back to get this movie done." Furious at this threat from an erstwhile ally, Scorsese shot back: "You will have to pull the script from my dying hands."[36] (In a more lucid moment, he contacted Ufland about remitting $15,000 to the William Morris Agency to renew his option through June 1986.)[37] It was their first serious quarrel, and the rift took nearly two years to heal, but Schrader claimed satisfaction with the outcome: Scorsese was again moving in the right direction.[38]

The rest of 1985 passed without serious movement on the film. Frixos Constantine of Poseidon Productions—an associate of Scorsese's friend Michael Powell, the British director—contacted the Soviet film ministry about money for shooting *Last Temptation* in Tashkent.[39] Later, in September, Constantine traveled to Athens, where his proposal for filming *Last Temptation* in Greece was well received by Minister of Culture Melina Mercouri.[40] Neither initiative, however, went beyond the talking stage. In 1986 Ufland tried another round of U.S. production and distribution companies. Copies of the script were sent to Carolyn Pfeiffer (Island Alive), Mitchell Cannold (Vestron), Greg Cascante (Interaccess Film Distributors), Tony Thomopoulos (United Artists), Brian Grazer (Imagine Films), and John Daly (Hemdale).[41] Only Hemdale, a company known for taking on risky projects, went so far as to start negotiations on a production to be shot in Italy on a $7 million budget. Paramount agreed to restructure its deal again, moving a larger percentage of the money it was owed to the back end.[42] Harry Ufland's devotion to Scorsese was second to none, but he was increasingly preoccupied with the production company he cofounded in 1983 with Joe Roth and ultimately could not close a deal with Hemdale.[43]

Fifteen years after the novel passed into his hands, Martin Scorsese was coming face to face with an obdurate reality: *The Last Temptation of Christ* was now widely regarded as an impossible vanity project, a film that nearly everyone in the industry believed could not be made. The problem wasn't simply that it was an art film with slim commercial prospects; every year dozens of films fitting that description are able to find their way into production. Rather, it was a *religious* art film, burdened with a history of being despised sight unseen by untold thousands of Christians.

But Scorsese had come too far to give up on it. After spending several years of his life making other people's films on time and under budget to claw back to a place where a Martin Scorsese picture meant something again, quitting was unthinkable. With *After Hours,* he showed that he could make a stylish, commercially oriented film on a tight schedule. And *The Color of Money* delivered a solid hit to Disney. With these two movies Scorsese had managed to steer out of the vertiginous downdraft that threatened to crash his career and seemingly earned the right to call his next play, according to a key principle of the film industry's reward system—the one that gives artists who have scored a commercial success greater freedom to choose their next projects. And when the artist is one of the very few who are undeniably gifted, the principle applies with added force. As a former Universal executive put it, "When you have a talent like Marty Scorsese, who has a burning desire to make a movie, then you've got to let him make the movie. . . . The same way Universal reacted when Steven Spielberg came to them and said, 'I've a burning desire to make *Schindler's List,* a black-and-white movie about the Holocaust.' You know, when you've got a filmmaker of that stature saying, 'I must make this movie,' at some point—especially if you want a relationship with them—you give it to them."[44]

The Walt Disney Company was the logical firm to reward him for *The Color of Money,* but now that they were at the helm of this most family-sensitive of media corporations, Eisner and Katzenberg were loath to go near *The Last Temptation of Christ* again. No one wanted to refuse Scorsese his burning desire, but no one wanted to assume its risks, either. It was evident that if the project had any chance of being made, it would have to be guided into a space of possibility by a special ally, by someone with the clout to represent Scorsese's interests forcefully. In the fall of 1986, the talent agent Michael S. Ovitz walked into that role.

"It's the oddest thing," Scorsese later admitted. "*Everything* changed at the beginning of 1987, when I signed with C.A.A. and Mike Ovitz. To this day I'm not quite sure what happened. . . . All I know is someone says they're going to try to do something for me and they come through. Ovitz is a very supportive man."[45] And speaking in 1997, Jon Avnet said: "Michael Ovitz, who is not du jour today, made that film happen. He willed it into existence. He did what few people can do, which is, he took a filmmaker's dream that no one wanted to touch and he did everything he could to make that happen. It's the story no one wants to write about Ovitz at this point in time because it's not fashionable. But he was brilliant. He protected Marty, he protected the movie, he was just brilliant."[46]

There is no doubt that Ovitz made a crucial difference in Scorsese's professional life for years to come; notably, the making of *Kundun* and *Gangs of New York,* two of the director's most personal films, were testaments to Ovitz's influence and his loyalty to Scorsese. But as a hard case, *Last Temptation* was in a league of its own, and to believe that one person could vanquish all of the movie's difficulties would be to succumb to the hyperbole surrounding the agent who was called by the *Wall Street Journal* "the most powerful individual in Hollywood."[47] Even Michael Ovitz understood that if he was to win a studio deal for *The Last Temptation of Christ,* he would need his own special ally.

IT HAD BEEN only eleven years since five talent agents—William Haber, Ron Meyer, Michael Ovitz, Rowland Perkins, and Michael Rosenfield—were fired by the William Morris Agency and formed a new agency on a $21,000 bank loan.[48] Housed at first in a sparsely furnished Wilshire Boulevard office, the Creative Artists Agency (CAA) quickly gained a foothold in the highly competitive talent market by selling a game show package to ABC and two variety shows, *The Rich Little Show* and *The Jacksons,* to ABC and CBS, respectively.[49] None of the shows lasted more than a few months, but they produced enough income to start CAA on its fabled ascent.

By the end of 1986, president Michael Ovitz was commissioning the world-famous architect I. M. Pei to design the agency's new headquarters. If anything announced CAA's arrival as a mature company, fully intending to stay at the top of the entertainment world, it was this audacious marble and glass structure enclosing 65,000 square feet of office space in the heart of Beverly Hills. In little more than a decade since the agency's founding, CAA had put nearly six hundred clients under contract—including such luminaries as Paul Newman, Sylvester Stallone, Dustin Hoffman, Robert Redford, Jane Fonda, Sally Field, Robin Williams, and Robert De Niro—and its gross billings eclipsed those of the other top baronies of talent, William Morris and International Creative Management (ICM). The upstart achieved something else that seemed even more inconceivable: CAA managed to convince a large segment of the film community that it had supplanted the studios as the prime mover of new projects. Not since the MCA of the early 1950s had a talent agency been so deeply involved in content development, and not since MCA's legendary president, Lew Wasserman, had the head of an agency instilled such awe and fear in studio buyers as Michael Ovitz.

Early on, CAA decided to focus its growth strategy on the exploitation of story material. The firm established ties with a number of literary agencies; the key one was the New York agent Morris Janklow, who represented such popular authors as Judith Krantz, Danielle Steel, Sidney Sheldon, and Jackie Collins.[50] These sources fed CAA a steady stream of book, magazine, and script properties that it could "package" with other elements—typically, CAA's own actors—and then sell to the networks as prime-time series and made-for-TV movies. Ovitz himself was often given credit for the practice. (Packaging, gushed a 1993 *Time* story, "is practically an Ovitz invention.")[51] But packaging goes back to MCA's founder, Jules Stein, and his music act bookings of the 1920s. Stein's protégé, Wasserman, later adapted it for radio and television network deals.[52] What CAA did accomplish to great effect was the use of the story properties it acquired to leverage deals for its clients. The agency slashed its TV packaging fee to only 6 percent of a show's total revenue, undercutting the fees charged by its rivals William Morris and ICM, but it more than made up for this discount with the personal service commissions, which stayed at the customary 10 percent. The intelligent crafting of packages became CAA's specialty, and this, in turn, elevated the status of its agents. As CAA's Steve Roth told the *Los Angeles Times,* "There's a great myth that agents are not creative. Take a look at some of the packages we put together—that's creativity. It's also good business."[53]

The success of this formula in television led Ovitz by the early 1980s to make the move into movie packaging. In the film business, more than in any other field of endeavor except politics, real power tends to follow shifts in perceived power, and the mystique of Ovitz—combined with the aggressive tactics used by him and his corps of agents—was disturbing the established order. Star actors were severing ties with their longtime representatives and flocking to CAA, drawn both by the agency's growing clout and by its stylistic difference from other agencies. Ovitz encouraged a Zenlike selflessness among CAA agents by dividing profits equally among them and by carefully identifying new hires who could fit in with the company's egalitarian concept.[54] Internecine rivalries among agents were discouraged; they were replaced by an ethos that put the client in the hands of the whole company. CAA's agents assiduously looked after their clients' interests, cultivating the impression that the fulfillment of their creative desires was at least as important as helping them reach new financial heights. The smoothly persuasive Ovitz even performed the hat trick of making it seem that the packaging process worked at the behest of the client, not the other way around. As he explained it to the journalist Michael Cieply: "[The clients] become the motor, and we really are like the body around the car. We try to shape it with them. But they make the choices. We make suggestions, there's no question. But we never make singular suggestions. We suggest alternatives. If there's a director, we suggest an actor. If it's an actor, we suggest a director. If it's just an idea, and an actor, we'll suggest a writer. . . . You see the permutations."[55] It became apparent to Ovitz that directors could be the most important "motor" of all, particularly the coterie of directors who tend to originate their own material and whose esteem among star actors can accelerate the chances of a project's being green-lit.

By the mid-1980s, Creative Artists Agency had built a large stable of A-list directors, including Sydney Pollack, Barry Levinson, Oliver Stone, Jonathan Demme, Ron Howard, John Landis, Joel Schumacher, and Ivan Reitman.[56] By this time, too, Ovitz had begun to lay the groundwork for intersecting CAA's and Martin Scorsese's paths. CAA represented Walter Tevis, author of *The Hustler*—the 1961 film starring Paul Newman as the pool shark Fast Eddie Felsen—and its sequel, *The Color of Money*. Newman, who also happened to be a CAA client, was taken with *Raging Bull* when it came out, and in the sort of personal touch for which he is justifiably known, Ovitz encouraged him to write a frankly admiring letter to the director.[57] When Newman showed interest in being part of the sequel, Ovitz managed to separate the rights from Twentieth Century Fox and took *The Color of Money* to Disney as a package deal that included Newman and another CAA client on the rise, Tom Cruise, with a non–CAA element, Martin Scorsese, attached.

Ovitz saw that Scorsese, if given the proper attention, was a unique motor who could make certain types of projects happen. "Marty was a passionate director who developed very few films," Ovitz recalled. "His ratio of developed to made films was very, very high, which at that time in the eighties was very tantamount to being successful. And because of that, I felt that he could get done almost anything he wanted to do so long as he focused on the development of very few projects. . . . And then I found out that he was very unhappy with his current representation. The change of representation was part of a very natural evolution all centered around discussion of the projects that he wanted to do, including *The Last Temptation of Christ*."[58]

The courtship commenced in earnest the evening of October 17, 1986, when Scorsese stopped by Ovitz's home after the Los Angeles premiere of *The Color of Money.* Ovitz, recalled Scorsese, promised to straighten out his life. Boosting his compensation to the level he was due as a world-class filmmaker was part of the plan. "You know, Marty," Ovitz teased him gently, "you could get paid for being a film director."[59] But the agent had much more in mind than brokering higher directing fees. Ovitz prodded Scorsese to think expansively about his future, to open up about his dreams—a suite of offices and editing facilities of his own; a production enterprise that would enable him to pursue a whole range of projects; a foundation dedicated to the cause he had been championing for years, the restoration and preservation of the classic films deteriorating in studio vaults.

As to what he most wanted, Scorsese had a simple answer: he wanted to get *The Last Temptation of Christ* made. Scorsese recounted the conversation: "And then Ovitz said, 'How much will it cost?' I said, 'We're talking about a European-style budget, not much lower than seven million. In Morocco, probably. Got most of the cast. Got some of the costumes. But there's a problem. A political problem with the picture.' I said it may be that theaters won't show it. And he said, 'Okay.' And he thought about that. And he didn't say anything. And I figured, well, that's just the usual [response] I've had all these years."[60]

Ovitz, in fact, wasted no time trying to satisfy Scorsese's most fervent desire. He knew almost instinctively where to start. Just two days earlier, on October 15, a new chairman had taken the reins of the MCA Motion Picture Group and its flagship label, Universal Pictures: Thomas P. Pollock, cofounder and senior partner in the law firm Pollock, Bloom, and Dekom. Over the course of a fifteen-year career, the forty-three-year-old Pollock parlayed formidable negotiating skills and an extraordinary grasp of film financing into a position as one of the town's top lawyers. More important, he was instrumental in redefining the entertainment attorney's sphere of influence. As the cost of films spiked in the late 1970s, and as the ancillary revenue streams from home video, cable TV, and foreign distribution swelled ultimate profit lines, creative talent began to look to their lawyers for innovative ways of putting projects together. Tom Pollock's particular insight was that movies could get approved more readily if talent gave up front-end fees for a larger share of the back end—a strategy that spreads out the risk and delivers potentially huge windfalls for the stars and directors who "invest" in their own pictures. *American Graffiti* was the archetype of this kind of deal. Representing the then-unknown director George Lucas, Pollock persuaded Universal to give his client 20 percent of the picture's net profits instead of a salary, and in lieu of charging a fee for his legal services, he took 5 percent of Lucas's share.[61] The gamble paid off spectacularly. Released in 1973, the $750,000 picture grossed $67 million, and Lucas's proceeds bankrolled his Star Wars Corporation, the launching pad for the celebrated trilogy. On *Star Wars*, Pollock aided Lucas in retaining the sequel, music, television, and eventually merchandising rights, in exchange for taking a lower director's fee.[62]

By the 1980s, Pollock, Bloom, and Dekom was shepherding deals for many of the industry's key players, among them Dino De Laurentiis, Don Simpson, Jerry Bruckheimer, Walter Hill, Ivan Reitman, Arnold Schwarzenegger, and Sylvester Stallone. The firm even helped several clients set up their own companies—most notably, Brian Grazer and Ron Howard's Imagine Films Entertainment. Pollock himself was profiled in *California Magazine* as one of the state's most powerful lawyers and prominently featured in a *New York Times* story on the new breed of Hollywood superstar lawyers.[63] "As one of the architects of the complex way movie deals are made today," the journalist Karen Stabiner wrote in 1988, "Pollock virtually guaranteed himself the chance to run a studio. He is one of a handful of people in town who actually understand what's going on."[64]

Ironically, it was another George Lucas project for Universal, the famously disastrous *Howard the Duck,* that prompted MCA's president Sidney Sheinberg to consider Pollock for the post of studio chairman. The scene was Sheinberg's Beverly Hills home, where he and Pollock were arguing over some of the money that Universal owed on Lucas's contract for the $35 million flop. Though Pollock didn't budge on the original terms, Sheinberg nevertheless admired Pollock's intelligence, his tenacity, and the relationships he had with many of the producers and talent with whom Universal did business. "In the course of this meeting," Sid Sheinberg told an interviewer, "I looked at him, and it occurred to me that he was really a terrific guy to run the motion-picture group. . . . I turned to him. And I said, 'I really think this is something that you could do and do well.' "[65] Sheinberg would later say that the reason he offered Tom Pollock the job of running Universal was that he would rather have Pollock working for him than against him making deals like *Howard the Duck.*[66]

Pollock had resisted many such overtures in the past—"It was something I was interested in doing later. In five years. It was always something that was five years away"[67]—but Universal Pictures needed new leadership immediately. By 1986 Universal had fallen to last in market share among the majors, and spending had risen to an average of $31 million both to make and to market each of its movies (compared to an industry average of $25 million).[68]

Moreover, the stormy relationship of the studio chairman, Frank Price, with Sheinberg was thought to be partly responsible for the slowing of new project planning to a virtual standstill. (Upon assuming office, Pollock was aghast to find only thirty-two films in active development, about one-sixth the number normally in the pipeline.)[69] After three days of thinking about the offer, Pollock decided to give up the security of his law practice and take on the challenge of turning Universal around. The appointment was announced on September 18, two days after Frank Price submitted his resignation.[70] His top priorities, Pollock told the press, were, first, to foster a more collegial climate inside the studio and with other MCA units;[71] second, to seek creative ways of financing films, exploring "all kinds of arrangements with talent besides paying them as much as they want";[72] and, third, to look at ways of leveraging MCA's varied assets when selecting and marketing movies.[73]

Still, Tom Pollock hardly fit the idealized image of a mogul. With his dark, bushy head of hair, mustache, and oversized glasses, he resembled a rumpled, cerebral Groucho Marx. And if he had a perceived weakness going into the job, it was his inexperience in moviemaking. The more natural candidate for replacing Price, according to some observers, was Universal's production president, Sean Daniel—who, coincidentally, Pollock was then representing in his contract re-up negotiations with Universal.[74] Pollock, however, was more attuned to the creative requisites of the chairman's job than many realized. "He was extraordinarily well read," recalled Sheinberg, "very much interested in what was being made, more so than many of the lawyers in town who have a way of only being interested in the deal and the money. He was one of these guys that read all the scripts and had opinions on them."[75]

One of the scripts he had read just months before was *The Last Temptation of Christ.* At the time he was representing Harry Ufland, who needed legal help in his negotiations with Hemdale. So Pollock was not entirely surprised when Michael Ovitz called him in October to discuss the possibility of a relationship with Martin Scorsese. The two men had known each other for years. When CAA was getting established, according to the journalist Michael Cieply, "Ovitz and company, desperate for business, cultivated Hollywood's entertainment lawyers as a then-undervalued source of information and clients. . . . C.A.A. had no staff and supposedly saw kindred souls in the so-called '5-percenters,' a generation of hungry young lawyers—[Barry] Hirsh, Thomas Pollock, Jacob Bloom, Peter Dekom, Kenneth Ziffren, Harry (Skip) Brittenham—who shied away from litigation and focused on deal-making in return for a percentage of the client's take."[76] Over time their businesses became even more intertwined as Pollock repped a number of clients on the legal side whom Ovitz served on the talent side.

As Pollock moved into the buyer's role, Ovitz noticed that Universal was plotting a new course of securing long-term relationships with directing and producing talent. Much of the output from Steven Spielberg's Amblin Entertainment was already flowing through Universal's television and motion picture divisions, mainly by virtue of Spielberg's special relationship with his early benefactor, Sid Sheinberg. But Pollock aimed to make it more of a priority by bringing many of his former clients, such as Robert Zemeckis, Ivan Reitman, John Hughes, and the Howard-Grazer team, into the fold. A modified version of the classical Hollywood system, when studios held talent under exclusive contracts, filmmaker relationships were thought to yield benefits for both parties. The studio was assured of first looks at new scripts, if not a minimum number of developed projects, and the directors and producers enjoyed "favored nation" status.

Ovitz guessed, correctly, that his call to Pollock couldn't be better timed. Universal had the opportunity to add Martin Scorsese to its roster of top-line talent; CAA could attach its actors to the films of a prestigious, highly efficient director; and Scorsese himself might see his long-delayed passion come to life. Ovitz told him that Scorsese was seeking an overall deal that would involve a number of directing and producing projects. "*Last Temptation* was in the group of projects that we discussed," Ovitz recalled. "It wasn't just the one project. . . . [But] Marty focused on *Temptation* because it was something that he always wanted to do. It was a very important project for him, creatively, so we focused on it. I always thought that project would be difficult. But I felt that if the film was done for the right price, then Marty could get it done."[77]

Part of the proposed deal involved favorable terms for office space for Scorsese's company in an MCA–owned building located at 445 Park Avenue in New York City. Ovitz wanted Universal to finance the overhead on the space, which eventually grew to occupy half of one floor and accommodate editing facilities and a screening room. Additionally, Universal later agreed to contribute to Scorsese's film foundation, which was created in 1990. But the critical piece—indeed, the predicate for the overall deal—was the film no one would touch.

"Marty will make a home at Universal if you can figure out how to do *Last Temptation*," Ovitz said to Pollock. "And, Tom, you and I will work together to get Marty to do a mainstream commercial movie, because that will be really good for his career and good for your studio."[78]

As he took notes during the conversation, Pollock realized that what Ovitz was proposing was a reversal of the order by which rewards—in this case, the small personal film—are typically dispensed in Hollywood. "What was unusual about *Last Temptation*," recalled Pollock, "was the chicken came before the egg. . . . In Marty's case, vis-à-vis Universal, he hadn't yet earned the right to make *Last Temptation* in the way that it usually works."[79] In effect, Universal would hand over one of the most valued chips before the director had generated a dime of revenue for the company. And for the freedom to make what? This, after all, was the film that had brought the vitriol of religious conservatives down on the previous studio that had had the temerity to try to make it.

The insistence on making *Last Temptation* before delivering a more commercial picture would have been coldly treated as a deal stopper by most studio bosses. But Ovitz and Scorsese were fortunate to have in Tom Pollock a singular executive who not only was comfortable discussing philosophical ideas, but had also read *The Last Temptation of Christ* at an early age. As a nineteen-year-old taking a comparative religion class at Pomona College, he had found the novel intriguing and immensely powerful.[80] It let loose a series of unfathomable questions for the young Pollock, starting with the root question of what it means to be both human and divine. How much does the human self know about the divine self? Are they united in purpose, or are they tortured? Kazantzakis' conclusion was that Jesus was tortured—at least until he went into the desert and realized that the divine nature he had been fighting was part of himself and in fact his true calling. How then did Jesus deal with this knowledge?[81]

As Pollock read the script again, thinking about how it would work with movie audiences, he returned to an idea that was apparent to him from the beginning: the story Kazantzakis tells is a religious variation of *It's a Wonderful Life*. The Frank Capra movie remains so powerful decades after it was made precisely because it unleashes an enormous emotional charge when George Bailey (James Stewart) realizes what the world would be like if he had not been born, the difference that any one man makes in the world. Thus, a strong what-if element lay at the core of both *Last Temptation* and *It's a Wonderful Life*. But unlike the vast number of movies employing the device ("What if dinosaurs could be cloned?"), Kazantzakis' novel and Capra's film induce people to imagine the most profound what-if's of human experience. What if we had never existed? What if we could choose to live our lives differently? What if we said no to God's will? Reflecting on the analogy, Pollock said: "I always felt that what was going on in *The Last Temptation of Christ,* both as a book and a movie, is that the temptation Satan offers on the cross is the ultimate temptation, . . . the temptation to give up the divine and to live out your life as a human. There is wonderful pleasure in that. The satisfaction of living a really good life that is radically different from the pleasure one gets from the ups and the downs, and the ins and the outs, the highs and lows of life as you go along. . . . So Satan has tempted Jesus with the triumph of his humanity over his divinity. And when he says No to this, and chooses instead to die in agony on the cross—"[82] Years later, when talking about the pure selflessness of the act, Pollock could still feel overcome with emotion.

If audiences could identify with George Bailey's despair and cheer for him when he finds his way back to his family, why shouldn't an equally skillful film impel them to think and feel deeply about Jesus' earth-shattering choice? The key to the picture, in Pollock's view, would have to be Jesus' self-awareness of what he is doing. His sacrifice on the cross has no redemptive meaning unless he is free not to go through with it. And if he has the strength to overcome the last temptation and choose the right path, as he eventually does, it is a model for all of us in our own everyday temptations. If Scorsese could put that idea on the screen with all his considerable vision and craft, it might move those in the audience who had lost (or never found) their faith. It could even spark a spiritual awakening, Pollock thought—and, in turn, make at least a modest profit.[83]

The script went to Sean Daniel for his evaluation. On first reading, he found it to be clearly, intensely personal to Scorsese.[84] Compared to most of the material he read, the script did not disclose how certain images that were part of people's religious upbringing—images, Daniel recalled, that "in one way or another they knew, or *felt* they knew in their own way"—would be depicted, and in that sense it seemed to be a script that would never be complete until filmed. The core audience, Daniel thought, would be film enthusiasts, overlapping with an urban, university-based segment; there was the chance of attracting a certain type of Christian viewer, open to a new take on Jesus—all together, an audience big enough to justify the investment.[85]

Fortunately, *The Last Temptation of Christ* played into Tom Pollock's philosophy of production that was then taking shape in his first weeks on the job. Pollock, recalled a former Universal marketing executive, Perry Katz, preferred "to produce [either] big tent-pole, marketing-driven movies—[Ivan Reitman's] *Twins* is a perfect example—or more controversial movies where you don't have to spend a lot of marketing dollars because the inherent nature of the project would create the buzz. [Spike Lee's] *Do the Right Thing* was a perfect example of that. And certainly if you were to make those [controversial] kinds of movies, you would make them at a different price level than if you were to make the bigger tent-pole movies, where you're talking about movie stars and big budgets. And I think Tom very much held true to that philosophy of production. . . . He always felt that where you got killed was kind of in the middle, where you made a middlebrow movie at a middle-level price with middle-level stars.''[86]

Pollock and Sean Daniel were of similar minds about this philosophy, and both saw a commercially exploitable vein of controversy in *Last Temptation*. "There was always the assumption," said Daniel, "that a personal vision like this—an admittedly controversial book in the hands of a major filmmaker who had long wanted to tell this story because it was personal to him—that this would get the attention of the film community, the film media, and be written about and, if you will, 'covered' on a lot of different levels."[87] Movies about Jesus always draw attention, but *Last Temptation*'s difference from previous treatments would surely be noticed by serious media outlets and opinion makers. Presumably the film would stir debate, resonate with the new evidence and theories then coming out about the historical Jesus, and push public discourse to a plane that few films reach. This off-the-entertainment-page publicity, so the thinking went, would create awareness of the movie on its own accord, thereby lowering the advertising costs that a movie normally requires to open.

Universal's front office was well-versed in Paramount's agonies with *Last Temptation,* however, and no one could discount the possibility that the same forces would resurface to wage war against MCA. The political muscle wielded by evangelical Christians had not waned appreciably during the 1980s. Christian activism was intensifying on several fronts—from protesting outside abortion clinics, to scapegoating gays for the AIDS epidemic, to supporting Attorney General Edwin Meese's efforts to criminalize the pornography industry. Whether *Last Temptation* would get caught in these currents could only be surmised, but MCA did know it wouldn't be released in a cultural vacuum. The film would elicit *some kind* of reaction.

Nevertheless, Pollock's game plan was more about Martin Scorsese than about the movie itself. If agreeing to back *The Last Temptation of Christ* would clinch an overall deal with the director, he would see that Universal's risks on the picture were brought down to the lowest possible level. "What was going on in my mind," said Pollock, "is that—aside from the fact that I did believe in [*Last Temptation*] from a commercial standpoint as well as an aesthetic standpoint—if I could figure out a way to do it at a price that made sense, not only would I bring him to Universal, but we would be able to work on more lucrative films."[88]

When Ovitz first told him of Universal's interest, Scorsese was skeptical. He could not recall meeting with anyone at Universal in the 1970s.[89] The studio reacted ponderously to the changes then afoot in the New Hollywood, and though Universal eventually rode to great success with a spate of hit movies— among them *The Sting, American Graffiti, Jaws, National Lampoon's Animal House,* and *E.T.: The Extraterrestrial*—it was still not known for nurturing young talent or taking artistic risks. In the minds of many, Universal was the film industry's dark force; for its avaricious reach into nearly every sector of the entertainment business, Universal's parent company, MCA, was known as the Octopus, and its fifteen-story, dark-paned executive office building was dubbed the gothic-sounding Black Tower. Presiding at the top of the tower was MCA's tough, politically connected chairman, Lew Wasserman, who was renowned for wringing every conceivable concession from a negotiation. By the early 1980s, Universal Pictures' reputation began to turn around. Under the stewardship of Bob Rehme, Frank Price, and Sean Daniel, the studio showed a new, creative-friendly face. Some of this progress was set back in 1985 by a flagrant episode of studio interference in which Sid Sheinberg's lack of enthusiasm for the director Terry Gilliam's political fantasy, *Brazil,* led to a yearlong tug-of-war over the film's final cut. Most of the town's critics and creative community sided with Gilliam in "the battle of *Brazil,*"[90] as the journalist Jack Matthews called it, and some writers, directors, and producers worried about whether the MCA president would get "aggressively involved" in their projects.[91]

Though Scorsese found it hard to envision a supportive home at Universal, Ovitz was telling him that Tom Pollock was different. One of those differences was that Pollock actually *wanted* to talk about *The Last Temptation of Christ.* "I would take meetings on *Last Temptation* anywhere, any time," Scorsese said.[92] And he knew that such opportunities were getting scarce.

Ovitz began trying to set up a meeting with Tom Pollock and Sean Daniel after the official start of CAA's representation of Scorsese, on January 1, 1987. Since Scorsese and his wife and producer, Barbara De Fina,[93] would soon be traveling with Robert De Niro to the French Polynesian atoll of Tetiaroa to discuss a comedy project with Marlon Brando, a meeting at Universal City was arranged for their one-day stopover.

They flew to Los Angeles on February 19, and Ovitz briefed them about the next day's lunch with Pollock and Daniel. That evening Scorsese was seized by anxieties about the meeting, and he called Ovitz back: "I said, 'I don't know about this picture. It was so hard. So many things I didn't expect. I just want to make a serious picture about the nature of who we are.' And [Ovitz] said, 'Look, go in there. You make the best picture in the world. You just go in there and you're going to make that best picture.' It was a very strong pep talk. But it wasn't even a pep talk. He doesn't couch it in those phrases. He works a different way and locks something in my head. And I went into the meeting the next day and it was fine."[94]

Sitting in a dining room adjoining the Universal commissary, Scorsese and De Fina quickly realized they did not have to pitch the movie to Pollock.[95] He was already very familiar with the material. What Pollock really wanted to discuss was the physical production. The film would probably be shot in Morocco, a country with no union regulations on film companies, using natural locations in the style of films by Pasolini and Ermanno Olmi. Much of the preparation from 1983, such as shot lists and wardrobe designs, could still be used. The performers would work for scale and Marty would take a fraction of his customary fee, minimizing above-the-line costs and putting almost all the money up on the screen. Everything De Fina and Scorsese said lined up with Pollock's own thinking, and they came away with the understanding that if the project could come in at close to $7 million, it was something Universal would consider.[96]

The conversation shifted to the other movies Scorsese wanted to do. Pollock, it turned out, was not only a fan of his work, he was genuinely curious about what Scorsese would do with different kinds of material. Other than *Wise Guys*, Nicholas Pileggi's best-selling account of Mafia life, already in development for Warner Bros.,[97] there was a Jay Cocks script called *Gangs of New York* about turf wars between Irish and Nativist gangs in nineteenth-century Manhattan, and a George Gershwin biopic written by Paul Schrader. They also talked about doing a commercial picture. On this occasion the discussion was inconclusive, but three years later Universal got its payback when Scorsese agreed to direct a remake of the 1962 thriller *Cape Fear,* a property co-owned by Universal (which produced the original) and Gregory Peck.[98] Released in November 1991, *Cape Fear* was Universal's second-biggest grossing movie of the year, earning almost $80 million in domestic receipts. His most profitable film until *The Departed, Cape Fear* provided Scorsese the freedom to pursue his own projects for the rest of the 1990s; however, it was still a genre film and one that he probably would have bypassed had not Universal been guaranteed a commercially designed project after *Last Temptation.*

Not long after Scorsese and De Fina departed for the South Pacific, Pollock walked two doors down the hall from his office on the fifteenth floor of the Black Tower to tell Sid Sheinberg about his interest in making the movie. There was little reason to fear a veto, even for this one. Neither Sheinberg nor Lew Wasserman was given to the same despotic impulses as Gulf + Western's Martin Davis, and particularly after the *Brazil* dustup and his very public dispute with Frank Price, Sheinberg was eager to avoid even the appearance of micromanaging MCA's film and television divisions. Wasserman and Shein- berg's management style, according to Pollock, went something like this: "[They would say,] 'Give us a plan, tell us what you're going to spend to make movies . . . and what you think you're going to make. And at the end of the year . . . we'll see how close you came, and if you exceeded it you'll be rewarded, and if you don't you'll be punished. But we're not running your division for you. It's your job to run your division.' And basically that was how MCA ran."[99] So Pollock, like the heads of the company's other units, enjoyed a great deal of operating authority; all Sheinberg expected in return was to be kept informed of his plans.

When he was told about *Last Temptation,* Sheinberg failed to see any upside coming from it. He knew it as the film that created problems for Para- mount, and controversy was not something that he readily associated with religious pictures—or with commercial success, for that matter. Yet he did not warn Pollock away from pursuing the deal. "To my credit, or my detriment," Sheinberg recalled, "it was not my policy to stop people from doing things. . . . I've always been a believer in the autonomy of division heads to run their divisions, particularly in a project like [*Last Temptation*], which was not a big, expensive, gigantic project. I didn't really see myself in the role of somebody who should stop him, particularly since my opinion would have been based on more of a concern with the reaction than anything else."[100]

Pollock next set in motion a number of initiatives intended to contain the project's risks. Without the possibility of each of these moves coming to fru- ition, individually and in combination, it is doubtful that Pollock himself could have rationalized the decision to go ahead with the film. The first arose out of a concern (also felt by Paramount in 1983) that *The Last Temptation of Christ* could turn into a runaway production, which—notwithstanding Scor- sese's new credentials as a cost-conscious filmmaker—was a plausible scenario once shooting got under way in North Africa.

Universal's solution was to take *Last Temptation* as a "negative pickup." The key factor underlying a pickup deal is a shift of production-cost risk. The studio agrees to distribute a film on the basis of its script, budget, production plan, and creative team, and using this distribution agreement as collateral, the filmmakers can raise money from nonstudio sources (usually a bank loan). The filmmakers must also purchase a completion bond, ensuring that the project will be finished even if the original financing proves to be inadequate. Upon delivery of the negative—hence the term negative pickup—the studio pays the agreed-on price (enabling the production company to pay back the lender) and takes ownership of the film.

A negative pickup, therefore, affords filmmakers all of the freedom of an independent movie. For its part, the studio does not have to worry about cost overages, nor is it out any money if the production goes totally off the rails. Those risks are assumed entirely by the completion guarantor. But no movie is risk-free. In the case of a pickup, the studio is obligated to pay even if the quality of the film doesn't live up to expectations. *Last Temptation* was unlikely to be substandard from a technical standpoint, or uninteresting in purely aesthetic terms. But with Scorsese exercising near-total creative control, it was certainly possible that not all its commercial potential (as Universal conceived it) would be fulfilled in the production process.

Pollock determined that the benefits of going the pickup route outweighed the risks. *Last Temptation*'s production budget was calculated at $6.5 million, plus the completion bond and a 10 percent contingency fund—capping the studio's liability at about $7.2 million "all in" (compared to an average cost of $20 million for making a major studio movie in 1987).[101] Tom Pollock had locked in the right price ("absolutely chicken feed!" he told Mary Pat Kelly),[102] a remarkably right price for a film being made in a Third World country nearly six thousand miles from California.

The next issue Pollock faced was far more consequential for *Last Temptation*'s chances. Recalling the tactics used against Paramount, he concluded that exhibition, again, might be the weakest link. Although Salah Hassanein was about to leave his position at United Artists, removing one potential impediment to the film's release, theater owners collectively are not a courageous lot.[103] Without a critical mass of theaters pledging in advance to play *Last Temptation*, green-lighting it was akin to stepping off a high ledge in hopes that a net would magically deploy before hitting bottom. Asked whether anyone at Universal was concerned about being able to show the film, Michael Ovitz was unequivocal: "Absolutely. They were all nervous."[104]

Once more, timing was critical to the project's advancement. Just the previous year, in early 1986, MCA had paid $239 million to buy 49.7 percent of the outstanding shares of the Cineplex Odeon Corporation, a Canada-based theater chain. It was the first significant purchase of theaters by a major studio since the epochal 1948 Justice Department decrees that ordered the Hollywood studios to divest the exhibition arms of their operations. That ruling effectively ended the vertically integrated studio system and paved the way for greater market competition by independent film companies and so-called mini-major studios. By the mid-1980s, however, the deregulation-minded Reagan Justice Department signaled to the movie industry that it was relaxing enforcement of the decrees. In short order, several studios went theater shopping. MCA led the way, followed by Gulf + Western, which acquired the 360-screen Mann Theatres circuit, and Tri-Star's purchase of Loews' 250 screens. The logic of these acquisitions was simple. As the construction of multiplexes exploded in the 1980s—there was a total of 19,571 indoor screens by August 1986—the studios wanted to ensure access of their films to the best locations.[105] "The most important asset the major studios have is their relationship with the theaters," noted Carolco's head, Peter Hoffman. "Buying theaters is a defensive strategy to avoid losing those ties."[106]

The lodestar of that expansionist period was Cineplex Odeon. Founded with a Toronto theater in 1979, the Cineplex Corporation was initially an exhibitor of second-run and art film fare. (It was shut out of first-run bookings by the major U.S. distributors.) After flirting with bankruptcy in 1982, Cineplex's brash, ambitious CEO, Garth Drabinksy, took the company public, aided by an infusion of capital from the Bronfman family. Drabinsky embarked on a tear of theater buying, starting with the 297 screens of the Canadian Odeon Theatre circuit, the chief competitor on his own national turf. Operating under its new nameplate, Cineplex Odeon pushed aggressively south across the border. The 574-screen Plitt Theater chain was purchased in 1985 for $65 million, and during the next three years Drabinsky bought up more than a half dozen smaller chains—ending up with 1,675 screens in approximately 500 locations.[107] These holdings also included an estimated 40-60 percent share of the movie admissions in New York City, Chicago, Los Angeles, and Toronto, North America's most important markets.[108]

Cineplex Odeon was clearly ripe to become MCA's foothold in exhibition, an asset boldly symbolized by a lavish eighteen-screen complex at Universal City that Drabinsky was building in 1987. Moviegoing, he always said, should be as much about "the experience" as the films themselves. So the Universal

City Cineplex Odeon would be tricked out in many of the company's signature amenities—plush seats, an atrium lobby, Italian marble floors, original art on the walls, cappuccino cafés, football field–long concession stands that served real butter on the popcorn.

Meanwhile, Drabinsky was restless to take Cineplex Odeon beyond the exhibition arena. Earlier in his career, he had speculated in "respectable tax-shelter films" such as *Silent Partner* and *The Changeling*, and now film production beckoned again.[109] He set up a subsidiary company, Cineplex Odeon Films, for buying negative pickups and investing in coproductions that would keep his theaters stocked with movies. Toward that end, later in 1987 Drabinsky formed joint ventures with Robert Redford and the director Taylor Hackford for producing inexpensively priced films, and he also entered into a distribution agreement with Universal for its Oliver Stone film *Talk Radio*. But before any of these deals came to pass, Tom Pollock called him about buying a piece of a new Universal film.

It was vintage Pollock-style deal making: if Cineplex Odeon invested in *The Last Temptation of Christ* as a 50 percent equity partner, the company would get Canadian distribution rights in all media as well as the first opportunity to play the film in all U.S. markets where Cineplex Odeon had theaters. At one stroke, the deal halved Universal's investment in *Last Temptation* and assured the cooperation of one of the nation's largest theater circuits to show the picture. The only revenue stream MCA was giving up was the Canadian markets.

Drabinsky read the script while he vacationed at the Los Brisas resort in Acapulco. "It seemed a no-brainer," Drabinsky wrote in his autobiography, *Closer to the Sun.* "Pollock's analysis showed little exposure for either party, because of MCA's lucrative network-TV deal, projected home-video revenues, and a substantial pay-TV deal that could be struck as part of the M.C.A. package to HBO or Showtime."[110] He was assuming, of course, that *The Last Temptation of Christ* would be deemed fit for play on network television, that it could be packaged for pay cable, that a big video chain like Blockbuster would put it on its shelves. This was not the last time Garth Drabinsky underestimated the troubles that the film would encounter. In any case, *Last Temptation* broke new ground as Universal's first foray into vertical integration; this was also the first time the studio asked an exhibitor to invest in one of its films.[111] Said Pollock of the deal: "I doubt we would have made the picture if we had not been a partner with Cineplex."[112]

Finally, Pollock had to confront Paramount's investment from 1983, a sum that, if paid in full, would wreak havoc with the financial model he had built. He had Michael Ovitz go to Paramount and try to get the costs deferred. When it began to look as though the standoff in negotiations would delay the film's start date, Paramount relented and sold the turnaround rights to Universal for a promise to pay back the $4 million once the film got into net profits (which it never did).[113] According to Scorsese, Paramount's chairman, Frank Mancuso, did not want to stand in the way of his dream project: "[Mancuso] said, 'I'm doing this because I know you really want to make this picture. But I don't particularly like what we have to do.' . . . And that was Frank."[114]

At last a narrow space opened up for *The Last Temptation of Christ*. By working their respective sides of the deal, Michael Ovitz and Tom Pollock managed to thread the eye of the needle. Ovitz saw that the way to bring Universal and Scorsese together was to show that the director was willing to think in mainstream terms; only then did *Last Temptation* become a less bitter pill for the studio to swallow. And thanks to Ovitz's ability to gain Scorsese's confidence on this project, the man who is by consensus America's greatest living film director moved to the Creative Artists Agency. The rest of it was Pollock's doing, aided by some extraordinary timing and other strange accidents of fortune. If any of the deal's underpinnings had gone the other way—if Pollock had not already been familiar with the Kazantzakis novel and favorably disposed to it; if Pollock had not been a new movie division chairman, ready to embark on a new policy of securing filmmaker relationships; if Pollock had been unwilling to let Scorsese make *Last Temptation* before delivering a commercial project; if MCA had not been a company that granted wide latitude to its division heads; if Pollock and Daniel hadn't been so motivated to structure Universal's risks at an acceptably low level; if Frank Mancuso had been intransigent about the money owed to Paramount—if even one of these pieces had not fallen into place, the film's chances of being made would have been severely diminished.

In the end, the alliance with Cineplex Odeon was decisive. "To have a leisure company and not take advantage of its resources is crazy," declared Pollock when he was named studio head.[115] Now he could pull all of MCA's levers—financing, distribution, and exhibition—to force *The Last Temptation of Christ* into the nation's theatrical markets, if it came to that.

In early March Scorsese and De Fina were still on Tetiaroa. They had initially planned to stay for a few days, but as the languorous rhythm of life on the island took over, their stay stretched to two weeks.[116] Scorsese began to hear from his new agent that Universal was moving on the project. "There was only one phone on the island and we only made a couple of calls, but Mike was saying to me, 'You know, Marty, these people may make this film, so you'd better come back here.' I didn't realize the power involved here, how he could work deals, reason with people, and give them the feeling they've pretty much come out with what they wanted."[117]

They flew back to Los Angeles on Thursday, March 5, and after a weekend recovering from jet lag, had a Monday meeting at Universal. Sean Daniel said that a deal was in the works and told them to go on a location scout just as soon as they could get organized. They were simultaneously giddy and surprised, De Fina recalled: "We kept saying, 'I don't believe they really want to make it'—it was like Sally Field saying, 'They really, really like me.' 'I guess they want to make it,' we said. 'They're sending us to Morocco.'"[118]

4

Morocco

WILLEM DAFOE was in Northampton, Massachusetts, working on the play *Wrong Guys* with the Wooster Group, when his CAA agent got him on the phone. Marty Scorsese wants to talk to you, he said. He's doing a film of this Kazantzakis novel. The actor asked what Scorsese wanted him for and what the role was. "Well, actually, Jesus," said the agent.[1]

Through most of the summer of 1987 Scorsese waited on Aidan Quinn to say whether he would return to play Jesus, but Quinn was in the throes of making *Robinson Crusoe* in the Seychelles Islands, an ordeal that left him exhausted and reluctant to go off on another overseas shoot. Scorsese had to move quickly, and among the names that came up was Willem Dafoe. Earlier that winter Dafoe had received a best supporting actor Academy Award nomination for his role as the martyred Sergeant Elias in Oliver Stone's *Platoon,* which bolstered his stock for leading-man parts, but at that point Scorsese had seen him only as the villainous counterfeiter in *To Live and Die in L.A.* Compared to Quinn, the thirty-two-year-old Dafoe would bring different qualities to the part of Jesus. "There was an innocence about Aidan, and a charm, you know," said Cis Corman, the casting director, "and Willem I always thought of as being stronger and deeply emotional."[2] There were also differences in the actors' physiognomy; Dafoe's face was angular, masklike but highly expressive. In part because of his face, many of Dafoe's most memorable portrayals have been repellent or morally dark characters, such as Bobby Peru in *Wild at Heart,* Max Shreck in *Shadow of the Vampire,* and Bob Crane's pal John Carpenter in *Auto Focus.* "This is the face of a psychopathic killer, not the face of our Lord," director Sergio Leone famously said about Dafoe when he saw *Last Temptation.*[3]

But Scorsese liked what he saw and heard when they met in New York City. "He looked like Jesus as we know him in religious images," Scorsese said about the actor's blue eyes, light hair, northern European features.[4] Dafoe also had the acting chops to play the gamut of emotions the part called for. When Scorsese got around to viewing it, Dafoe's performance in *Platoon* confirmed his sense that Dafoe could play a deeply compassionate character. He called Oliver Stone and asked what the actor was like to work with. Don't worry about Willem, Stone told him—he is a fearless professional, willing to "do anything you want, as long as it's legitimate for the film."[5]

As for Dafoe himself, the process was simple and direct. Scorsese, he recalled, "told me about his approach, which was to get a human side as well as the divine side of the character. And he asked me to read the script. I read it, I thought it was really right, and I thought it was perfect timing, and I felt like I was exactly the right guy to do it. There was no negotiation about money or anything."[6]

Most of the actors cast for the Paramount production were enthusiastic about coming back, but a few were lost to scheduling conflicts—Paul Sorvino's CBS series *The Oldest Rookie* was only halfway through its episodes;[7] Kathy Baker, who was then filming *Clean and Sober,* had to yield the part of Lazarus's sister Martha to Peggy Gormley;[8] and Sting, who was committed to an Amnesty International concert tour, was replaced in the role of Pontius Pilate by David Bowie.[9] Lew Ayres, originally slated to play the guardian angel, was dropped because the role itself was reconfigured. In order to give the last temptation sequence a novel look, Scorsese decided that the guardian angel should be an innocent-looking young girl.[10] From casting sessions in London he selected Juliette Caton, a pale, red-haired teenager who had trained at the Redroofs Theatre School but never before worked in film.

The only casting issue raised by the studio was Harvey Keitel in the role of Judas. In Scorsese's mind, it was a personal—and nonnegotiable—choice: "Harvey and I would read one word of the [Kazantzakis] book and we'd start talking for hours. And we just had the passion for it. And he also understood being Jewish. . . . We were soul mates, so to speak, over the years, Harvey and I. I just couldn't see doing without him."[11] He argued in long phone conversations with Tom Pollock that Keitel's Brooklyn accent was the contemporary equivalent of ancient Galilean speech, and if it bothered anyone who expected Biblical characters to talk like BBC newsreaders, so much the better.[12] Pollock, however, was unconvinced: "I was one of those who did not want Harvey Keitel as Judas. I thought the accents would be totally jarring and take you out of the movie. Marty had an idea that somehow this would show that the people who followed Jesus were the proletariat of the time, the common workingman. I said, 'All right, Marty, I get it, but why do they have to talk like they're the common workingmen from the *Lower East Side?* What's wrong with just sort of straight-on American?'"[13] Though Universal technically had final approval on the major parts, in the end it wasn't a fight worth having.

Making *Last Temptation* as a negative pickup gave Scorsese the freedom he craved, but it came with a sobering caveat. As Pollock paraphrased the instructions he gave to the filmmakers: "'You have a total amount of money to spend. You bring back a finished film for that, and we don't care how you spend it.' So Marty had a lot more freedom than he might otherwise have had. He simply didn't have a lot of resources. So you have to be entrepreneurial."[14] The starting point for everyone's calculations was a fifty-five-day shooting schedule, essentially the same number of days as the revised plan that Jon Avnet submitted to Paramount in late 1983, but without the second unit. (Not only was it too costly to field two units at once, but Scorsese preferred to put his own time into filming inserts.) If they were to finish shooting in under two months, the filmmakers would have to combine meticulous planning in the States with what Scorsese termed a "commando operation" in Morocco.[15]

Accompanied by the production designer John Beard, Scorsese and De Fina arrived in Casablanca on April 7 for a ten-day scout. When the Arab location manager looked at sketches of the sets that were originally to be constructed in Israel, he pointed them to Meknes, one of Morocco's four imperial cities. There they walked through the seventeenth-century ruins of the royal stables of Sultan Moulay Ismael, which Scorsese saw could be used as the Temple, the Passover baths, and the palace of Pontius Pilate. The absence of ceilings in parts of the stables not only meant less interior lighting was needed, but also created possibilities for overhead shots. Just outside Meknes stood the third-century Roman ruins of Volubilis and the forested valleys and slopes of the western edge of the Atlas Mountains. It was in this region that the Crucifixion and the last temptation sequence would be shot. Next they crossed the mountains to the desert outpost of Quarzazate, with its high-walled casbah. This location was dropped because it would take too much time to move crew and equipment across the mountains and back again.

The Marrakech area was last on their itinerary. They returned to the village of Oumnast, which had changed little in the years since Scorsese and Boris Leven had walked its streets. It was still untouched by the clutter of modernization: no power lines, TV antennas, paved streets, or commercial signage. The crew worked in and around Oumnast for the first five weeks, utilizing different parts of the village for Nazareth and Magdala, and filming the Sermon on the Mount, the John the Baptist scenes, the monastery, desert, lakeside, and other scenes in the outlying country. The clear, unpolluted light and the colors of the arid wilderness—reds, warm yellows, beiges, and browns—lent a stark beauty to Jesus' early ministry and contrasted with the greener Volubilis region. The geographic arrangement of all the locations in relation to the shooting script suggested that much of *Last Temptation* could be shot in continuity, a rare circumstance in film production.

The shot list from 1983 was still largely serviceable. About a third of the shots had to be altered because of the switch from stage sets in Israel to natural locations in Morocco and the restoration of scenes that were cut at Paramount. Scorsese wrote copious annotations to the script: descriptions of shots that supplemented the directions in the screenplay (in some instances stipulating lenses and film speeds), along with "pencil drawings, little storyboards with thumbnail sketches of shots," as first assistant director Joe Reidy characterized them.[16] Reidy and the cinematographer Michael Ballhaus studied every page of the annotated script before going to Morocco, and again the evening before, and the morning of, every shooting day, to plot out all the setups. The result was that Scorsese and the crew always knew what they were supposed to be doing during the shoot, and each shot was timed to a predetermined number of minutes.[17] If a given day's shot number 3 was supposed to take twenty minutes, and it was taking twenty-five minutes, they were heading for trouble. The shot had to be picked up quickly, or they would have to abandon it and move on.[18] Due diligence could take them only so far; pure, unforgiving force of will would have to be summoned to pull them across the finish line.

The production also saved resources by hiring a regionally based crew. Other than the cast, the only Americans going to Morocco were Scorsese, De Fina, Reidy, and a camera assistant; the rest of the crew—except for Michael Ballhaus, who brought his sons Florian and Sebastian, and the camera operators David Slama and David Dunlap—were Italians and Moroccans. The Italian crew, assembled by Laura Fattori, the production manager, made up the higher ranks of technicians as well as managers and other workers in the production office. The Moroccans, many of whom had worked on films shot in their country, filled out the laborer cadre and mid-level positions in the various departments. The first few days on the set were a veritable Babel of nationalities and tongues. Most of the Italians were bilingual in either English or French, the colonial language of Morocco; Fattori, who was fluent in all three languages, often translated for the Americans and acted as intermediary to the Moroccan authorities. Communications with the Moroccan crew and extras usually went through a second assistant director, Ahmed Hatimi, who spoke English, French, and Arabic, as well as the local Bedouin language.[19]

Nearly all the film's extras were Moroccans, and directing them could be a complicated matter. The Moroccans knew it was the story of Christ that was being filmed, a person as historically real to them as the prophet Mohammed, but they did not always understand what was happening during the filming, especially in such intense moments as the brutality of the Crucifixion. Scorsese bemoaned the loss of comprehension that crept into their eyes, which became most noticeable when they stood close to the camera.[20] Ahmed Hatimi worked carefully with the extras to try to get them to produce meaningful looks, and Michael Ballhaus had to be ready to get quick shots of these reactions. In some of the crowd scenes, the second assistant directors mixed in with the Moroccans and cued them to respond in a certain way; in other situations, Hatimi stood off to one side and used hand signals. The most proficient of the Moroccan actors were cast in four of the twelve apostle parts. Although they had no lines to speak, these men were given special attention to help them blend in with the principal actors; they took direction well, said Reidy, and "were able to interact eventually with their English-speaking partners as disciples."[21]

Like the many actors before him who had faced this assignment, Willem Dafoe began to grapple with how he would play a man who walked the earth nearly two thousand years ago and who was survived by four slim volumes of ostensibly eyewitness accounts and the unshakable faith of hundreds of millions of people. Dafoe decided to work his way into the part from ground zero. He tried to purge himself of any preconceived notions, get free of personal responsibility for any of the imagery that the audience might bring to the idea of Jesus. "I felt responsible for *this story*," Dafoe recalled, referring to the Kazantzakis version, "and my way into the story was more a process of letting go. The character in this story is very reactive. He has something from the outside come onto him and he has to deal with it. And as we shot the movie, I had to sort of sit with all the events and I had to deal with them and not get ahead of myself or have a notion of how the character was supposed to be. . . . The whole idea was this guy with this awesome responsibility, how he felt about it, how he approached it."

Dafoe was acutely aware that even as a work of fiction, the script did not stand isolated from its scriptural sources: "Because we're riffing off of actual events that are recorded in the Bible in all of these different accounts, I would read all the accounts. I'd look at our script and I'd try to see what the 'through line' of all of them was and see if there was any common ground that all of these accounts keep on returning to or pointing to. So I just sort of did my own Bible study in order to feel the inner life of the character. To try to make articulate his internal considerations."[22]

Assisting him in this quest was a set of scholarly articles on the subject of forgiveness that Scorsese discovered in the August 1987 issue of the theology journal *Parabola*. Because Jesus' teachings of forgiveness were so critical to the triad at the heart of *Last Temptation*—Jesus, Judas, and Mary Magdalene—Scorsese provided Dafoe, Harvey Keitel, and Barbara Hershey with copies of the journal.[23] (Some of the actors pursued their own courses of study; Keitel, for example, became engrossed in the writings of the New Testament scholar Elaine Pagels.)[24] The *Parabola* articles afforded multifaceted views of the concept. In "Living in Communion," Father Thomas Hopko wrote of forgiveness as the letting go of one's self, the path to communion with the other, and the only way of "breaking the chain of evil."[25] D. M. Dooling's "This Word Forgiveness" is a meditation on the mystery and grace of forgiveness. "[Forgiveness] is not ours to give," he wrote, "but to receive; the human being cannot create it. We can be certain only that it is beyond us, above us—and we can never entirely know anything on a level higher than our own."[26] The notion that God's forgiveness is unconditional and cannot be earned by anything we do is the foundation of Paul Tillich's sermon "To Whom Much Was Forgiven." "Nothing greater can happen to a human being than that he is forgiven,"[27] wrote Tillich, because forgiving heals our estrangement from God and our own selves. Collectively, the articles were intellectually exciting to Dafoe, helping him understand why Jesus acted as he did.[28] The articles also helped him and Keitel deal with the complicated relationship between Jesus and Judas as it evolved up to the betrayal.[29]

Right before shooting began, Dafoe and Keitel lived with a family in Oumnast, "just to settle into our sandals and know what living without electricity was about, to know what eating with your hands is like, to know what sitting on the floor is about."[30] Their Muslim hosts did not speak any English, and Dafoe recalled a comical moment on the first night when Keitel pulled him aside and whispered that, if they were asked the next day about their nationality, they should say through the translator that they were Canadian. Keitel, said Dafoe, "was a little nervous because of his Jewishness. Here we were in a North African country and he was thinking they might strangle us in the night if they thought we were New York Jews."[31]

Principal photography began on Wednesday, October 7, with Ballhaus shooting some of the Moroccan desert and moon in the night sky. Three days later, the first scene—a traveling shot through rustling trees, Jesus writhing on the ground with a migraine induced by God—was filmed in a half day. Finally, on Monday, October 12, the production of *The Last Temptation of Christ* kicked off like a gunshot. With the crew still adjusting to the drive time from Marrakech, the language barriers, and the problems of credibly recreating the first century, they had three days and more than 120 setups to shoot several pages of script. "When I saw our Roman soldiers come up," Scorsese recalled about that first day, "I said, 'Oh my God, this is not going to work. These guys are all clean!' We had to roll the extras in the dirt, mess up their uniforms, give them scars, rough them up. That's how we spent that first morning! Then . . . everybody in the picture was covered with a light patina of African dust. They blended right into the soil."[32] Moving at breakneck speed, the crew got all their shots by the end of the third day.[33]

One of the reasons they could function like a crack commando unit was the German cinematographer working close by the director's side. In 1983

Willem Dafoe as Jesus, in Morocco, 1987.

Scorsese's first choice had been the Italian director of photography Guiseppe Rotunno, renowned for his collaborations with De Sica, Visconti, and Fellini.[34] When Rotunno turned down the offer, Scorsese was referred to Michael Ballhaus, who had just emigrated to the United States after several years of working almost exclusively with the recently deceased director Rainer Werner Fassbinder. Scorsese needed a camera that would invade Jesus' space, moving in close when doubts and dread weighed on him, circling around his body as he performed miracles, fencing with him and St. Paul in their highly charged encounter during the last temptation sequence. Scorsese screened several of the Fassbinder films and saw that Ballhaus's fluid style ("a spontaneous, sensuous control of motion more evocative of dance than machinery," wrote one observer)[35] perfectly matched his blueprint for shooting *Last Temptation.*

After the plug had been pulled at Paramount, Scorsese consulted with him about the feasibility of doing *After Hours* for less than $4 million. Scorsese, recalled Ballhaus, "called me, showed me his shot list, and asked if we could do it for that kind of money. I really wanted to work with him, so, of course, I said yes. We captured sixteen to eighteen shots a day, and in forty days we filmed the entire thing."[36] *After Hours* and their next film together, *The Color of Money,* featured some of the most visually exciting sequences in any of Scorsese's movies, and Ballhaus was duly credited as the best interpreter yet of the director's vision.

Ballhaus's European training prepared him for coping with an impoverished production, a movie so stripped down to essentials that they couldn't even afford to bring a crane to Morocco for high-angle shots. Instead, they substituted a Panther jib arm that took the camera up fourteen feet, just high enough for scenes like the olive grove where Jesus and Judas slept side by side.[37] Nearly every scene was filmed on dusty streets and hillsides and ruins. The only exterior sets they built were several monastery huts made of dried-mud bricks, wood, and animal skins; the monastery interiors were built in the Moulay Ismael stables in Meknes.[38] The only optical effect was that of the lion entering Jesus' circle in the nighttime desert scene; the insidiously seductive look of the column of fire representing Satan was created by burying a gas jet in the sand, filming it at high speed, and later double-printing the frames.[39] To get snakes to "perform" in the monastery and desert scenes, they recruited one of the snake charmers who entertained tourists in the main square in Marrakech.[40] He came with his cobras and flute and charmed the snakes while Scorsese, terrified of the reptiles, sat in another room watching a video monitor.[41]

There were never enough stunt men. To multiply their numbers in a Temple scene, Scorsese resorted to an old silent movie trick. Five Italian stunt men clattered down stone steps, outfitted as soldiers with swords drawn; in the next shot, five more soldiers were seen in silhouette overhead; the camera swish-panned and another five rose up menacingly. They were same five men in each shot, creating the impression of a legion of soldiers surrounding Jesus' followers after the shots were edited together. When the Italians had to play both Roman soldiers and Jews in one sequence of shots, their faces were wrapped in scarves so the audience wouldn't know the soldiers were the same people they were confronting.[42]

Getting enough light presented a fierce challenge and one that grew worse through late autumn. Early in the shoot, crew members left their Marrakech hotels before dawn and tried to work at the Oumnast locations until 6:00 in the evening. But inevitably, as the days grew shorter, they found themselves fighting the oncoming darkness by 4:30. Joe Reidy remembers a typically agonizing struggle at the end of the Sermon on the Mount scene: "We got this shot, a close-up of Barbara Hershey's foot with Willem Dafoe stroking it, with the last light. In essence, the light was so low that it was basically just hitting the foot. And as the sun was going down, we had minutes to get it. There was only *a ray of light* on that foot. But that would be how our day would go. We'd have to get these shots in and plot it out to get it done as fast as possible."[43]

Even waiting thirty minutes for clouds to move meant cutting back on the number of takes or reducing the time that Scorsese could talk with his actors. Whenever inclement weather shut them down for more than a few hours, as it did when hailstorms and torrential rains hit in November, a whole additional day would have to be squeezed into the mercilessly tight schedule. Often they went right on shooting through light mismatches, hoping to correct the problem later in the color timing at the lab. Occasionally, the solution to a lighting problem was found on the set. During one of the Temple scenes, when Jesus rides into Jerusalem on a donkey, the light changed suddenly from sunny in the first part of the scene to deeply overcast in the second part. What they needed was another shot to bridge the change in the light. As it happened, there was an emotional change in the scene itself, as Jesus' triumphant entry to the city shifts abruptly to a confrontation with the high priests. Scorsese suggested that at the point where Jesus got off the donkey, they shoot from a camera already positioned on a dolly track above the Temple's arches. Ballhaus framed a high overhead shot, lit for day. Just as Dafoe dismounted, the crew flagged all the lights. The light change happened *within* the shot, so that after

Martin Scorsese on location in Morocco, 1987.

the sequence was edited it appeared as if a cloud were passing across the sun just as Jesus' attitude shifted, giving the scene a feel that was thematically true to the story.[44]

When Ballhaus and Scorsese first looked at dailies—the shots of the moon and landscape taken on the first day of principal photography—Scorsese remarked on the beautiful clarity of the shots, enhanced by the lack of interference from the earth's atmosphere in the high desert. He then looked closer. "But the moon seems to be on the wrong side of the frame, Michael. Didn't I ask you to do it—" They then realized that they were looking at the image upside down. The Moroccan projectionist was so untutored that he had threaded the film backward in the projector.[45]

From that point on, Scorsese stopped looking at dailies, not only because of the primitive conditions in Morocco, but also owing to the expense of flying the film to New York City for processing and back again. He also had to forgo meetings with his longtime editor, Thelma Schoonmaker. Ordinarily, when he filmed in New York, she would join him at the end of the day at the Brill Building and he would talk through the screenings, telling her what he liked or didn't like, relating how he had encouraged an actor in a certain direction, discussing camera moves that were too slow or fast, pointing out things that happened accidentally, and responding with delight to a wonderful performance or being savagely critical of what he had done. Schoonmaker used her notes from these screenings to catalogue Scorsese's "selects" in descending order of his preferences. Later, when he came into the cutting room, Schoonmaker would show him the first choice, then his second or third choice if he didn't like the first, or she would tell him why she thought the first choice wasn't working.[46] On *Last Temptation*, however, Scorsese was virtually flying blind. He had only a black and white video assist to determine on the spot that he had gotten the shots he needed.[47]

When phone connections permitted, and especially when he was concerned about whether a sequence had turned out right, he would call Schoonmaker to inquire about the dailies. One evening he called about the Crucifixion scene. She was so moved by the footage that she wept. The only other time Schoonmaker had been so emotionally affected by the dailies was when she first saw the scene near the end of *Raging Bull* in which Jake La Motta encounters his estranged brother on the street and hugs him. "When Marty called me, and I tried to tell him about the Crucifixion, I kept bursting into tears—and I couldn't talk. And he got terribly frightened. He said, 'My God, what's happened? Have we blown it? Did we get it on film?' And I had to hang up. It was very difficult to make phone calls from Morocco, so he tried the next day and got through, and I burst into tears again! And finally the third time I was just able to tell him what I thought, and he was terribly relieved because he thought something horrible had happened."[48]

The scenes for Golgotha were staged on a rocky hill several miles outside Meknes. Originally the Crucifixion was to be shot in three days and eighty-plus setups. But with the schedule slippage from bad weather, Scorsese, De Fina, Ballhaus, Joe Reidy, and Laura Fattori huddled in a trailer and managed to cut it down to fifty-five setups in only two days. Cast and crew gathered in the dark each morning, waiting for the first light to break through. They had a limit of ten, fifteen, or twenty minutes to get each of those shots—shots that Martin Scorsese first imagined when he read the book more than a decade before, shots he formulated in a room somewhere in Los Angeles in 1983, entire sequences of shots he had replayed in his mind for years and now had only a few chaotic hours to get. All the love and care he had lavished on this material for fully a third of his life were momentarily forgotten; the making of *Last Temptation* had devolved into an exercise in brute efficiency. Scorsese recalled, "All those things are designed exactly so that when you go in that morning, you say, 'Okay, we've got to get these three shots real fast. Change the lens, you know. Just bang. Same thing. . . . Okay, take another lens, and higher speed.'"[49] At one point during the shooting of Golgotha, they did a nearly 180-degree turnaround of camera angle and found all their equipment piled up in front of them. "Let's get this stuff moved!" Scorsese yelled, and he ran out with the other crew members, picking up gear. "I have to say," said Reidy, "I've never seen a director move like him on those days."[50]

The work took a physical toll on Willem Dafoe. He broke three toes, three of his toenails were torn off, and while being beaten and scourged by Roman soldiers, he had to fall repeatedly on a stone floor, naked.[51] The narrow seat on which he was forced to sit upon the cross was designed after a description of Roman crucifixion practices that Scorsese had found two years earlier in *Biblical Archaeology Review*.[52] Called a *sedile* in Latin, its apparent purpose was to prolong the agony of the victim until asphyxiation caused death. Perched on the sedile, knees turned sideways, Dafoe was able to stay on the cross only for the length of a shot before his ability to breathe began to falter and assistants rushed up with a ladder to bring him down. He "never complained," said Scorsese, "and he was always able to deal with his body in such a way that the whole body was in the role."[53]

The Crucifixion was staged brilliantly and yielded the film's most stirring imagery. Flanked by Roman soldiers, Jesus staggers up Golgotha and the camera moves in to frame the face of a man who realizes that this is the moment his entire life has pointed toward. The soldiers lift the crossbeam from his shoulders and yank off his sweat-soaked robe. He stands dazed and alone.

"Father," he says in an intimate voice-over, "I'm sorry for being a bad son." They lead him by the arm to the cross lying on the ground. They maneuver him onto it and tie down his wrists with rope. Ballhaus's jib-mounted camera moves slowly across Dafoe's blood-streaked body, lingering briefly before cutting to a perfectly timed montage of a hammer raising up in three successive shots, driving down on the spike, Jesus' face clenched in pain, blood spurting out a side view of his pierced hand. Arms and shoulders lean into the cross from behind. The cross pitches skyward. We are suddenly lifted up to Jesus' level. All around him, the hills recede to the horizon like waves on a sea. Below, a mob jeers while Roman sentries stand by. His female followers, in dark gowns, gather at his feet. His face slack with desolation, Dafoe whispers, "Father, forgive them." A gust of wind blows in, churning up red dust at the base of the cross, and from behind the angrily gesturing crowd, the camera tracks the tableau of deep blue sky and leafless trees, the forlorn figure at its center. With roaring wind and thunder breaking out on the soundtrack, Ballhaus frames Dafoe in a close shot and tilts his Arriflex so far sideways he can no longer put his eye to the viewfinder. "This incredible moment," Ballhaus said about the shot that took forty minutes to get, "breaks all the so-called 'rules' of composition, but people accept it because when it's right for the emotions they don't feel that something is wrong with it."[54]

In the rush to finish, the film magazine containing the last take of the Crucifixion, the one of Dafoe crying, "It is accomplished," was mishandled, and the footage was partially exposed. The leakage spilled ribbons of color onto the final frames of the scene and the rest was consumed by edge fog. Nevertheless, when he saw the take later in the editing room, Scorsese decided it was the one he wanted. "Leave it; that's the resurrection!" he said.[55]

Shooting of the Crucifixion wrapped up on November 22. Seven days behind schedule and with Christmas closing in fast, the company had no choice but to crank up the already furious pace. Up to that point, everyone had Sunday off; Scorsese would sometimes unwind by watching videos flown in from New York, the CBS show *Pee Wee's Playhouse* among them, formatted for the European PAL television system.[56] By December there was no time left for such dispensations. From now on, they had to shoot all week, every week. "The last twenty-one days of shooting," recalled Scorsese, "were probably the worst we've ever encountered, Joe Reidy and myself."[57] They threw the schedule to the winds and plunged into the rawest form of guerrilla filmmaking, tumbling daily through the remaining scenes, shooting in whatever order made logistical sense at the moment.[58] The weather turned colder and wetter.

Scenes that were supposed to be exteriors—the scene of Mary Magdalene dying; Jesus carrying the cross through the streets of Jerusalem—had to be shot inside the granary section of the Moulay Ismael stables.[59] Scorsese faced new crises every day: shortages of stunt men and extras; not enough costumes to go around; takes, camera angles, and scene coverage he had to sacrifice. Several days before Christmas, he looked up and saw the Italian sound crew leaving the set, bidding him good-bye—"Ciao, Martino, Buon Natale." They were going back to Rome for the holidays. "Who's gonna do the sound?" Scorsese asked. "Well, the Moroccan guys," he was told.[60]

Despite the adversities during the production's stretch run, spirits remained high and the actors and crew felt united by Scorsese's sense of mission.[61] There were moments, however, when Scorsese realized that he was just scratching the surface of what he wanted to do, even for an austere European-style production.[62] To Schoonmaker, Ballhaus, and others, he privately confessed his disappointment about lacking the resources commanded by the likes of Bernardo Bertolucci and Steven Spielberg, whose respective films, *The Last Emperor* and *Empire of the Sun,* were just being released.[63] Schoonmaker recalled, "He was terribly afraid that he was not going to be able to give enough power to the film. But what came out of it was his own tremendous emotional and philosophical commitment to the material, and the actors themselves were of course giving so much that it was being done right anyway, even though he didn't have the money he needed."[64] In Jay Cocks's view, *The Last Temptation of Christ* may have actually benefited from its hardships. "When you're working at that kind of energy, under that kind of time stricture, you really can get a kind of a boldness that might not come through otherwise if you're a little fatter and a little slower."[65]

This boldness was evident in one of the last scenes to be shot. Lying on his deathbed, the elderly Jesus is confronted by an angry Judas, who exposes the guardian angel as Satan. Jesus then drags himself off his bed and crawls to a balcony overlooking the destruction of Jerusalem, and he begs God to forgive him and return him to the cross. The night before, Keitel had asked Scorsese what kind of shot it would be when he made his entrance.[66] *Last Temptation* was being filmed in 1.85:1 aspect ratio—not the anamorphic wide-screen format Scorsese would have used for a grander, more epic approach—and this entailed tighter compositions.

Motioning from his waist up, Scorsese said, "It's going to be from about here, and you're going to come forward, and you do your speech at the foot of the bed."

"Why don't you just let me do what I feel I should do?" Keitel said.

"What are you going to do?"

Scorsese knew that Keitel would come up with something fascinating, but he worried whether it would be in the frame. Keitel had a contained space in which to act and if he didn't hit his marks, there would be no set in the shot. Inwardly Scorsese cringed, thinking about the days they were behind schedule and the very real possibility that the production's nearly depleted contingency fund would run out.

The next morning, the first thing Keitel did was ask Dafoe if he wouldn't mind if Scorsese was the one lying on the pallet while he delivered his speech. With the film rolling, Keitel, as the aged Judas, came through the entranceway, advancing slowly toward the director stretched out before him.

"Traitor!" he shouted. "Your place was on the cross. That's where God put you. When death got too close, you got scared and ran away and hid yourself in the life of some man. We did what we were supposed to do. You didn't! You're a coward!"

What Keitel had hinted at the previous evening turned out to be a blast of emotion that started out on a high withering note, then turned sorrowful: "Rabbi, you broke my heart. Sometimes I curse the day I ever met you. We held the world in our hands. Remember what you told me? You took me in your arms, do you remember? And you begged me. 'Betray me, betray me. I have to be crucified. I have to be resurrected so I can save the world.'"

After the take, he looked at Scorsese and said, "Well, okay?"

"Yeah, okay. That was good," he admitted.

"You want me to take it down a little?"

"Yeah, take it down," said Scorsese, laughing. But now he understood that they had to go there for Keitel to be able to calibrate his performance.

Willem Dafoe's part of the scene was arguably even more of a challenge. When Jesus becomes aware of the guardian angel's deception, Dafoe must suddenly shift his character against the tide of the entire film. In that moment Jesus had to take control of his destiny and drive the story out of the satanically inspired hallucination and back to the cross. What made the scene technically difficult was that Dafoe had to manipulate the externals of the character—the acting techniques for playing an eighty-year-old man—yet also find a way to bring a strong emotionality to the movie's moment of truth.

"I felt it deeply because of the expectation that it's the climax," Dafoe said of the scene. "And that was the kind of thing that Marty couldn't necessarily direct me in. He could only tell me when it was wrong and that's what he did.

And I suppose for that moment, that sense of failure and that sense of frustration became the fuel for what ended up being the scene. And I won't judge whether it was successful or not, but whatever we ended up with was better than the first take I did."[67]

ONLY A FEW OUTSIDERS entered this insular world that the filmmakers created in Morocco—a photographer from Rome flew in to take publicity stills (one of the delivery requirements to Universal);[68] a German documentary film crew, friends of Michael Ballhaus, showed up for a few days;[69] and the musician Peter Gabriel, who was commissioned to score the film, visited on the last day of shooting. Otherwise, the movie was made in splendid isolation. Scorsese never liked having journalists on the set, but in this case he really didn't. The apostles often sat together in makeup and robes, joking and playing cards and smoking cigars while they waited for Scorsese to decide whether he needed them in a shot. Pictures of this off-camera bonhomie would not do the film any good if published out of context.[70]

Nondisclosure clauses in actors' contracts are a routine way of controlling information coming out of a movie set, and *Last Temptation* was no exception. But before Scorsese and company left for Morocco, Universal decided that another measure was needed to stave off stories in the press that might produce the kind of pressure by outside groups that had plagued Paramount. The studio asked the director to come up with a working title for the film in order to lower its public profile and thus provide everyone cover for the duration of the production. "So we decided," said Scorsese, "to call it *The Passion,* because it is full of passion. It is my passion. So let's just do it, and that's what we did. Just to let it be."[71]

By the time Scorsese and De Fina boarded their December 23 flight back to New York, news about *The Passion* had been appearing for months. Announcements of Universal's deal with Scorsese were published in July,[72] and in September a substantive article about the production then getting under way appeared in *Variety.*[73] The new title didn't throw anyone off the trail, however. "For lo these many years," noted the *Los Angeles Herald-Examiner,* "director Martin Scorsese has been hot to make a movie titled 'The Passion' out of Nikos Kazantzakis' book 'The Last Temptation of Christ.' Now rumors are rife that he's to begin filming in Morocco in October."[74] A mid-November *Chicago Tribune* story even poked fun at the faux title: "Martin Scorsese is reportedly going to change the name of 'The Last Temptation of Christ' . . .

to 'The Passion.' Same project, but the latter sounds so much more, um, commercial, doesn't it?"[75]

By December the studio was handing off responsibility for *The Last Temptation of Christ* to its marketing group, the entity that mounts the publicity and paid advertising campaigns for the studio's slate. During the first full year of Tom Pollock's administration, the top echelon of the marketing team underwent a facelift, starting with Edward G. Roginski's appointment as president. In March 1987 Perry Katz joined the company as vice president of marketing research, followed the same month by the arrival of an Amblin Entertainment publicist, Sally Van Slyke, as the new vice president of West Coast publicity, promotion, and field operations. Six months later, David Sameth was hired as vice president of creative advertising. Roger Armstrong, who came on board as director of national publicity in October, recalled being consumed by *Batteries Not Included*, *Midnight Run*, *Gorillas in the Mist*, and "the other pictures on our plate. . . . Nobody was really focusing on *Last Temptation* in that way."[76]

Adding to the fluidity in Universal's marketing group was Roginski's AIDS diagnosis only a few months into his tenure. As the illness began to take its toll, he came to the office less often, and there came a point when a de facto triumvirate of Katz, Van Slyke, and Sameth was virtually running the department.[77] Before the day arrived that Roginski went home and never returned, he shared with Sally Van Slyke his concerns about a spectral presence on the near horizon. "Ed Roginski and I used to have these profound talks at seven o'clock at night," said Van Slyke. "He'd either go home—he was just really ill—or sit in his office, and we'd talk. And he looked at me and said, 'You know what's coming down the line?' "[78]

She knew *The Last Temptation of Christ* was coming. Van Slyke had been getting some stills and prepress materials from the unit publicist. "Nobody paid a great deal of attention to it," she said. "It was a small film off in the middle of the desert getting shot."[79] Roginski, however, who had once studied to be a Catholic priest, gave her a more detailed understanding of what the Kazantzakis novel contained. Before the project was green-lit, said Van Slyke, "[Roginski] went to Tom Pollock and said, 'Please don't make this movie. There are just some things that big corporations the size of MCA shouldn't get into.' "[80]

Roginski's pleas went unheeded, but when his replacement, Simon Kornblit, was named during the third week of November, the time to plan seriously for *Last Temptation*'s release—especially the question of how to manage its potential for controversy—was very much upon them. From his command post in Tupelo, the Reverend Donald Wildmon had been following the trade coverage of the resuscitated production. Claiming that "someone with an entrée into Universal's business affairs" had tipped him off about the film, Wildmon urged his friends in the former National Federation of Decency—now sporting its new, benign-sounding name, the American Family Association—to make their concerns known to MCA/Universal, just as they had done to Gulf + Western/Paramount in 1983.[81] Initially, the letters arrived at Universal in isolated batches. But by late fall of 1987, they came streaming in by the hundreds weekly.

For Universal's executives, just getting *Last Temptation* into production had been an achievement. The subsequent steps they took to sequester the picture were supposed to buy time until Scorsese was ready to show them a rough cut. They now found themselves having to figure out, much sooner than expected, whether the flow of letters and calls was just a blip, a microburst of angst that would exhaust itself before the film came out, or whether—like a seismic event far out at sea, triggering a tsunami that streaks underwater for thousands of miles before reaching shore—it was the first sign of a thunderous conflict already advancing on the studio.

5

Fevers Under the Veil

AS 1987 DREW to a close, and a presidential election year loomed on the horizon, evangelical Christians were in a dispirited mood. Seven years earlier, Ronald Reagan had been elected to the presidency with their overwhelming support. Although Reagan himself had no "born again" experience, his sunny optimism and the conservative values he espoused had won them over. The newly ascendent Christian right—personified by the televangelists Jerry Falwell, Pat Robertson, and Paul Robison, but also powered behind the scenes by Paul Weyrich, Beverly LaHaye, Phyllis Schlafly, and other movement activists—had gotten behind Reagan's campaign and helped him achieve a resounding victory over the authentic evangelical in the race, President Jimmy Carter.

Not without reason, they held high expectations that the "Reagan revolution" would usher in a host of desired social changes. Overturning the right to abortion topped the list. Not far behind was an array of other "traditional family" policy issues demanding action: the restoration of public school prayer; tuition tax credits for parents with children in private schools; and laws forbidding the use of federal funds to promote homosexual or feminist values. They also wanted the administration to get out front on fighting moral decay in the media—especially what they saw as a flood of pornography, violence, and antireligious bigotry. But after two terms, the White House had done little more than offer symbolic gestures of support to this agenda. "Although it raised millions of dollars and received enormous amounts of media attention, the Christian Right of the 1980s cannot be deemed a success," wrote the sociologist Clyde Wilcox. "Reagan was more interested in enacting the agenda of the financial and foreign policy conservatives than those of the Christian Right."[1] Partly to fulfill this agenda, Pat Robertson, the genial host of the Christian Broadcasting Network's *700 Club,* announced in October 1987 his candidacy for the Republican presidential nomination. Running as a pure social conservative, Robertson began assembling an "invisible army" of supporters in his bid to win the Iowa caucuses.

Meanwhile, evangelical Christians were unhappy about the embarrassing behavior of their own leaders. First, in January, the Pentecostal preacher Oral Roberts invited public scorn and ridicule when he told his viewers that God would "call him home" unless they donated $4.5 million to help keep his ministry afloat. Then, on March 19, Jim Bakker, who, with his wife, Tammy, headed the popular PTL cable network and Christian theme park, Heritage USA, revealed that he had committed adultery with a church secretary, Jessica Hahn. Bakker immediately resigned his post and announced that Jerry Falwell, the founder of the political action group Moral Majority, was taking over the PTL empire. The soap opera continued to unfold over the course of the year. PTL went bankrupt, a weeping Jim Bakker was led off in handcuffs, and Falwell himself resigned in October after a court allowed PTL's creditors to file their own reorganization plans. And just around the corner, another scandal was waiting to explode. In March 1988, Jimmy Swaggart of Assemblies of God was brought down by his admission that he had visited a New Orleans prostitute. To the dismay of parachurch organizations and other nonprofit groups, these events were having an effect in Christians' loss of confidence in their leadership and, more alarmingly, a drop-off of donations.

But not everything was bleak in the Christian world. The 1980s witnessed the takeoff and acceleration of a full-blown evangelical subculture. Sprawling megachurches were built on the outskirts of cities, catering to the spiritual and lifestyle needs of young families and single adults. Many of these churches established Christian academies so that their members' children would be given a biblically based education. Christian bookstores sprang up in shopping malls, and the new genres of Christian fiction, contemporary Christian music, and "family values"–inflected movies and videos poured into the marketplace. Believers also connected with each other through increasingly popular computer-based services such as bulletin board systems and e-mail. But the biggest change in Christian media—bigger even than the much-publicized televangelist shows—occurred in the "old" medium of radio. In 1973 only 111 stations were airing at least twenty hours of religious-oriented programming weekly; fifteen years later the number of religious radio broadcasters had soared beyond one thousand.[2] By far the hottest format was Christian talk. Talk radio was the subculture's underground railroad—a loose confederation of listening posts for information and viewpoints that the mainstream media didn't report. Listeners tuned in to commune with hosts such as Dr. James Dobson and to get the Christian perspective on what was happening in the world. And when hot political issues came along, there was no more forceful way to "telegraph the need for urgent action," as one author put it[3]—actions like calling elected officials, signing petitions, joining boycotts, sending money to advocacy groups—than radio. Thus, by the end of the 1980s, the glimmerings of a new Christian paradigm could be discerned in the melding of political activism with a robust, values-driven consumerism.

But in November 1987 few people in the top corporate posts of the major film studios had more than a superficial understanding of—or interest in—these changes. At Universal Pictures, the only major change in progress was the transition to a new executive vice president of marketing. To fill the vacancy left by Ed Roginski's departure, the studio hired Simon Kornblit, a thirty-three-year veteran of the advertising agency D.D.B. Needham. One of Kornblit's immediate priorities when he took over was to resuscitate the faltering release of *Cry Freedom*. Richard Attenborough's drama about the anti-apartheid activist Steve Biko and his friendship with a white South African journalist was green-lit by the Frank Price administration at a time when South Africa's racist policies were a topic of debate in the United States. "By the time the movie came out," said Pollock, "nobody could care less about apartheid."[4]

Employing the services of John Scanlon, one of the premier crisis fixers of his day, who had earlier advised studios on social issues films such as *Silkwood* and *Absence of Malice,* Universal set out to create an attention-getting tempest around *Cry Freedom*. On November 25 Tom Pollock issued a formal challenge to the South African government, calling for the film to be shown uncut and in its entirety in fully integrated theaters in every part of the country; Universal promised to donate any profits received from showings of *Cry Freedom* to a UNICEF fund benefiting the children of South Africa.[5] Pollock's challenge was designed to box the government's censorship board into a specific set of choices: it could reject the film, as everyone expected it would, thus spotlighting the regime's repressive practices; or it could grant *Cry Freedom* an exception to its policy of denying licenses to films critical of apartheid. No matter how the board's decision came down, *Cry Freedom* would make news back in the States.

Two days later the South African censorship board cleared *Cry Freedom* for exhibition in the nation without cuts or restrictions.[6] Pollock could barely contain his ebullience. He vowed that Universal's international distributor, UIP, would book the film everywhere in South Africa. "We want to make a big deal out of it. . . . We're going to do all the things we can to make the film the event it ought to be in South Africa. This is going to be fun."[7]

Universal's jousting with the Botha regime had the immediate effect of improving *Cry Freedom*'s U.S. box office take by 50 percent over its opening weekend, but the publicity had a brief half-life. Without the resonance of apartheid as a front-burner issue, Pollock recalled ruefully, it was "just a noble movie about a noble white guy who helps a noble black guy."[8] The studio quickly cast about for other ways to promote *Cry Freedom* before submitting it to triage—which in all likelihood meant pulling the $21 million picture from theaters.

In early December Si Kornblit was given the name of a Burbank producer who might be able to help Universal with *Cry Freedom*. A tall Oklahoman with a big, outgoing personality, Tim Penland was a born-again Christian known to be on good terms with many of the major figures in the evangelical world. His producing career had been modestly successful at best; his most notable project was a 1975 Roy Rogers picture, *Mackintosh and T.J.* Penland's true talents lay elsewhere, in a newly forming niche in Hollywood's industrial ecology. In the early 1980s a handful of film companies and marketing firms began to concentrate on reaching the elusive Christian moviegoer. Much of their work was done for overtly religious (or "gospel") films. After more than a decade of neglecting religion as a factor in developing or marketing movies, however, Hollywood was becoming interested in the commercial possibilities of the approximately 80 million people who referred to themselves as "born-again" or "evangelical" Christians.[9] The studios needed a test case, and in 1982 they found one in Warner Bros.' *Chariots of Fire*.

The future Oscar-winner revolved around an obscure sport (long-distance running) in a period setting, featured a cast of unknown British actors, and served up a strong spiritual theme. Deciding that the only way to build popular interest in *Chariots of Fire* was to show the whole movie repeatedly,[10] Warner Bros. gave a religious film company, Inspirational Films, more than $2 million to screen it for religious leaders and church groups. Tim Penland, by then a vice president with Inspirational Films, set up *Chariots of Fire* viewing groups in a quiet, "underground" fashion to avoid having it labeled as a Christian-message movie.[11] "People who saw the film got inspired and motivated. They went out and told their friends," Penland said about the slow-building, grass-roots strategy. "And so when we opened with no seeming advertising, all of a sudden the theaters were filled with people and everybody was in shock."[12]

Four years later, he applied the same treatment to *The Mission,* Roland Jaffe's film about Jesuit missionaries and their martyred resistance to the slave trade in eighteenth-century South America. *The Mission* was not a breakout hit like *Chariots of Fire,* but both of them demonstrated that a studio-financed movie could pull in a faith-based audience if it had the right spiritual and narrative elements.

"You only have your credibility in this business," Penland once said, "and once you lose your credibility, you've lost everything."[13] Tim Penland's own credibility depended on taking those projects that had the redemptive values he believed in as a Christian—and turning down the ones that did not. When he saw *Cry Freedom,* Penland was impressed with the story of a friendship that transcends rigid racial boundaries. The protagonists' courageous struggle for human rights in an oppressive political system was also uplifting. But he told Si Kornblit that he could not help him. The film as a whole just did not seem to him to be the type that would appeal to a specifically Christian audience.

A couple of weeks later, Kornblit called Penland and asked him to come back to the studio for a conversation after the turn of the new year. There was another film they wanted to discuss with him.

When they met in early January, Kornblit and Sally Van Slyke, the vice president for publicity, told Penland about the new project. Martin Scorsese's adaptation of *The Last Temptation of Christ,* they said, was by no means a conventional interpretation of Christ, but the director assured the studio that it would be "faith affirming." Principal photography had just been completed. Announcements of the movie's release were coming out. Recently, however, people had been writing letters and calling Universal, apparently spurred by notices appearing in the newsletter of the American Family Association. Some of the letters were disturbing for their vehement tone and the writers' insistence that the film was blasphemous.

If it's a faith-affirming film, said Penland, there is nothing to worry about. Ultimately he might be proven right, but their problem then was more about the rumors spread by people who hadn't seen the film. Universal wanted to support Marty and protect the project. And toward that end, they thought a religious authority should be hired, someone who would be an advisor to the studio. Based on what he had done with *Chariots of Fire* and *The Mission,* they thought that he could be that person. They did not expect Penland to "sell" the film. Rather, they hoped he could make a connection to certain groups, to try to establish a constructive dialogue about the movie, to *build a bridge* between the studio and the Christian community.

Penland was intrigued—even a bit flattered—at the idea of Universal's coming to him for assistance, especially for a film about Christ directed by someone of Scorsese's stature. He said he did not know if he could help, but would certainly be willing to consider it.

Penland immediately got in touch with his friend Larry Poland, the president of Mastermedia International, a Christian ministry dedicated to changing the moral direction of the television and motion picture industries by building relationships with executive-level leaders. Tim Penland was a member of Mastermedia's "Key Man" group—a support group of Christian executives, producers, and directors. The men shared their life stories and bared their feelings about working in a business that constantly challenged their faith. In the Key Man meetings Tim Penland openly discussed his earlier struggles with alcohol and how God had helped him make a new start in life. Poland took a liking to Penland's sincerity and plainspoken southwestern manner: "Tim," he wrote, "said he had been led to Hollywood, and nobody doubted it. It was obvious that he was enough 'out of phase' with Hollyweird that if God hadn't brought him, he wouldn't be here."[14]

Penland told his friend about Universal's overtures and asked what he should do. Poland replied with a question: "Tim, you wouldn't be able to work on a film that attacks the character of Christ, would you?" Penland answered that of course he couldn't. But he looked forward to learning more about the project in a meeting that Van Slyke was trying to set up with Universal's chairman.[15]

Penland often turned to Larry Poland for advice. In this case, however, Poland became more than just a confidant. From Penland's first meeting at Universal, and continuing for the next few months, Poland created for himself the role of "shadow consultant." Poland listened to Penland's accounts of what the people at Universal were saying; he offered his own analysis of their motives; and he spoke privately—and, occasionally, bluntly—to Penland's conscience about what his involvement with *The Last Temptation of Christ* meant for his soul and for the future of everything the two of them held dear. Poland, in effect, became the behind-the-scenes counterpart to Penland's more public role, the superego to his ego. Whereas Penland depended on Poland's sage counsel and emotional support in times of isolation and distress, Poland gained from Penland a vicarious entrée to backstage conversations. In time Larry Poland became a player himself in the controversy, and later that year—with the benefit of Penland's diary—he wrote an insider-Christian's account of the bruising confrontation with Universal.

The meeting with Tom Pollock materialized in a matter of days. The studio chairman went into great detail about the Kazantzakis novel and the origins of the project. Pollock emphasized that the subject matter was very intimate for Scorsese as a Catholic. *The Last Temptation of Christ,* said Pollock, sets forth that Christ is both divine and human and does not deny anything that finally is important about the nature of Jesus. He said to Penland, "We know you're suspicious of Hollywood in general and of everybody's motives. We're not asking you to love the movie or even to endorse it. But we will show it to you. Please don't judge us until you see it. Don't judge it off of other things you've heard, or what other people tell you. See the movie and then judge it."[16]

They talked about the possibility of using one or more screenings of the movie as the linchpin of an outreach strategy. Penland said that he could go to certain people in the evangelical leadership circle—people like Billy Graham, Jerry Falwell, Lloyd Ogilvie, James Dobson, Donald Wildmon—and ask for their restraint until they had a chance to see the film in advance of its release. If they agreed to do this—and if their cooperation was announced publicly—most Christians would take it as a signal to hold their fire. Then, after the religious leaders saw what was actually in the movie, they could say and do anything they liked, including attacking it.

But if the film did dishonor Christ—or if the studio abrogated the terms of their agreement in any significant way—he would have no choice but to resign. This was the only way he could preserve his credibility.

Pollock enthusiastically embraced all these ideas. "I think we were all on the same wavelength," he recalled about the meeting. "We engaged Tim Penland to present our case to the right, the Christian right. And our case was: Don't judge us until you see the movie. Don't make suppositions. We'll show you the movie as soon as we can. Just wait. We went forward with that in good faith. I think Tim Penland went forward with that in good faith."[17]

Elated, Penland called Larry Poland with the news that he had "never seen anyone more earnest than Tom Pollock. He really sold me. . . . The world could use a film about Christ that dealt realistically with His humanity without denying His deity."[18] The euphoria of the moment even prompted Penland to think beyond *The Last Temptation of Christ.* This movie could be the first, crucial step in a broader rapprochement. It could take bridge building to a new level, helping close the chasm that had alienated Christian Americans from the secular media for so long.

First he needed to find out if the plan would be acceptable to the religious leaders. The person whose opinion mattered most was Donald Wildmon, whose campaign in 1983 had helped waylay the Paramount production of *Last Temptation* and who was now mobilizing another direct-mail attack against the film. In a phone call to Wildmon, Penland reviewed the key points of the deal. Three things in particular stood out for Wildmon: the opportunity to offer suggestions and comments after the screening; Penland's pledge to quit his consultancy if the film turned out to defame Christ; and a promise by the studio to hold the advance screening no later than early June. Wildmon agreed to the plan, he said later, "not because I trusted Universal . . . but because I trusted my fellow Christian, Tim Penland. . . . However, I told Tim that if Universal wanted to play games, then I would play games also. In our next conversation Tim assured me that Universal assured him that they were sincere, and not trying to play games."[19] Penland informed his Universal contacts that Wildmon was going to halt his direct-mail campaign; Larry Poland characterized their response as "stunned."[20]

In January Penland made the rounds at Universal, paying courtesy calls on some of the executives. He met briefly with Fred Mound, the senior vice president of distribution and a churchgoing Christian. The *Last Temptation* script had landed on his desk, as was the custom for movies on the studio's release slate; he glanced at it, briefly discussed it with others, and then forgot about it. Now Penland was telling him about the outreach he was organizing. Said Mound: "Quite candidly, I didn't give him much hope of bringing the Christian community around on the picture, even though I hadn't seen it at the time. But he had every confidence. And all I remember is, I told him, 'Well, be my guest, and I hope you do very well.'"[21]

DURING THE second week of January, postproduction work on *Last Temptation* got quietly under way in the Sound One facilities on the ninth floor of the historic Brill Building, at Broadway and 49th Street in New York. Scorsese had missed out on dailies during the shoot, so the first thing he and Thelma Schoonmaker did was screen all of the footage. "He didn't know yet whether he had it or not," said Schoonmaker. Filming in Morocco "had been hard, extremely hard, and he was troubled by that. But . . . once he started looking at the footage, he was reassured and got excited."[22]

They assembled forty minutes of clips, which Scorsese and Barbara De Fina took to Los Angeles on January 25, to show Tom Pollock and Sean Daniel. During the visit Pollock sat down with them and explained that he was getting outside help with the film's public relations. "It became apparent that it needed to be handled," said De Fina. "Obviously we're filmmakers, not corporate people. So [consultants] are the kinds of things that, if you feel the studio's on your side, which they were, whatever they suggested, we sort of went with."[23] One of the suggestions was for Scorsese to write a brief statement about the film and what it meant to him. The statement would be given to media representatives who needed quotes from the director and to answer people who wrote or called to express concerns about the film. The statement Scorsese wrote would serve as his only public comment on *Last Temptation* until that summer:

> "The Last Temptation of Christ" is a motion picture that I have wanted to make for over fifteen years. Both as a filmmaker and a Christian, I believe with all my heart that the film I am making is a deeply religious one. Although Jesus is tempted by Satan, what the movie says and what I believe is that Jesus resisted temptation and was crucified as told in the Bible. I have made a film which is an affirmation of faith and I urge everyone not to judge my film until they see it.[24]

Around this time, Universal's executives decided they needed another consultant to help flesh out the rest of the marketing campaign and publicize *Last Temptation* among religious "progressives"—believers who weren't biblical literalists, who were open to alternative interpretations of Christ. Ideally, this consultant would also have an understanding of the Christian right—not as a member of the movement, but as a knowledgeable observer—and thus be able to advise the studio on how to respond to its arguments, especially if the film was half as problematic as Ed Roginski had intimated the year before.

Sean Daniel called the only person who fit the totality of this job description: Josh Baran. He was then the president of the eponymous public relations boutique in Venice Beach, and his firm was known for counseling clients on the political and cultural left—among them, the People for the American Way, the ACLU, the Hollywood Women's Political Committee, the National Resources Defense Council, celebrities, entertainment companies, children's health causes, and various environmental and religious groups. Baran had helped promote some of the highest-profile events of the 1980s, such as pro-choice rallies and the Farm Aid concerts. He was also active in Democratic Party politics, having served as California press secretary for U.S. Senator Gary Hart's 1984 presidential bid.

Along the way Josh Baran had built an impressive list of contacts. As a movie industry acquaintance put it: "He knows a remarkable number of people from a remarkable number of areas of life. And you know, you say, 'Josh, I have this film about the unique way that Lithuanian women choose to give birth and I need to find out if there's a society of Lithuanian midwives out there.' And he knows it. And if he doesn't know it immediately, he finds it."[25]

The route he took to this expertise was unusual by the standards of the typical PR professional. Raised in the Los Angeles neighborhood of Brentwood, Josh Baran went to the Shasta Abbey in northern California at the age of nineteen to study Zen Buddhism. He recalled it as a dramatic transformation of his life: "I shaved my head, donned black monastic robes, and entered into this unknown world of meditation and discipline." For the next ten years he studied under the monastery's teachers and became a Zen monk and priest. Over time, however, he became disturbed at what he called "the shadow side of the Zen community." The authoritarian rule of the monastery stifled his questioning of certain tenets of Buddhism; even expressions of personal feeling were discouraged. For a while he tried to convince himself that the fault lay in his own lack of devotion and discipline. "But I soon came to realize that the problem lay not in me, but with the harsh and unkind culture of the monastery. It took me the better part of a year, but I finally mustered the courage to walk out the door."[26]

In 1977 Baran quit the priesthood. He moved to San Francisco, where he started working on a degree in religious studies from Antioch College. Said Susan Rothbaum, a close friend and a layperson then associated with the abbey: "Joshua went through a process of coming to terms with [questions like] what did he think, why had he left, what didn't feel right to him, and what did he then believe." Rothbaum herself left Shasta Abbey when she was given an ultimatum to cut off her ties to Baran.[27] She and Baran began talking with other ex-disciples of the alternative religions flourishing in the Bay Area. Many of them had gone through the same struggle of trying to reclaim their personal agency, a process often complicated by the efforts of the groups' gurus and membership to pull them back into line.[28] Together Baran and Rothbaum founded Sorting It Out (SIO), a Berkeley-based counseling center that helped "leavetakers" explore, and come to terms with, the meanings of their experiences.

Over a seven-year period, SIO assisted some 3,000 persons coming from more than 250 groups—including sects, convents, storefront churches, therapeutic groups, cults, and branches of Christianity, Buddhism, and Hinduism.[29]

The hours he spent listening to the SIO participants sharpened Josh Baran's understanding of how people behave when they feel their beliefs and sacred images are threatened. He gained a realistic view of how and why true believers can go off the edge psychologically. By the same token, he learned that it was vital not to try to "deprogram" anyone, but instead to show respect for—indeed, to encourage the free expression of—differing viewpoints.

By this time Baran was also getting involved in California's nuclear disarmament movement. Much of his volunteer work was done for Ground Zero, a major antinuke group, and he soon discovered that he had a knack for developing communication strategy. As before, he was promoting the ideals of compassion, nonviolence, and social change one person at a time, only now the persons with whom he spoke—reporters, scientists, policy makers, and other influential types—had the ability to carry these messages to thousands or even millions more people. Josh Baran seemed ready to embark on a new career of producing enlightenment on a massive scale. Publicizing the imminent destruction of mankind seemed as good a place as any to start.

In May 1982 the ABC television network announced that it was going to broadcast *The Day After,* a movie-of-the-week drama that would depict the detonation of a Soviet nuclear weapon on Kansas City. This news came just as nuclear freeze advocates were ratcheting up opposition to the Reagan administration's plans to deploy cruise missiles in Western Europe. *The Day After,* Baran realized, could be an unparalleled opportunity to focus the nation's attention on the need to stop the nuclear arms race.

Working out of the Berkeley house he shared with Susan Rothbaum, Baran geared up a campaign with the ambitious goal of making *The Day After* the biggest media event of 1983.[30] In April—seven months before the movie's November 20 air date—he helped form The Day Before Project, an ad hoc organization funded by Ground Zero and Physicians for Social Responsibility. The project organized community gatherings across the country, as *Newsweek* reported, "in order to transform the film's voltage into consciousness-raising and constituency-building."[31] Meanwhile, Baran obtained bootlegged copies of the film from sources inside ABC and screened them for peace groups and the media.[32] Rothbaum herself was pressed into service, ghostwriting an op-ed piece by the mayor of Lawrence, Kansas, one of the real-world sites of the fictional cataclysm, and writing a study guide for schools and community groups nationwide. In the days before the telecast, Baran seemed to be everywhere at once—helping produce a television ad featuring Paul Newman;

staging candlelight vigils in Lawrence and Kansas City; coordinating hundreds of group viewings the night of the broadcast; constantly talking to the media about the danger of the arms race and what his fellow activists were doing to alert people about the movie—"because," he was often quoted saying, "the way we feel about it is, it's still The Day Before, and there's still time to do something about it."[33]

The Day After, recalled Rothbaum, was almost terrifying in its size and scope—"the first example of Josh *really goes large.*"[34] Through his savvy co-opting of ABC's own publicity campaign, he had pioneered the concept of "piggybacking" a public issue onto the release of a commercial media product.[35] Within months of this triumph, Baran set up his own public relations shop in Los Angeles.[36] During the next two decades he helped promote many more mega-events, such as Earth Day 1990 and the Dalai Lama's 2000 talk before fifty thousand people in Central Park. Entertainment companies also sought his help in handling scores of films with socially sensitive or volatile themes, such as *Do the Right Thing, Basic Instinct, American Me, Henry and June, New Jack City, Betrayed, Kids,* and *Seven Years in Tibet.* But nothing brought out the adrenaline—or the warrior—in Josh Baran like direct combat with those forces in American society that would seek to deprive people of their personal liberties or deny media companies their constitutionally guaranteed freedoms to produce and distribute content.

Josh Baran's experience with Sorting It Out prepared him for operating in this battlefield. He had seen the dark side of religious commitment, the tendency of some of its strains to erect a system of beliefs that denies the validity of other ways. Intolerance of any path but the one "true" way follows a similar story line everywhere, whether it is a cult's perfect master demanding followers' fealty to an ideal of spiritual purity or religious leaders asserting that the United States is destined to be a Christian nation. Baran saw it as his mission to use the tools of the public relations discipline to open up a space in people's minds for the concept of freedom of expression—to remind them that it is legitimate in America to write and read varied interpretations of art and religion, to have one's own internal definition of what is true.

He viewed it as a fight that, in one fashion or other, had been carried on since the founding of the republic: "Ultimately this is . . . a cultural war that's been going on for a long time and will go on forever probably. And that's the forces of the reactionary right against an open society. . . . They might say that they're not against freedom of speech, but they are. They believe in heresy as if it were a legal term, and it's not. They would like to tell us what to see.

They're kind of the thought police. And so, to me, this is one more skirmish in an ongoing war. That's what the *Last Temptation* was for me. And I wanted to win it."[37]

Baran had read the Kazantzakis novel as a college freshman, before he set off for Shasta Abbey. He remembered having a good feeling about it then. As he reread the novel, he was horrified to find the prose embarrassingly florid, almost unreadable, in fact. But it was the script that raised red flags for him. He read it through once, then again. He checked in with several of his colleagues. Their opinions confirmed his own: "It became clear to me that this was going to be the most controversial film ever released by any studio in the history of the movie business. . . . In fact, I couldn't sleep a couple of nights. I just thought, this thing is going to *explode*. They have no idea what they have here. They have no clue. And my initial reaction was a little bit like—I can't believe they're making this movie. And the thought was—Who approved this, and how did this happen? What was going through their minds when they decided to make this film?"[38]

In his first meeting with Tom Pollock, recalled Baran, the Universal chairman wanted to know if he could help the studio make it more controversial, if necessary. Baran told him not to worry. The script departed from the Gospels on so many key points that it would push every button imaginable for any biblically oriented Christian. The firestorm that *The Last Temptation of Christ* sets off, Baran said, will hit Universal like a nuclear bomb.[39]

When Pollock reacted with skepticism to this prediction, Baran went back to his office and started working with his associates on a memo outlining the issues that the studio would face before the movie's release. They analyzed the script in terms of dialogue and actions that conservative Christians would see as "tantamount to blasphemy, heresy, the Devil incarnate, the worse thing they'd ever seen in their entire lives . . . many, many points of theological elements that would drive them absolutely insane." They projected the difficulties that would probably ensue once the activists rallied their troops. There would be a flood of protest letters and hundreds of thousands of calls jamming the phone lines. There would be demonstrators assembling at the studio gates, maybe as many as a hundred thousand for a single event. Hundreds, if not thousands, of MCA's 16,800 employees were Christians who would be deeply offended by *The Last Temptation of Christ*. Some would quit their jobs over this film, some would try to weaken the company's morale by bad-mouthing the executives. A few of them might even try to sabotage distribution of the film. Finally, MCA's other divisions could be affected by a concerted boycott effort. This rarely happens, Baran noted, but "there's a possibility of boycotts being called against a video division or the toy division or the theme park. The theme park was extremely vulnerable to this kind of attack."[40]

The process of writing the memo convinced Baran of the inevitability of major problems arising from *Last Temptation.* "This was going to be an *extremely* contentious, difficult time for the studio and for the movie industry and there was no way around it. This film was coming out, and [the threats outlined in the memo] were going to happen, and we had to get prepared for it."[41]

Baran then learned that the studio had hired a Christian marketing expert for the *Last Temptation* project. It struck him as an absurdity that this film could ever pass muster with the people Tim Penland represented, or that any objections or suggestions produced by such a group would have a chance of persuading Universal Pictures and Martin Scorsese to edit the picture to its satisfaction—"because if he looked at this script, and the content of the movie, there is no way that the film could in any way be significantly changed enough so that any conservative or even middle-of-the-road Christian could support this movie."[42]

But Penland had signed on without reading the script and was moving forward with his outreach. Accompanied by Larry Poland, he was traveling in early February to Washington, D.C., for the annual convention of the National Religious Broadcasters. He pitched the trip to Pollock, Kornblit, and Van Slyke as an opportunity to tell an important group of "influencers"—the representatives of about 70 percent of the nation's religious radio, television, and cable outlets—about the studio's desire to make a serious film about Christ. The setting for his prepared remarks was a session on Hollywood and religion organized by Ted Baehr, chairman of the Christian Film and Television Commission and publisher of *Movieguide,* a movie newsletter for Christians. The featured speakers were Barry Reardon, president of distribution for Warner Bros. Pictures; David Puttnam, former president of Columbia Pictures; the film and television producer Ken Wales; the director Ron Maxwell; and Penland.[43] A big turnout was expected for the session.[44]

Josh Baran was tipped off by Universal about the session and decided to go to Washington and place himself in clear view of Penland. "I walked in the room and sat there and watched him. First, I wanted to make it clear that if you say anything, it'll get back to the studio. I didn't want him to be two-faced about what he was doing. And I wanted to know what the buzz in the room was, what people were saying. And the truth at that point was that they weren't saying a lot yet. It was too early, and it wasn't on their radar screen."[45]

Writing in his book *The Last Temptation of Hollywood*, Larry Poland perceived the same event—and the other consultant, Josh Baran—quite differently.

> Universal leadership must have had some doubts about Tim, the statement he was to make, or the dynamics of the NRB, because they dispatched another paid representative to the NRB for purposes known only to them. Tim knew this guy was from another public relations firm and that he was assigned to the same Universal project. Tim and I wondered aloud if he was checking up on Tim, but dismissed the idea because we had nothing to hide. At times, though, it was a little funny, because this guy was philosophically and by lifestyle like a fish out of water with more than four thousand evangelical Christians. . . . When Tim got back in communication with the Universal bosses upon his return to California, they indicated in rather extravagant terms how pleased they were with his performance at NRB and with the statement he had made. . . . [Universal] apparently got good words from their "observer" at NRB.[46]

Within days of the convention, the pace of the outreach quickened. Penland submitted to Universal his list of key leaders to invite to the special screening: James Dobson, prolific author and founder of Focus on the Family; Jack Hayford, nationally known pastor of the Church on the Way, in Van Nuys, California; Lloyd John Ogilvie, pastor of the First Presbyterian Church of Hollywood; Bill Bright, president of the Campus Crusade for Christ; and Donald Wildmon. (He also suggested Archbishop Roger Mahony of the Los Angeles Catholic archdiocese, but Universal reportedly told him that it wasn't necessary to invite him.)[47] In letters dated February 29, 1988, Universal formally invited these individuals and notified them that the screening would occur within seven days of the studio's receipt of the finished film, then projected for late June.[48]

The first public result of Penland's activity appeared in a story in the March 4 issue of *Christianity Today*, the largest and most influential magazine catering to conservative Christians. After observing that "Universal Pictures began receiving critical letters, calls, and boycott threats after announcing plans to distribute the movie," Steve Rabey, a reporter, quoted Tim Penland: " 'The desire of Universal and director Martin Scorsese is to make a faith-affirming movie. . . . We're asking Christians not to prejudge the film, and not criticize it until they can comment intelligently.'" In closing, Rabey alluded to the impiety of the Kazantzakis novel and the dark themes pervading Scorsese's work and pointedly noted Penland's intent to resign his consultancy if the movie turned out to be blasphemous or damaging to the cause of Christ.[49]

Universal was pleased with the overall tenor of the piece, especially Penland's remark about not prejudging the film.[50] For a couple of weeks it even seemed to have the effect of stanching the flow of complaining letters.

Heading into the spring of 1988, Universal's strategy of dual-track public relations consultancies was up and running. Moving along one track was the evangelical Christian who was hired to vouch for the studio's good intentions and persuade his constituency—a good number of whom were predisposed to be critical of the film—to withhold their judgments of *The Last Temptation of Christ* until it was ready to be viewed. Going down the other track was the Zen Buddhist hired to make an approach to groups whose philosophical orientations made it likely they would accept, if not embrace, the concept of a challenging film about Christ. By engaging the services of both, Universal hoped to penetrate the most important religious markets for *The Last Temptation of Christ.*

But the consultants had their own understandings of where all this would lead. Tim Penland was hoping that a new spirit of reconciliation might come out of the project. If the content of the picture matched the studio's professions of goodwill, it could even signal a historic bridging of the chasm separating Hollywood from the values of mainstream, religiously observant America. Josh Baran considered the idea of reconciliation naive, at least as far as *Last Temptation* was concerned. This film could be a replay of *The Day After,* only this time the capital of the entertainment industry—not Kansas City—was being targeted by a warhead. Taking no chances on the outcome, Baran was already plotting how to navigate the studio through the conflagration.[51]

ALTHOUGH TIM PENLAND had some early success in restraining the Christian right's activists, there wasn't much he could do about rumors percolating up from the grassroots. The strangest, and most troubling, was the rumor of a pornographic film about Jesus Christ.

Its origins go back at least to 1980, when the office of the Illinois attorney general found itself suddenly inundated with letters (many of them form letters) and petitions warning that a film titled *The Sex Life of Jesus* was on the verge of being filmed, or had already been produced and simply awaited a

Tim Penland and Larry Poland, 1988. (Courtesy of Larry Poland)

distributor. Some versions of the rumor had the film portraying a "gay Jesus," or Jesus as a "swinging homosexual." The attorney general's staff traced the source of the rumor to an article in the November 1977 issue of *Modern People,* a weekly magazine published in Franklin Park, Illinois.[52] The story was not entirely apocryphal. The project did exist, although its real title was *The Many Faces of Jesus.* Originating in the fertile imagination of a Danish author and filmmaker, Jens Jorgen Thorsen, whose credits included an oft-banned 1970 adaptation of Henry Miller's novel *Quiet Days in Clichy,* the script for *The Many Faces of Jesus* dealt with Jesus' supposed love for various women, especially Mary Magdalene, and featured homosexual trysts with the apostle John.

Attempts by Thorsen and others in the mid-1970s to make the film in France, Denmark, and Sweden collapsed in the face of outraged reactions from Protestant and Catholic clerics.[53] Thorsen then tried England. The announcement that he was "in the late stages of negotiation for making the movie in the south of England" triggered denunciations by the queen, Prime Minister

Josh Baran, 1988. (Author's collection)

James Callaghan, and the archbishop of Canterbury, Donald Coggan.[54] In February 1977 the director was barred entry into England for having a copy of the script in his possession. The trail of *The Many Faces of Jesus* finally went cold in early 1978, when the office of U.S. Senator Mark Hatfield took an interest in thwarting Thorsen's attempts to set up the movie in the United States.[55] By 1985 an estimated million people had sent letters and petitions to civil authorities in the United States—including a very large number to the Illinois attorney general's office in Springfield—demanding that the film be stopped.

As mail decrying *The Sex Life of Jesus* reached a high-water mark, the letter-writing campaign against Paramount's production of *The Last Temptation of Christ* was also taking off. Both sets of letters came from fundamentalist churches in every region of the country and used much the same vituperative language.[56] Rumors about the two films even appeared to cross paths. Unaware of the existence of the *Sex Life of Jesus* rumor, Paramount and Gulf + Western officials were dumbfounded by letter writers' claims that the Jesus Christ in Kazantzakis' novel would be shown in the film as a homosexual.[57] But Paramount kept publicly quiet about the content of the letters. Denying the validity of a rumor can sometimes be riskier than staying silent, especially in the case of *Last Temptation,* which had not even gone into production, thus making the charges so much more difficult to refute.

The rumor of a Jesus sex film lingered in a state of dormancy for the next several years. So it came as a surprise to a Los Angeles radio talk show host, Rich Buhler, when he began getting on-air calls in February 1988 about a movie that his listeners said had Jesus Christ engaging in sexual acts. A radio professional who was also a pastoral counselor, Buhler designed KBRT-AM's *Talk from the Heart* as "a genuine forum where people can genuinely talk."[58] The show was cutting-edge Christian programming: a call-in show dealing with topics like finances, marriage, addictions, and other "emotional injury" issues, all advice dispensed with a Christian flavor.

Buhler was also an amateur investigator of the Christian rumor circuit and knew all about *The Sex Life of Jesus.*[59] When he first heard from his callers about *Last Temptation,* he dismissed it on the air as a replay of the discredited Jesus sex film rumor. Then he got a call from Larry Poland, who told him there was something more to the story. The film did exist, Poland said. Or, he corrected himself, it would exist *unless* it turned out to be dishonorable to their Lord and Savior. Buhler soon went back on the air with a different message. "Hey folks," he said, "We've been hearing about this, and here's some more information about it. It apparently does have some substance to it. This is not just a Jesus sex film rumor being recirculated."[60]

That same month, John Stewart, a radio personality at Christian station KKLA-FM, located just a short distance from Universal City, took the helm of a new talk show called *Live from LA.* An attorney who had gained some visibility when he negotiated on behalf of Jessica Hahn just before the PTL scandal broke,[61] Stewart ran *Live from LA* as a hard-news show. During most of the week he had a producer and interviewed authors and newsmakers, but on Friday afternoons he threw the show open to calls.[62]

During his first weeks on the air, Stewart took calls from people wanting to talk about rumors of a film portraying Jesus in blatantly sexual situations. Unlike Rich Buhler, John Stewart had the instincts of an activist. He recognized that the story had all the elements of an issue he could ride for a long time. It had a mysterious, possibly sacrilegious film no one knew much about; a novelist and filmmaker who had fallen out of their respective faiths; and a pact struck between a servant of Christ and a secular entertainment giant. In April he had Tim Penland as a guest on his show. Penland counseled patience, as he always did. But Stewart was openly skeptical about "whether such an unmitigated piece of sordid mischaracterization as Kazantzakis' book could be adapted in a way acceptable to Christians. . . . The more I thought about it and discussed it with my radio audience, the more preposterous the notion became."[63] Stewart took the measure of the amazing effect this movie was having on his listeners' emotions and decided it was the kind of white-hot issue that could propel his new show out of obscurity.

While talk of the movie increasingly raised the hackles of Los Angeles radio audiences, Tim Penland went quietly about his business, sitting for media interviews and listening to what was being said in Christian leadership circles. Universal's marketing people liked him personally and welcomed the input. Penland got along especially well with Sally Van Slyke. He would come around to her office in the late afternoon, and they sometimes fell into deep talks about God and what it meant to have a relationship with Jesus. Coming from an Episcopalian background, Van Slyke enjoyed hearing his approach to Christianity. "He was so absolutely sure we were going to answer for our actions in the end, that good people were going to heaven and the other people were going to hell. . . . So we got into long discussions about that, and heated ones, but very friendly ones."[64] Some of her colleagues in marketing didn't know what to make of Penland's declamations, but for Van Slyke his talk about the dire consequences for her soul of working on a Christ-defaming film offered a window into the thinking of evangelicals.

By early April Penland's colleagues were clamoring to see some footage from the work in progress, or anything they could use to assay the truth of the rumors. There was, however, little news coming out of Martin Scorsese's cutting room, and no one at Universal could tell Penland anything about what shape the film was taking. Scorsese habitually walled himself off from the world while he edited, not giving interviews or showing the film to anyone until he and Thelma Schoonmaker got close to a final cut. It wasn't until April 21 that the two of them viewed a very rough cut, then at a running time of three hours, twenty-two minutes.

The first ominous report of a "religious backlash" surfaced in the April 17 edition of the *Los Angeles Times*. The reporter Pat Broeske quoted John Probst, head of a Christian ministry to the entertainment industry, as objecting to the script's "wimpy, almost milquetoast kind of characterization" of Jesus and the dishonor it brought on "the deity of Christ."[65] (In the coming months, "wimp" was often used as shorthand for the allegedly indecisive, ineffectual personality of the film's Jesus. Sometimes the term was used without quote marks in mainstream press articles.) The head of the National Association of

Media Evangelism was also quoted saying that the film's Jesus is shown "totally against the historical view—as a person confused about his identity, who has an affair with Mary Magdalene."[66]

Broeske's article was followed a few days later by an AP story picked up by the *Dallas Morning News, San Diego Union-Tribune, Orange County Register, Atlanta Journal,* and other dailies. Among the parts of the article that greatly disturbed Universal was the notion—unsubstantiated, but presented as established fact—that the film showed Jesus "pondering homosexuality." Penland's plan to hold an early screening was duly noted, but for the first time in a nationally distributed article, the Reverend Donald Wildmon was quoted on *Last Temptation.* Wildmon rattled his cage menacingly, warning that millions of Christians stood ready to protest. "MCA has businesses that Christians do business with, such as Universal Studios. . . . We will do everything possible to knock the financial props out from under Universal. We will be prepared to fight it with everything we've got. And it would be an easy battle to win."[67]

Wildmon was on the phone to Tim Penland almost daily. He was getting pressure from his constituency about why he wasn't taking action this time. Wildmon told Penland that if Universal was deceiving them just to buy time, he would crank up a protest campaign unlike anything he had ever launched. Penland's associates also felt that Universal was either stonewalling them or not taking their concerns seriously. Some of them wondered what kind of consultant Penland was if he couldn't get access to any of Scorsese's footage. Even his friend and "shadow consultant," Larry Poland, urged him to go to Universal and insist on seeing the film. Poland recalled saying to him, " 'Tim, I can't imagine that Universal doesn't have anything to show you, so that you can represent them well. How can they expect you to speak with authority on their behalf if you don't even know with precision what is in their film? I think at some point you are going to have to demand to see what they have finished.' "[68]

Finally, Kornblit's office sent a copy of the shooting script by courier to the consultant's Burbank office. Although he had the script for only one day, it was enough time for Penland to peruse the document and compile a list of concerns. On 80 of the 120 pages he marked scenes that he considered problematic. Many of them were mildly offensive, such as the nudity in several scenes. But others lacked any foundation in the Gospels—for example, the scene of Jesus making crosses for the Romans' executions; the instances in which Jesus resists God's call or refers to his own sins; Jesus' visit to the Magdalene's brothel; and numerous incidents in the last temptation sequence. One of the most disturbing passages was near the end of an important scene with John the Baptist, shortly before Jesus departs for the desert. Bidding him farewell, the Baptist kisses Jesus on the mouth. Jesus says, in voiceover, "His tongue felt like a hot coal in my mouth."[69] To many of the Christians who were horrified to read this line (which was not included in the film), it could refer only to a homosexual proclivity on the part of Jesus.

Penland recommended a number of changes, but Universal apparently regarded his notes merely as issues that they should be aware of. He realized that the film was going in a direction that would be anathema to Bible-believing Christians. But in asking his brethren to hold off any protest actions until the movie could be seen, he had put himself, at least to some degree, on the studio's side. And that was a troubling place for Tim Penland to be. The role he once thought of in noble terms—the bridge builder, the peacemaker, the facilitator of dialogue—he was now finding to be a test of his soul. Every day he prayed that he was doing what the Lord wanted him to do. He constantly rehearsed his resignation statement, just to clarify in his mind that he was still serving Christ.[70]

To Universal's consternation, Penland seemed at times to be perilously close to going off the reservation. In Broeske's *Los Angeles Times* article, Penland made an unsettling remark about *Last Temptation:* " 'Who can say what will happen . . . though if you think what's happening with 'Colors' is something, just wait. . . . There are 150 million Christians [the figure encompasses Protestants, Roman Catholics, and members of the Greek Orthodox Church] in this country. A lot of them will have something to say.' "[71] (The recently released urban gang movie *Colors* was raising concerns about its potential for provoking violence at theaters.) Instead of trying to subdue anxieties about the movie, he seemed to be throwing gasoline on them. Tom Pollock reportedly passed the word down the line to remind Penland whom he was working for.[72]

A few weeks later Penland came across as a more self-possessed advocate for the studio. Quoted in a May 20 column in the *Chicago Tribune,* he was fairly brimming with confidence. "First of all," he said, "Universal is acting to relieve paranoia about the film's content and to calm fears that the film will be made, hidden for a while, and then sprung on an unsuspecting public. And, I think they will show at the screening that this is not a sleazy film exploiting the life of Christ, but a powerful film with a positive message for Christianity. . . .

"If it is positive, I don't think Universal will be able to contain the crowds."[73]

This was the Tim Penland that the studio's executives preferred to see showing up in print. If he continued being quoted like this, he would be worth every cent of the fees they paid him.

IN APRIL Josh Baran flew to New York City for the first of many trips on behalf of Universal Pictures.[74] He had lined up appointments with officials of such denominations as the United Church of Christ and the Roman Catholic Church, interfaith organizations such as the National Council of Churches, and groups with a history of counteracting the Christian right, such as Fundamentalists Anonymous and Americans United for Separation of Church and State. He also paid visits to influential personal acquaintances: the Jesuit priest-poet Daniel Berrigan, the mystic and author Ram Dass, and the Episcopal bishop of New York, the Right Reverend Paul Moore. They talked about the Kazantzakis novel and how Scorsese would adapt it. He told them how the studio perceived the film and what was likely to happen before its release.

In the words of Michael Sitrick, one of Hollywood's leading crisis managers, a cardinal rule of spin is that the "news media abhor a vacuum: if you don't tell your story, someone else will tell it for you."[75] In a case like *The Last Temptation of Christ*—a film with pretensions to reenvisioning the religious figure most revered by Americans—studio flacks are hardly qualified to discuss the fine points of Christology. It is much better to have credible third parties, and Baran was recruiting them for an early look at *Last Temptation*—essentially, the liberal religious counterpart to the screening that Penland was working on. "You don't need a lot of them," said Baran about these allies, "because the media will go to those people if you tell them where to go. . . . Because they're looking for quotes, and they're not going to call every church in the country when they haven't seen the movie. So, usually, with a little bit of pushing from my casual manipulation, they will find somebody who's seen the movie."[76]

Baran also made the rounds of news organizations. He was well aware that reporters are supposed to be unbiased; but it is also common knowledge that most journalists in Hollywood and the national media are personally unsympathetic to the political agenda of the Christian right. Accordingly, Baran wanted editors and writers to think about what was at stake, so that when the battle was joined, the tide of media opinion would flow toward Universal. "So, right away," he said, "I would sort of encourage them to understand what this was about. That ultimately this is about freedom of expression. . . . It may not be the government doing it, but nonetheless it is the idea that there are ideas that [the Christian right] want to be able to destroy and they don't want out there. So I definitely wanted to move it to a First Amendment footing."[77]

There was more to Baran's strategy than currying the goodwill of clergy or encouraging journalists to think of the movie as a bulwark of free speech. Eventually the studio itself would have to answer for the film. And that could be a defining moment not only for the fate of the film, but for the public image of MCA. It could even have ramifications for the way all Americans—regardless of their religious allegiances—view the motion picture industry and how it discharges its social responsibilities. When it came time to account for its actions, the studio had to be ready to do it with eloquence, integrity, and intelligence.

To assist him in this part of the work, Baran turned to one of the best writers he knew, Susan Rothbaum. He told her that an uproar over the film was coming and, because of the intense pressure, the studio might be forced to withdraw it.[78] They had to anticipate all the objections to the film and be ready to counter them. Said Rothbaum, "I understood my position to be to take the moral high ground, as opposed to, 'We're sacrilegious blasphemers smearing religion and stomping on it.' And I found that came very natural."[79]

Her first assignment was to analyze the novel and the screenplay, comparing their points of similarity and dissimilarity. "Joshua thought that would be useful because people would be reading the book and therefore attacking the movie without having seen the movie. And so it was important to be able to distinguish the book from the movie, and what the book did, and what the movie did."[80]

In ten single-spaced pages, Rothbaum compared the book and film scene by scene. The bottom line of her analysis was that, though both contained controversial elements, the screenplay omitted or softened many of Kazantzakis' more radical deviations from the Gospels. For example, the screenplay left out Matthew's role as scribe, which is used in the book to suggest that the Scripture authors fabricated some of the events of Jesus' life. Whereas Kazantzakis emphasized Jesus' triumph over human limitations, "the flavor of the screenplay is one of penitence and submission to God's will, a more conventionally Christian view."[81] Other differences focused on particular modes of depiction, such as the book's portrayal of Satan as a Negro boy, which Scorsese changed to the less disagreeable figure of a young girl.

The next assignment Baran gave her was to review the historical sweep of humanity's march toward freedom of expression. The purpose of this research was to situate *Last Temptation* in a tradition of free religious expression in liberal democracies. Rothbaum spent several days at the Berkeley Public Library, looking up sources and copying by hand information from books, articles, and court cases, which she then incorporated in the flow of her own thought. The thirty-plus-page document, dubbed the "positioning paper," was coolly received by the studio. "Universal found this kind of a waste," she recalled. "They didn't really see what the point would be, because they were not anticipating the same kind of furor that Josh was expecting."[82]

The opening sentences of the paper laid out the general strategy: "Opponents of 'The Last Temptation of Christ' would lock the argument into a dispute over religious doctrine, and paint those involved in it as blasphemous, sacrilegious villains. The line of argument presented here aims to take the argument out of their court by framing the central issue as one of freedom of expression and religion."[83]

Rothbaum made her way to this "moral high ground" one step at a time. She traced the origins of the nation's religious and artistic freedoms in writings of the authors of the Bill of Rights, including Thomas Jefferson's early experience of religious intolerance and James Madison's belief that freedom of conscience was essential for a healthy democracy. She examined the motives and behavior of censors, which had not changed in any substantial way since antiquity. She noted some of the famous (and not-so-famous) works that have been suppressed throughout history, from the burning of Dante's *Divine Comedy* during the Inquisition, to the Nazis' banishment of modernist art and architecture, to the American Library Association's 1984 withdrawal of exhibition space at one of its conventions from a man who had written a book claiming that the Holocaust never happened. She described the legal and societal justifications for film censorship leading up to the landmark *Miracle* case in 1952 (the Rosselini film starring Anna Magnani). She argued that charges of sacrilege and blasphemy cannot be used as a basis for controlling religious expressions without abridging everyone's rights. Even within faith communities, she wrote, "there have always been and there continue to be irreconcilable differences. Only in societies ruled by a single, all-powerful church/state are such standards enforceable."[84]

In the section entitled "The Film Industry's Affirmative Responsibility to Support Freedom of Expression," Rothbaum arrived at the core issue Universal would have to confront:

If it were only one film at issue, one expression of one man's vision, we might say that the hazards of courage were not worth the possible gain. But much more is at stake here. This fight is part of a larger battle to preserve our right to be guided by conscience rather than by dictators in matters of religion; our right to explore new territory through art and creative expression and to offer the fruits of those explorations to others; our right to choose for ourselves what we wish to see, hear, and say. The American way of life depends on the free expression of many voices, many points of view. To cede these rights would be to threaten them in all. We have no wish to offend the religious views of any group, but we will support the equal right of Martin Scorsese, and all Americans, to express their own.[85]

In other words, the law is of no use if citizens—or media companies—are afraid to exercise the freedoms it guarantees. It is precisely the most challenging films that the industry must stand up for if it is to protect the creative process for *all* its projects. Despite Universal's initial reservations, the positioning paper became a key resource for crafting the studio's position in the controversy and communicating it to the press, religious leaders, and the public at large.

In Tim Penland's world farther down the Pacific Coast, *The Last Temptation of Christ* was still a phantom object in anxiety-filled conversations. His phone rang with callers wanting new information about the movie, and the voices on the other end were getting insistent. The Evangelical Sisterhood of Mary—the Arizona nuns who were so instrumental in stirring the protest against Paramount in 1983—struck Penland as the most determined group he had yet heard from. "I can't tell you what to do but to be obedient to God," he told them. "You will have to do whatever he directs. I am just asking you to consider holding off."[86]

The Reverend Donald Wildmon was nervously eyeing the calendar. He wasn't sure how much longer he could control his people. He reminded Penland that he needed at least three months' lead time to assemble his forces. If Universal held the screening on or before June 10—the date he always maintained that he was promised—he could still launch his multistage campaign so that it reached maximum effectiveness before the film's expected September release.[87]

KKLA's John Stewart did not feel bound by any such agreements. With each passing day, audience response to the anti-Christian film saga pegged higher and he was devoting more time in his show to the latest rumors. Stewart gave out the names and phone numbers for Universal personnel on the air and exhorted his listeners to call them.

Penland himself was pessimistic about whether any of the script changes he had recommended were being made. "It looks like they duped me," he said to Ted Baehr. "They had no desire to make changes. This was all just a ruse."[88] Without evidence of what the film actually contained, he felt squeezed between the studio's expectations and the suspicions of his own people. But there was never any doubt which side he would choose, if it came to a decision. It was just a matter of knowing what the action-forcing event would be.

For more than a month, various people said they had a copy of the screenplay of *Last Temptation*. It wasn't clear to Penland which script they were talking about. Universal guarded the shooting script so closely that even he was given just one day to examine it. One day Wildmon called Penland with the news that he had obtained a script.[89] He would send it by overnight mail. He also told Penland that hundreds of copies were being duplicated that very day, in preparation for a massive mailing.[90]

When they opened the package, Penland and Poland pulled out a ninety-nine-page screenplay—fully twenty pages shorter than the shooting script that the studio had earlier provided. Unlike Universal's version, this one came with a quote from Nikos Kazantzakis' *Saviors of God* placed starkly in the center of a cover page: "It is not God who will save us—it is we who will save God, by battling, by creating and transmuting matter into spirit." Much of the material in this script paralleled the shooting script, but they also found "new" scenes or scenes that were written differently. On page 4 they were confronted with Mary, mother of Jesus, crying out: "Forgive my son! He's crazy! He doesn't know what he's doing. He has problems. Ever since he was a baby. He's not well in the head." On page 73, in the Last Supper scene, the disciples cough up the bloody flesh of the first Eucharist. And on pages 81 and 82 Jesus and Mary Magdalene are shown making love in a Judean house at night. Kissing her breasts and lips, and convinced that he has found the road to happiness, Jesus is moved to say, "A woman is God's greatest work. And I worship you. God sleeps between your legs." All while a guardian angel watches them.

The litany of scenes and dialogue they marked as patently offensive seemed to go on forever. "Never in almost 12 years of fighting the media's bias against Christian values," Wildmon later wrote about this script, "had I ever come across a more blatant attack on Christianity than this movie. I realized that if there ever were a time for Christians to let the Hollywood elite know that the entertainment industry's constant Christian-bashing should stop, this was it."[91]

It did not take long for the studio to identify it as one of Schrader's first drafts from 1982. They told him that it was a pirated script, a bootleg; the "new" scenes were not in the final shooting script. Without actually seeing the film, Penland could not be sure which script was the operative one, and he certainly couldn't advise his associates what to do or believe. He immediately went over to Sally Van Slyke's office. If these outrageous scenes were not in the film, he needed to know about it so that all of them could try to resolve the problem. They offered to give him the shooting script again to prove they weren't misleading him. But Penland said he needed to see the film. Otherwise, his constituency would understandably doubt Universal's motives and the whole arrangement would fall apart.[92] The studio demurred, explaining that until Scorsese delivered the negative, the film did not even belong to Universal Pictures.

No one knew for sure how the early Schrader script got into circulation. Scorsese suspected that it may have slipped into the wrong hands during the 1983 auditions. "The problem with the script that was being protested," Scorsese told the *Oregonian* in 1988, "was that it wasn't really a script. I wouldn't even have used it as a preliminary script to show to a studio to get financing. It was truly a work in progress, a set of ideas for the eyes of the writer and myself and no one else. There was a lot of shorthand-type stuff in there, ideas we wanted to consider between ourselves but had no intention of putting on screen."[93]

The surfacing of this early script threw the studio's plans into turmoil. When the Schrader script got out, said Tom Pollock, "the truth [started] to change around. Tim Penland claims that we betrayed him and that . . . he could no longer do the job—because they no longer believed him. He was losing his credibility with that constituency if he didn't turn on us. . . . And no matter what we said—'Tim, this isn't the script, you *have* the script for the movie. This is the script for the movie. Here it is. Right here. We swear to you this is the script of the movie.' It didn't matter at that point because *that* script was out there."[94]

BY THE MIDDLE of May Martin Scorsese and Thelma Schoonmaker had cut *The Last Temptation of Christ* to a running time of two hours, forty-six minutes, and they were ready to show it to a group of friends. The first screening was held on May 13 at Sound One. Scorsese and Schoonmaker settled into their customary seats in the back of the screening room, where they could talk quietly. When it was over and the lights came on, Schoonmaker's husband, Michael Powell, stood up in front of them and turned around. His face was bathed in tears. The only other time she remembered him reacting so emotionally was when the Berlin Wall was torn down. She looked over at Scorsese. "The look on his face was like he was slapped. He couldn't have wanted anything more than that."[95]

Scorsese consented to Tom Pollock's suggestion that they start showing the movie to people outside his inner circle. On May 31, Pollock, Sean Daniel, and Sid Sheinberg gathered to watch *Last Temptation* in a Magna screening room in the old United Artists headquarters on Seventh Avenue. Sheinberg remembered muttering as he walked out of the room, "My God, people are going to be outraged."[96] He also thought it was too long. Scorsese had rights to the final cut, as on all his films since *Raging Bull,* but only up to a certain length imposed by the studio; for *Last Temptation,* Universal gave him two hours and ten minutes. "The length they give me isn't bad," he has remarked about studios generally. "The problem is that you have to fight for that extra footage, and you do."[97]

Another studio screening was booked for Magna just seven days later, Tuesday, June 7. That day, executives from Universal and Cineplex Odeon were flown in to view the film before starting work on it. In addition to Van Slyke and Baran, the guests included Universal's head of creative advertising, David Sameth, the president of distribution Bill Soady, and Fred Mound, the senior vice president of distribution. Sameth was having a first look at *Last Temptation* before receiving a black-and-white dupe to start cutting the trailer. Soady's job entailed choosing the release dates and methods of distribution for the studio's slate of movies; *Last Temptation* was tentatively set to roll out in a late September platformed release, just behind Universal's *Gorillas in the Mist* and *Moon over Parador,* and in close proximity to other specialty films such as Orion's *Eight Men Out* and Warner's *Running on Empty.* One of the few practicing Christians in Universal's upper management, Fred Mound had already expressed deep concerns about the picture, and Tom Pollock specifically asked him to call in his reaction the minute he walked out of the screening.[98]

Scorsese told the group that he was planning to cut another five to seven minutes—not for any major scenes, but for running time and pacing. David Sameth recalled, "I don't remember how very often you see a film in a much rougher form than it would be finally. We saw it with temp music. The music was being done concurrently with our being there, that's how fast things were going."[99]

When the screening was over, the audience members paused to collect their thoughts about what they had seen. Josh Baran didn't like it. "I just thought the film was kind of tortuous and overly long and confused. . . . So it could have been a great movie, and I just don't think it really was, ultimately."[100] Sameth considered the film a work of art, "which, you know, in this business you don't see too often. More often, the question is, does it fulfill its commercial intent?"[101]

A senior distribution executive asked the head film buyer for Cineplex Odeon if he found it offensive. "Nothing offends me," he said blandly. "I have no opinion on it whatsoever."[102]

Several of them phoned in their reactions to Tom Pollock in Los Angeles. Van Slyke fumbled around for a few seconds, then blurted, "This is trouble. This *is* trouble. But you may pull it off because it's artistic."[103]

Fred Mound dutifully placed his call to Pollock, whose first question was whether Mound felt it was blasphemous. "My response to [Tom] was that certain segments of the Christian community would take it that way. I personally did not take it as blasphemous. Did I accept the nature of the picture? No. Did I like the picture particularly? No. . . . But I told Tom at the time that I felt it was going to be very, very controversial, not only with our customers, but with the general public. And he knew that. Tom knew that, I think, all along."[104]

Pollock then asked Mound about his willingness to work on the film. "You've seen the movie," he said. "Do you feel morally constrained that you can't work on this movie? Because if you feel you can't, you don't have to. And I understand. I'm not going to force you to do something if you think this is religiously repugnant to you."[105]

No, Mound replied, he could work on *Last Temptation*.[106] He did not approve of the movie. But he didn't think it was so wrong that it would interfere with his job.[107]

Though the film was closer to being locked, a significant amount of work remained: some additional trimming of the movie; the design and shooting of the title sequences; Peter Gabriel's score, which the composer had begun recording on the floor below Scorsese's cutting rooms; overdubbing of voices and sound effects; and, lastly, the sound mix. Scorsese told Pollock that, everything considered, he needed two more months—a time line that conflicted with Universal's promise to hold a June screening for Penland's group of religious leaders.

Meanwhile, the studio's attitude about the Penland situation had taken a decisive turn. Josh Baran always maintained that any intelligent analysis of the screenplay or novel would show there was no way Tim Penland could get behind the movie. The way Baran saw it, Penland had been seduced by an ideal. Captivated by the vision of bringing Christian America and Hollywood together, Penland did not look closely enough at the unvarnished nature of what he was being asked to vouch for. "The devil is in the details," said Baran. "In this case, that's a very good analogy: the devil *was* in the details, as far as they were concerned, ultimately."[108]

A new theory of the opponents' motives was gaining credence: not only was *Last Temptation* emerging as a "scapegoat" for the Christian right's long-standing issues with the media, but the activists saw that it was in their interest to make it an object of controversy. Tim Penland himself had laid out the key premise when he sat in Roger Armstrong's office and told him, "You people don't understand. Christian evangelicals need something to rally around, to get them focused again. And there's nothing greater for that movement to rally around than Jesus Christ. And this movie directly impugns the integrity of Jesus Christ. And you've got to be careful."[109] Many of those in the higher ranks of Universal did believe that the Christian right would try to rebound from the recent televangelist scandals—and rebuild its lagging fund-raising—by yoking *Last Temptation* to the time-tested theme of Hollywood's insensitivity to Christians. If this was true, then nothing the studio did or said would stop them from attacking the film.

By the first week of June, suspicions on both sides had metastasized to such an extent that when Van Slyke informed Penland that the screening might have to be postponed until July, or even August—because of postproduction delays in New York—he knew what he had to do. Penland had been girding himself for the moment of his resignation. Now he put it in writing. He drafted a memo making June 12 the date he would quit unless certain conditions were met. First, the screening for Christian leaders had to be rescheduled for no later than mid-July. Second, the film's release had to be delayed by the same length of time as the delay in the special screening.

Within days, even this pretext for going forward was overtaken by new events. A story appearing in the June 4 edition of the *Philadelphia Inquirer* hinted that "a series of secret New York screenings" of *Last Temptation* had taken place. To Penland this could only mean that Universal had lied when it said that the film wasn't ready to be shown. More insulting to Penland person-ally was the article's suggestion that he had been hired "to shepherd the movie past possible objections of religionists."[110] Many of the Christian activists were now convinced that Universal was reneging on its original promise; what galled them most, however, was the idea that Penland unwittingly helped the studio by keeping the critics at bay for several months.[111]

Concerned about the proliferation of the pirated script, Universal bypassed Penland and on June 7 faxed a letter directly to Wildmon. It read, in part: "We are very distressed to learn that you are circulating copies of an early version of the script of 'The Last Temptation of Christ.' Martin Scorsese, the director of the film, advises us that he believes these scripts differ from the film in a great many key and important ways. . . . We continue to move ahead with our plans to screen this film for you and other religious leaders well in advance of the release date. The filmmaking process is sometimes slow and painstaking. We ask for your continued patience so that your final judgement will be based on fact and not rumors."[112]

But it was too late. The first salvo of approximately 250 copies of the early script had already been launched from his Tupelo headquarters to ministers and church officials across the country, and with them went Wildmon's asser-tion that the script corresponded point-to-point with the film. Larry Poland's staff at Mastermedia also began reproducing hundreds of copies and sending them to the Christian media professionals and ministries on his mailing list.[113] According to Poland, every person who received a copy made at least a dozen more. Whether those numbers were correct, there is every indication that copies of the early script of *Last Temptation* spread throughout southern Cali-fornia religious circles during the first weeks of June.

On June 8 Van Slyke called Penland and told him that the screening for evangelical leaders was postponed indefinitely.[114] The studio also declined to delay the film's release date, citing its commitments to exhibitors. Finally, on Monday, June 13, Universal was told by Scorsese's production office that the film's delivery date was being moved to August.[115]

These developments made it impossible to satisfy the conditions in Pen-land's memo. On Tuesday, Penland met with Van Slyke and Kornblit to work out the language of his resignation. Given out later that afternoon, the state-ment cited the problems with the pirated script and the delayed screening; it ended by stating, diplomatically, "Mr. Penland determined he could no longer serve the best interests of Universal Pictures and the Christian community."[116]

Moving quickly to try to salvage the screening Penland had brokered, the studio faxed letters to the five religious leaders, inviting them to view the work in progress in New York City on July 12 at a 10:00 A.M. screening. "Please be assured," the letter said, "that it will be the first screening of its kind to take place."[117] This was technically true. Scorsese, however, had already agreed to stop postproduction that day to show the film for the people that Baran was lining up.

All five of them rejected the offer. It was seen in that poisonous atmosphere as just another ploy to get them to hold off on their criticisms. They also took umbrage at the alleged mistreatment of Penland. The story of the consultant's exploitation became one of the chief indictments against Universal and showed just how far Hollywood would go to abuse people of faith—a claim that became almost as much a rallying point as the movie itself.

Afterward, Penland pleaded innocence about his role in the breakdown. "I was nothing more than a peacemaker," he told the *Los Angeles Times*. "Then I had the tools removed from my hands."[118] But many of those at Universal who worked with him held a less charitable view. Said one, "He took the coward's way out and quit and turned on us, even though he knew that [the pirated script] was not the script. . . . He could have said, 'All right, I'm compromised, I won't work anymore,' and simply not taken our money."[119] Most saw him, however, as a good, well-intentioned man who was guilty of nothing more serious than accepting a fool's errand. A former executive reflected, "Tim came into this thing with his eyes open. We showed him the script. No one was trying to pull anything over anybody's eyes. And then at some point, you know, he had to cover himself. He had his business and his constituency, and he wasn't going to burn any bridges. And I recognized that. So if he said things that sometimes might be contrary to what we might say, I understand his motives. You know, I can't be critical."[120]

When Tim Penland quit, not only did one of the rails of Universal's dual-track consultancy drop away, but the narrative of the release of *The Last Temptation of Christ* changed decisively, now following a logic dictated more by who could command images and language in the media and less by a deliberate effort to come to terms with the underlying issues. Suddenly, the struggle over the film took on the surreal quality of a civil war, threatening to tear apart the unspoken rules and understandings that bound Hollywood to the rest of the country.

6

Summer of the Locust

THE SUMMER OF 1988 was shaping up as the hottest in years. Earlier that spring, meteorologists saw a high-pressure dome of hot, dry air settle over the Plains, which disrupted the flow of the jet stream, responsible for bringing moisture and variable temperatures to the continent's midsection. Unlike normal weather patterns, the system didn't move. By the third week of June, temperatures in the Midwest were topping a hundred degrees, and much of the nation plunged into a severe drought, one of the worst since the Dust Bowl of the 1930s.[1]

In politics, Massachusetts Governor Michael S. Dukakis swept the four primaries held on June 7, and his resulting delegate total of 2,249 put him over the top for the Democratic nomination. Most national polls showed Dukakis holding a substantial lead over Vice President George H. W. Bush. More troubling for Bush was the discontent surfacing in his party's base. Conservatives worried openly about whether the vice president shared their core values on such issues as abortion, prayer in schools, and the traditional family. There was little risk they would bolt the Republican ticket and vote for Dukakis. "The real danger for Bush," reported the *Christian Science Monitor,* "could lie in losing the grass-roots campaign work of such 'worker bees' as supporters of former conservative candidate Pat Robertson."[2]

On June 18 Bush finally showed his hand about the kind of campaign he intended to run in the fall. Speaking to the Illinois Republican state convention, he harshly questioned whether the Democrats could be tough on crime. The vice president then asked what the governor of Massachusetts was thinking when he gave weekend furloughs to convicted murderers, "even after one of the criminals brutally raped a woman and stabbed her fiancé? . . . I think Gov. Dukakis owes the people of the United States of American an explanation of why he supports this outrageous program."[3]

Hollywood was living its own trial by fire. A strike by the 9,000-member Writers Guild of America lurched into its fifteenth week, and the issues underlying the work stoppage—revolving mostly around the residuals paid to writers when television shows go into syndicated reruns—were no closer to being resolved. The effects of the strike went well beyond the deprivations of WGA members or the postponement by the networks of the fall season. The production shutdown also threw legions of actors, makeup artists, costume makers, carpenters, office workers, and other personnel out of work, and it depressed the commerce of the restaurants, caterers, dry cleaners, and other businesses that depend on the entertainment industry.[4]

While Hollywood coped with its labor problems, Americans by the millions were going to the movies, seeking a respite from the heat. The weekend of June 24 promised yet another round of diversions: *The Great Outdoors,* a family-vacation comedy with Dan Aykroyd and John Candy; *Bull Durham,* a comedy-drama about life and love in the minor leagues, starring Kevin Costner and Susan Sarandon; and an inventive film from director Robert Zemeckis, combining live action and animation, called *Who Framed Roger Rabbit?* Most people gave no more than passing attention to newspaper articles about the latest Scorsese film, not due out for three months, but for a small corps of readers, the stories of a consultant's resignation signaled that the way was clear to go to war, unfettered by any more experiments in "bridge building."

The Reverend Donald Wildmon, who had been chomping at the bit since the end of 1987, was the first to go. "I've waited six months and I am not waiting any longer," he was quoted saying in the *Los Angeles Times.*[5] In situations like this, Wildmon slipped easily into a familiar role: the underdog defender of America's Christian values. And nothing pleased this cultural gladiator more than going against a foe who underestimated him. "What Universal wanted was controversy," Wildmon wrote to John Dart of the *Los Angeles Times* in July. "They wanted it to help fill the theaters. They had intentionally used me for several months. Now they were ready for the controversy. . . . I was finally going to protest. Unfortunately for Universal, what they expected and what they are getting are two different things. They expected a single Volkswagen. They are getting a convoy of hundreds of Mack trucks."[6]

In June 1988 Wildmon was already making headlines by demanding that CBS cut three and a half seconds out of a Ralph Bakshi cartoon that allegedly depicted Mighty Mouse snorting cocaine. Later that summer, CBS capitulated and removed the cartoon for reediting. As gratifying as that victory was, it was an easy one compared to the goal of stopping a studio from releasing a nearly finished picture made by one of the nation's preeminent filmmakers. The American Family Association's multipronged push to stop *The Last Temptation of Christ* grew larger and more intensive than any previous campaign. The release of the bootlegged script was merely the opening round. The Methodist minister taped a three-minute spot to run on 800 Christian radio stations, decrying Universal's betrayal of Christians. A half-hour television program attacking the film was rushed into production, intended for airing on more than 50 Christian cable networks and television stations. His staff reset the layout for the July issue of the monthly *AFA Journal*—which reportedly had a circulation of 330,000, including 170,000 churches—so that Wildmon could present a front-page story about the unfolding crisis and issue "clear instructions about how to protest the movie."[7]

The most effective weapon in his arsenal was direct mail. This time it would be used on an unprecedented scale. The centerpiece of the campaign was AFA's "action packet," which consisted of a blistering letter, emblazoned with a boldface banner, "Stop Universal Studios," that exhorted readers to stand up for Christ and oppose Universal Pictures; a "script sheet" ("a sampling of scenes and quotes from the script"); a petition for gathering signatures to be delivered to local theaters; and a "torn ticket stub" designated for MCA's president, Sidney J. Sheinberg, who would thus be informed that "it will be a long time—if ever—before I pay to see another Universal Studio's produced movie." The entire run of 2.5 million action packets took weeks to be printed and launched in waves from the Tupelo post office. The man who often boasts that his middle name is "boycott" was getting his constituents ready for the day when they would be told to refuse to patronize MCA's businesses, ranging from MCA's music and television divisions to Spencer Gifts, G. P. Putnam's Publishers, and Yosemite Park and Curry Company at Yosemite Park.

This style was not business-as-usual for the parachurch organizations— Campus Crusade for Christ, Focus on the Family, and Mastermedia International, among others—that went along with Tim Penland's effort. Theirs is a more conciliatory style. Their chief mission is ministering to people, healing lives by bringing them into a relationship with Christ. Normally, they would defer to AFA and other watchdog groups, such as Morality in Media and the Traditional Values Coalition, to lead the charge on issues of decency in the media. But when Penland's pact with Universal fell apart, they made common cause with Wildmon and anyone else who opposed the film. Whether it was because of the film's treatment of the Savior; or because of the studio's behavior, which most of them thought set a new standard in bad faith even for Hollywood; or because they wanted to give the laity something to feel strongly about after months of disappointing news about its national leaders—the decision to form a united front against *The Last Temptation of Christ* and MCA was made surprisingly fast. During the rest of June and into early July, they strategized together and supplied their memberships with news about the movie. The Campus Crusade for Christ was one of the first to alert staffers and members. "We'd like to make this the last temptation of Universal to make a film that is going to defame the name of Jesus Christ," said CCC's communication director, Don Beehler, in a June 18 *Los Angeles Times* article. Southern California's conservative ministries, churches, and activists decided they had no choice but to try to stop *The Last Temptation of Christ* from being released.

Not all Christians, especially those based in California, granted the American Family Association a leadership role in the emerging ad hoc coalition opposing the film. For one thing, its Mississippi headquarters was far from the center of the action. But a major reason seemed to be Wildmon himself. His Southern fundamentalist style stood in the way of closer ties with the evangelicals in California's media industries. A radio producer in Los Angeles put it this way: "There are a lot of people who don't respect him. Because he's kind of a redneck, you know? He handles himself in ways that I don't like to identify with. And he comes across as a kind of a reactionary."[8] Not surprisingly, Larry Poland emerged as the main catalyst and linchpin in the early days of the campaign. Formerly one of Bill Bright's top vice presidents in the Campus Crusade for Christ, Poland knew all the California players. As a "shadow consultant" during Tim Penland's star-crossed time with Universal, Poland was privy to some of the studio's internal thinking about *Last Temptation*. Poland also placed himself at the nexus of information pouring in from hundreds of Christians in the media industries that he claimed to be in touch with. Still others came unbidden to him with reports of studio meetings, conversations, and management decisions—which fed the protesters' growing appetite for "intel" about their adversary's next moves.

They soon had plenty of material to work with. One informant told Poland that Tom Pollock vowed at one point, "The Christians aren't going to stop us from releasing this film!"—an incendiary statement of defiance coming from a Jewish studio head. Poland quoted the line twice in a "fact sheet" he sent out in early July. (In mid-July, a humbled Larry Poland publicly apologized to

Tom Pollock when it was revealed that the Universal chairman never made that statement.) Poland's militaristic rhetoric—he called Universal's "surprise attack" on believers "the moral equivalent of the Japanese raid on Pearl Harbor"[9]—appeared in the newsletters of several groups and helped set the tone for the coming debate. "As Tim and I talked strategy," Poland wrote in *The Last Temptation of Hollywood,* "we determined that we had to act fast, and we had to get the word of Universal's planned release of this monster out to as many Christians across America as rapidly as possible. . . . More than one source inside Universal and inside the industry tipped us off that they were gunning for an early release to capture the peak of the controversial free publicity."[10]

The strategy involved the launching of several "preemptive strikes," as Larry Poland termed them.[11] Poland and his colleagues knew that the "liberal" news media would line up on the studio's side. Their only hope for counteracting Universal's public relations juggernaut was to act quickly and aggressively to get their grievances aired, and thereby rally millions of Christian believers nationwide to make their voices heard.

All the "strikes" were timed to go off the day before, or the day of, Universal's July 12 screening for mainstream clergy in New York. The first of them was a full-page advertisement placed in the *Hollywood Reporter*. The ad was intended by Poland and his fellow *Last Temptation* fighters to plant their flag of conscientious objection squarely in the middle of the creative community; another purpose of the ad, no less important, was to help steel the resolve of the town's Christians. As Poland later wrote, "We felt it would be a good watershed point for some of them who had been 'secret agents' or 'woodwork Christians' in Hollywood for years. If they came out identifying themselves as Christians . . . there would be no turning back."[12] The difficulty was getting enough of them to go public. For days, Poland, Tim Penland, and Mastermedia's members scrambled to find a respectable number of media professionals who were willing to sign their names to the ad and, therefore, openly associate themselves with the protest. Twenty-four hours before the deadline, they had collected just fifteen names. But they forged ahead, hoping—as Poland put it—for a "miracle." Their late-hour efforts produced the desired miracle. On the morning of July 11, *Hollywood Reporter* readers opened the inside front cover to find sixty-one names listed under a message that stated, in part: "Today Universal Pictures is planning to release a Martin Scorsese film based on the Kazantzakis novel, The Last Temptation of Christ. This film maligns the character, blasphemes the diety [*sic*], and distorts the message of Jesus. As professional members of the film and television community, we ask that this film not be released. . . . Our Lord was crucified once on a cross. He doesn't deserve to be crucified a second time on celluloid."

The second "strike" originated from the Pomona, California, studios of James Dobson's daily radio program, *Focus on the Family*. The show had gone on the air eleven years earlier, and its audience—and Dobson's own influence—had grown spectacularly. By 1988 Dobson was being heard on more than a thousand stations, more than any radio commentator except Paul Harvey.[13] In some urban markets, listeners could tune into *Focus* broadcasts as many as two dozen times a day.[14] Known to his millions of admirers as "Doctor Dobson," the avuncular child psychologist gained a reputation for integrity unequaled among the leaders of the Christian right. The show became the main vehicle for Dobson's agenda and the base from which the rest of the Focus on the Family empire sprang. Topics usually concerned parenting styles, child development, marriage and divorce, and other family issues, all of them informed by Christian values. On those occasions when Dobson tackled political issues, the effect could be huge—and difficult for public officials to ignore. Just the previous year, the White House found itself deluged with a hundred thousand letters after Dobson expressed anger in his broadcasts about the way in which a Health and Human Services official was treated for her antiabortion decisions.[15]

The Last Temptation of Christ was one of those subjects that drew James Dobson's ire. The reputed content of the film was enough to justify comment on his show, but Dobson also felt personally insulted by the way Universal had mishandled the early screening for evangelical leaders. He and his producers decided to tape a show on *Last Temptation* on June 30. To comply with the need to put it on the air as soon as possible, the show was slotted for July 11's broadcast, several weeks ahead of schedule. His guests were Larry Poland and Tim Penland.

After telling his listeners that he was preempting the regularly scheduled broadcast—something he did only for urgent topics—Dobson opened with his own take on the situation:

> I cannot describe at the top of this program just how strongly I feel
> about what we're getting ready to talk about. . . . If you've been reading
> your papers, you are aware that this movie was coming. You may not
> have known how bad it was. I will confess to you I had no idea how evil
> it was. I still have not seen it. And yet I am getting bits and pieces now

of what's in this film. And it would appear to be the most blasphemous, evil attack on the church and the cause of Christ in the history of entertainment. . . . And we're on the verge of having this film released, around the world really.[16]

Tim Penland described how Universal sought his help in reaching out to Christian leaders, and, in Dobson's words, "the duplicity and the lies and the disrespect that has characterized Universal's approach to the Christian community in this issue from the beginning." He and Larry Poland talked about the apparent sincerity of the studio's appeal, the promise of a new day in Hollywood, and the complications that followed. Penland said he knew he had been "used" by Universal when an eyewitness who had seen the film assured him that "the most liberal Unitarian minister would probably not be able to sit past the first twenty minutes in the film."

The film, Poland stated flatly, has "no redeeming value." Its "twisted view" of Jesus, he said, would not sway the faith of "solid Christians." But it would have a deleterious effect on the millions of moviegoers looking for the truth about Christ. The problem with the movie, and the reason why people would find it intriguing, said Penland, is that it is a different interpretation. "In other words, if this were another film on the life of Christ, it would probably not be seen by a lot of people. It'd be a yawner. But this is a *sex film* about Jesus Christ . . ."

Dobson mused about why Christians should be subjected to the kind of disrespect that would never be shown to any other minority or religious group. His voice lowering a bit, Dobson pondered the situation that Universal had gotten itself into: "You know, I would hate to be in their shoes, to tell you the truth. Because they really haven't taken on us. I mean, who cares? They've taken on the king of the universe. *God is not mocked.* And I don't know how long it will take him to speak. But he will speak. The universe has a boss. And you don't do that to him. I have a profound respect for the authority and the majesty of God. And I would hate to be on the other end of that one."

As the show neared its end, Dobson asked his guests to chart a strategy for keeping the film out of theaters. Poland and Penland urged people to boycott all Universal's movies and MCA's retail enterprises, call Cineplex Odeon theater managers, and petition the owners of other theaters. Dobson told his audience about Poland's "fact sheet" listing MCA's holdings and the decision makers one should call with complaints about the movie. They repeated the main phone number at Universal four times.

"Let me make one last thing clear," said Dobson. "You all have had some inside information as of last night that came to both of you from different sources as to what is actually in this film. We're not guessing. Except for the fact that they could change it. They can always change it. But it was screened as it is going to be released. And it is worse than you feared."

"Exactly," Penland agreed. "It's much worse than I feared from the report we got."

Minutes after *Focus on the Family* ended on the morning of July 11, Universal's switchboard lit up. "All hell broke loose," recalled a marketing executive. "And when I say that, I mean the studio started being inundated with phone calls."[17] The Dobson program marked a watershed, the point at which awareness of the movie exploded among conservative Christians nationally. By the week's end, the studio had hired more operators and installed special lines for handling the high volume of *Last Temptation* calls. But Tom Pollock, Sally Van Slyke, and other Universal executives were not in Los Angeles to witness the outpouring. They had left Los Angeles, flying to New York City to attend a screening that signaled the start of the studio's counteroffensive.

ON JULY 12, at the Cineplex Odeon theater on 23rd Street, Universal staffers made preparations for two showings of *Last Temptation*. The 10:00 A.M. showing, originally intended for the evangelical Christian leaders, now went ahead as a sound-check screening. Joining Scorsese at the morning showing were Paul Newman, Robert De Niro, a *Time* magazine reporter, Sally Van Slyke, and the president of the Motion Picture Association of America, Jack Valenti. Recognizing that *Last Temptation* was fast becoming an issue with implications for the entire industry, Valenti wanted to familiarize himself with the material. When the film was over, Valenti recalled, "I was quite candid with Marty. I thought, first, artistically, it was a brilliant piece of work. . . . But I also said, 'I can understand why you're going to get criticism on this, because you're cutting right to the nerve edges of people's religious rubrics. And that is going to cause a lot of people to come out of the woodwork.' He understood that."[18]

The main event was a special afternoon showing for approximately forty theologians, clergy, religious officials, and others, nearly all of whom were drafted into duty through the studio's "diplomatic campaign," as one of them put it.[19] Josh Baran's connections with Norman Lear's People for the American Way (PAW) yielded two Lutheran ministers: the Reverend Charles Bergstrom, an Evangelical Lutheran Church pastor and one of the founders of PAW; and the Reverend Robert E. A. Lee, head of public relations of the Lutheran Council Office for Governmental Affairs. Several interfaith organizations—the National Council of Churches, the United Church of Canada, and the World Council of Churches—sent their communication executives. Major religious faiths were represented by, among others, the Right Reverend Paul Moore, Episcopal bishop of New York; Bishop Anthony Bosco, chair of the communications committee of the U.S. Catholic Conference; Eugene Schneider, deputy director of communications for the United Church of Christ; Kathleen LeCamera, a United Methodist minister who was media critic for the weekly U.M.–produced television program *Catch the Spirit;* the Reverend Robert Thompson, an American Baptist pastor in Evanston, Illinois; Michael Morris, a Catholic professor; and members of the Union of American Hebrew Congregations. Baran also invited Daniel Berrigan, Ram Dass, ex-Jesuit Terry Sweeney, Jim Luce and Richard Yao of Fundamentalists Anonymous, and Robert Maddox, the executive director of Americans United for Separation of Church and State.

The only conservative Christians to accept Universal's invitation were two senior staff members of the anti-pornography group Morality in Media. The notes they took constituted the sole eyewitness report to go out to protest groups until shortly before the film was released. "The demand for copies [of the transcript of their notes]," Morality in Media reported later, was "tremendous. It was circulated among outraged clergy and lay persons from coast to coast."[20]

The secrecy measures were remarkable for an advance screening. None of the guests learned of the other participants' identities until they met for a noon luncheon at the Grand Bay Hotel, on West 51st Street just off Sixth Avenue. After lunch they gathered in the hotel lobby, where passes were handed out to prevent anyone with ill intent from sneaking aboard the four vans parked outside. Only the driver of the lead van knew the destination. "I half expected to be blindfolded so that I wouldn't be able to read the street signs," said Morality in Media's Evelyn Dukovic.[21] But information about the embarkation point had somehow leaked out. When the group went outside to get into the vans, they were met on the sidewalk by people carrying signs in the shape of crosses that read "Universal Crucifies Christ."

As the last van pulled away from the curb, one of the studio's executives lowered a window and yelled at the picketers, "No, you've got that wrong. It isn't Universal that crucifies Christ. It's Universal and *Cineplex Odeon!*"[22]

The protesters hopped into a nearby car and followed in hot pursuit. "The ride to the theater," commented Michael Morris, "was out of a Keystone comedy."[23] The vans negotiated the mile-and-a-half trip through midtown Manhattan in twenty minutes, pulling up to the 23rd Street Cineplex Odeon just ahead of their pursuers. The guests were hustled into the theater while a Universal staffer was dispatched to a nearby coffee shop to get Scorsese.

The security team conducted another sweep of the theater. After the guests were let into the auditorium and settled in their seats, Scorsese walked to the center of the stage. He said nothing to attract the audience's attention, and some stopped chatting only after noticing the filmmaker standing in front of them, already part of the way through his remarks. The previous day, Rothbaum, Baran, and Van Slyke had written a list of themes they wanted Scorsese to address in his short speech. "Nothing he hadn't said before," said Rothbaum, "but he'd given Sally an earful. Not wanting to leave editing, he was already two days behind schedule and he wouldn't apologize for the film."[24]

But now Scorsese touched on all the important points. He told the audience his personal story, growing up as a Catholic, and why it had been his passion for more than twenty-five years to make a film about Christ. He said that making *Last Temptation* was, for him, "an act of faith and a labor of love."[25] He stressed that the picture was a work of fiction based on a novel by Nikos Kazantzakis, not an accurate portrayal of the Gospel accounts. Almost as an afterthought, he said that he would be interested in hearing their impressions of it. And then he exited.[26]

The guests watched intently and quietly. "It was a long, demanding film," Daniel Berrigan said that afternoon to the reporter John Dart, allowing that he needed a few days to think about it before he could comment further.[27] "Part of it was kind of hokey and part was on pretty shaky ground theologically," confessed Robert L. Maddox in the *New York Times*. "But the overall impact was powerful on me."[28] William Fore, of the National Council of Churches, was quoted in the *Washington Post* as saying that the film's major doctrinal problem was Jesus' attainment of messiahship through the force of his own will, although he was of the opinion that "even the messiahship problem can be viewed as consistent with strands of Christian thought emphasizing that 'God depends on all of us for his will to be done.'"[29]

"I was really quite taken with it," recalled Robert Thompson. "I just thought the artistry, the texture of images, the portrayal of Jesus as one who struggles with voices of the mind and with himself—you know, a whole vast array of elements that were present in the film that violated prior cinematic representations of Jesus—were very appealing to me. Because it has been my view, as long as I have been a minister, that people need to be shaken out of whatever kind of preset images they have about him. And that's the path to truth and growth."[30]

Then, just at the point in the Crucifixion montage at which the nail is driven into Jesus' hand, the projector abruptly stopped. For a few seconds, the audience sat stunned and silent in the dark. Thinking something could be seriously wrong, Baran bolted from his seat and rushed Tom Pollock out of the auditorium.[31] At the time Van Slyke was sitting on the stairs, eating from a bag of popcorn. When the lights flashed out, she screamed and ran toward the auditorium. She reached the door just as Pollock came rushing out, exclaiming, "The film is dead! It's off. It's dark in there."[32] Baran took Pollock into a holding room and locked the door. By then technicians were running up to the projection booth to see what had happened.

A Universal representative came out and announced that there had been a power failure. This news was greeted by the guests with laughter. There were mutterings in the audience about acts of God and jokes about a fundamentalist conspiracy. As Van Slyke walked back in, the auditorium's lights came on. Daniel Berrigan turned to her and said, referring to the Crucifixion scene, "It's okay, Sally, this is where the story ends for me anyway."[33]

Richard Yao of Fundamentalists Anonymous said to Susan Rothbaum, who was sitting nearby, that it was a good thing no fundamentalists were present. His fellow FA member Jim Luce could not understand from what he had seen so far why the film was being called blasphemous.

"You'll see. Trust me," said Rothbaum. "There have already been a number of things that don't square with the Gospels."

"I'm not familiar with the Gospels," Luce said.

"What kind of ex-fundamentalists are you?" asked Rothbaum incredulously.

"Well, as I tell people—we didn't read the Bible. We just worshipped it."[34]

Power was restored and the film resumed. Thirty-five minutes later, at the end, the guests rose to their feet and applauded the filmmaker.

Everyone who was present that day seemed to have his or her own explanation of what caused the projector to go out at the crucial moment. Some thought it was due to a thunderstorm that was moving through the city that afternoon.[35] "I was told that a circuit broke," said Pollock. "We checked for sabotage. It didn't appear to be that. . . . But, nonetheless, it absolutely fed into the paranoia."[36] Van Slyke was certain that there was a conspiratorial plan afoot: "There was a projectionist or somebody paid off to turn off that film. There was some kind of hanky-panky going on there, no doubt."[37]

Scorsese, who was outside the theater when the incident happened, had his suspicions. He knew what projectionists were capable of doing. For *The Last Waltz*, he recalled, "We kind of arrogantly put up a title right before the United Artists logo, which read, 'This film should be played loud.' All the projectionists immediately turned it way down. We did *Raging Bull* and we killed ourselves on the mix. Three and a half months of mixing. Thelma Schoonmaker goes to check it on Broadway at a theater the first day it's open. She can't hear the sound. And she went in and said, 'What are you doing?' [The projectionist] said, 'I don't like the way they treat Italians in this picture.'"[38]

Over time the testimony of the guests in attendance spread out—to radio and TV talk shows, church publications, and newspapers and magazines—and helped guide the public conversation in the direction preferred by Baran and the studio. Most of them not only had impressive religious credentials, but were also the only "civilians" (non-industry professionals) who had seen the film. So, when the press contacted them—and Baran made sure the press knew where to find them—they were able to talk knowledgeably about the film. Moreover, these "allies" did not have to give the movie their unqualified blessing, or even necessarily like it, to be of value to Universal. Indeed, they often functioned best when they simply defended the rights of artists to create different forms of religious expression.

Apart from the power failure at the Cineplex Odeon theater, the presence of picketers at a supposedly secret location was a puzzling coda to the day's events. This was not the first time the film's opponents seemed to have obtained knowledge of confidential matters; Poland, Penland, Wildmon, and others spoke about being briefed about the film's content by an unidentified source inside Universal Pictures.[39] Speculation about who the leak might be traveled through the studio grapevine, but the person's identity couldn't be pinned down until one day in July, when an unusual memo appeared on Sally Van Slyke's desk. It was a signed memo—in effect, a tip letter—revealing what seemed to be pertinent facts about the informant.[40]

She carried the memo to Tom Pollock's office and gave it to him. "It's out of my hands," she said. "I never saw it. I'm not doing anything with it. You do something with it."[41]

"You're giving it to me?"

"Yes, and do what you want with it." Pollock laid the memo on his desk and never said another word to her about it.

The memo identified a son of one of Universal's executives as the person who had passed details about the film to people outside the studio. An employee on the Universal lot, the son was also actively involved in an anti-*Temptation* group. The son went to Penland and Poland in June, citing his father's account of the film's content and postproduction status as proof that Universal was lying when it said the film was not yet finished.[42] "And we were glad he did," recalled Larry Poland. "We needed a providential act."[43]

Pollock confronted the executive with the allegations, who denied that he engaged in deliberate sabotage of the company's efforts to release *Last Temptation.* "It caused some controversy between Tom and me," he recalled. "My son was free to do what he wanted to. I mean, he had a very strong belief about this. This was inside my own family, and other people, I'm sure, went through some of that at their houses."[44]

Pollock looked further into the matter but never found evidence of the father's complicity.[45] For his part, the executive demonstrated his loyalty by working closely with other MCA executives on the film's release. That fall, Tom Pollock rewarded him with a promotion.

JUST ONE HOUR before Universal's chosen few entered the 23rd Street Cineplex Odeon, Larry Poland and other members of the "offended brethren," as they called themselves—Tim Penland, Bill Bright, Dr. H. Lloyd Ogilvie, and the Reverend Jack Hayford—mounted the dais in Ballroom C of Universal City's Registry Hotel to denounce *The Last Temptation of Christ.* This was their third "preemptive strike," following the previous day's *Hollywood Reporter* ad and *Focus on the Family* broadcast. Despite the haste in pulling it together—press releases started going out only twenty-four hours before the event—the execution was impeccable. Not only did the open forum of the news conference compare favorably with the cloaked character of Universal's private screening, the 10:00 A.M. start time meant that the news conference would get on the noon, late afternoon, and evening television newscasts in Los Angeles.

The location for the news conference was also astutely chosen. By staging it in MCA's own backyard, the organizers served notice that they would take the fight directly to the studio. Moreover, in a stroke of high symbolism they had not foreseen but were delighted to capitalize on, they had booked the same room in which Pope John Paul II had spoken the previous September to more than a thousand members of the country's entertainment elite. On that occasion, MCA's chairman, Lew Wasserman, who had emerged from colon cancer surgery just two months earlier, introduced the pontiff by saying, with a straight face, that he and other industry leaders often lost sleep wondering if the decisions they made were morally right ones for the public.[46] The pope told his audience that they were "the stewards and administrators of an immense spiritual power," and he called them to use their influence to "cultivate the integrity consonant with your own human dignity. You are more important than success, more valuable than any budget."[47]

Now it was Larry Poland's turn to stand at a lectern in Ballroom C. Arrayed before him were reporters from *USA Today,* the *Los Angeles Times,* the *New York Times,* AP, UPI, CNN, the broadcast networks, and dozens of other news outlets, as well as a number of nuns and priests dressed in religious regalia, including several from the Greek Orthodox Church sitting in the front row. In his prepared remarks, Poland spelled out the reasons for the anguish that Christian believers felt. The film, he said, portrayed Jesus Christ as "mentally deranged, a lust-driven man . . . whose own mother Mary declares him crazy and, in a dream sequence, comes down off the cross and has a sexual relationship with Mary Magdalene." He told the assembled media about Universal Pictures' duplicitous behavior, about how the studio had hired Tim Penland to reach out to Christians, only to violate all its promises. This badly broken situation, however, could be made right if Universal agreed to "abandon its plans to release the movie." The film, he said, "[should] be destroyed to prevent its future release or sale."[48]

Tim Penland was next to speak. Acknowledging that coming out so publicly against the film could risk "playing into the hands of Universal's marketing," he said the group had no choice. "We come from a personal standpoint, there comes a time you have to stand up for what you believe . . . and we do know the film has to be stopped."[49]

He criticized the screening that Universal was holding that day in New York. The studio, said Penland, was doing it only to gain the approval of mainline Protestant and Catholic churches, thereby circumventing the community of evangelicals.[50]

The other panelists took their turns at the lectern. In the most quoted line from the news conference, the Reverend Lloyd Ogilvie called *Last Temptation* "the most serious misuse of film craft in the history of moviemaking."[51] Bill Bright regretted that it had to come to this. But Universal had left them no other option. Unburdening himself of thoughts that he said left him sleep-deprived for several nights, Bright feared that "a handful of people with great wealth and depraved minds" might make decisions that would invite the wrath of God.[52]

The Reverend Jack Hayford deplored Universal's unprovoked attack on Jesus, saying the movie "violates the soundest lines of tradition."[53] He continued, "If you were to make a film distorting the life of a Moslem leader, you would hear an outcry and rightly so. Or if you were to attack an ethnic group, such as making a slur against the black or the hispanic communities, a protest would go up. . . . What makes these people think that Jesus Christ is fair game?"[54]

The fusillade of "strikes" reached their targets. The *Hollywood Reporter* ad delivered a message of principled resistance to the creative community; the James Dobson show awakened Bible-believing Christians across the country, most of whom had not yet heard of the film; and the news conference focused the attention of the local and national media on the underlying "facts" of the crisis. All three of these well-scripted forays spoke boldly about what they wanted from Universal: the movie had to be shelved. Invariably, the next question was, how would they achieve this? What could possibly cause Universal to acquiesce to this extraordinary request?

During the news conference's question-and-answer session, Poland denied he was calling for a consumer boycott of MCA, although he did admit that a recent Mastermedia newsletter listed the company's ownership interests and products. In a labored explanation, Poland said the information was published so that "the discretion and positive and responsible actions of Christians nationwide [could] express their concerns to Universal in a way they will hear and understand and take accountability for their decisions."[55] Donald Wildmon, however, who declined to take part in the news conference, was not coy or convoluted in his own answer.[56] Wildmon told an AP reporter, "The decision makers at Universal may not care about offending Christians, but they do care about making money. If this movie is released, we will do all in our power to reduce their income."[57]

At first the call by protest leaders for Universal to withdraw the film was phrased as a request. This was clearly not going to happen without a struggle or, at a minimum, a very strong inducement for the studio to cooperate. Soon an act of divine intervention supplied the solution. According to Larry Poland's account in *The Last Temptation of Hollywood*, Bill Bright was so troubled by the film that he couldn't sleep for several nights. "During one of those sleepless nights Bill slipped to his knees to seek God's direction as to what to do about this hideous character assassination of his cherished Lord. . . . Then, as if being projected by a laser beam onto the silver screen of Bill's conscious-ness, came the message, 'OFFER TO BUY THE FILM!' A rush of excitement flooded Bill's soul! As he often says, 'Every corpuscle in my being stood on tiptoes!' This was the answer, 'OFFER TO BUY THE FILM!' "[58]

The revelation was received joyously by many of Bright's colleagues. They considered it a stroke of genius, "the kind of genius that only our God could originate."[59] The figure they arrived at was ten million dollars, which they calculated to be the movie's negative cost. Concluding that the money could not legitimately come from the coffers of Campus Crusade for Christ or any other ministry, they would instead solicit contributions from their constit-uents. The money would be placed in an escrow account to make sure it was used only for the intended purpose. Once the transaction with Universal was done, all the prints of Scorsese's film would be in the hands of the Campus Crusade for Christ, or a consortium of Christian groups. "We would then own it," wrote Poland. "We could do with it what we wanted. We could probably have a public celebration and burn it."[60]

Although Bill Bright and the others were undoubtedly sincere about want-ing to avert the "hideous character assassination," of Jesus Christ, the Campus Crusade for Christ had another incentive for taking *Last Temptation* off the market. In the late 1970s, the organization had teamed up with the British producer John Heyman to film a two-hour movie of Christ based almost entirely on the Gospel of Luke. Distributed in the United States by Warner Bros., *Jesus* opened in October 1979 to mixed reviews and a yearlong theatrical run that reached about four million Americans.[61] But that was merely a pre-lude to an extraordinary distribution plan unlike anything that had ever been conceived. Campus Crusade began dubbing the *Jesus* film into the world's languages; by 1988 the film had been translated into 110 major languages, which made it the most prolific multilingual motion picture in history. Prints of *Jesus* were taken by mission agencies to the planet's remotest places to win souls for Christ, as reported by the Jesus Project's promotional literature: "The *Jesus* film is carried by elephants in Burma, on carts in India, river boats in the Amazon and on shoulders of workers in parts of Africa. Film team workers have been beaten, stoned, burned with firebrands and attacked by Muslim extremists. Yet the message goes out to hundreds of thousands each night."[62] Rich Buhler of KBRT-AM personally witnessed the phenomenon of the *Jesus* film: "You set that thing up under the wing of an airplane in a Third World country, and the whole village comes and watches. And they're touched by it. They weep. It's very powerful."[63]

In Campus Crusade's accounting, by 1988 *Jesus* had been viewed by more than 285 million people and led to 30 million "salvation decisions" for Christ.[64] When Bill Bright died in 2003, the film was said to have been shown in more than 800 languages and its cumulative audience estimated at 5.1 billion.[65] *Jesus* was arguably the most lasting legacy of Bright's quest to fulfill the Great Commission. The idea that this evangelistic tool could be diluted or compromised by a blasphemous Hollywood film—especially if *Last Temptation* itself turned out to be an attractive, compelling work—was anathema to Campus Crusade and its supporters.[66]

Initially, Bright and his colleagues asked for a private meeting with Lew Wasserman. When the request was promptly—and predictably—denied, Bright wrote a letter to Wasserman. He formally presented a proposal "whereby I would personally be responsible for reimbursing Universal Pictures for the amount already invested in the movie *The Last Temptation of Christ*. In exchange you would provide me with all of the copies of the film (which would promptly be destroyed) and its distribution rights." The funding, he wrote, would come from "concerned individuals across America who will pool their resources in order to cover your costs."[67] For good measure, Bright quoted at length from Pope John Paul's September 15 speech, in which the Holy Father entreated the entertainment industry to accept moral and spiritual accountability for its actions. Bright asked Wasserman for his response by Tuesday, July 19. He sent copies of the letter to Pat Broeske and John Dart of the *Los Angeles Times,* and it was hand-delivered late on Friday afternoon, July 15, to Tom Pollock's office.

Ever since the evangelical leaders had declared their desire to see the film destroyed, Universal's executives had been expecting a proposal of some kind. But Bill Bright's letter took their collective breath away. Not only was it an affront to MCA, but it betrayed a cynical attitude toward his own people. They found it appalling that someone of Bright's stature was willing to shift the burden of paying for the film onto his followers—in effect, saying, as one of them put it, "'Send me ten million dollars in quarters, you poor people, and then I'll have enough money to buy it back.'"[68] Impulsively, Pollock replied to Bright, asking him to back up the offer: "We sent him back a telegram, saying, 'Where's your check?' And we weren't serious about it. Because we were as serious as we thought his offer was. It was mostly our way of saying, 'Blank you.'"[69]

Historically, there have been very few instances of a studio pulling a film for reasons other than poor box-office performance. Typically, this occurs only under the duress of highly negative publicity or difficult exhibition conditions. The hostage-taking episode that marred the opening of *Mohammed: Messenger of God* in 1977—the same film that so exercised Sallah Hassanein during *Last Temptation*'s first incarnation—prompted Paramount to withdraw it temporarily from theaters. More commonly, a studio puts a problematic project into turnaround while it is in development—or, if it is finished, refuses to release it. In 1998 Universal decided not to release Todd Solondz's *Happiness,* which had been produced by its October Films label, because of the movie's sympathetic portrayal of a pedophilic character. That decision, however, was motivated by exhibitor reactions. The notion that a studio would seriously consider selling one of its films to a hostile party lay far outside the boundaries of rational thinking in Hollywood.

There was, however, at least one fugitive from rational thinking in Universal's ranks—someone who felt the film should be sacrificed if it meant saving the company from harm. One evening, while he was in New York for the *Last Temptation* screening, Roger Armstrong got a call from a colleague staying at the hotel, asking him to come down to his room. "The first thing out of this person's mouth was, 'We've got to destroy this film.' And I said, 'What are you talking about?' And the person said, 'It's growing so out of control. It's becoming so dangerous, it's hurting Lew, it's hurting the studio, we've got to destroy the film. We've got to convince Tom that the film can't be released. The negative can be destroyed, something can happen to the film, but we've got to do something . . .' And that kind of statement lands like a couple of very large loads of dynamite. And I sort of sat there, and the room was real quiet for a minute. And my response was, "You can never, ever say that again. You certainly can't say that publicly. You've got to let that go. That's never going to happen. And you can't tell anybody else you feel that way." And I talked for about an hour to finally get this person turned around. . . . Whether you agree with the message [of a film] or not, there are still very powerful creator, First Amendment issues in terms of a filmmaker's right to say something. That's why that kind of statement in the creative community is so shocking. And that's precisely what my response was—You can never say that."[70]

As Josh Baran, Sally Van Slyke, and others dissected the ramifications of Bright's offer, it dawned on them that they had been handed an opportunity, not a problem. If the sense of violation they felt could be conveyed with the appropriate gravity, and if they could articulate the vital principles that were at stake, then the studio's reply to Bill Bright could help them reclaim the "moral high ground" in the controversy. Legally, of course, there was nothing in Bright's offer—or any other peaceful actions aimed at inhibiting the film's release—that constituted censorship. But as the studio well knew, there was also nothing more sacred in the civic life of the country than the U.S. Constitution, and if they could surround the film with the aura of the freedoms of speech and religion, then the legal specifics would not much matter. "You know, we all hide behind the First Amendment when it's necessary to do it," Pollock said later.

The studio had to be careful about how it framed these issues. Baran's analysis earlier in the spring suggested that it might not be the wisest strategy for the studio to claim responsibility for Scorsese's vision; after all, reasonable people could agree that it did in fact violate the Gospel accounts in a number of important ways. Thus, in communicating the studio's position, the artist's vision had to be distinguished from the studio's right to show it. Universal would go to the wall to defend the latter. About the former, people could make up their own minds—but only if *Last Temptation* was allowed to be shown in theaters. It may be a fine distinction for the public to understand, but it was nevertheless the only path open to them.

Baran called Susan Rothbaum in Berkeley the evening of July 15 and asked her to write a letter for the studio. The letter was intended to reply to Bill Bright, but Baran was thinking of using a variation of the text as a full-page advertisement to be placed in major newspapers.[71] Rothbaum said she couldn't do it. She just didn't have the time that weekend. "So he started offering me more money," she recalled, "and I finally said, 'Okay, you bought me.'"[72]

He faxed Bright's letter to her and during the next two days Rothbaum wrote Universal's reply. The basis for the ideas—and the source of most of the poetic language she composed—was the positioning paper she had drafted that spring. Like a lawyer giving a summation, she paraphrased (or quoted) each of Bright's concerns and then proceeded to rebut them, or show why his concerns were misplaced:

UNIVERSAL PICTURES   July 20, 1988
Mr. Bill Bright
Campus Crusade for Christ

Dear Mr. Bright,

We, at Universal Pictures, have received your proposal in which you have offered to buy "The Last Temptation of Christ" which you would then destroy so that no one could ever see it. While we understand the deep feelings and convictions which have prompted this offer, we believe that to accept it would threaten the fundamental freedoms of religion and expression promised to all Americans under our Constitution.

You have quoted Pope John Paul II on the film industry's "accountability to God, to the community and before the witness of history." Those who wrote the Constitution believed that all of these were best served by protecting freedom of speech, freedom of press and freedom of religion. As Thomas Jefferson noted, "Torrents of blood have been spilt in the old world in consequence of vain attempts . . . to extinguish religious discord by proscribing all differences in religious opinion." The Twentieth Century has provided us with further evidence of the abuses which occur when monolithic authorities regulate artistic expression and religious beliefs. Though those in power may justify the burning of books at the time, the witness of history teaches the importance of standing up for freedom of conscience even when the view being expressed may be unpopular.

You have expressed a concern that the content of films be "true." But whose truth? If everyone in America agreed on religious, political and artistic truths, there would be no need for our constitutional guarantees. Only in totalitarian states are all people forced to accept one version of the truth. In any case, Martin Scorsese has stated clearly that his film is a work of fiction and that it is based on a novel, not the Gospels. It makes no claim whatsoever to be any more than a reflection of his own personal exploration.

In your letter you state that your position "embraces all the major branches of Christendom." But there always have been and continue to be many viewpoints among Christians. Many religious leaders of different denominations who attended our July 12 screenings in New York, which you declined to attend, were not offended by the film and even felt that it could be a tool for fruitful discussion. The constitutional guarantee of freedom of religious expression was provided precisely to protect such diversity of opinions, including the highly personal views of Nikos Kazantzakis, Martin Scorsese, the film's writers and artists.

In the United States, no one sect or coalition has the power to set boundaries around each person's freedom to explore religious and philosophical questions whether through speech, books or film.

The key arguments finished, she dropped down a line and gave the studio's answer to Bill Bright's offer:

These freedoms protect all of us.
They are precious.
They are not for sale.
We cannot accept your offer.
Universal Pictures[73]

On Sunday evening, she went to a copy shop and faxed the text to Universal. The next morning, Sally Van Slyke was running into a meeting with Pollock, Sid Sheinberg, and Lew Wasserman; the *Los Angeles Times* had broken the story about Bright's offer on Saturday and they had to discuss it.[74] Baran told her that he had something she could use in the meeting. "Here's a first draft," he said, holding up Rothbaum's letter, "but we haven't worked on it yet." There was no time for fine-tuning. Van Slyke snatched the letter and took it with her.

Nearly ten years earlier, Lew Wasserman had begun to cede day-to-day operational responsibilities to Sheinberg. Since then he rarely, if ever, got involved with decision making on a Universal picture. Still, nothing of any consequence happened in Hollywood without the seventy-five-year-old chairman's notice. Wasserman, said a longtime observer, "used to meet the message and delivery trucks with the trade papers, sometimes in his bathrobe. He had read every newspaper and trade paper he could get his hands on before he came to the office . . . so he came to work with a head of steam up."[75] He certainly would have been receiving internal reports of the *Last Temptation* problems for weeks, if not months, before Bill Bright's offer. He could not have failed to notice the first street demonstrations against the movie, held outside the studio gates on Saturday, July 16. And he was on the phone often with his friend the Catholic archbishop of the Los Angeles diocese, Roger Mahony, who expressed concerns about the damage to interfaith relations that the controversy could cause.

By all accounts, the last king of Hollywood—the last power broker to truly identify with the industry—was less concerned about any attacks on himself than about protecting the reputation of his company. Yet no one really knew what the notably reticent Wasserman thought of the movie that was making a lightning rod of MCA. Pollock didn't know, but he had an idea of what that opinion could be: "I'm sure in my heart he looked at it and said, 'I don't hire Tom Pollock to make art movies. Why is he making an art movie?' *Not,* why is he making *this* movie, and what is all this controversy about? He had to know that our job here is to make *Jurassic Park* and *Apollo 13,* not *The Last Temptation of Christ.* He never said that. But it would not surprise me if that's what he was thinking, because Lew believed very strongly that we're not here to be artists. We're here to build the company, and to do so artistically, but . . . the first thing you have to do is make money."[76]

Even Jack Valenti claimed not to know his mentor's thoughts about *Last Temptation,* although, characteristically, Valenti praised Wasserman's steady, statesmanlike conduct in the whole affair. "I must say I was quite impressed with the courage of Mr. Wasserman. He had people coming and staging demonstrations outside his private home, disrupting his personal life. But he never wavered. I don't know what he felt personally about the film. But he was committed that a director making a film under the banner of his company should have the right to take that film to the marketplace, even though he may or may not have agreed with the film, its premise, its characters, its story, or whatever. And I was quite proud of him."[77]

When Sally Van Slyke arrived at his office, Wasserman wanted to know how they were going to respond to these people who said they wanted to buy the film and burn it.[78]

Pollock said they had prepared a reply which was designed to take the issue out of the opponents' court—a disagreement about religious beliefs—and move it to a position on freedom of religious expression. In Van Slyke's recollection, Pollock felt unsure of himself at the meeting. "Tom was humiliated by the entire thing at that point, and realized what he'd gotten everybody into," she said.[79]

Pollock then read Rothbaum's letter aloud. The room fell quiet when he finished. "Well, you know, it's just a rough draft," Pollock shrugged.

Wasserman disagreed. "That's not a rough draft. That's done." Whoever wrote this, he said, did an "A-plus job."

The only revision Wasserman made was to the layout. When Van Slyke returned later that afternoon, he reminisced about his early, pre–MCA days as a publicist in Cleveland. Running ads back and forth between newspaper offices and the Mayfair Casino, he would block the copy in different ways, trying to find the best way of putting across the point of an ad. He turned the copy of the letter around on his desk so that it faced Van Slyke.

"Don't you want, Sally, to say, 'They are not for sale.' And you want that line to stand out, so drop it down." He then scratched out the last line, "We cannot accept your offer."

When she heard about Wasserman's revisions, Rothbaum recognized the good sense of ending on a note of principle, rather than a refusal to an individual. She admitted, "My writing always has one sentence that needs to be cut at the very end of it."[80]

Wasserman agreed that the best use they could make of the reply to Bright was to print it as a full-page "open letter." He asked Van Slyke for her thoughts about where to run it. She and Baran had already decided that ad space should be purchased in the trade papers, *Variety* and the *Hollywood Reporter,* as well as in the *New York Times, Washington Post, Los Angeles Times,* and *Atlanta Constitution.* The Atlanta paper was included because the Democratic National Convention would soon be opening there.

Wasserman balked, thinking that placing it in all these major outlets might make the Bright offer seem more significant than it deserved.

This was no time to be timid, argued Van Slyke. "Mr. Wasserman," she said, "if you don't think you've got a problem here, let's all think again."

Van Slyke was surprised at her own outspokenness, but she had been up for nearly all of the previous seventy-two hours and felt frustrated that no one seemed willing to grab hold of this nearly uncontrollable situation. Decision making on the film was being pulled in tightly and the studio was still unsure about how to handle relations with the media.

"Nobody wanted to be quoted," recalled Baran. "You look at that ad from Universal. It doesn't say MCA at the top, it says Universal. It's not real letterhead. No one signs it. They're trying to distance themselves a little bit, probably too much actually."[81]

On Thursday, July 21, Universal's reply to Bill Bright ran in the front sections of the newspapers. The next day, the *Washington Post* reported on Universal's "unusual public defense of its own picture"; an unidentified Universal spokesman said the ad would be the studio's only public comment on the controversy until the picture was released later in the fall. "Much of what [the protesters] are saying is inaccurate and exaggerated. . . . This is censorship. People have a right to choose for themselves whether or not to see this movie, and to form their own opinions of it."[82] The studio's advocacy of religious

expression won plaudits in editorials and op-ed columns and was quoted liber-
ally in the trade press, newspapers, and television news programs. For the first
time in a long time, Universal's people had reason to be proud of what *The
Last Temptation of Christ* had wrought. Said one, "It was a very eloquent letter
and I think anyone who read it had to be moved by it."[83]

The themes enunciated in the ad were rapidly picked up by the industry
representatives who spoke out for Scorsese and MCA, beginning appropriately
with Jack Valenti. The very next day, July 22, Valenti released a statement on
behalf of the member companies of the MPAA, supporting "MCA/Universal
in its absolute right to offer to the people whatever movie it chooses. . . . The
key issue, the only issue, is whether or not self-identified groups can prevent
a film from being exhibited to the public. . . . The lawyers call this 'prior
censorship.' It is an odious intervention by whatever name it is called." A few
days later, Valenti went on CNN's *Larry King Live* to debate a feisty Catholic
nun, Mother Angelica, again using artistic freedom as his major argument to
defend MCA/Universal and the movie. *Variety* also reported that the board of
the striking Writers Guild of America was "discussing a motion of solidarity
with [Universal] in its anti-censorship stand."[84]

Publicly, the anti-*Temptation* activists were dismissive of the ad and what
they considered its smug, self-serving invocation of religious and artistic liberties. But privately, some were upset by the insulated decision-making process
that led to Bill Bright's buyout idea. To Coleman Luck, the offer emboldened
the industry's natural impulse to make the objectors look like censors: "What
it did was actually solidify everyone's position here because they were all very
much concerned with First Amendment rights and all the rest. . . . On the part
of the evangelical leaders, the ignorance was abysmal and inexcusable."[85] In
Rich Buhler's view, the offer displayed financial ineptitude; if MCA had
accepted the offer, he said only half jokingly, it might have created a market
for conspicuously sacrilegious films. The biggest problem with the idea was
that it was simply the wrong thing to do. Although Buhler would have been
quite happy if the film was never distributed, he did not wish to see its access
to the marketplace taken away, "any more than I would want [MCA] to come
and buy out all of Billy Graham's TV shows because they didn't like people
being evangelized."[86] The buyout offer also prompted the media to further
emphasize in their stories that people were branding the film blasphemous
without having seen it.

The Los Angeles and national media were clearly swayed by the First
Amendment argument, and a new image of Universal began to be limned—

the image of a staunch civil libertarian. "This film has made idealists of Universal," observed Ram Dass on the sidewalk of the Cineplex Odeon theater after the July 12 screening. "And I thought that was very accurate," said Susan Rothbaum of his remark. "It was like, all of a sudden, Universal *was* taking this moral high ground."[87] To the industry insiders who knew it as one of the toughest, most cynical companies in Hollywood, the reputational makeover seemed almost unbelievable.

THE EXPONENTIAL INCREASE in media attention brought a raft of rumors, new and old, out into the open. Donald Wildmon told *Baptist Press*, the news service of the Southern Baptist Convention, that Universal had two versions of the movie in hand—a sanitized work in progress that was shown in the New York screening, and a far more objectionable version intended for the public.[88] Universal spokespeople denied the claim. A Baptist newsletter in Oklahoma reported that Universal had already released *Last Temptation* in selected cities on July 15.[89] Universal called this report false, too. Another rumor had Universal preparing 70-mm prints of the movie for exhibition on the nation's biggest screens—a story the studio neither confirmed nor denied. And the July 15 issue of *Christianity Today* reported Tim Penland's resignation and cited his concerns about the script, including a scene of Jesus "engaging in homosexual activity with one of his disciples."[90] As reports filtered from Christian media and direct mail to the grassroots, innuendo of a homosexual Jesus sprang up everywhere. Some Christian clerics declared that the movie's Jesus was not just wimpy, but a "limp wimp."

Such rumors fed the pressures that were already building on theaters. An "informal survey" conducted by the *Los Angeles Times* found many of the nation's theater chains extremely cautious about committing themselves to book the film.[91] "There is a real possibility every theater booking the film will have pickets protesting outside of it," noted the head film buyer for the California-based Pacific Theater chain.[92] Some exhibitors echoed what the opponents were saying about *Last Temptation,* even before they had a chance to see it. One of Universal's distribution executives was constantly on the phone with theater owners, learning about their concerns firsthand. "What happened was that the Christian community organized themselves, and not only were writing to the studios, but were writing to exhibitors, calling exhibitors, saying we can't, shouldn't play that film. So [the exhibitors] got very nervous about it. And they actually started to send us copies of the correspondence they got on it. And some of the letters were very threatening. It wasn't, 'God will get you.' It was, you know, 'We'll blow up your theater.' "[93]

The explosive events of mid-July forced the studio to reassess its options. Universal and Martin Scorsese had earlier reached an agreement with Joanne Koch, executive director of the New York Film Festival, to give *The Last Temptation of Christ* its American premiere on September 23, the festival's opening night. But with the rapid escalation of the protest, everyone was having second thoughts. "According to Scorsese's office," reported *Newsday* on July 19, "the festival plans could be derailed if Universal decides to debut 'Last Temptation' before the festival premiere."[94] If they waited two months, giving the opposition time to build to full strength, the protest could easily eclipse the one that afflicted the festival debut of Jean-Luc Godard's *Hail Mary* three years before, when more than a thousand demonstrators gathered at Lincoln Center's Alice Tully Hall. Studio officials began talking to Scorsese and De Fina about speeding up postproduction, just in case the release plans had to be changed.

Meanwhile, as the threats on *Last Temptation* mounted and the media clamored for more information about the movie, it became evident that the studio's communications had to be tightly controlled. It was a sensitive situation, said a person knowledgeable about *Last Temptation*, "just because there was too much concern [people] would *die* if they talked. I mean, they would become such a target."[95] Accordingly, it was decided that Sally Van Slyke would function as *Last Temptation* project leader and company spokesperson on most press inquiries about the film.[96] (An early quote she gave to the AP drew the attention of individuals with untoward fixations, to put it mildly; thereafter, the press honored her request for non-attribution for the duration of the controversy.) Pollock continued to be quoted by name when a personal response from the Universal chairman was needed.

Something also had to be done to make it clear that *The Last Temptation of Christ* was not supposed to be an accurate depiction of Christ. The studio could say all it wanted about the freedom of religious expression, but to the average person this rhetoric could sound akin to Scorsese or the studio reserving unto themselves the right to change the Gospels. Baran elaborated: "If you have a framework that says, these are the Gospels, they're perfect as they are, they're the Word of God, and you don't do anything with them—[then] you can't touch them. There's another [framework] which talks about religious poetry, religious imagery, religious fiction, which is a whole different approach. And I wanted people to think about Kazantzakis and start saying, here is somebody who was a religious writer, has religious themes, and then this is an interpretation of that. So that was the reason—to further position the film."[97]

The idea of attaching some sort of disclaimer to the front of the movie began to be discussed with Martin Scorsese. Because he had creative control, only Scorsese could allow it. Jay Cocks was against the idea: "I didn't think that we had anything to explain, and to my reckoning, perhaps very defensive reckoning, it came close to apologizing."[98] To Scorsese, it was a small concession to help people understand the movie in the way it was intended. "I thought it was good idea, actually," he said. "I liked it because it kind of set a tone in Kazantzakis's words. . . . I want everybody to know it's not the Gospels, it's not a regular pageant."[99]

The passage they selected for setting the tone came from the book's prologue: "The dual substance of Christ—the yearning, so human, so superman, of man to attain God . . . has always been a deep inscrutable mystery to me. My principle anguish and source of all my joys and sorrows from my youth onward has been the incessant, merciless battle between the spirit and the flesh . . . and my soul is the arena where these two armies have clashed and met."[100]

"To show how much pressure we were under," said Scorsese, "we got the word 'principal' spelled wrong. . . . Supposed to be 'pal.' We put 'ple.' "[101]

The words of the prologue scrolled down the screen, leading the audience to the statement: "This film is not based upon the Gospels but upon this fictional exploration of the eternal spiritual conflict."

This sentence, forever a part of the film, wouldn't have been added had it not been for the controversy. But it seemed unlikely that admitting the film was fiction—saying, in effect, that Kazantzakis and Scorsese decided to invent their own Christ—would assuage those who believed that the Christ of the Bible was the one, true, perfect Christ. For them, any other Christ was a lesser Christ, and the disclaimer gave them one more reason to stop the film from being released.

7

Teeth Bared, Knuckles White

IN THE WEEK following James Dobson's *Focus on the Family* broadcast, the escalating war of words between Universal and an ad hoc coalition of evangelical Christians dominated the news about *The Last Temptation of Christ*. Where one side considered the movie a slander on Christ's character, the other side called it an affirmation of faith; where one found evidence of betrayal, the other said that its intentions were honorable; where one was determined to do everything in its power to keep the film out of theaters, the other vowed to release it. Despite these profound—and probably irreconcilable—differences, both parties had so far managed to steer clear of personal attacks on each other. But on July 16 the protest "took a new twist," as *Variety*'s reporter Amy Dawes characterized it.[1] On that warm, hazy Saturday morning, a rogue element interjected itself into the unfolding drama, which had the effect during the next few days of upending the coalition's carefully scripted brief against the film and opening up a whole new set of problems for the studio.

Just before 11:00 A.M., about two hundred members of a downtown Los Angeles church, the Fundamentalist Baptist Tabernacle, quietly assembled at the Lankershim Boulevard entrance of MCA/Universal. Led by their pugnacious minister, the Reverend R. L. Hymers Jr., they formed a picket line along the sidewalk. Several of the church members unrolled a long banner reading, "Wasserman Fans Hatred toward the Jews with 'Temptation' Movie." Others held up neatly lettered placards—"Wasserman Fans Anti-Semitism," "Wasserman Endangers Israel"—decorated with pictures of the Star of David or a caricature of Lew Wasserman. A light plane circled overhead, towing a long banner with a message accusing Wasserman of inciting hatred toward the Jewish people.

Reporters gathered around the short, stocky minister. Asked why he thought Lew Wasserman endangered Israel, Hymers said matter-of-factly:

"These Jewish producers with a lot of money are taking a swipe at our religion. Of course, it's going to cause a backlash." The MCA chairman, Hymers explained, "puts himself in the position of ridiculing a region in which he did not grow up. . . . It isn't good for interfaith relations. Why throw gasoline on the fires of religious intolerance? Particularly in this time, when Israel needs the support of the Christian community." Wasserman, he continued, "should go back to being the nice old man who introduced the Pope last September."[2]

When reporters tried to engage his parishioners in conversation, Hymers would not allow it, saying that some of them might not understand why they were protesting Lew Wasserman, or even know who he was. "They know there's a bad movie about Jesus," he said, but "they may not understand the subtleties of it."[3]

Before the Baptists dispersed at noon, Hymers gave out copies of a press release announcing his next event: a demonstration scheduled for 11:30 A.M. on Wednesday, July 20, at the corner of Foothill Road and Sunset Boulevard in Beverly Hills, about fifty yards south of Lew Wasserman's home.

For the entertainment beat reporters who covered the scene at Universal City, the protest seemed to come out of nowhere. But for those familiar with the forty-seven-year-old preacher's combative style and penchant for publicity, Hymers's attacks on Lew Wasserman could not have been very surprising. Indeed, events like these were becoming an annual occurrence. Two years earlier, Hymers and his flock had prayed publicly for the deaths of two U.S. Supreme Court justices who supported abortion rights. A year later, they crusaded against a local Christian college for allowing critical teachings of the Scriptures. Jews were an object of special fascination for him. According to an investigative article in the July 1988 issue of the *Jewish Journal,* the Fundamentalist Baptist Tabernacle ran an outreach program to convert Jews to Christianity. In addition, the journal reported, Hymers "boasts that 8 percent of his inner-city congregants are Jewish; his principal aide is a converted Jew; and he was married six years ago to a Salvadoran women by an old friend, Moishe Rosen, of Jews for Jesus, an organization his church is said to support financially."[4] Hymers's activities followed in a tradition of Jewish evangelization dating to the early nineteenth century in America. According to Jonathan Sarna, a scholar of Jewish studies, the Christians who advocate such conversions often say they do it out of love for the Jewish people. "Still," wrote Sarna, "those who sought to convert Jews could not escape casting aspersions on the religion they wanted Jews to leave. . . . By definition, a conversionist had to believe that Jews were beset by faults that only conversion could cure."[5]

Like nearly all the conservative Christians who received copies of the boot-legged *Last Temptation* script, Hymers recoiled at the sacrilege of the text. After being informed that Jews filled the top echelon of MCA's management, Hymers fixated on Lew Wasserman as a target of his next crusade. He sent the church's minister of education, C. L. Cragan, to public libraries to compile a dossier of information on Wasserman. Cragan did not learn much about the publicity-shy chief executive, but in searching through real estate records and the society pages of city newspapers, he did find Wasserman's home address. Hymers began to confer with his New York friend Moishe Rosen about the best way of focusing public attention on Lew Wasserman's culpability in the *Last Temptation* matter. Hymers later wrote about these phone conversations, "It was Moishe who had come up with the idea of protesting in front of Wasserman's home. . . . Over two months ago [in mid-June] he had suggested that I rent a large van and park it in front of Wasserman's house, with a sign on the side reading, 'Lew Wasserman, the man who attacks Jesus Christ, lives at XXX Foothill Road.'"[6] By July the somewhat more imaginative idea of a mock Passion Play had formed in Hymers's mind.

On the morning of July 20, Hymers and a small group of fundamentalists gathered in a quiet, wooded Beverly Hills neighborhood, carrying signs of protest and chanting, "Paid for with Jewish money!" Hymers, dressed in a dark suit and white shirt, stepped forward to address the media. "There should be an outcry from the Christian community when these Jewish people bankroll a film that makes Jesus look insane. . . . It's dangerous for the Jewish people to have this film put out." His voice rising in a preacher's cadence, Hymers thundered indignantly, "In the name of God, and in the name of decency, do not put out this film!" Then the street theater began. Four members of the church picked up an eight-foot wooden cross at the curbside of Lew Wasserman's home. A Hymers aide carrying a two-way radio directed them to a place on the sidewalk where, surrounded by other expressionless congregants and a crowd of reporters and onlookers, they set the cross down. A long-haired young man wearing a white robe spattered with fake blood lifted the cross on his back and took it several yards farther. The "Jesus" figure halted and assumed a kneeling position under the main beam of the cross. Another young man approached. Attired in a business suit, his hands covered in fake blood, he evidently played the part of "Lew Wasserman." "Wasserman" then hooked one of his legs over the cross, planted his shoe on the back of "Jesus," and held the pose for the cameras.

This bizarre Christian kabuki took an unexpected turn when several members of the militant Jewish Defense League arrived on the scene. With microphones and cameras crowding in close, the tall, imposing JDL national chairman, Irv Rubin, shook his finger at the minister: "This was an easy target—'Let's go get the Jew in Beverly Hills.' Huh, Hymers? It isn't going to cut it. . . . Don't make this a Jewish thing because then you're the anti-Semite." Momentarily thrown off-stride, Hymers extended his hand. "Shake hands! I don't want to be an anti-Semite!" Rubin refused the gesture. For a few disconcerting seconds, it was unclear whether the exchange was happening spontaneously or was just the next act in a scripted performance. Both men came to their roles so naturally that the distinction seemed almost unimportant.[7]

Hymers's bellicose accusations, reported on Los Angeles television stations that evening and in newspapers the next morning, sent alarms ringing throughout the local Jewish community. Before then, wrote Leo Noonan in the *Jewish Journal,* "the film . . . did not cause more than a ripple in the Jewish community, where the prevailing attitude was a mixture of curiosity, fear, outrage, *and* profound respect for what the non–Hymers/Falwell-types of protestors [were] trying to accomplish."[8] Now, outrage and trepidation were loosed, not only in reaction to the incident at Wasserman's home, but also because of remarks made earlier in the week by the Reverend Jerry Falwell. Echoing the substance of Hymers's charges, Falwell predicted that *Last Temptation*'s release would "create a wave of anti-Semitism in this country."[9] Falwell said he feared that many Christians would blame "Jewish leaders" in the entertainment industry for a film they considered to be a blasphemy of Jesus Christ.

National Jewish organizations were appalled at the disingenuous idea that Universal was in any way responsible for fomenting hatred of Jews. By raising the issue of anti-Semitism at all, Hymers and Falwell seemed to courting the very outcome they warned against. The protests against Universal, said Robert M. Jones, a senior official of the National Conference of Christians and Jews, "have deteriorated into an all too familiar scapegoating of Jews."[10] Seymour D. Reich, president of the B'nai B'rith, the world's largest Jewish organization, said in a news release, "This kind of vigilante mentality is in the tradition of book-burning and witch-hunting we hoped had long since disappeared from the American landscape."[11] Acknowledging that people offended by the film had recourse to the same First Amendment freedoms as the film's producers, Robert K. Lifton, president of the American Jewish Congress, and its executive

director, Henry Siegman, said in a joint statement that "the exercise of constitutional rights by both sides in this dispute does not create license to engage
in bigotry and use it as an opportunity for anti-Semitism."[12]

The potent combination of Jerry Falwell's statement, Hymers's flamboyant
tactics, and the reactions of Jewish leaders gave an irresistible new hook to
coverage of the developing *Last Temptation* story. During the week of July 18,
the controversy played out in newspapers across the country and landed on
the evening newscasts of CBS on July 22, and ABC and NBC on July 25—all
of them showing vivid footage of Hymers's demonstrations. Hymers himself
soon came under critical scrutiny in the press. The *Los Angeles Times* and the
Jewish Journal interviewed former associates and members of his church who
told stories about Hymers's erratic temperament and his allegedly abusive
behavior toward congregants.[13] Undeterred by this attention, Hymers zeal-
ously pursued his white whale. In the coming weeks, he staged more public
denunciations of Lew Wasserman—first at the Jewish Community Center on
July 27, where he accused Wasserman of having "gangster connections"; then
again at Wasserman's residence; twice at the Wilshire Boulevard Temple,
where he hoped to accost Wasserman as he went to synagogue; and, during
the week of the film's release, a final rally outside the Universal studio lot,
where he and his followers staged a crucifixion of Wasserman in effigy.

Privately, many of the Christian leaders of the ad hoc coalition seethed
with anger. Hymers's tirades threatened to hijack the legitimacy of their own
message and clash with their goal of forming a multifaith front against the
film. Ultimately, such well-known orthodox Jews as the radio host Dennis
Praeger and film critic Michael Medved joined in criticizing Universal's
release of *Last Temptation*, but not before "anti-Jewish themes" began showing up in protest literature and demonstrations in other parts of the country.[14] "He was a wild man," said Larry Poland about Hymers. "And we did
everything we could to silence him in his veiled and not-so-veiled references
to the Jewish factor."[15] Tim Penland spoke for many of his colleagues when
he told John Dart, "It grieves us to see this."[16] Donald Wildmon agreed, "It's
very unfortunate."[17]

In their own rhetoric, however, some of the protest leaders were already
questioning the personal religiosity of MCA's executives. Wildmon, for example, was quoted in the same *Los Angeles Times* story about the Christian reaction to Hymers, saying that "hostility toward Christians" was a common
"pagan" attitude among "the Hollywood elite."[18] Writing more directly to his

The Reverend R. L. Hymers's congregation protesting against Lew Wasserman in Beverly Hills, California, August 1988. (Corbis)

constituency, Wildmon described Universal as "a company whose decision-making body is dominated by non-Christians."[19] Later, in an open letter to Sid Sheinberg published in the *A.F.A. Journal*, he asked how many of the executives in MCA's top echelon were Christian.[20] Arguably this coded language telegraphed a view of Hollywood's leadership that might have encouraged some people—especially those inclined to decode terms like "elite," "pagan," and "non-Christian" within a particular ideological framework—to take the next step, of blaming Jewish studio officials for a film slandering Christ.

The playing of the Jewish card evoked feelings in the media community ranging from shock and anger to embarrassment, regret, and sadness. For the first time in his storied career, Lew Wasserman was the object of widespread sympathy from his peers. Whatever people thought about the wisdom of making the film, many industry professionals thought it was grossly unfair for Lew Wasserman, who was highly regarded in Los Angeles for his civic contributions and philanthropic projects, and whose hosting of Pope John Paul II the previous year had underlined his dedication to the cause of interfaith dialogue, to be singled out for such abuse.

Hollywood was also taken aback at how readily the controversy tapped into wellsprings of prejudice dwelling below the surface of the fundamentalist psyche. The studio and the press relentlessly pointed out—but apparently to little effect—that the author of the novel was Greek Orthodox, the screenplay's author was Dutch Calvinist, and the film's director was Roman Catholic. The allegation that *Last Temptation* would cause a backlash against Jews made sense only in the context of ancient stereotypes of Jews as Christ killers; as economic exploiters; as a rootless "tribe" that lacks ethical bearings or any sense of moral obligation to a wider community—images that had given rise to countless acts of prejudice against the Jewish people throughout American history.[21] Since the early twentieth century, the film industry largely avoided the worst of this bigotry, despite the disproportionate number of Jews in its executive ranks. As Neal Gabler documented in *An Empire of Their Own,*[22] the Jewish émigrés who founded Hollywood, as well as later native-born moguls like Harry Cohn, Irving Thalberg, and Harry and Jack Warner, not only tried to assimilate themselves and their companies in secular Gentile society, but also made movies that exalted, in Gabler's words, "a genteel American vision—a powerful wish fulfillment that idealized America and sanctified its values."[23] The insular character of the film colony also played a part in lowering the profile of its Jewish movers and shakers. They felt relatively secure in their own surroundings. Anti-Semitism was something that happened in the rest of the country, not to the executives of media companies. Even Tom Pollock had no personal acquaintance with it: "I'm one of these people who never had an anti-Semitic experience in my life until [*Last Temptation*]. I never was discriminated against. Not knowingly. Nobody ever called me a name. . . . I mean, I knew it existed. I just didn't experience it."[24]

The Jewish issue muddied the waters considerably in the studio's efforts to take the "moral high ground." It was of particular concern to Archbishop Roger Mahony. Only days earlier, Mahony had received a preliminary report from the United States Catholic Conference (USCC) Department of Communications, two of whose members were at the July 12 New York screening of *Last Temptation,* that the film would probably be classified "O" (signifying an "offensive" film that should be avoided by Catholics). And now, with the Pandora's box of anti-Semitism pried open, the always delicate fabric of interreligious relations in Los Angeles was suddenly at risk. Mahony wrote a formal letter to Wasserman, which, according to a knowledgeable source, encouraged him to find a way to stop the film's release. The archbishop, this source said, was feeling pressure from the Vatican to bring the situation under control.

Meanwhile, Mahony and his public affairs office drafted a statement designed to clarify his position on the film, entitled "Archbishop Mahony on 'The Last Temptation of Christ.'" Released to the press on July 20, Mahony's statement was given substantial coverage in the *New York Times, Los Angeles Times,* and other major newspapers. Tom Pollock recalled, "His Eminence called Lew to tell him that he was going to have to do this beforehand. Lew apologized for it, because I believe [Mahony] is certainly among the more conservative Catholics, as that goes."[25]

"The proposed release of the film," said Archbishop Mahony in his statement, "has generated far more heat than light."[26] Noting that *Last Temptation* was likely to be rated "O" by the USCC, he observed: "That would hardly be a compliment to the makers of this film which purports to portray a segment in the life of Jesus Christ, the Son of God. . . . It is always dangerous for authors, artists and film makers to portray any fictional or apocryphal aspects of Christ's life, whether it be dealing with His divinity or His humanity." Alluding to his back-channel conversations with the MCA chairman, Mahony said, "I have the highest esteem and regard for Mr. Lew Wasserman and I am confident that he would not allow any film to be released through his studios which would be offensive to a large segment of the American film-going public." But as Universal's response to Bill Bright made abundantly clear, that was not about to happen.

With so many events coming to a head during the fourth week of July, *The Last Temptation of Christ* had become a national cause célèbre. The media decided that the film's opponents had a point of view to express, something more coherent to say than just the brief, chopped-up quotes appearing in "objective" news stories. Cultural conservatives were given a chance to lay out their arguments in longer, unfiltered formats—editorials, op-ed columns, commentaries, and radio and TV talk shows. One of the issues they wanted the public to consider was this: Is it appropriate to engage in artistic speculation about a historical figure, especially a figure revered by religious believers? Especially among those Christians whose beliefs shaded to a view of the Bible as an inerrant text, all fictional treatments of Jesus are pale imitations of the sacred Word. They could be dangerous if created with malicious motives or ill-conceived methods. As the Reverend Donald Wildmon put it in a guest editorial in *USA Today:* "*The Last Temptation of Christ* is, by definition, a sermon about Christ. However, it has no biblical substance. It is not true to what we know of the biblical and historical Jesus. It finds reference to Christ only in the twisted mind of someone's imagination."[27]

In this view, *Last Temptation* was an *insufficiently representational* fiction. It conjured events that did not happen—and, in the case of scenes like the one of Jesus making crosses for Roman executions, events that never could have happened. The danger was greatest, argued Jonathan H. Wilson, a Presbyterian pastor, in the *Los Angeles Herald-Examiner,* for "all the millions of impressionable young people who are trying to see the film and who may have inadequate Christian education to be able to divide truth from fantasy."[28] On this point, nearly every conservative religious critic agreed: the separation of truth from fantasy is not an issue for those who already have a biblical understanding of Jesus. But for those whose only source of information is the movie, it could inflict long-lasting damage to the cause of Christ—which is to bring all people into a faith relationship with him.

There was also the issue, explored on a more theological plane of discourse, of what it meant for Jesus to be human, and more specifically, what it meant for him to be "tempted." Did Jesus experience the same choices as the rest of us to do right or wrong? How much did Jesus share of the fallen nature of man? At the far end of religious opinion were those who believed Jesus was completely incapable of having "impure" thoughts[29]—even if those thoughts did not eventuate in impure action. This position sometimes tipped over into the heretical Docetist view of Jesus Christ as a divine being who merely assumed a human appearance during his time on earth. For other Christians, it was more a matter of the type and degree of temptation. The cinematic rendering of temptation, especially by a director like Martin Scorsese, who is interested in dealing with the concept on his own terms, was bound to upset people whose ideas of Jesus' humanity were either abstract or at a far remove from their own everyday fears, doubts, and desires. Sexual desire, in particular, seemed to be a quality that Jesus could not be allowed to have. Even the framing device of a hallucinatory reverie induced by Satan did not excuse the transgression. In a *Washington Post* column, William F. Buckley Jr. chastised Scorsese's handling of sexuality in the last temptation sequence: "On the cross, [Scorsese] gives us a Christ whose mind is distracted by lechery, fancying himself not the celibate of history, but the swinger in the arms of the prostitute Mary Magdalene. The blend of the ultimate altruist seeking in primal agony the fantasy of hot sex is something far from what a Sen. Bilbo would have dared to do to Stepin Fetchit in a smoker in the '30s, let alone on huge Hollywood screens with hawkers outside shilling for big juicy audiences to get a shot of impiety while projecting Artistic License."[30]

According to the theologian James Gustafson of the University of Chicago, who was asked about *Last Temptation* by an *Atlanta Constitution* reporter, if Jesus was in fact outfitted with the same human physiology as the rest of us, he must have responded to his desires similarly: "Jesus undoubtedly had a penis. He had testicles. He was a good Jewish man. Are you going to sit around and tell me that Jesus was never sexually aroused?"[31] More generally, theologically moderate or liberal clergy had a difficult time understanding why Jesus' humanity in its fullest possibilities was so hard for Christians to grasp or accept. In an opinion piece in the *Los Angeles Times,* Maurice Ogden, a Unitarian minister, asked: "How can you say Jesus 'sacrificed' his life . . . if he had no attachment to life, experienced no doubt or pain or terror at losing it? If he had no genuine human temptations, how can he be a meaningful model of resistance for those who are tempted?"[32]

Eventually, most conservative Christian commentators got around to asking the same set of questions—Why did the movie have to be made? Why is the studio defending it so aggressively? Why does Universal seem to be so deaf to the wounded voices of Christians? The answer to all those questions usually settled on the ever-widening gulf between Hollywood and the Christian community; charges of Universal's complicity in this one film rapidly accelerated into an indictment of the value system of the entire secular media industry.

The opinion piece that most forcefully advanced this viewpoint was Patrick J. Buchanan's column "Is It Art or Sleaze?"[33] Widely reprinted in newspapers during the summer of 1988, Buchanan's column reassembled all the disturbing pieces of the controversy into one bold manifesto. After reading it, Christian traditionalists could have no more doubts about Universal's motives or what *Last Temptation* portended for their own lives.

After quoting Jack Valenti's First Amendment justification for releasing the film, Buchanan drew a series of analogies:

> Under the First Amendment, the Protocols of the Elders of Zion are surely protected, as would be the anti-Semitic Nazi tracts of Julius Streicher. Would Mr. Valenti defend their distribution by, say, Waldenbooks? Would Mr. Valenti defend a film titled The Secret Life of Martin Luther King, that depicted the assassinated civil rights leader as a relentless womanizer, a point of view with more foundation in truth, and, surely, less of a profanation, than showing Jesus of Nazareth as a lusting wimp? . . . Of course not.[34]

If the inference that a reader should draw from these analogies was not clear enough, Buchanan drove home the point:

We live in an age where the ridicule of blacks is forbidden, where anti-Semitism is punishable by political death, but where Christian-bashing is a popular indoor sport; and films mocking Jesus Christ are considered avant-garde. . . . And the reason Universal Pictures and Mr. Scorsese are doing this is because they know they can get away with it. Their Hollywood chums will laugh and whisper, "Right on! Stick it to 'em!" Their clerical camp followers at the National Council of Churches will provide the religious cover. And the controversy will guarantee big profits all around. Who cares if the Christian community is outraged, or individual Christians are hurt and offended?[35]

In saying that Universal did not make the movie for all the normal reasons—for profits, for prestige—but because it could "get away with it," Buchanan was suggesting that the liberal media are ruled by a different ethos from the rest of us. They will go to great lengths to protect their own icons from being sullied, but they show no compunction about ridiculing the most revered religious figure of "America's unfashionable majority."[36] This majority, Buchanan asserted, was actually being treated like a despised minority group. And the ones giving offense—especially the movie studio wielding *The Last Temptation of Christ* like a sharp stick in the eye of Christians—enjoyed doing it.

In the closing paragraph, Buchanan depicted the movie as a gauntlet thrown down by the entertainment industry: "What all of Hollywood, now rallying around Universal Pictures, is saying with its unqualified endorsement of 'The Last Temptation of Christ' is: 'Hey, you Christians, look here: we're showing your God and your Savior, Jesus Christ, having sex with Mary Magdalene; now, what are you going to do about it?'"[37]

Buchanan's column was one of the most skillfully written—and certainly among the most provocative—opinion pieces to blame Universal for the film. But it was just one of dozens being published in newspapers across the country in July and August. The studio decided that it had to do something more to present its viewpoint. The July 12 screening yielded a large pool of religious leaders and church officials who could speak knowledgeably—and favorably—about the film, and in the days and weeks after the screening, most of them did give interviews to a variety of religious organizations and news media about their impressions of *Last Temptation.* Not all of them, however, had the time to do it on a sustained basis—or, for that matter, had the ability to do it effectively on television. What Sally Van Slyke and Josh Baran needed was a few articulate clergymen who weren't afraid to go on the road and plunge into the controversy, debating the critics on behalf of the film, Martin Scorsese, and freedom of religious expression. Within days of the New York screening, the studio found three Protestant pastors who enthusiastically embraced this role: the Reverend Robert Thompson, the Reverend Charles Bergstrom, and the Reverend William Fore.

A dynamic, boyish-looking thirty-nine-year-old minister of an American Baptist church in Evanston, Illinois, Robert Thompson was passionate about social justice and the possibility of interfaith comity. He had been alarmed during the Reagan years by the fundamentalists who used literal readings of the Bible as a basis for pursuing unjust policies on a whole range of issues, from AIDS and women's reproductive rights to aid to the poor. Now the strident reactions to *The Last Temptation of Christ* took this effrontery to another level. "I've waited for a long time to say that there's more than one voice in the Christian faith, and it feels good to finally say it," Thompson said at the time about why he decided to act.[38]

Upon returning to Chicago from the July 12 screening, he called the *Chicago Tribune*'s religion writer, Michael Hirsley, whose column in May about the incipient controversy prompted Thompson to get in touch with Universal. The reporter was eager to hear the pastor's eyewitness account. That Sunday, July 17, Hirsley's story in the *Tribune* ("Churchmen at Odds over 'Temptation'") quoted Thompson extensively about his perceptions of this hotly debated and heretofore unseen movie. "This film is not pornographic," Thompson said in the article. "It does not appeal to prurient interests. What it does is violate the traditional images of Jesus and depict Him as struggling to achieve His divinity. The film was clearly a reaffirmation of my faith."[39] Rich Samuels, a reporter with Chicago's NBC affiliate, WMAQ, called Thompson that afternoon about doing an interview. Hours later, Thompson sat for a videotaped interview in his church office. Samuels's package aired on WMAQ's Sunday night newscast, then was shipped to Los Angeles and shown on KNBC the following evening. On Tuesday morning, little more than forty-eight hours since his remarks first appeared in the *Tribune,* Sally Van Slyke was on the phone with Thompson, asking how he would feel about doing more interviews. "I said, 'Oh, it would be a lot of fun!' She said, 'Well, we'll have somebody get in touch with you.' So, Josh Baran then called me."[40]

"I talked to him several times," said Thompson about his interactions with Baran. "He told me they had three people that they wanted to be going around, talking about [the movie]. . . . He said they were going to set up some interviews. So, fine. And the next thing I remember was receiving a call from [ABC's] *Nightline*. . . . That didn't work out. Next thing I knew, I got a call from the CBS morning news program. They wanted me to come do a live thing in their studio, in three or four days. Pack your bags. So, I did that. . . . And then there was the [CNN] *Crossfire* interview."[41]

Thompson went to his church board to ask for advice and guidance, since doing the interviews meant being absent occasionally from his pastoral duty. The board members, he said, gave their blessing, seeing it as an opportunity to take the church's progressive voice to a wider audience. "The month of August is slow anyway," he added.[42] All told, Thompson did more than forty television, print, and radio interviews in a span of about thirty days. Well-spoken and possessing a deep baritone voice, Thompson was particularly effective on radio and television. His joint appearance with the Reverend Hymers on CNN's *Crossfire* sparked one of the wildest exchanges seen on national television. But he kept his cool, even as Hymers caustically questioned the tenets of his faith. Frequently, his anti-*Temptation* counterparts challenged Thompson about his ministerial judgment, asking, for example, whether he would want the "little old ladies" in his congregation to see Jesus pull out his bloody, pulsating heart. "I thought that was so patronizing. . . . The little old ladies in my congregation are very sophisticated people."[43]

With regard to the kind of coaching Baran gave him, he recalled:

I was told, "Just say what's true for you. We like what we've heard, we just want you to go ahead and talk like that." We all shared a similar perspective. And there were times when I asked how it came off, and if there was a better way that I could say that. And I also took it as an opportunity to refine my communication skills, too. . . . One of the things [Josh] asked that I would say, and that was to talk about, you know—This is a free country and people have a right to see what they want to see. Which *is* my position. He wasn't asking me to say something that I didn't believe in. . . . Actually, what I always tended to do is get into the theological symbolism of the film. He didn't want me necessarily to do that. But [he laughs] I couldn't help myself.[44]

The Reverend Charles Bergstrom pursued an equally busy itinerary on the *Last Temptation* talk show circuit. Whereas Thompson in the span of a few days catapulted from obscure Baptist pastor to proponent of a major motion picture, Bergstrom already had a record of public service at a national level. After a career as pastor of Lutheran churches in New England, Bergstrom spent more than a decade as director of the Lutheran Council Office for Governmental Affairs in Washington, D.C. In 1980 he and the television producer Norman Lear cofounded the People for the American Way (PAW), an organization that championed church-state and civil liberties issues and acted to counter the growing influence of the religious right. Bergstrom was appointed chairman of the executive committee and he started traveling around the country, representing PAW in meetings and speaking engagements.

The attempt to squelch *The Last Temptation of Christ* was just the sort of issue that PAW was designed to weigh in on. Josh Baran set up a late July screening at Norman Lear's home, attended by Pollock, Van Slyke, PAW officials, and former California governor Jerry Brown, who had just spent a year in India working alongside Mother Teresa. (According to Tom Pollock, Brown liked the film so much that he said that he would contact Mother Teresa. "Well, Mother Teresa did *not* endorse the movie," said Pollock.)[45] Because of his clerical credentials, his public speaking experience, and, not least of all, the impression he gave of a kindly, older minister, Bergstrom became a sought-after defender of the film. Scarcely a day went by that he did not have a *Temptation*-related event on his calendar. Between a July 13 interview with John Dart of the *Los Angeles Times* and a guest spot on *The Oprah Winfrey Show* on August 16, Bergstrom was enlisted for thirty-eight print and broadcast interviews and other appearances.[46]

Bergstrom, like Thompson, was often matched up with such antagonists as Donald Wildmon on *The Oprah Winfrey Show* and John Stewart on KABC-FM. If Thompson found himself "caught in the crossfire" with R. L. Hymers, Bergstrom's Waterloo occurred on the August 12 *Kelly and Co.* show in Detroit, at which the leader of the Eternal Word Television Network, Mother Angelica, mercilessly upbraided Bergstrom's viewpoints on religious tolerance in front of an adoring studio audience. Bergstrom ruefully recalled the show as "the only one I felt that was kind of loaded, in terms of everybody cheered for her, [and] almost booed me, in terms of my presentation."[47] He did not receive as many negative phone calls and letters that summer as Thompson (who had to get an unlisted home number after receiving a number of harassing calls). A prominent, nationally syndicated columnist did take the time to condemn him in rather extravagant terms, however, after one of his television appearances. According to Bergstrom, the man wrote, "Your sickening, lying remarks on *The Last Temptation of Christ* make me want to puke. You are a disgrace to the cause of Christ. A perfect example of a kind of person Christ said wasn't fit even for a dung hill."[48] As it turned out, abusive language was the least of the worries faced by many of the people who spoke out for Universal and the film.

INEVITABLY, the firestorm set off by *The Last Temptation of Christ* impinged on the organizational culture of MCA/Universal. An executive involved with the project recalled, "There's no doubt that *Last Temptation* was our particular cause at that moment because there was so much surrounding it, and so much hatred of it—I liken it to being in a snow globe. When somebody shakes it up and you're standing inside of the snow globe, there's an awful lot going on. But when you're standing outside that snow globe, your world hasn't changed very much."[49] Most of MCA's employees did their jobs unfazed by the controversy. But to those standing in the snow globe—the circle of those in the theatrical film division who were working on *Last Temptation*—it was a nearly all-consuming blizzard.

Much of the initial onslaught was absorbed at the studio's portals to the public, which in this pre-Internet era were the mail room and the phone system. Early on, when the volume was still low, the complaining letters were often read and passed around among executives. Some of these individuals took satisfaction in the ones that blamed the studio for exercising bad judgment; they would show these letters to colleagues, saying, I told you we shouldn't have done this. But after the James Dobson radio show, the floodgates opened and a massive tide of letters, cards, packages, and petitions poured in unabated for the next five weeks. Sally Van Slyke kept count of the mail for at least part of this period, but the data did not survive. Dan Slusser, then the senior vice president and general manager of Universal City Studios, remembered estimates ranging from 800,000 to 5 million pieces of mail. "The best I could document was a million and it was all in a very short period of time—I'd say, in a thirty-day window."[50]

The greater number of missives, Tom Pollock recalled, "prayed for our souls, which I consider a perfectly appropriate and good Christian response. . . . Of course, a sizable percentage of them were anti-Semitic hate mail. . . . Lots of them were death threats. You know, you're going to die, you stupid ignorant Jewish scum."[51] Roger Armstrong remembers letters praying for him as well as letters damning the filmmakers and the studio. He also received more than fifty Bibles.[52] After the July deluge, no one had time to read all the letters. The overwhelming majority of them were opened, kept in cardboard boxes for four or five months, and eventually thrown in the trash. Only a small portion was set aside for response by a form letter or, more rarely, a personal reply. Parcels were X-rayed and opened only after mail room employees made judgment calls, based on packaging and distinguishing marks, that they were not dangerous.

Universal's main switchboard number, which was being announced daily on Christian radio and television and in thousands of direct-mail pieces, came under a disabling attack for a few days. The company quickly installed new lines and hired extra operators; the bulk of the *Last Temptation* calls were diverted to these "hotlines" and screened for legitimacy.[53] At first the company's executives were shielded by their direct lines, but it did not take long for protest groups to discover the extension numbers for Wasserman, Sheinberg, Pollock, and others. "We didn't want any direct calls to go to Sid or Lew or Tom," said Slusser, "so we went through a screening kind of a process and tried to set up lines that would literally take the burden off the system."[54] The calls ultimately stopped at a secretary's desk, who was instructed to take the callers' names and thank them for their concern.

Marketing alone got hundreds of *Last Temptation*–related phone calls every day, many of them asking for Sally Van Slyke by name. Occasionally, after hours, somebody would get her on the phone, and if she had time, Van Slyke would listen to his or her spiel. "Some of them," she said, "were—How could you do this? You all are going to burn in hell. . . . There were other people who wanted sincerely to discuss [the film] and wanted to know what was behind it and whatever. You know, it was a mixed bag. You couldn't be impolite because people have a right to their own opinions."[55] One day Roger Armstrong picked up the phone to hear a familiar voice on the other end of the line: "Hey, Roger, this is Don Wildmon. I'm just wondering when I'm going to be able to get a look at this picture?" Armstrong replied, "Well, I'll do the best I can, but I'm not sure that's going to happen."[56]

Call screeners and mail handlers noticed an extremist element among the thousands of phone calls and letters—an element that some at the studio labeled "lunatics," "nut cases," "religious fanatics" coming "out of the woodwork." Amounting to far less than 1 percent of the total, the messages nonetheless suggested that certain people might decide to act on their emotions and attempt to penetrate the studio and disrupt its operations, harass the executives, or, most disturbing of all, cause bodily harm. The studio's security system was better equipped to cope with these threats than it had been just a few years earlier. Until the mid-1980s, Universal was widely known as a "leaky" studio. Guards at the studio gates sometimes waved visitors through even when the authorization to issue a drive-on pass had not been received. The vulnerabilities began to be addressed with the appointment of Mike Lanzaroni, a former deputy chief of the Los Angeles Police Department with twenty-six years of law enforcement experience, as head of studio security. In short order, a new cadre of professionals—consisting largely of retired FBI and DEA agents, county sheriff's officers, and LAPD officers—was hired, communications with the gates tightened up, and a layer of supervision was put in between Universal's senior security management and Burns Security, a protective services agency that MCA had contracted with.

Still, the task of protecting the Universal City campus was daunting. Movie studios are often called an "attractive nuisance"—high-profile sites that attract intruders and mischief makers—but the characterization is particularly apt of Universal. At 413 acres of contiguous property, surrounded on all sides by the city of Los Angeles, it is the largest physical plant in the entertainment industry. (By comparison, the Disney studio lot in Burbank was only 44 acres.) The property bordered the Hollywood Freeway, Warren Boulevard, and the Los Angeles flood district overflow area, which meant that a significant length of perimeter had to be patrolled. Universal also had more access points than any other studio, with gates on Lankershim and Warren Boulevards and at the Universal Studios Tour. The theme park—the only major tourist attraction on the grounds of a studio—welcomed hundreds of thousands of visitors annually. On occasion, people jumped off the trams to shake hands with an actor or try to run into a soundstage. As Slusser put it, "Everybody in the world tries to get on [the lot]. Everybody wants to see a movie star. But at the same token, you don't want to irritate those people who have appointments such as network executives. . . . So you have to work a delicate balance."[57]

The *Last Temptation* travail put that balance to the test. In mid-July the security presence was beefed up noticeably. "There are suddenly guards here that weren't here before," one employee was quoted in *People*.[58] The tour's security force, attired in plain clothes so that the park would not feel like a fortress, was increased substantially.[59] In several of the studio's buildings, two guards were stationed on the ground floor and a guard posted on every floor above.[60] On the fourth floor of the "producer's building," where the marketing department was housed, bulletproof glass was erected at the reception desk. (A year later, security installed a windowed scenario for buzzing people into the office suite.)[61] The executive office building was buttoned up tighter than the other buildings. MCA employees going into the Tower, even those known personally to the guards, were required to show their badges.[62] Lanzaroni posted four officers on the fifteenth floor, where Wasserman, Sheinberg, Pollock, and Tom Wertheimer, the television division head, had their offices. Next to the elevator, an armed guard sat behind a bulletproof glass door and monitored people coming off the elevator. The film itself was always under surveillance. Jim Fredrick, an editor for the trailer vendor InterLink, recalled the unusual circumstances of working on *Last Temptation:* "They would not allow a print of the movie to leave the premises. So I basically had to cross picket lines. There were people protesting with placards when I went to the studio. I mean, it was in full-bloom craziness. And there was a guard outside my editing room. . . . I can tell you that has never happened before or since."[63]

Senior executives were the object of vicious threats. "It was a scary time, in all candor," said Sid Sheinberg. "It was scary not only for us, but for our children and our families. . . . Bloody pigs were delivered to my house. A dead pig delivered in a package. . . . There were pictures taken of my beach house from the top with telephoto lenses and sent in the mail, saying 'You may think we don't know where you are at all times, but we always know where you are.' And there were other kinds of intimidating things. There was some paraphernalia found in an elevator at Universal that was suspected of maybe being part of an assassination plot. And you know, you don't know what is prank, and what isn't."[64]

In another chilling incident, Mike Lanzaroni learned from the FBI special agent in charge of the Los Angeles office that the Aryan Nations, a prominent white supremacist group based in Hayden Lake, Idaho, had put Wasserman, Sheinberg, and Pollock on a list of corporate executives designated for assassination. Lanzaroni and his second in command went to Wasserman's office to lay out the nature of the threat. According to Sheinberg, they could be mysterious sorts. "A short conversation with [Lanzaroni and his deputy] can scare you pretty good," said Sheinberg. "They were always alluding to sources they had, and by the time you had finished a meeting with them, you were afraid to leave your office."[65] This time, the threat was credible: information about the alleged plot came from FBI sources who had infiltrated the Hayden Lake compound. Years earlier, the company had established "countermeasures" for protecting Wasserman and Sheinberg.[66] Perimeter intrusion detection systems were installed at their homes, and they were often driven around town by ex-police officers who were trained in evasive driving techniques and authorized to carry firearms. But the Aryan Nations threat called for more protection. For the next several weeks, bodyguards accompanied each man at home and on the studio lot. Lanzaroni himself made a series of trips to Idaho to consult with agents in the field. Ultimately, they found no evidence to indicate that the assassination plan was ever put in motion.

Below the triumvirate of Wasserman, Sheinberg, and Pollock, the executive who attracted the most attention of the rabid fringe was the studio's spokesperson, Sally Van Slyke. Van Slyke, said Slusser, "was a very active, very polished, very professional executive, and when the shit hit the fan and she started to get the threats, and they started to use her name and she became more high profile in a sense, she became very emotional."[67] Death threats addressed to her came in regularly, an anti–*Last Temptation* group tried to intimidate her secretary, and, to her horror, a writer friend on a book tour came across her name and phone number written on the wall of a public restroom in Utah. The most terrifying incident occurred in late July. One morning, a guard at the main gate saw a suspicious movement on the lawn near the Smith Barney brokerage on the first floor of the Black Tower. Approaching the area, he found two boxes, about one foot in length, lying on the grass. Inside one of the boxes was a male doll dressed in a suit, resembling Lew Wasserman, with a knife piercing the chest. The other box contained a doll with red yarn for hair, unmistakably meant to resemble Sally Van Slyke. The doll was covered with blotches that looked like dried blood and a knife was driven through the crotch. A note read, "Sally Van Slyke—This is what's going to happen to you." Both dolls were attached to crosses.

More than an hour passed before police examined the dolls, and by then, so many people had handled them that little useful information about who placed them could be determined. News about the "voodoo dolls" spread rapidly through the studio, but—like the other threats on individuals—it was kept out of the media. These intrusions into her private life infuriated Van Slyke. When Wasserman heard about the state she was in, he called and asked her to come up to his office. When she arrived, he said, "Look, I'm prepared to do anything I can to help you out of this. What do you want me to do?"

"Well, I don't know, Mr. Wasserman, do you think they're going to kill me?"

He paused and said calmly, with a hint of a smile, "Oh, probably not. I don't think they'll kill you." Wasserman, Van Slyke recalled, "did the greatest schmooze job on me, but with great sincerity. It was wonderful."[68]

Lanzaroni and Slusser came to her office and asked what they could do to give her a feeling of comfort and security. Up to that point, they had managed to sway her to their basic viewpoint, which was that the protesters were essentially unhappy Christians who were trying to voice their objections, and that she need not fear for her life. "And every time we said that," said Slusser, "an incident occurred that would change her mind."[69] After the doll episode, they equipped her apartment with motion detection sensors and alarms, and assigned two bodyguards to watch her residence and go everywhere with her on a twenty-four-hour basis.

"They came and went in shifts," she said of the bodyguards. "They answered my doors. When we went out, one of them got in the car with me. What really made me just nuts was that they had to get down on their hands and knees and look under my car before I got in. If I went to a store to buy panty hose, they were with me. . . . They were very loving and kind to me. . . . One of them made me breakfast every morning. One would put on coffee and the other one liked eggs and toast, and the two that came in the morning drove two and a half hours to get to me."[70] Several weeks later, when the bodyguards left and things returned to normal, Tom Pollock gave her a bonus for hazard duty—which, she pointed out to him at the time, wasn't nearly enough compensation for what she had gone through.[71]

After the security measures were in place, the enemy outside the studio gates became somewhat easier to monitor. The opposition within, however, posed a different set of challenges. Universal, like any large company, had a sizable contingent of Christians in its employ—not only mainline and evangelical Christians, but Jehovah's Witnesses, Seventh-day Adventists, Mormons, and devout people of other denominations. Many of these believers met on their lunch hours for Bible studies and fellowship. Their ranks swelled during the summer as Christians began to feel caught between loyalty to their employer and loyalty to their Lord. Normally they were not bothered by the movies produced by the studio, but *Last Temptation* crossed into an area that many of them considered inviolable. They also started getting blowback from their own churches. Their pastors railed against Universal from the pulpit, and friends questioned why they tacitly participated in the release of the blasphemous movie.

Most of Universal's Christian employees, even those who found the idea of the movie repugnant, stayed true to the company during the furor. Some forthrightly told their bosses that it was wrong for MCA to be backing this film. And others responded to the cross pressures they were feeling—and the inner voice of their conscience—by helping the opposition. One of the people who was keen to avail himself of these allies was Larry Poland. At first, rank-and-file Christians were wary of trusting him and Tim Penland, who were known to be cooperating with the studio on the project. Poland himself tried

Sally Van Slyke and Lew Wasserman at Universal Studios, August 1988; Van Slyke's bodyguard is in the background. (Author's collection)

to be scrupulous about the ethics of asking for information that might hurt Universal—or endanger the employees' status with the company. As he later commented: "We felt it would be a violation of our integrity and a conflict of interest for us in any way to be soliciting information about what was going on inside the company while we were in their employ. And even after we terminated our consulting relationship with Universal, even then we felt this was not good behavior to try to pry information out of [these people]. So we never did. But we didn't have to. Because they called us. . . . When they would call us with information on their own volition and say, 'I felt led by God to tell you this,' we would listen."[72]

Some of it was information of a general nature—conversations about plans to release the movie that differed from what was publicly announced; or rumors about Lew Wasserman's or Sid Sheinberg's personal reactions to the controversy; or observations of how terrorized some of the people inside the studio were feeling. They also reported on details gleaned from memoranda, purchase orders, invoices, and other hard-data sources. (Dan Slusser recalls Tom Pollock joking that the protesters seemed to know more about the film than he did.)[73] Sometimes they had no idea whether the information they were passing on would be useful. And some were fearful it might cost them their jobs.[74] But the idea that they could contribute *something* to the protest effort spurred them on, empowered them, gave them a sense of purpose that overrode everything else.

Studio management soon began to realize what was going on. By the third week of July, an "extraordinary veil of secrecy," as one put it, descended on the project.[75] Information about *The Last Temptation of Christ* was now disseminated on a need-to-know basis. Roger Armstrong recalled, "Over the last three or four weeks [before release of the film], things were really closed down tight, including me and my staff. I mean, we just sort of sat around and reacted when we were told to jump."[76] Only the departmental vice presidents—and the public relations consultant Josh Baran—participated in sessions focusing on the critical issues of media strategy, security, and release dates. Long memos virtually disappeared and the paper trails on *Last Temptation* were closely guarded. Like the rest of them, Baran took precautions: "I never faxed [my memos]. Usually they were hand-delivered, and I took the copies with me. I didn't allow them to be filed. Most of what was done was verbal in the end."[77] Many of the movie's marketing issues were translated into "corporate" decisions and kicked upstairs to Sheinberg and Wasserman. Said one of the marketing executives, "It's unusual to have Sid Sheinberg and Lew Wasserman involved in the release of a movie. But again, normally you don't have protests that are targeting all divisions of the corporate parent."[78]

The department heads also gave their employees the option of not working on the picture, without any repercussions. This policy, one of them noted, had never been adopted for any film before *Last Temptation*. Sally Van Slyke, for example, brought her staff together, including the eighty-five people under her supervision in seven field offices across the country via phone conference. "Now listen," she said, "here's the situation. I am not going to discuss with you the religious implications of this film. I am going to tell you that I stand in support of the First Amendment. I believe anybody has the right to make any film. . . . So, please understand, here's where I'm coming from. If you want to quietly come into my office, close the door, and tell me that you do not want to work or have anything to do with this film, I will honor that. Nothing will be said, and we will just keep it between ourselves."[79] During the next week, several people did come to her. Workers in other offices sought the same relief from their bosses. By this show of concern, the studio probably earned at least a modicum of goodwill from some of its Christian staff members; it may have also reduced the possibility of leaks.

Despite the polarization of opinion about the movie erupting all around them—or perhaps because of it—the majority of MCA employees in "the snow globe" rallied to the studio's side. Despite their varied feelings about the movie, they banded together to get through this trying time because, as one put it, "the Indians had surrounded the wagons."[80] The raw, bigoted attacks on Lew Wasserman, a man respected, if not revered, up and down the corporate hierarchy, only deepened the sense of solidarity. Some also got caught up in the idealism of the moment, the feeling, said a Universal publicist, Catherine Leach, "of being part of something that was happening that was, you know—the First Amendment, protecting filmmakers."[81] Invariably they took pride in MCA's stand on behalf of Martin Scorsese and all film artists.

The stress of working in the ambient noise of a full-throttle controversy wore on many in the MCA organization, and a few of them were convinced that nothing less than their professional survival or personal safety had been put at risk. Probably no one, except for Sally Van Slyke, felt pushed closer to the precipice than the man who green-lit the movie. Years later, Tom Pollock spoke about how the *Last Temptation* crisis affected him personally:

> The only time I ever felt close to losing it, losing my job, was when this movie came out and the people started personally attacking Lew Wasserman at his house. . . . And I'm thinking, What have I done to this man? And, of course, never once, never once did he say to me, How could you have done this? All I ever heard from him was, We have an obligation to back you and back this film. . . . He gets my total and undying love and support for that, because I, of course, never intended for any of that to happen to him. I'm not naive. I knew there would be some controversy about the movie. But neither I nor anybody else ever expected what happened and that it would become as personal, as anti-Semitic, and as ugly as it became.[82]

BY THE THIRD WEEK of July, Universal's marketing team and trailer vendor, Interlink, were furiously at work on the movie's advertising materials. It was decided early on to focus on an iconic image of some kind as the centerpiece of the one-sheet, or theatrical poster, since *Last Temptation* was the type of movie for which "the most important thing is to set a tone, not to tell a story or to refer to any of the publicity that's going on," said David Sameth, the creative advertising director.[83] They created a number of different looks—including one of Jesus' face bleeding through a desert scene[84]—but settled on a visually abstract piece in the style of famed graphic designer Saul Bass: a tangle of black thorns on a red background.

The same approach carried over to the theatrical trailer, usually the most important tool for generating the public's first impressions of a movie. "We tended just to sell the emotionality of it all," said the trailer's producer, Jim Fredrick, "rather than try to do a traditional trailer where you have a narrator telling you how to think and what to feel and here's what the movie's about."[85] In addition, said Fredrick, "The religious aspect of this movie was something that we didn't feel we needed to drill into the public's consciousness."[86] Certain sexually charged or brutal scenes were excluded at the outset, not only because of the likelihood that the MPAA ratings board would nix them, but also because the studio wanted to avoid any hint of inflammatory imagery. The scene of Willem Dafoe, as Christ, etching a circle in the desert sand with a stone, was used as a "grid"—that is, as a scene that the rest of the trailer kept cutting back to. The title cards were designed with the movie's "pedigree" in mind, announcing the acclaimed novel by Kazantzakis and Martin Scorsese as the director of the film. They also had the luxury early in the trailer-cutting process of being able to use pieces of Peter Gabriel's score, which lent a "hip, ethnic" quality, as Fredrick characterized it, to the two-minute montage.

"We had to produce the trailer immediately and get it out as soon as possible," recalled Sameth. As it turned out, the trailer played only in isolated instances—and exclusively in theaters owned by Cineplex Odeon—owing to the secrecy shrouding the studio's decisions about when and where the movie would open. Thirty-second television advertisements, typically the backbone of a studio film's advertising campaign, were also made, but not a single TV spot was run. "This movie was such an anomaly and so far outside of the process," commented Perry Katz, that normal rules did not apply.

In fact, the marketing of *Last Temptation* veered about as far from the model of a traditional, advertising-driven Hollywood "product" as a major studio dared to go. From the start, Universal conceived *Last Temptation* as a classically "review-driven" picture, albeit one whose controversial aspects would bring out moviegoers on a broader scale. With Tim Penland and Josh Baran activating their social networks and media contacts on the right and left ends, respectively, of the ideological spectrum, the plan was to bring multiple groups to the theater: the religious moderates and liberals who were eager to see Martin Scorsese's vision of the Christ mythology and would probably be the most willing carriers of good word of mouth; and the evangelical and fundamentalist Christians—the biggest target audience in terms of sheer numbers, but the group least likely to embrace a revisionist interpretation of their Savior.

Much of this plan had been derailed by the rush of events. Several months' worth of publicity, some of it improvised reactively, much of it spinning out of anyone's control, had already been crushed into the two weeks since July 12. Every day brought new developments on the protest front, or a statement by a political or religious figure. Yet even as the studio kept trying to shore up its position with religious constituencies and other groups, it tried to stick to elements of the original marketing plan. Earlier in the year, Tom Pollock made it known that he wanted *The Last Temptation of Christ* to be on the cover of *Time* magazine. Although Josh Baran knew it was a tall order, and certainly not something that was in his power alone to fill, it made perfect sense for this movie. "Okay, we'll get you the cover of *Time*," Baran said.[87]

Choosing a cover—including its subject matter, visuals, and caption—is one of the most important decisions a magazine editor can make. The cover is a driver of newsstand sales, which, Linda Williams noted in the *Los Angeles Times,* not only helps a magazine meet its circulation guarantees to advertisers, but also "[tells] editors what interests people in general." The covers of news magazines—especially those of the segment leader, *Time*—deliver a value that is as much cultural as commercial. A *Time* cover can stimulate vibrant public conversations and validate the social importance or political weight of a person, issue, or trend. In a typical year, no more than a half dozen *Time* covers come from the world of entertainment. Consequently, the odds of a motion picture getting on the cover of *Time* are long, and longer still if it has neither A-list stars nor a strong expectation of becoming a blockbuster. The only hope for such a movie vaulting past all of the other cover ideas vying for the editors' approval is if it is certifiably controversial—in other words, if it is emblematic of a breaking nonentertainment issue.

During one of his trips to New York, Josh Baran met with Richard Ostling, *Time*'s religion correspondent. He discovered that Ostling had already pitched a cover story to his editors about the latest scholarly investigations of the historical Jesus. The whole area was undergoing one of its periodic upheavals, driven by new archaeological finds in Israel and internecine debates about the use of scientific methodologies to sift the real Jesus from the Christ of faith.

Moreover, a group of liberal biblical scholars, calling itself the Jesus Seminar, had recently grabbed the media spotlight by conducting "votes" on the authenticity of the sayings of Jesus Christ—such as the Lord's Prayer, which, the Jesus Seminar announced later in 1988, was largely the invention of early Christians. The time was ripe, Ostling argued, for a fresh look at what these scholars and theologians were saying.

But *Time*'s editors disagreed, contending that the historical Jesus disputes were not of substantial interest. When Baran heard about the impasse, he told Ostling, "I have your hook. The movie is your hook. You can have your cover if you use this movie."[88] (Initially Baran was afraid that an earlier *Time* article about the *Last Temptation* situation, published in the July 25 issue, would "kill" the cover, but it turned out not to be a deterrent.) Ostling saw the logic of what Baran was saying: "The controversy over the movie in religious circles was a natural way to pitch a cover idea that I had failed to sell earlier."[89] The editors also saw the possibilities: the controversy clearly lent the force of urgency to issues about the identity of Jesus, while the latter provided context to the hysteria surrounding the film. They approved a cover package coupling Ostling's "Who Was Jesus?" story with a long piece by John Leo examining the movie and the unfolding controversy and a glowing review of the film by *Time*'s critic Richard Corliss. Meanwhile, Sally Van Slyke tried to cajole *Time*'s Los Angeles representative into using a movie still for the cover (reportedly, a photograph of Willem Dafoe nailed to the cross), but the magazine opted instead for a collage of classic artwork depicting Jesus.

The "Who Was Jesus?" issue was *Time*'s top-selling cover of 1988 and elicited 2,121 letters (more than two-thirds of them critical), more than double the amount of reader mail of any other issue that year, and the seventh-highest total in the magazine's history. Twenty readers expressed their disapproval of the cover story by canceling their subscriptions; one noted that "he was not going to 'meet our Lord as a subscriber to TIME.' "[90]

Another magazine cover that Universal was cooperating with was already well advanced by late July. *Premiere*'s chief editor, Susan Lyne, decided to do a big story on *Last Temptation* for its October issue, timed to the movie's projected late September release. It was going to be about the making of the film and the prerelease politics, the kind of story that *Premiere* liked to do, and for the first time in the magazine's short life, a photograph of a director would be on the cover. Lyne dispatched a staff writer, Steve Oney, to the Brill Building in May, weeks ahead of the outbreak of the controversy, to sit with Scorsese and Schoonmaker while they edited the film and engage the director in talks about the movie's long, difficult journey. The studio resisted giving Oney or anyone else from *Premiere* access to the film. "A film like this ordinarily would be the kind of movie we would have seen early," said Lyne. "I think Universal was just being exceedingly careful about not letting people see it, just hoping they could dull a little bit of the negative controversy around it."[91] Meanwhile, the magazine spent more than $100,000 for photo shoots. Oney finished his interviews with key players involved in the saga, including Donald Wildmon, and wrote the piece. "Because *Premiere* was on this long deadline," he recalled, "I had to sit and wait for the rest of the world to catch up."[92]

It was during this interval that Sally Van Slyke gave Lyne a rude shock, informing her in a phone call that Universal didn't want the cover after all. Van Slyke had just come out of a meeting with Wasserman, Sheinberg, and Pollock, and she knew that the timing of *Premiere*'s cover story was going to be off. "I would have done anything I could to back her off. . . . I knew that we were going to open before her cover was going to break. And she thought I was the biggest idiot she ever talked to. She thought, What is wrong with this woman?"[93]

The original release strategy had *Last Temptation* premiering at the New York Film Festival, then going into a limited number of urban markets before widening out to the rest of the country. An early fall release was supposed to work in the film's favor, since it would be one of the first important films to come out after the summer season; by that point, said Pollock, the entertainment press is "so tired of seeing action films that they overpraise the serious ones."[94] The major question was what kind of environment the film would confront if it opened as originally scheduled. One scenario depicted the protesters as growing steadily in skill, resources, and support. Rallies on or near the Universal lot were already taking place on an almost daily basis. By far the most effective rally leader was KKLA-FM's talk show host John Stewart, whose first rally on July 20, organized with several members of a West Covina church, drew an estimated 2,500 people—purportedly the largest demonstration against a film in the history of Hollywood to that time.[95] Just a few days later, the same coalition (soon to give itself the name Citizens for a Universal Appeal) announced a much more ambitious demonstration at Universal City. Designating August 11 as the date for the combined news conference and rally, the coalition crafted logistical plans for communications, traffic control, a sound system, and transporting people to the rally site. Another eight weeks could give them time to organize even bigger rallies. It would not be an unbroken upward slope—there would probably be miscues and miscalculations along the way—but the momentum of their rage could conceivably carry the protesters forward and keep them engaged until something dramatic happened: perhaps a series of spectacular demonstrations climaxing on the day of the movie's release, or, more to their liking, the studio's bowing to popular demands to withdraw the movie.

It also seemed plausible that the controversy was about to peak. If that was the case, the studio needed to act immediately, while public awareness of the movie was still at a phenomenal 80 percent, as reported in a poll in early August.[96] The logic of this move, said Fred Mound, was that the media attention "would probably go downhill, . . . [so] why not take advantage of it while we were at the peak of the controversy?"[97]

In a series of discussions taking place about July 24, consensus tended toward the idea of a quick release. Perry Katz summarized the key argument for showing *Last Temptation* as soon as possible: "We always felt that the best spokesperson for the film is the film. That if people would see the film, they would realize that it's not this subversive diatribe against the church. That it was in fact an act of faith on the part of the filmmaker, and that a large part of the teeth of the protest would be taken away."[98] There was also a pragmatic argument: if it was allowed to go on, the controversy would continue to sap the studio's human and physical resources.

The decisive voice in these deliberations belonged to Lew Wasserman. In Sally Van Slyke's recollection, the trigger was a comment by Pollock that he wanted to bring out 70-mm prints in certain markets, to signify that *Last Temptation* was an "event film." Wasserman, said Van Slyke, who was present at the meeting, "went on the roof and peeled himself off. He said, 'You don't think you have an event film here?' . . . I've seen a lot of people scream, but he was furious. And he said, 'Now I'm telling you, you get those prints and you get them in theaters. What is the first possible date that you can ship enough of those prints and get it open?'"[99]

Pollock convened his marketing and distribution people and asked how much time they would need to get the film into theaters. Mound recalled, "Bill [Soady] and I both said, 'We need at least fourteen days to make sure we get the right theaters set up for this thing.'"[100] Pollock then called Garth Drabinsky, chairman of Cineplex Odeon, and asked him if he could get the Ziegfeld Theater at West 54th Street in midtown Manhattan. Booking New York's biggest theater in midsummer is no simple matter, especially on short notice, and at the time the Ziegfeld was playing the year's biggest-grossing movie, *Who Framed Roger Rabbit?* During the next week, Drabinsky personally called Disney's president, Jeffrey Katzenberg, and persuaded him to end the movie's Ziegfeld run by the second week of August to make way for *Last Temptation.*

Next, Pollock called Martin Scorsese and asked him how soon he could finish the film.[101] The studio would pay whatever it took, Pollock explained; he just needed to know if it was technically possible to wrap up the "post" and finish work on the answer prints by the first week of August—about two weeks ahead of schedule. If it had been another studio head asking them to do something contrary to what they thought best for the film, the answer might have been different. But Scorsese, Barbara De Fina, and Thelma Schoonmaker were aware that the studio was under heavy attack, and Pollock had proven his mettle in numerous ways and circumstances over the past year and a half. Years later, Schoonmaker summed up their feelings about Tom Pollock at that juncture: "He deserves a great deal of credit for how he backed us up and never wavered until the very end, when he finally told us that we had to put the film out before I felt we were ready. And he said, 'You have to get it out as soon as possible.' So we completely agreed with him. But he was remarkable throughout. Just to have the courage to do it, period, you know, after all of the history."[102]

The next day Scorsese stood in a cramped booth next to one of Sound One's mixing studios, watching the crew work on the other side of the glass as he called Pollock. It could be done, he said. It meant buying more studio time, hiring more sound editors (for conforming the audio tracks to the picture edits), and paying overtime for the crew. They would have to run the cutting room and mixing studio around the clock for the next ten days—a headlong rush comparable to the last frenzied weeks of shooting in Morocco, seven months earlier. The acceleration in postproduction ended up costing Universal an additional $500,000, a major factor in pushing the total negative cost of *The Last Temptation of Christ* over $8 million. The extra expense was a minor consideration, however, compared to the mounting costs in security, the stress on the Universal staff, the neglect of the other movies on its release schedule, and potential damage to the parent company, MCA, if the entanglements with protesters continued to consume the studio's attention for another eight weeks.

Reflecting on those last days in late July and early August, Scorsese said: "I don't think any of us had ever experienced such a push to finish a film. None of us had. I remember being up almost day and night at the mixing room in the Brill Building, with Thelma and Gerry Peroni [an assistant editor]. . . . To this day Michael Ballhaus contends that the film is not really color corrected. . . . The prints that were struck were not very good. The mix was as good as we could get it. And I must say, Thelma and I looked at each other from time to time and said, We need another three months cutting. We still would have never made the New York Film Festival, but we would probably have a tighter picture. . . . I don't want to say it's a work in progress but it is as good as we could get it at that point in time."[103]

The shortening of postproduction meant that Scorsese never had time for a fine cut. With more time, said Schoonmaker, they could have "just given it a blast, a little shiver"—taking a few frames off the tail of a scene here, or trimming within a scene there, to quicken the pace.[104] It also short-circuited the normal process in which the studio holds test-screenings of a finished picture, as Universal had with Scorsese's *Cape Fear* two years later, to gauge audience reactions to characters, plot, structure, and ending. Certainly Garth Drabinsky and Tom Pollock would have been happier if more minutes had been taken off the film; but, said Scorsese, "I didn't feel any undue pressure. . . . [They were] normal concerns."[105]

Much of their effort in the stretch run was devoted to putting the finishing touches on the sound mix. Five weeks earlier, Peter Gabriel had arrived in New York with tracks he had been recording since January at his Real World Studios in Bath, England. *Last Temptation*'s score was the tonal equivalent of the film's mystical, Eastern look—a series of pulsating, brooding, soaring soundscapes. It seemed to come from a primitive, turbulent place, far from the stately hymnal sources of most Hollywood films about Christ.

Scorsese began forming his ideas about the music when he heard the venerable Moroccan band Nass El Ghiwane. The group's "traditional Moroccan songs, . . . Sufi chants and Berber poetry with hypnotic grooves," as one journalist characterized the music, even inspired him to visualize how he would design some of the scenes for *Last Temptation*. Peter Gabriel's solo work in the early 1980s, especially songs like "Biko," "Rhythm of the Heat," and "I Go Swimming," with their Middle Eastern and African influences, prompted Scorsese to ask him to compose and produce the music for the Paramount production in 1983. Scorsese was particularly taken by the layering of Gabriel's delicate vocals and synthesizer fills on top of pounding rhythms: "The drums reflected a kind of very basic, forceful humanity, you know. The flesh, in a way. And there's kind of an ethereal sound that pervaded it. . . . And those two combined together were very, very evocative for me."[106] Gabriel sampled dozens of pieces of ethnic music from the National Sound Archive in London, recorded the samples on cassettes, and sent them to Scorsese. According to Gabriel, "He'd say, 'This sounds great, this is right for this, this is right for that,' and that's how I started and picked out my palette."[107]

Gabriel took care to inform the musicians, most of whom lived and performed in Islamic countries, about the nature of the story before they agreed to work on it. Only a British boys' choir from Wells Cathedral, commissioned to sing on a track titled "With This Love–Choir," went uncredited on the film as well as on Gabriel's album of music from the film, *Passion*. Church leaders asked the filmmakers to grant anonymity to the choirboys after the bishop of Bath and Wells, the Right Reverend George Carey (later the archbishop of Canterbury), who had no direct control over the choir, began calling for a boycott of the film.

After Scorsese reported getting threatening mail at his Upper East Side brownstone, Universal added heightened security around the director and at the Sound One studio. "My assistants never really let me see exactly what it was. There were a couple [of letters] I saw. And so we had bodyguards in the

Peter Gabriel, Michael Powell, and Martin Scorsese during *Last Temptation* postproduction at the Brill Building, July 1988. (Courtesy of Thelma Schoonmaker)

mixing studio, and bodyguards at my house. And a new alarm system was put in by Universal for me."[108] Nevertheless, an esprit de corps grew in the Brill Building during the final weeks of postproduction. The sound rerecording mixer, Tom Fleischman, often led off the day by reading aloud a passage from the Bible. *Last Temptation* T-shirts were made, which many of the crew members wore proudly. Though focused on the urgent work at hand, they enjoyed the process of overdubbing voices and creating sound effects. Scorsese, said Philip Stockton, the dialogue supervisor, "gives us a list of what he wants but it's constantly being added to. . . . [At the same time,] we're free to go off and do what we want to do, and more often than not he likes it. He's always open to the ideas of those around him."[109] Scorsese blended his own voice with that of Leo Marks, the brilliant World War II cryptographer and author of the screenplay for Michael Powell's *Peeping Tom,* whose distinctively deep, velvety voice was used for Satan in the desert and last temptation scenes. Powell himself often came to the studio, bringing cakes and ice cream and cheering them on. "He was there as a real Rock of Gibraltar," said Thelma Schoonmaker.[110] The eighty-two-year-old Powell even stayed up with Scorsese, Schoonmaker, and Gabriel until dawn on the last day of the sound mix.

Of all his pictures, *The Last Temptation of Christ* was the only one Scorsese never tired of viewing. The many years of trying to get it made, the production problems he had to endure in Morocco, the ongoing attacks on his reasons for making it, and then the rush to finish it—none of this diminished how he felt about the mystery at the heart of the novel. If anything, the film's roughness honored Kazantzakis' story of the long, uncertain, but ultimately redemptive search for God, and it reminded Scorsese of a story about an Indian rug belonging to a priest. "[The priest] said, 'You like the rug.' I said, 'Yeah.' He said, 'It's made by Hopi Indians. They always leave a few stitches open to let the soul come through.' With 'The Last Temptation,' there's a lot of soul."[111]

8

The Big Wind-Up

AT 5:00 A.M. on Wednesday, August 3, Martin Scorsese delivered the final cut of *The Last Temptation of Christ* to Universal Pictures. Later that day he told Aljean Harmetz of the *New York Times* about feeling "a sense of loss and at the same time a sense of exhilaration. I anticipated opposition to the film, but not the flavor of the antagonism, not the anti-Semitism."[1]

The next morning, Universal announced that it had received Scorsese's film and would release *Last Temptation* in "select theaters in [the] U.S. and Canada" in seven days:

> Few motion pictures in recent memory have generated such heated debate, especially when so few people have actually seen the film. Rumors have proliferated; exaggerations, misconceptions, and scenes taken out of context have added fuel to the fire. Martin Scorsese believes he has made a very religious film and deplores the attacks waged by those individuals who have not seen this picture.
>
> "The best thing that can be done for 'The Last Temptation of Christ' at this time is to make it available to the American people and allow them to draw their own conclusions based on fact, not fallacy," says Tom Pollock, Chairman of the MCA Motion Picture Group. . . . Universal Pictures and Cineplex Odeon Films support Martin Scorsese's right to express his personal artistic and religious visions, and the right of individuals to decide what they will see and think.[2]

"The announcement," reported the *Los Angeles Times*, "came as a surprise strategic move in the escalating war between Universal and protesters of the fictional account of Christ's life."[3] The fallout from this bombshell was felt almost immediately in Hollywood and beyond. On August 4 *Premiere*'s editor, Susan Lyne, was on vacation in a remote area of Belize. She went downriver to make a telephone call to her office to make sure everything was on track. Her assistant broke the news that Universal was moving up the release date, which meant the film would already be in circulation for six weeks by the time *Premiere*'s October issue came out.[4] Lyne made a decision on the phone that day to drop the cover story in which she had invested so heavily and substitute a cover on the upcoming Sigourney Weaver film, *Gorillas in the Mist*. When she returned to California, Lyne called Sally Van Slyke, who had uncharacteristically fought her on the cover, and asked, "Why didn't I trust you?" Van Slyke answered, "Susan, I couldn't tell you because I was under sworn oath to keep my mouth shut."[5]

Universal's preemptive move also blindsided Christian activists, even those who had been siphoning information from sources inside the studio. Tim Penland, the Christian consultant who quit working for Universal in June, said about the early release: "What this means is that they're [Universal] fearful of the storm that's coming toward them. They're hoping to get the movie out before the storm hits."[6] Larry Poland, Penland's "shadow consultant" and a member of the ad hoc coalition of evangelical leaders, reacted angrily: "It's hard to construe this as anything but an act of aggression against so many millions of concerned people."[7] Focus on the Family mailed emergency bulletins to the managers of radio stations, warning that "very soon the name and person of Jesus Christ will be openly blasphemed 'at a theatre or drive-in near you,'" and urging them to air an audio cassette of *Last Temptation* "updates" taped by Poland and Penland.[8] The Reverend R. L. Hymers was his usual incensed self. Reached for comment about the accelerated release, he said, "My reaction to all this is—war!"[9]

The lion's share of media coverage of Christian reaction, however, focused on Jerry Falwell's press conference in the Murrow Room of the National Press Club in Washington, D.C. "This is Hollywood's darkest hour," Falwell asserted. "If we don't speak out, anything goes. . . . They'll do Mother Teresa next and then the Pope."[10] He proceeded to reveal his plans to educate millions of Americans in every available medium about the blasphemous content of the film; urge people not to see the film and "not to ever attend" any theater showing it; promote picketing of theaters around the country; and orchestrate "a massive letter writing and telephone campaign" against Lew Wasserman, Sid Sheinberg, and Tom "Pollack." "Finally, and perhaps most importantly," said Falwell, "we will urge and organize a boycott of MCA and all MCA business interests. . . . Be assured that I will work day and night during the next several months to see that it becomes unprofitable for any theater to show this film."

Falwell's advocacy of direct action came one day after the Reverend Donald Wildmon ratcheted up his own campaign. For weeks Wildmon's rhetoric had grown sharper and more confrontational, as though he had to go to extraordinary lengths to be heard above the din. On July 20, the eve of Hymers's demonstration outside Wasserman's home, Wildmon issued an ultimatum to MCA. Unless the picture was canceled by September 1, he warned in a telegram to Sid Sheinberg, "AFA will begin a boycott that will bankrupt MCA. You have my word on it." On July 25 he accused Universal of engineering the controversy for the sole purpose of selling more movie tickets. Predicting that Universal's refusal to capitulate to his demands would backfire, Wildmon quoted one of filmdom's most famous phrases: "If Universal wants to release this film, 'Go ahead, make my day.'"

Wildmon's defiant posture was producing tremendous results at the home office in Tupelo, Mississippi. AFA's barrage of "action packets" included appeals for "a financial, tax-deductible contribution to help pay the high cost of this nationwide drive to stop Universal Studios' movie *The Last Temptation of Christ.* . . . Please make your check payable to: AMERICAN FAMILY ASSOCIATION: or A.F.A. Thank you and God bless you." Cash donations poured into AFA headquarters in greater amounts than for any campaign it had ever mounted. The phones rang almost nonstop. People were calling the man who stood tall in the center of the storm, asking whom they should call, where they should picket, what else they could do to stop the anti-Christian film. Allen Wildmon, Donald's brother and AFA's associate director, remarked about the response: "We've never seen anything like this at the grass-roots level as far as people getting involved so quickly. We've had to hire 10 extra people to help us with the mail and catch the phones."[11] Donald Wildmon also marveled at the intensity of the chord they had struck. He was already wondering how he could keep the Christian community galvanized after *Last Temptation* passed from view, to fight pornography, televised violence, and all of the other, more permanent threats to the cultural security of American families.

If Christians read Universal's surprise announcement as a sign that the cause was lost, the result could be a sudden deflation of support for the most lucrative campaign in AFA's history. To avert this downturn, Donald Wildmon transformed the scope of the campaign. "History will prove me right or wrong," he said, "but my sincere belief is that this issue has transcended the movie, per se. . . . The issue is now Christian bashing by Hollywood."[12] Fighting *Last Temptation,* he was suggesting, was a way to counter the entertainment industry's wide-ranging attack on their values. And it would start by punishing any entity that supported, even indirectly, this blasphemous film.

Wildmon called for a one-year national boycott of MCA to begin immediately, focusing in particular on the output of MCA's media divisions and other retail assets. He also included any theater showing *Last Temptation* in the boycott. And, not to be outdone by Falwell, Focus on the Family, Campus Crusade for Christ, and any of the dozens of lesser lights calling for a boycott, Wildmon upped the ante. He told his constituents that they could strike a blow against MCA by voting against all Democrat candidates running for office in the fall elections. The justification for this electoral boycott was Lew Wasserman's role as a major fund-raiser for the Democratic Party, as well as the fact that Robert Strauss, former chairman of the Democratic National Committee, sat on MCA's board of directors.

With his years of experience instigating consumer resistance, Donald Wildmon surely knew that a boycott against an entire political party was impossible to pull off. In any case, it was just one more way to leverage the MCA boycott in Christian communities across the United States. With the proliferation of boycotts during the 1980s—from around twenty ongoing national boycotts when Ronald Reagan took office in 1981 to more than two hundred annually by the end of the decade[13]—there was no longer anything unusual about using tactical strikes on private companies to achieve political or social ends. Boycotts broadened out to an array of mainstream issues, and national organizations got into the act—such as the National Organization of Women's boycott of Domino's, for the pizza company's support of antiabortion causes, and the AFL-CIO's boycott against Coors Beer for its antiunion policies.

Still, it is never a simple matter to persuade people to reject products in large enough numbers to force a change in a company's behavior.[14] In particular, the use of a boycott to punish a large, diversified corporation like MCA requires enormous discipline on the part of citizen-combatants. For the boycott to work, people would have to begin paying attention to which of the hundreds of movies, television shows, and music recordings in the constantly changing media marketplace carry the Universal label. And since *The Last Temptation of Christ* was not representative of Universal's output—in other words, it wasn't part of an ongoing slate of religiously offensive films or TV programs—consumers had to be willing to deny themselves many entertainment options they ordinarily would have chosen and found pleasurable. Furthermore, following through on the MCA boycott meant identifying—and avoiding—the many MCA subsidiaries that do not carry the Universal label, such as Spencer Gifts, Motown Records, and the publishing houses G. P. Putnam's Sons, Grossett and Dunlap, Coward-McCann, and Berkley Publishing Corporation. In short, many of the factors that tend to make a boycott successful—a focus on only one or a few brands; targets that are easily identified; and changes in consumer behavior that are easily performed—were absent in the boycott called on MCA.[15]

Though a boycott of MCA may have been a quixotic notion—as was the call for MCA stockholders to sell their shares in protest, announced in a *Wall Street Journal* ad placed by Concerned Women for America—these actions kept the crisis on the front burner of media coverage and helped sustain the sense of purpose of people in all parts of the country. By the end of July, church groups and moral values organizations were busily collecting signatures in churches, grocery stores, shopping malls, and other public places. Most of these local drives freely made use of petition forms, quotes from the pirated script, and other materials supplied by AFA, Focus on the Family, Mastermedia International, and other national groups. In Louisville, Frank Simon, director of the American Coalition for Traditional Values, delivered more than eighty petitions by the third week of July to Louisville-area theaters.[16] San Antonio's Advocates for Family Values group also got an early start in its campaign to persuade Santikos Theaters, a chain controlling more than 90 percent of the city's screens, to pass on *Last Temptation*. In the Tampa Bay area, the activist David Caton drummed up opposition to the film as part of his drive to establish a Pinellas County chapter of the AFA; in Orlando the Citizens for Decency, led by the religious radio talk show host George Crossley, spearheaded a prayer vigil outside the offices of Universal Studios Florida that drew more than a thousand people. Simultaneously, the *Orlando Sentinel* invited calls from Floridians on the question of whether *Last Temptation* should be kept out of local theaters; in just two days, the newspaper took 8,548 calls favoring an embargo of the film and 4,711 calls opposing it—the biggest response in the history of the *Sentinel's* "Sound Off" feature.[17]

Some local governing bodies were taking it upon themselves to voice their displeasure in official proceedings. In late July the village board of Chicago Ridge, Illinois, voted 5–1 to formally ask area theaters not to show *Last Temptation*. That same week, the city commission of Winter Park, Florida, voted 2–2 with one abstention on a resolution calling on Universal to stop distribution of the film and local theaters to refuse to show it. Under state law, the abstention counted as an affirmative vote, and so the resolution passed on a 3–2 vote.[18] On August 9, "prodded on by dozens on onlookers," as reported by the *Orlando Sentinel,* the Titusville City Council passed a nonbinding resolution recommending that citizens not go to see *Last Temptation* and "congratulating theater owners who decide not to show it."[19] A few days later, the Melbourne, Florida, City Council followed suit. News of these groundswells of disapproval lapped up on the distant shores of Universal City, California. But the proximal target were the players on the front lines: local exhibitors and the executives of theater chains.

Universal's firewall in the exhibition arena was Cineplex Odeon. It was understood from the start that the studio's financial partner would, in the words of *Hollywood Reporter*'s Claudia Eller, "take the heat off the other circuits in the face of numerous threats being launched by religious groups to disrupt showings at theaters exhibiting the picture."[20] But as strong as Cineplex Odeon's position was in many of the nation's major markets—and, to some degree, in the Bible Belt, with locations in Tennessee, Georgia, Texas, Virginia, Florida, and the Carolinas—it operated in only twenty-one states. Universal needed the cooperation of other chains if it had any hope of *Last Temptation*'s becoming profitable. More important, after vigorously championing the rights of film artists to bring their work to the marketplace, it would be a pyrrhic victory at best if Universal could open the film only in theaters co-owned by its parent company.

The first exhibitors to succumb to the pressure were the smaller chains, especially those that did business in the South: Malco Theaters, operator of 110 screens; the Texas-based Premiere Cinemas; the Florida-based Wometco chain. A district manager for Consolidated Theaters, a chain operating 115 screens in five southeastern states, expressed a typical sentiment when he told a reporter, "If the movie has in it what they say it does, we're not going to run that garbage."[21] Contacted by a UPI reporter, a vice president of J-F Theaters, Inc., operator of more than 60 screens in the Baltimore area, said, "Right now I would say there are about 10,000 letters in my office. Does this tell you what's happening? There aren't any threats of picketing or violence in the letters, just simple requests to please not show the movie."[22] The vice president of the Greater Huntington Theater Group, a West Virginia chain, put his company's position this way: "We're not going to book the movie because the local community does not want the picture shown in the area."[23] Other exhibitors turning down *Last Temptation* included the Luxury chain, headquartered in Portland, Oregon, and Wisconsin's biggest circuit, Marcus

Theatre Corporation. Asked about its decision, a spokeswoman for Marcus said, "We have no comment on why. . . . We just aren't showing the movie."[24]

Universal's foothold in the South was further eroded by the defection of Carmike Cinemas, based in Columbus, Georgia. Known for its "Wal-Mart strategy" of setting up efficiently run locations in small and medium-size markets, Carmike had by 1988 become the nation's fifth-largest exhibitor, with 216 theaters and 670 screens in several southern states.[25] Carmike played to socially conservative tastes, and its president, Michael Patrick, wasn't about to alienate his loyal customers with a Christ-defaming movie. Patrick, according to a Universal source, was the only exhibitor to admit openly that Donald Wildmon could hurt him because of the proximity of AFA's Tupelo, Mississippi, headquarters to his theaters.[26] Another Universal executive recalls a story told about Mike Patrick driving through a southern town: "The sheriff pulled his car over. 'You're not going to play that movie, are you?' 'Well, you know, we haven't decided,' [said Patrick]. 'I wouldn't suggest you play that movie.' . . . He was very concerned about it, early on. He said in no uncertain terms that he was not going to play the movie."[27]

Universal had no illusions about where the priorities of theater operators lay. Although some operators took umbrage at the protesters' goals and methods, most of them did not consider it to be their responsibility to take a stand for artistic expression or religious pluralism. They leaned far closer to the opinion of Jack Valenti, who believed "any cinema artist ought to have the right to make any film that he chooses to make. By the same token, I'm very protective of the right of a theater owner not to play a picture he doesn't think is suitable for his neighborhood. I don't find that censorship. . . . Because the fact you make a film doesn't mean that you have an absolute right to force everyone to show it."[28] Generally, the exhibitors' greatest concern was the effect of *Last Temptation* on their long-range business planning. They were also concerned about the short-term disruptions that picketing at their theaters would cause. Universal soon realized that it was unrealistic and counterproductive to expect theater owners to play *The Last Temptation of Christ* at every location; instead, the studio simply hoped that they would decide on a case-by-case basis where the movie might play. Tom Pollock's message to the recalcitrant ones was, "Don't turn on the movie, [because if you do] you're turning on Universal. We have to back the movie, and you have to back us. . . . So, do not say you're never going to play this movie. Simply agree not to play the movie in any community where you feel that you're not being a good neighbor in the community."[29]

Despite the pleas to stick together, some owners did turn on the studio. On August 6 James Edwards III, president of the Edwards Cinemas of Newport Beach, California, a chain that owned half of the 189 screens in Orange County and another 60 screens elsewhere in California, announced that *Last Temptation* would not play at any of his locations. Edwards told the *Orange County Register,* "We made a decision some time ago [that] . . . as a businessman wanting to be responsive to our patrons and also as a Christian myself, we won't show a film that is in any way denigrating to the image of Jesus Christ."[30] It was reportedly the first time that the company had refused to book a studio film without screening it first. Evidencing astonishment at Edwards's decision, Universal's Bill Soady was quoted in the *Register* as saying, "I don't know how he can make that statement that he won't show a film that is denigrating to the image of Jesus Christ without seeing it. . . . Theater owners generally make decisions on what pictures they are going to play after they see them. That's part of their job."[31]

Another Southern California exhibitor that broke with Universal was Metropolitan Theaters. In the early going, Metropolitan's president, Bruce Corwin, told the *Hollywood Reporter,* "We want to see the picture and are not going to make any judgments on its content or whether or not we'll play it until after we screen the film."[32] Subsequently, Corwin declined to play the film at any of the circuit's nearly eighty screens. Universal was particularly upset at being shut out of Palm Springs and Santa Barbara, which the studio considered to be important markets for *Last Temptation.* Lew Wasserman did not easily forget slights like this. When Corwin gave out season passes in 1989 to his theaters, as he traditionally did for Universal executives, Wasserman, who had a residence in Palm Springs, refused to accept the gift. Wasserman, said a Universal executive familiar with the situation, "wrote Bruce a very curt note, nothing nasty, but just very short and curt, to the point, and returned the pass to him. He refused to accept it because [Corwin] would not play this picture [*Last Temptation*]."[33]

One of the studio's problems in lining up commitments to play *The Last Temptation of Christ* was the abnormal timing of its trade screenings. Ordinarily, these screenings are held anywhere from two to eight weeks before release; in addition, more than twenty states prohibit the practice of "blind bidding," thus requiring distributors to make a completed film available for viewing before a licensing agreement can be awarded. But trade screenings for *Last Temptation* took place only days before it opened, forcing a drastically telescoped time frame in which film buyers had to decide whether to bid on it. Several exhibitors who were desperate to find out something about the film heard that Fred Mound had seen it. He started getting their calls. "My general reaction, and Tom [Pollock] and I discussed this, was, 'I'd rather wait and let you see it yourself. I don't want to judge what I'm going to tell you.' So they then took that as a warning from me, which they shouldn't have, because I wasn't trying to warn them. . . . It's just a difficult picture to describe. . . . The primary thing exhibitors are interested [in knowing is] what kind of business will it do. And I didn't know what kind of business this picture was going to do, and I don't think anybody did at the time."[34]

When the challenges of booking a first-run theater became insurmountable, Universal was often left with no options except to negotiate with an independently owned theater. In most cases, these were "art houses" that normally booked specialty, classic, and foreign films. A senior distribution executive recalled, "Some people played it because they owed me or Universal favors. Some people played it because they weren't normally getting first-run product, and this might be an opportunity to place their theater into a longer-term relationship, or to show what kind of gross they can get in this specific theater."[35] Ultimately, *Last Temptation* ended up on independent theater screens in many of the biggest markets, including Philadelphia (the Ritz Five), Pittsburgh (King's Court Theater), St. Louis (the Avalon Theater), Kansas City (the Granada Theatre), New Orleans (the Prytania), Columbus, Ohio (the Drexel), and Memphis (the Fare 4 Theater).

One of the most important exhibitors to Universal was the nation's largest, United Artists Theater Circuit (UA), with 2,549 screens. The day before Universal's early release announcement, UA's president and CEO, Stewart Blair, informed the *Hollywood Reporter* that he would take the unusual step of personally screening the picture ("I've never done it before"), and he pointedly discounted the threats of ideologically motivated groups, and "picketing or nonsense like that," as a legitimate reason for refusing clearance.[36] Other chief executives also resented being the object of pressure tactics; two of them, Stan Durwood of American Multi-Cinema Entertainment (AMC) and National Amusements' Sumner Redstone, privately told Universal's executives that no one was going to tell them where, or where not, to play the picture.[37] Eventually, after viewing the film and gauging the post-release public reaction, most of the major chains—United Artists Communications, National Amusements, USA Cinemas, AMC Entertainment, and the Mann's Theater circuit—agreed to play *Last Temptation* at selected locations. According to Mound, AMC, the nation's second-largest chain, "bailed us out in a number of markets, and they extracted a price for it, and, you know, in retrospect they deserved to extract a price from us for it because they came under a lot of criticism."[38]

Another key circuit was General Cinema Corporation, the nation's third-largest and operator of 1,339 screens in thirty-two states. Universal recognized early on that General Cinema would be a difficult case. Cardinal Bernard Law of the archdiocese of Boston, where General Cinema's headquarters was located, supported a boycott of the film, and company officials were disturbed at the strongly negative response being registered at its regional offices. Universal put on a full-court press. Soady, Mound, and even Sid Sheinberg placed calls to General Cinema's president, Paul Del Rossi, on an almost daily basis. "The idea," said Mound, "was not to make him go against what he would have personally thought or believed"—Del Rossi was a Roman Catholic and disliked the film—"but in the markets where he had been a customer of ours, and we had serviced him, we felt that he was now deserting the company that supported his company. . . . But we couldn't bend him."[39] On August 10, after its top executives screened the film, General Cinema announced that it would not play *Last Temptation* at any of its venues.[40] The company never commented officially on the reasons, but according to sources at Universal, Del Rossi insisted that his own religious convictions did not enter into the decision.

General Cinema's defection rankled Tom Pollock a great deal. "It wasn't the only circuit [they expended effort on trying to keep], but it was the main one that really bothered us," said Mound.[41] Years later, Fred Mound was cleaning out his files at home and came across a letter Del Rossi wrote on the occasion of Mound's retirement from the presidency of distribution at Universal. In the letter Del Rossi warmly thanked him for their years of working together, despite the occasional disagreement—and in parenthesis, he wrote, "('Last Temptation of Christ')." Mound called Del Rossi that day and said he was going to have the letter framed. Referring to the *Last Temptation* episode, Mound said to his friend, "You know, you were wrong, don't you, Paul?" Del Rossi simply said, "Nope."[42]

UNTIL EARLY AUGUST, most of Josh Baran's waking hours had been consumed with using Universal's superior advantages in media relations (and pulling the strings in his own spheres of influence) to shape the terrain of national opinion about *Last Temptation*. With the movie's release date locked, he could leave most of the publicity tasks in the hands of the three staff members at Josh Baran and Associates who worked full-time on *Last Temptation* (augmented by several temp workers hired for the project). Now, as opening weekend approached, the climate of intimidation surrounding *The Last Temptation of Christ* was in full bloom. In a number of communities where the film was expected to open, battle lines were being drawn—and the lines ran right through the middle of movie theaters.

Baran was adamant that no theater would be shut down and no showing canceled because of these difficulties. It became his personal mission to prevent the "reactionary right" from encroaching on an open society: "[The movie's opponents] will not shut down one screen. Not one theater, ever. If they don't like it, they don't have to pay any money for it. They can picket. But they don't shut [it] down, they don't stop a film being seen by someone who wants to see it. I'm an absolutist about it. . . . When we shifted into the release of the film, that was my job: Not one showing should be canceled because of these people. Not one showing. . . . And we're going to hold those theaters. I was in a war and I was not going to lose it to those people."[43]

Increasingly he worried that "those people" would come directly out of the pro-life movement, since the movie's release coincided with Operation Rescue's own turn in the media spotlight that summer. Led by its charismatic, media-savvy director, Randall Terry, Operation Rescue activists descended on Atlanta during the Democratic National Convention and laid siege to abortion clinics over a period of weeks, and hundreds were arrested.[44] Operation Rescue and other antiabortion groups tapped a militant core of Christians who were willing to take direct action for a righteous cause. The techniques used by these activists—such as human blockades of clinic entrances and aggressive "sidewalk counseling" of pregnant women—had the potential, if adapted to the site of the movie theater, to disrupt the flow of business and frighten away moviegoers. Baran also feared that radical antiabortionists could go well beyond passive acts of civil disobedience. By the mid-1980s, clinics had been invaded and vandalized on a number of occasions. The 1984 bombings of the National Abortion League headquarters in Washington, D.C., and Planned Parenthood and abortion clinics in Maryland served notice of the lengths these extremists would go to achieve their ends.[45]

If Universal had any doubts that similar assaults could happen at *Last Temptation* showings, they were dispelled on August 6, when Hymers brought about one hundred of his followers to a spot outside the Wilshire Boulevard Temple, in the mistaken belief that Lew Wasserman worshiped there. He set up an eight-by-ten-foot movie screen displaying the words "Sex Scene," in reference to the sequence in the movie in which Christ makes love with Mary

Magdalene. Predicting that the film's release would "cause damage to theaters and to the owners of theaters"[46] unless the scene was edited out, Hymers took a can of red spray paint and drew a large "X" across the screen. He then slashed the screen with a box cutter. It was both a warning and, in the words of a Baran staffer, a "show and tell" of how to vandalize theaters.[47] "If [MCA executives are] going to leave the sex scene during the dream sequence in," Hymers said to print and television reporters, "they can probably expect violence."[48]

The only recent point of comparison to the dangers facing *The Last Temptation of Christ* were the outbreaks of violence that sometimes accompanied the exhibition of "urban action" films. The February 1979 release of the gang warfare movie *The Warriors* was marred by fatal attacks on teenagers in three separate incidents, which prompted several theaters to pull the movie and others to hire security guards.[49] Street fights involving hundreds of young people followed Long Island, New York, showings of the rap music film *Kush Groove* in 1985,[50] and in April 1988—not long before *Last Temptation*'s release—a suspected gang member shot and killed a Stockton, California, teen who was standing in line to see *Colors,* a film depicting two Los Angeles cops who engage in battles with neighborhood gangs.[51]

But the applicability of these cases to *Last Temptation* is tenuous. The violence erupting at a gang movie is usually triggered by the kinds of people it attracts and the spontaneous combustibility of situations outside theaters. In contrast, the hostility surrounding *Last Temptation* was being channeled toward the theaters themselves, and if a catastrophic event were to happen, it was likely to be the result of careful planning.

"Universal's expectations," recalled Dennis Walto, who worked closely with Baran on the film's crisis management, "were nothing short of a true 'apocalypse-now' scenario at theaters across the country. . . . We were hoping for just massive protest in the best of scenarios. The worst scenarios involved mass casualty incidents, theater damage, and confrontational violence."[52] They quickly realized it would be irresponsible for the studio not to pay the price—no matter what the price turned out to be—to ensure that moviegoers were not put in harm's way. As one executive put it, "We didn't want to have anything that, for lack of a few dollars for hiring security, would come back on us."[53]

MCA/Universal was embarking on the most security-conscious opening of any movie in American history. It proved to be a complex—and very expensive—undertaking. Before *Last Temptation* opened in a market, the studio would alert the police department about inspecting the theaters' entrances and exits for malicious activity and investigating credible threats received by the theater staff. Universal assumed responsibility for what happened on theater property. Security guards protected the print of the film every step of the way. They conducted sweeps of the theaters before daily showings began—sometimes with bomb-sniffing dogs—and checked moviegoers for weapons and other dangerous objects as they entered. They cordoned off areas for protesters to hold their demonstrations, thus providing customers with safe, unmolested passage from the parking lot to the theater. The studio also indemnified theaters against any property damage or legal costs attributable to *Last Temptation.*

For some of the openings, Universal and Cineplex Odeon contracted with Intercon Security, Ltd., the largest Canadian-owned security firm. At other locations, theaters hired their own security forces, usually off-duty policemen, and billed Universal for the cost. On the basis of information supplied by Universal's regional field offices about the expected turnout of protesters, the studio came up with estimates of how much security was needed for an opening weekend. Nevertheless, the studio discovered that spending on security was virtually impossible to predict or control. "If we found after the first couple of days that we needed to beef up security," said Fred Mound, "we did it immediately and the security costs [were] just astronomical. I can recall areas where we did a tremendous gross . . . and we didn't make a penny because security just ate us alive."[54] The theater owners sometimes haggled over the number of guards. Mound recalled, "What they wanted was a security guard every twenty feet, because they said the [protesters] were harassing the people standing in line, which we thought was ridiculous. We finally compromised with a security guard every fifty feet."[55] The studio also suspected some of the owners of trying to make a profit off the security by charging Universal for more guards than they were actually hiring.

Even when attendance dropped off sharply, usually after the first week or two, Universal did not pull all the guards. Everyone feared a lone terrorist lying low, waiting for a theater to relax its vigilance. In all, the security costs for *Last Temptation* came to nearly a million dollars. "It wasn't a budgetary item," said Pollock. "You simply spent what was necessary when there was a crisis going on and you stopped when it was over."[56]

It soon became apparent that just dropping security into the midst of an inflamed movie opening would not solve all the problems. This movie, after all, had been the object of escalating, almost nonstop vilification by church leaders, radio and television personalities, and moral values defenders. With the encouragement of the likes of Donald Wildmon, James Dobson, and Pat Buchanan, many people had begun to think of *The Last Temptation of Christ* as a stalking horse for the entertainment industry's grand designs for changing the core values of their culture. For those on the other side of the ideological divide, the abuse heaped on the film symbolized everything that was wrong with the self-appointed censors of the Christian right. It was one thing for these camps to square off against each other in the relatively safe confines of newspaper op-ed pages or radio talk shows. It was quite another for theater managers and security officers—few of whom were skilled in crowd control or conflict resolution—to cope with physical confrontations in front of a multiplex. "The theater chains were *incredibly* worried about this," Baran recalled. "Some of them didn't want to take the movie, but if they did, they really wanted Universal to say, 'We will protect you, we'll take care of this.' "[57]

For months Baran had contemplated various ideas for "taking care" of besieged theaters. As the prospect of disruptive acts came sharply into focus, he settled on the idea of deploying a *field crisis team*—a team of people who could "hit the ground running" without a lot of guidance or supervision; people with a mania for detail work; people who knew how to deal with a crisis; people who had the skills to negotiate with all the parties contending to be heard and seen upon *Last Temptation*'s arrival; people who would appreciate Universal's desire that the security effort not create the appearance of a fortress or dampen the public's eagerness to see the film.

"This was a new model," said Baran. "This had never been done before. Because normally what happens is, the studio distributes the movie, it's the theater's responsibility to sell [it], and if anything happens, it's their problem. . . . But it takes a special effort, special people that have the know-how to [manage a volatile situation.] . . . So, we basically created a new model for a kind of corporate studio responsibility in terms of controversial product."[58]

Who were these "special people"? Early in his public relations career, Josh Baran had become aware of the existence of a species of political operatives called advance teams—the people who go out ahead of a candidate, oversee all the preparations for an event, and then, on the day of the event, make sure everything goes off as planned. One practitioner has defined it this way: "Advance is moving people through events that advance creates." The statement is a tautology, but it captures the idea that advance people design a ritual structure that allows social actors to play their parts naturally and convincingly. Building and shaping crowds, organizing motorcades, handling the media, making peace with local politicos, and guiding candidates through a visit are among the nearly endless tasks of advance. Many advance people, especially those who work at the presidential level, are adept at orchestrating the visual symbolism of events. They know how to create backdrops, how to light a set, how to figure out camera sight lines, how to choose the props and the "cast" surrounding a candidate. Crucially, they also have ways of dealing with protesters or anything else that threatens to disrupt an event. And through it all, advance people remain silent and invisible. Even the fact that the event has been "advanced" is typically off the record. "We're not supposed to exist," said Robin Schepper, an advance woman who worked on *Last Temptation*. "Things are just supposed to happen. They're supposed to look like they happened by themselves."[59]

Baran's first choice for the job of heading up the field crisis team was tracked down in Denver. But he needed someone who lived in Los Angeles or could relocate there temporarily. Baran's Denver acquaintance referred him to a more "geographically desirable" advance man, Dennis Walto. Walto had in fact only recently moved into a Venice Beach apartment a hundred yards or so from Baran's office on Pacific Street. After receiving the call, he put on long pants and walked down the road to see Baran. Walto recalled, "My knowledge of *The Last Temptation of Christ* was limited to one or two newspaper articles. . . . Following my first meeting with Josh, I became a *Temptation* expert. We immediately drafted a concept paper on how to use advance people in opening *Last Temptation*. It was essentially Josh's idea. I just needed to 'tangibilize' the concept, and make it happen."[60]

Few people were better qualified than Dennis Walto to "tangibilize" the idea. In little more than four years he had become, in the words of a colleague, "one of the great advance men of his generation"[61]—an intelligent, resourceful, fast-responding operative. He got his start in late 1983 as a twenty-four-year-old volunteer for Senator Gary Hart's insurgent campaign for the Democratic presidential nomination, handing out leaflets on snowy New Hampshire streets and helping organize Hart's appearances. After Hart's surprise victory, Walto got swept up in the rapidly expanding campaign and was swiftly promoted to the national advance team. In the years until the next election cycle, he found steady employment as an organizer for nonprofit causes; his first intensive experience with Josh Baran came when Baran hired him to be the media operations manager at the Farm Aid III concert in 1987. Walto had stayed closely associated with Hart, becoming his personal aide and one-person advance team in early 1988, when the senator's second presidential campaign briefly restarted following revelations of his affair with Donna Rice. Later that spring Walto joined Jesse Jackson's campaign as it wound through Michigan. He discovered that to perform well in the chaotic Jackson campaign, he had to be at the top of his game. "Although we were hired to do 'advance' for Reverend Jackson, we found that working with the Jackson campaign was more a training ground for what we came to call 'simultaneous.' This meant just going into a 'situation' and turning it into an 'event.' To the Jackson campaign, crisis management was a way of life." In time, Walto realized that steering *Last Temptation* through its first difficult openings was again doing "simultaneous"—only now for money.[62]

Walto's first order of business was to recruit members of the field crisis team. Partly because of the hiatus in campaign activity between the end of the Democratic convention and the start of the general election, it was easier to lure them than might otherwise have been the case. Part of the appeal, too, was the change of scenery the assignment offered. "Having just finished [Jesse] Jackson, just finished the convention, I was actually kind of relieved to have the chance to do something a little bit different," said Laura Quinn.[63] But other motivations were at play. Baran asked for, and got, substantial budgetary leeway from Universal for the "special effort." Compared to the $100 a day that advance people typically made on the campaign trail, they were paid $2,000 a week, plus per diem, to work on the movie. Advancing *Last Temptation*, noted one team member, Kevin Sites, was "a very good-paying gig . . . and it appealed to our sense of financial survivability."[64] Several of them were glad to have a reason to opt out of working for Michael Dukakis, who was considered an inept and uninspiring nominee. The job's ideological implications were a secondary factor, albeit one that resonated for some. All the team members were affiliated with the Democratic Party and more than a few had worked for progressive causes opposed by the religious right. One of the advance people, Steve Rabinowitz, summarized the group's viewpoint: "If [*Last Temptation*] had offended any of our personal or religious sensibilities, I'm sure people wouldn't have done it. But the fact that it pissed people off that we other times found as political antagonists of ours was just a bonus."[65]

Walto was not unaware of the potential dangers and knew that his cohorts could be risking their lives for a film. He addressed this issue with each person who went on the road; none of them, he said, "freaked out or refused to go."[66] It was perhaps less a manifesting of courage than just the routine attitude of young, single people who lived adventurously from one gig to the next. Robin Schepper, already in her early twenties a veteran of several campaigns, said of the nomadic lifestyle, "You travel with your pocket knife, your duct tape, your XLR cable, and then your clothes."[67] They were accustomed to working in the cauldron of partisan politics, and other than the fact that they would be advancing a movie instead of a candidate, many of them saw little that was new in what was being asked of them. That perception would change for those who ventured into the hottest spots of *Last Temptation*'s tour through the country.

In the interest of getting everyone "on the same page," Josh Baran set up a two-day briefing at the Universal Sheraton. While he and his assistant, Shana Weiss, were busy with the preparations for the briefing, Dennis Walto hit the phones. "It was no difficulty to gather twelve high quality advance people at twenty four hours notice to come to L.A. for a meeting," he recalled. "That's the nature of advance work. It's not 'keep your bag packed,' it's just be ready to move."[68] Most of the recruits flew into Los Angeles on the evening of August 5. They were pleasantly surprised to find that Universal had dispatched limousines to pick them up; said one, "Frankly, we weren't flattered so much as we appreciated that the studio obviously gave a shit, that they were trying to do the right thing by us, even if it was standard procedure for them."[69] After checking into the hotel and dining together in a banquet room, they filed into a screening room to have their first look at the movie. The reactions were mixed. Some criticized the movie's length and plodding pace; others expressed admiration for what Scorsese had done. "What we saw didn't seem to be offensive," said Elizabeth Stevenson. "I didn't see what the problem was. But, you know, I could see where other people could have a problem."[70]

The next morning they convened in one of the hotel's conference rooms. A big U-shaped table occupied the center of the room. The advance people sat on the long sides of the U, and Josh Baran, who moderated the meeting, sat at the head of the table. Several Universal executives had walked over from the studio lot, and representatives from Universal's regional field offices took seats behind the table. "The feeling I got," recalled one of the advance people, "and I don't know if it's true or not—but they just didn't know what to make of us."[71] Dennis Walto spoke first, then had all of them introduce themselves and say something about their backgrounds. As the introductions went around the table, the advance people began naming the high schools they had attended. Everyone laughed as it became evident that about half of them had gone to Catholic schools—Sacred Heart, St. Ignatius, and so forth.

When it came her turn to speak, Sally Van Slyke could not resist asking a question that was undoubtedly on the minds of other studio officials. "But what is it that you *really* do?" The room fell quiet for a moment. One of the advance people, John Toohey, then looked at his friends around the table and deadpanned, "Well, we'd tell you, but then we would have to kill you."[72]

"And that broke the place up," said Walto. "After that, it was just kind of assumed that we knew what we were doing. You know, we had the résumés, we had been in these situations before."[73]

The mandate of the field crisis team was simple in conceptualization: they were to go into a city and work with theater managers, news media, local law enforcement, and any groups that were organizing protests against the film. The advance person would be the liaison, the interface, the calm person at the center, coordinating with all the parties that had a stake in the film's opening. Baran stressed the importance of managing the emotional temperatures of everyone: to allay the fears of theater managers about the heightened security; to give direction to the off-duty police; and to preserve the people's right to demonstrate near the theater. Above all, Universal wanted a safe environment for moviegoers. If a critical situation did arise, the studio wanted to be assured, in John Toohey's words, that there was "somebody on the ground who could take the crisis and, one, dissolve it, and two, put the best face on it, without [that person] becoming the story. Which is really what we've been sort of *bred* to do, for lack of a better word."[74]

If the idea seemed simple, its execution promised to be far more nuanced. The studio's executives wanted the film eased into markets without a lot of fanfare, but they also made it clear that they stood behind the movie and felt there was nothing to apologize for. What they wished to avoid was a situation in which *Last Temptation* would be met with a very unbalanced set of critiques. Indeed, said Laura Quinn, "They thought their best defense against most of the criticism was to get more people in to see the film. And, you know, getting more people in to see the film was good for ticket sales."[75] Accordingly, one of their jobs was to prescreen the film for religious leaders in selected markets—essentially, local versions of the July 12 New York screening—as a way of defusing dangerously speculative talk and making sure the film got a fair shake.

The advance people understood that they would be dealing with unhappy people, some of whom might be in a state of panic about the film's arrival. They were advised to monitor the theater staff, especially devout Christians whose loyalty could not be taken for granted. They ran through a variety of the hypothetical situations, such as the employees calling in sick on opening day, or an in-house sabotage of the projection equipment. "A big issue was the safety of the film," said one of the advance people. "You know, when it's delivered and when it's sent to different cities. . . . You know, the film is like the candidate. It comes on an airplane, and you make sure it gets to the right place."[76]

Interactions with the media were a delicate issue. It was the advance person's job to link up reporters with the religious leaders who saw the movie; at the same time, the media were not to be trusted with confidential information about the movie. The advance people were expected to help facilitate media coverage at the theaters, but were not to be quoted as Universal spokespeople. The "special effort" itself had to remain a secret. During lunch, someone from the studio told the group not to discuss it with anyone, even their closest friends. Robin Schepper recalled, "All of us kind of looked at each other and laughed and said, 'These *are* our closest friends.'"[77]

The rest of the day was filled with seminars and breakout sessions. The advance people practiced "talking points" to use with the press for different kinds of situations. They were shown videotape of the Reverend Hymers demonstrating how to spray paint and slash a movie screen. It made a big impression on them. At one point in the afternoon's proceedings, Cineplex Odeon's Garth Drabinsky was introduced by conference call from Toronto. Drabinsky addressed the group from an AT&T Merlin speakerphone sitting on the table, giving what one of them called "a bit of a pep talk . . . a kind of a rah-rah, we're-counting-on-you, go-get-'em talk."[78] Although Drabinsky acknowledged that they were doing important work for the film and the cause of freedom of speech, the advance people noticed a dismissive tone. "I got the impression that he kind of thought the whole worry was overblown. He didn't seem particularly worried about it," said one of them.[79]

Josh Baran was taken aback by Drabinsky's implication that there would not be serious problems. "Garth," he said loudly at the speakerphone, "let me go over who's attacking the film, and let me explain the last two years in terms of abortion clinics." He recited the statistics on abortion clinic attacks and reminded Drabinsky about the volume of letters received at the studio, the bodyguards placed with Universal executives, and the threats on theater chains. "This film is hugely controversial," Baran continued. "The theaters *will* be attacked. And we're going to do this. We *have* to do this!"

It was obvious they had more work to do to convince Drabinsky of the value of the "special effort." Two days later, Walto flew to Toronto to personally discuss the crisis team operation with the Cineplex Odeon leadership and the security firm Intercon.

By the end of the briefing, some of the advance people detected the slightest of openings for them to practice the sort of "soft-hand manipulation" they knew from the campaign trail. There was clearly a fine line to walk, but if they could contain the more volatile elements, what could be the harm of manipulating the scene in ways that might benefit the movie? As Dennis Walto noted, "Who better to manage a crisis than someone who can create a crisis? Or better yet, who better to spin a situation into a crisis and come out with an event worthy of news coverage? Why, advance people, of course. And while we were all on our best behavior for the first couple of weeks [of the movie's release], once the team became indoctrinated into the issue, we carefully manipulated situations into events. No one had to ask or even imply, it's what we do."[80] "The more exposure the film got through these protests," a member of the team said, without irony, "obviously, the better it was for our client."[81] In the coming weeks, as they got a feel for the controversy, some members of the team did manipulate it in the manner they knew. Universal did not ask them to do this, but they surmised that the studio would not be displeased if it did happen—so long as their names stayed out of the news.

By the time the briefing ended, the advance people readily grasped how their expertise would transfer to the challenge of opening the movie; the field crisis model seemed an eminently logical model to apply, almost "second nature" to them. The next day, Sunday, August 7, Walto gave the team members their opening weekend assignments. They picked up their plane tickets and rolled out of Los Angeles that evening.

ON MONDAY, August 8, Universal and Cineplex Odeon announced that *The Last Temptation of Christ* would open Friday at nine theaters owned by Cineplex Odeon: the Ziegfeld Theater in New York; the Biograph in Chicago; the Place du Canada in Montreal; the Cooper 2 Theatre in Minneapolis; the Cinerama in Seattle; the North Point in San Francisco; the York in Toronto; the Wisconsin Avenue multiplex in Washington, D.C.; and in Los Angeles, the Century Plaza Cinemas (chosen instead of Cineplex Odeon's Universal City venue, owing to security considerations). Over the previous weekend, the MPAA ratings board had assigned it the "R" classification, primarily for scenes of frontal nudity, simulated sex, and graphic violence. It was the first motion picture about Jesus Christ to receive an R rating.

The studio's disclosure set off a rush of activity on all fronts. Universal began making arrangements to screen it for exhibitors, critics, and religious leaders. After months of maintaining a shroud of secrecy, the *Washington Post* reported, "Universal has cautiously gone on the offensive, showing the film over the weekend, and for a couple of days early this week . . . holding virtually nonstop screenings from 10 in the morning until almost 11 at night."[82] Those who were invited had to give the names of their guests to security guards—"an unprecedented step for large-scale preview screenings." Canadian film critics were shown *Last Temptation* at the Toronto offices of Cineplex Odeon, with security guards stationed outside the locked doors of the room. The screenings for New York critics happened to take place at a building with the address of 666 Fifth Avenue. Universal's publicity executive Roger Armstrong recalled this detail with bemusement: "Like, we needed that. Could be at 656? Nope, we're at 666."[83] At one of the evening showings, the sound system failed. The next day Scorsese told *Newsday,* "I'm suspicious about that projector breaking down"; it seemed all too reminiscent of the mysterious power failure at the July 12 screening.[84]

Universal was particularly interested in accommodating the representatives of church organizations, many of whom had been requesting information from the studio for weeks, usually to no avail. Larry Braidfoot, general counsel of the Southern Baptist Life Commission, was one such frustrated church official. Since June 26 he had placed two telephone calls and sent ten letters, including two express-mail packages, to Universal offices and received no response. In one recent letter to the studio, he referred to the groups advocating a comprehensive boycott of MCA and noted, "It is entirely possible that this office might issue such a call to our 15 million members. . . . We want to be very cautious in doing so."[85] A screening of *Last Temptation,* he wrote, "would assist us in forming opinions objectively on the basis of firsthand viewing rather than on inferences from an original script or secondhand reporting." Then, on August 5, a spokesperson for Sally Van Slyke contacted the Southern Baptist leaders to confirm that Universal would honor their long-standing request: "They will be shown the final print, exactly what will be shown in theaters. . . . [The purpose of the screening] is not to determine whether we will release the film. That has already been determined. The screening is set up to give them a firsthand opportunity to see the film."[86]

Six days later, Braidfoot attended a screening with two colleagues in Washington, D.C. Although Braidfoot was troubled by the film's treatment of women, the role of Judas, and Jesus' indecisive demeanor, he told his fellow Baptists that some of the most egregiously offensive parts of the bootlegged script were not in the film.[87] Reports such as Braidfoot's assisted Universal's goal of getting information about the film's actual content disseminated as rapidly as possible so as to let some of the steam out of the forces mobilizing against the picture.

The screenings also gave Universal the satisfaction of turning away two of its most vocal detractors, Wildmon and Falwell. In a letter to Wildmon that it released to the media, the studio said it was denying him admission to a private screening "because you have chosen to speak out against M.C.A. Inc. and Universal Pictures with regard to the film without seeing it, and because you rejected our earlier offer to see the film on July 12."[88]

On Tuesday, August 9, the Roman Catholic Church weighed in with its judgment. An eighteen-member board of the U.S. Catholic Conference communications committee issued the "O" rating (for "morally offensive") in consideration of the film's graphic violence, sexually explicit scenes, nudity, and deviations from Catholic orthodoxy. The board also passed judgment on the film's artistic merits, criticizing its "muddled script, shallow characterizations and flat dialogue."[89] The council's action was not unexpected. Ever since Roger Mahony had commented disapprovingly about *Last Temptation* in July, the studio regarded the "O" rating as a foregone conclusion. The committee chairman, Bishop Anthony G. Bosco, however, went beyond normal protocol. Bosco issued his own toughly worded memo with the apparent motive of giving church officials additional "talking points" for publicly addressing the film. In one passage from the memo, he wrote, "Mr. Scorsese has indicated that he tried to depict Christ as a loving Savior. There is precious little love in this film. . . . I looked in vain for the message of love. Scorsese has given us an angry Christ, a bumbling Christ, a Christ more of this world than the next."[90]

Roman Catholic leaders across the country clarified their positions on the film during the next three days, most of them falling in line behind the USCC's official condemnation. Cardinal Law of Boston termed the film "morally offensive and repugnant to Catholic belief";[91] San Francisco's Archbishop John Quinn declared it "an outrage and a stinging offense to the religious sensibilities of Christian believers";[92] and Bishop James H. Timtin advised Catholics in his Pennsylvania diocese to boycott the movie. The leader of the Greek Orthodox Church in the Americas, Archbishop Iakovos, deemed the film "the fantasy of a sick human imagination," and he called on "the merchants of such unspeakable perversions to come to their senses and to reevaluate the consequences of their actions."[93]

There was also a statement issued on August 9 from Mother Teresa, the Catholic nun who worked with the indigent of Calcutta: "If Catholics will intensify their prayers before Our Eucharistic Lord in the Blessed

Editorial cartoon commenting on the tendency of Church officials, such as Cardinal Bernard Law of Boston, to criticize *Last Temptation* without having seen it. (Dan Wasserman, *Boston Globe*, reprinted with permission)

Sacrament. . . . If they will implore the Power of God through increased recitation of the Holy Rosary. . . . Then, Our Blessed Mother will see that this film is removed from the land."[94]

In an interview for *Newsday,* Martin Scorsese answered the bishops' denunciations by saying, "As a Catholic, I am, obviously, even more saddened by their reaction than I am by the response of the fundamentalists. . . . They feel they have to protect the people [from interpretations of Jesus' life]. . . . So I am disturbed by it, upset by it, saddened by it. But I understand their political motives. They had to do it."

Later on Tuesday evening, Scorsese agreed to go on ABC's late-night news program, *Nightline.* It was only after he arrived for the taping that the show's producer informed Scorsese that Donald Wildmon would be joining the show from Memphis, along with the film critic for the *Christian Science Monitor,* David Sterritt. Already nervous about the studio setup for the interview—

when he looked into the camera to respond to questions from the show's host, Ted Koppel, he couldn't see Koppel's face—Scorsese disliked the point-counterpoint format. "'This is something deeper than political issues,'" he recalled telling the producer. "'I don't want to get into a situation where I'm in a screaming match. . . . I mean, we're not going to convince each other, in this manner at least.' And so I was very careful about making that clear."[95] His anxiety mounted as he watched the opening segment: a three-minute overview of the controversy, including clips of Larry Poland, Tim Penland, Tom Pollock, Charles Bergstrom, and others. "That's when I realized it was all over," he said of the futility of trying to discuss the film rationally in the middle of a firestorm.[96]

For most of the program, Ted Koppel acted as an intermediary, first questioning Scorsese about the outrage the film had provoked, then asking Wildmon a series of questions about the legitimacy of his protest. Finally, Koppel gave Scorsese and Wildmon "an opportunity to talk to one another right now . . ."

KOPPEL: Let's see if what it is the two of you have to say to one another, if anything at all, that might add something to what is really the substantive issue here, which I think is whether filmmakers have a right to make a film like this, and whether the public has the right to choose whether to go and see it. Mr. Scorsese?

MR. SCORSESE: Well, I just feel that we have a right—I'm a Catholic, raised Catholic—we have a right to explore God in our own way. I feel that some people may be offended by that, and I sincerely understand their taking offense to it. . . . My feeling is that I think there are people out there who want to see it, and want to have this spiritual experience, I believe a moving experience. And by having it, by seeing this film and having that experience, they'll get to know Jesus or God better.

KOPPEL: Mr. Wildmon, ultimately, I suppose, the point is, just as the book has been around for 40 years, and those who wanted to read it could buy it, pick it up, get it in their lending library, those who didn't want to, who might be offended by it, could avoid it. There's no one holding a gun to anyone's head and saying, "You've got to go to this movie, you've got to watch it."

REV. WILDMON: The bottom line is this. Mr. Scorsese has every right to do the film, Universal has every right to release that film, but those of us who are Christian, who are offended by what you've done, or—I'm sorry, not you—but what has been done to our Lord have every right to protest this film. . . . I find it incredible how anyone could go to the film knowing the historical Jesus and the biblical Jesus. The Jesus here in this film is not that Jesus.[97]

Scorsese was in a gloomy mood after the broadcast. He called Tom Pollock, saying, "Look, I understand, you guys are taking this for me. Just shelve it. Shelve it." Trying to assuage his feelings, Pollock said that no group of people with fundamentalist views could force them to pull a film that they all knew was a serious work.[98]

The first wave of critical reviews revealed a divided set of opinions about the film. *Sneak Previews'* Michael Medved pronounced it a colossal failure. "It is the height of irony that this level of controversy could be generated by a film this awful," he wrote. *Hollywood Reporter's* Duane Byrge was dismissive of the film's "arid point/counterpoint" structure and predicted, "Martin Scorsese's aesthetically graceless and philosophically turgid big-theme offering will be a dry hole at the boxoffice."[99]

Last Temptation fared better in the judgment of critics writing for the major newspapers, many of whom praised the film's art direction and cinematography, the intensity of the performances (especially those of Dafoe and Keitel), and the serious purpose underlying Scorsese's exploration of Christ's humanity. But they also concluded that the sum of the film's brilliant parts fell short of fully realized greatness. "'The Last Temptation of Christ' is a probing, unflinching film," wrote the *Washington Post's* Hal Hinson. "And Scorsese's motive here is to stimulate and provoke, not to sensationalize. The director's failure, though, comes at the most basic level. In spite of all he accomplishes, he is unable to bring Jesus close to us, to realize his stated goal of creating a universal figure who symbolizes the spiritual anguish of all men."[100] Although she faulted the film's "stilted, showy quality . . . often more apt to announce its ideas than to illustrate them," the *New York Times'* Janet Maslin admitted at the end of her review that she was won over by *Last Temptation's* "sense of absolute conviction," which culminated in the emotionally moving and "mightily affirmative" final sequence.[101] All the major critics did hold one opinion in common: the sexuality in the film, especially the fantasized marital lovemaking of Jesus and Mary Magdalene, was dramatically justified and not in the least salacious.

As for whether the furor hurt or helped the film's commercial prospects, the days before *Last Temptation's* release yielded mixed clues. Harold Vogel, an entertainment industry analyst for the brokerage firm Merrill Lynch, told *Variety* that he expected the controversy to give the film a boost at the box office.[102] In a sign of swelling interest, bookstores across the country reported an increased demand for the Kazantzakis novel. Anticipating this surge, Touchstone Books placed the movie's thorns design on the cover of the paperback edition and ordered a new print run of 200,000 copies.[103] (By the third week of September, the reissue occupied second place on the trade paperback best-seller list.) But there were counter-indicators of the controversy's effects. A national telephone survey conducted in the second week of August by Ethridge Marketing Research, a Lincoln, Nebraska, public opinion research firm, found 78 percent of all respondents (both those who had heard of the film and those who had not) reporting that they would probably not go to see the film. Among the survey's other findings: 61 percent opposed the movie coming into their areas, and 28 percent said that they would boycott for one year any theater showing *Last Temptation.*

On Wednesday three U.S. congressmen, all Republicans, attempted to drag that deliberative body into the fight against the movie. William E. Dannemeyer and Robert K. Dornan of California, and Clyde Holloway of Louisiana, cosponsored a "sense of the Congress" resolution (H. Res. 517) that called for Universal to refrain from releasing *The Last Temptation of Christ* and for citizens who were offended by the film to "ask their local theaters and film distribution companies not to show it, and refuse to patronize Universal Studios and those businesses that have associated themselves with the film."[104] According to Rep. Dannemeyer, whose understandings of the film were based on articles published in the Focus on the Family's magazine, the bill did not constitute federal censorship. He told *Variety,* however, that "Congress as an institution can express the outrage of the American people at the sacrilege of Jesus, the Savior of the world."[105]

On Thursday, August 11, all attention shifted to Los Angeles and the massive rally and march at MCA's headquarters. Turnout expectations were originally in the range of five thousand people. But when Universal changed the release date to August 12, an act that the Citizens for a Universal Appeal organizers hailed as "providential," the event reaped the benefits of a tidal wave of publicity.[106] On the day of the rally, the *Hollywood Reporter* noted that "up to 15,000 people from various religious organizations are expected to be busing in from across the country to picket Universal Studios en masse." Even that number turned out to be on the low end of the final estimates, and if the thousands who reportedly couldn't reach Universal City because of traffic congestion and closed freeway off-ramps are factored in, the total number of people who physically set out to march that day could have exceeded 30,000.

One hour before the news conference, the principal participants met with one of the chief organizers, John Stewart, at the studios of KKLA radio station. "After committing the rally to the Lord in prayer," recalled Stewart, "we made an unforgettable journey down Lankershim Boulevard. Everywhere we looked there were people walking toward the site of the news conference and rally and up the hill to the entrance of Universal Studios."[107] The emotional high point of the news conference came when Steve Gooden, an articulate twenty-four-year-old African American singer who had just signed his first recording contract with MCA, walked up to the lectern. Gooden said, "I would like to encourage and challenge other young men and young women that are signed in the industry, that are associated with companies, to make a decision to put their conscience and convictions of Christ before their own personal gain. . . . I tear this contract in the name of my Lord and Savior, Jesus Christ!"[108] He then ripped up the document. The thousands of onlookers roared their approval as Gooden, choking back tears, turned around and walked into a bear hug from the former football star Rosie Grier.[109] Compared to the authentic drama of Gooden's performance, many of the speeches that followed, from Wildmon, Bill Bright, Trinity Broadcasting's president, Paul Crouch, and others, seemed scripted and didactic. Indeed, Gooden's sacrifice posed an implicit challenge to those who not only gave up little of their privilege and material well-being to engage in their protest campaigns, but actually stood to gain significantly from the controversy in terms of broadcast ratings or monetary contributions.

In the early morning of Friday, August 12, Dennis Walto arrived at the offices of Josh Baran and Associates to begin monitoring the openings via phone updates from the field crisis team. Since the Los Angeles briefing, the advance people had dispersed to their various cities. They faxed diagrams of the theaters' lobbies to Baran's office and conferred with police about where to put "designated protest areas," how to arrange the rope cordons, stanchions, and barricades. Baran's office also fed them information about the opposition. In a routine that would be refined in the coming days and weeks, Shana Weiss and other staffers monitored religious broadcasts, got on the mailing lists of fundamentalist organizations, scanned local newspapers, and even called some of the activists to inquire about their plans. "We were looking for who the lead organizers were," said Weiss. "We were looking for what kind of targets they would select. . . . We were trying to figure out which communities were more vocal, which communities were more likely to be targeted."[110] Finally, everything seemed to be in a state of readiness. The first showings of *The Last Temptation of Christ* were only a couple of hours away.

Barbara Hershey and Willem Dafoe made appearances on the network morning shows in a final push to get the movie's best face out in front of its embattled openings. Interviewed on NBC's *Today,* Dafoe admitted to being perplexed about the negative reactions: "I just think this is a beautiful, powerful, positive film. Some people that for the most part haven't seen it are coming out against it—that I don't understand."[111] (That day, the UPI interviewed Dafoe's parents, who lived in retirement in the Orlando, Florida, area. "He is from a good Christian home and he believes in God," Muriel Dafoe said of her son. "I can't believe he would do anything blasphemous.")[112]

Street protests were on the rise that day, even in cities not yet identified as candidates for *Last Temptation* openings. In suburban St. Louis, about 400 protesters carrying signs excoriating MCA marched along the perimeter of the parking lot of Crestwood Plaza shopping mall, which the group's leader said was targeted because "they have all the stores that carry MCA products, and it's the company we're after."[113] In Dallas, a crowd estimated at 150 picketed the studio's regional office. And in Orlando, about 700 people gathered at the Universal Studios Florida to conduct a prayer vigil and listen to George Crossley, who as leader of the rally exhorted them to "declare economic war on Universal Studios."[114] In dozens of other cities and towns, the imminent opening of *Last Temptation* sent activists scrambling to redouble their efforts to put pressure on theater owners and local government officials.

Also that morning, delegates to the Republican National Convention were flying into New Orleans to bid farewell to the party's paterfamilias, Ronald Reagan, and to entrust to his successor, George H. W. Bush, their hopes for holding on to the presidency. Later in the day, several of the Christian right's biggest stars—among them Jerry Falwell—spoke at a dinner sponsored by a coalition of social conservatives. Falwell told the assembled faithful that he was obsessed with three things, but the one that was uppermost in his mind was *The Last Temptation of Christ.* "I think we can drive it out of existence in the next few weeks. . . . We're going to bruise him so badly," Falwell said of Martin Scorsese, "that the others are going to pull back and let him die alone."[115]

Falwell's remarks betrayed a basic misunderstanding of how Hollywood behaves when one of its own is "bruised," particularly by someone perceived

The latest temptation of Christ.

Editorial cartoon suggesting the un-Christian nature of some Christians' protest of *The Last Temptation of Christ.* (Tribune Media Services, Inc., reprinted with permission)

as hostile to civil liberties and religious pluralism. For more than two weeks, Directors Guild of America (DGA) executives and members had been talking about doing something to show their solidarity behind MCA/Universal and the filmmakers. After conferring on the phone with Sid Sheinberg, Scorsese, and others, DGA's president Frank Schaffner and executive director Greg

Gumpel determined that it made sense for the DGA to defend Scorsese's right to make the film of his choice.

"It's not a difficult call," said Gumpel about the decision to hold a news conference. "The community feels threatened, and to the extent that beyond the instance of this film, the issue really in this community is that films wouldn't get made if the chilling effect could take place when directors, writers, and others [are] making presentations or pitches to the studios. If the thought would be that we really have to be careful of all these groups, these films wouldn't see the light of day, clearly. So, it goes beyond the one film. And it goes beyond defending a work of art, if you want to call it that. It goes to the fact that [films] wouldn't be made in the first place. The brushes and the paint would disappear, and the canvas would disappear, because the money would just dry up. That's the real issue."[116]

Starting on Thursday morning, calls went out from the DGA's publicity consultant, Chuck Warn, and other Guild executives to a variety of directors who might be interested in participating. Warn himself was just back from traveling with Jon Voigt in the Soviet Union. He had taken prints of *E.T.* and *Coming Home* to show to the Supreme Soviet as part of an initiative to open up the country's marketplace for U.S. films. After seeing firsthand the cultural liberalization going on in the land of America's Cold War adversary, it seemed bizarre to Warn to come back to Los Angeles and witness a holy war being waged against Scorsese's movie.[117] Most of the directors who were in town and had no scheduling conflicts readily agreed to speak. Warn regretted that he did not get in touch with Richard Brooks, an active Guild member and respected director of films, such as *Blackboard Jungle* and *Elmer Gantry,* that had generated heated debate in their day. "I apologized to him numerous times afterwards for the oversight," said Warn. "And he let me know in his inimitable way that he would have loved the opportunity to express his opinion on the subject. . . . It was really a failing on my part not to have had Richard at that press conference, because he would have been, even more than some of the ones we had there, able to express with his unique passion the issue that we were talking about."[118]

Shortly before noon on August 12, a rare gathering of prominent directors joined Glen Gumpel on the dais in the DGA's boardroom and voiced their unequivocal support for Martin Scorsese and MCA/Universal: John Badham, Warren Beatty, Peter Bogdanovich, James L. Brooks, John Carpenter, Martha Coolidge, Randa Haines, Walter Hill, Michael Mann, Penny Marshall, John Milius, Sydney Pollock, George Sidney, and Elliott Silverstein. It was one of the last of the major news conferences to be held in the old DGA headquarters on Sunset Boulevard (the new building opened in early 1989), and—in Warn's memory—a unique undertaking by the Directors Guild.[119] In his introductory remarks Gumpel spoke of the Guild's support for "every artist's commitment to his or her creative work. The right of the artist to create in an atmosphere free from interference, meddling and innuendo is an inherent American right."[120]

"It makes me a little frightened and sad to see something like this happening," said Sydney Pollock, "because what's at stake here is the very essence of what we think of when we talk of a free society. . . . There would *be* no Christianity if people thought this way before Christianity. . . . and certainly Martin Scorsese's $6.5 million film is no threat to it."[121]

Martha Coolidge compared the protesters' actions to book burning and Michael Mann argued that Scorsese's "very sincere, deeply religious and inquiring motion picture" was being attacked by groups he referred to as "thought police."[122] Warren Beatty said that he had purposely not seen the film in order to keep the issues they were addressing separate from the theological questions raised by the film. Noting that film artists are often at odds with the large companies that employ them, Beatty applauded MCA's defense of *Last Temptation* and said he hoped to see the studios "continue to finance and distribute subject matter that is controversial."[123]

Several directors were openly critical of General Cinema and the other chains that turned down *Last Temptation*. Drawing a parallel between Scorsese's movie and another recent Universal film, Randa Haines said, "We were all outraged and disappointed when the government pulled the film *Cry Freedom* from theaters in South Africa. . . . And we must feel as disappointed and frightened when people in our own country are crying for censorship and a major theater chain yields to that pressure."[124] In his turn at the podium, Peter Bogdanovich read statements from several filmmakers who were unable to attend.[125] He concluded with Clint Eastwood's single-sentence message: "Freedom of expression is the American way." "That's pretty succinct," noted Bogdanovich.[126]

The words of support from Scorsese's peers gave the film a well-publicized send-off as it headed into uncharted territory. No one knew what to expect, in terms either of the strength of the opposition or of the reception the film would get at the box office. At that moment, all that anyone connected with *The Last Temptation of Christ* wished for the picture was for it to get through the first weekend unscathed.

9

Trouble in Flyover Country

I T MAY HAVE BEEN the best opening weekend conditions that could have been devised for *The Last Temptation of Christ*. By premiering the picture in the nation's media centers—New York, Chicago, and Los Angeles—and the cosmopolitan Canadian cities of Montreal and Toronto, Universal was hoping *Last Temptation* would attract enthusiastic audiences and win the praise of influential critics. The film was also set to open in four of the most politically liberal urban markets in the United States, all with relatively low percentages of evangelical Christians: Washington, D.C., Seattle, Minneapolis, and San Francisco. Even with these home-field advantages, the nine Cineplex Odeon theaters braced for a situation of unnerving volatility: the all-but-certain arrival of large groups of protesters in a state of high dudgeon and the possibility of disruptive incidents—including the worst-case scenario of mass casualties.

The Canadian openings were largely peaceful. At Toronto's York Theater, a contingent of more than a dozen Metro police officers and Intercon security agents outnumbered the seven protesters at the sold-out 1:00 P.M. showing.[1] A different atmosphere prevailed at Montreal's Place du Canada theater, owing in part to the history of separatist violence in the predominantly French Catholic province of Quebec. A bomb threat was phoned in that morning, and police found a container of flammable liquid leaning against an outside wall of the theater. They quietly disposed of the device and the showings went ahead on schedule.[2]

Most of the opening-day performances in the United States were sold out, although long lines and security procedures often kept screenings from starting on time. At San Francisco's North Point Theater, near Fisherman's Wharf, every show was delayed for as much as an hour as guards inspected the purses, shopping bags, and knapsacks of people filing into the spacious lobby.[3] But the Sisters of Perpetual Indulgence—a troupe of men who often appeared at

Bay Area religious events attired in nuns' habits—entertained moviegoers and tourists alike with a flamboyant sidewalk act and a Ten Commandments prop that read, "Thou Shalt Not Censor."[4]

The early evening show at Minneapolis's Cooper 2 Theatre drew four hundred demonstrators, chanting and praying, passing out literature about the "real Jesus." The hardiest among them vowed to stay at their posts throughout the night. There was just one slip-up in Universal's field operation that day. The *St. Paul Pioneer Press* identified the advance person assigned to Minneapolis, Rob Johnson, as a "spokesman for Universal Studios," and quoted him by name discussing the security detail protecting the theater.[5] Recalled Johnson, "The reporters, especially in the earlier weeks, were just going crazy to get us to say something. . . . And what I always did was try to get them to call the Universal spokesperson [in California]. But at some point, when they're following you around all day, they *are* going to pick something up."[6]

Approximately four hundred demonstrators gathered outside Seattle's eight-hundred-seat Cinerama, which was filled with "near-capacity crowds" for the first day's showings.[7] But when the advance person, Elizabeth Stevenson, had arrived in town earlier in the week, she discovered that the local police had no plans for issuing public gathering permits outside the theater. More disconcertingly, the police seemed nonchalant about the impending protest. "So I started making telephone calls to local churches with a pseudonym, just to find out if they [planned to picket]—you know, from an interested participant's point of view." Stevenson would ask them, "'I'd like to come out to a demonstration and, you know, where are you gathering? Are you having buses coming in? . . . Where are people meeting?' And also, you know—'I have a sister or a relative or a friend in this other town. Is anybody coming from there?' I found out that there were buses coming from Spokane and other areas of the state." She came up with an estimate of the number of out-of-towners coming to Seattle for the protest. "And when I informed the police of that, they were pretty surprised and were able to cordon off the sidewalk across the street from the theater so that there wouldn't be direct confrontation with the people trying to come in and see the film."[8]

When Dennis Walto heard about the investigative techniques that Stevenson used in Seattle, he encouraged other team members to do the same. "These people are self-identifying. They are not media-shy," said Walto about the protest planners generally. "So, two or three strategic phone calls to would-be spiritual leaders, leaders within the community of that particular sect or following, would suddenly give you a blueprint as to what the plans were for protests."[9]

In Washington, D.C., Christian protesters taunted the ticket buyers who stood outside the Cineplex Odeon Circle Avalon Theater in sweltering 98-degree heat. "Hey people!" shouted a woman wearing a T-shirt sporting the word BLASPHEMY! "This is not the greenhouse effect you're feeling—this is the wrath of God!"[10] Walking slowly in a circle in a protest zone patrolled by officers from the District of Columbia's Special Chemical Weapons Unit, the seventy-five opponents carried signs ("This movie degrades God!" "Scorsese Busters!"), played hymns from a boom box, pushed a life-size mannequin of Jesus on wheels, and gave out religious literature—including an open letter from the Washington Redskins' head coach, Joe Gibbs, championing a boycott of the movie.[11] Here, as in other cities, they were confronted with a band of counterprotesters: a group of teenagers called the Youth Idealists who passed out leaflets produced by "People for the Separation of Government and Morality." In an encounter not atypical of the tenor of dialogue between the groups, one of the Idealists questioned a protester, "Why are you doing this?"

The protester, a leader of a local antipornography group, replied, "Well, if you loved your mother, would you want to see her degraded up on the screen?"

"But my mother's not the issue here."

"You obviously don't love your mother," the protester retorted.[12]

Before the day was out, one protester was arrested for crossing a security line, and police officers conducted a sweep of the theater after a bomb threat was phoned in. No bomb was found, but the police continued using dogs to search the theater for explosives each day before showings began.

In Los Angeles, the first incident occurred before dawn. At 5:00 A.M., guards at the Cineplex Odeon in Century City discovered a theater window and a poster for the film spattered with yellow paint. By the time the studio limousine carrying Tom Pollock, his wife, Peggy, Sally Van Slyke, and Perry Katz pulled up for the noon premiere, approximately one hundred demonstrators were corralled in front of the theater and closely watched by ten police officers. The driver accidentally deposited Pollock and company on the curb next to the protest area. They had to walk by the picketers to get to the theater doors, but no one recognized the face of the Universal Pictures chairman who had just appeared on ABC's *Nightline*.[13]

Inside, uniformed guards were stationed on either side of the screen to protect it from attack during the movie. Finally, the lights went down. "I remember the chills that I got when the Universal logo came up, and the audience gave the [company] a standing ovation for having the courage to release this movie," said Perry Katz.[14] Unbeknown to him and others in the audience, Intercon agents intercepted a group trying to force its way through the theater's rear exits; the theater staff also encountered another act of vandalism shortly after the movie began: someone had poured thick glue on the floor of a women's restroom. Midway through the show, one of the agents came down to Pollock's row and whispered that he had heard there would be a disruption at the temptation scene. "So, here I am," said Katz, "not knowing what to expect. What's going on in my head is that I'm sitting next to Tom, and, gee, if someone wants to take a shot, and he's a sad shot—"[15]

When the temptation sequence began, a man dressed in a black T-shirt suddenly stood up and shouted, "I think it's been a pretty good movie until now but I feel that I have to say: This is blasphemous!"[16] As others in the audience told him to be quiet, agents moved in and hustled him out of the theater. Outside, the man identified himself to reporters as "Bobby Bible," minister of an obscure Long Beach church; for his assertive act inside the theater, and particularly for having been forcibly ejected, Bobby Bible's status among his fellow protesters on the sidewalk was elevated considerably. The Christians and other groups allied in their cause—among them an ultraconservative Catholic group, the American Society for the Defense of Tradition, Family, and Property—hoisted placards, passed out religious tracts, and heckled people going into the theater. Some of the moviegoers brandished slogans of their own: "Relax, It's Only a Movie," and "I love Jesus but that doesn't stop me from having an open mind."[17]

By evening the exchanges between protesters and the ticket buyers grew testy, often escalating into yelling matches. The crisis team member on duty, Steve Barr, made a point of trying to forge a friendly relationship with the protesters: "I think they thought I was like a lawyer. An ACLU one. I think someone actually made that comment. . . . Even though I disagreed totally with what they were saying, I did respect their right. And I would talk in those terms, not to say I disagreed with what they were saying, but just explaining their rights. And when there were flashes of anger from the [theater] management people, I would actually calm them in front of the [protesters] and kind of say, 'Look, this is their right to be out here.' And I think the protesters thought I was on their side. So I think that defused some of it."[18]

The most impressive show of official force that day was on display in midtown Manhattan. New York police set up a "situation room" in a van parked near the Ziegfeld Theater, cordoned off a block of West 54th Street, and deployed a hundred-officer detail to maintain order around the theater. Two bomb threats were phoned in, and both times the police took dogs into the theater to search for explosives. Universal's advance person on the scene, Craig Livingstone, was struck by the moviegoers' reactions: "A lot of people in the line waiting to buy tickets, or standing in line with tickets at the Ziegfeld, thought it was really cool that the bomb dogs were going in before them. . . . I thought that was bizarre. But people were so keyed up into the craziness surrounding the event itself that [the bomb dogs] almost became a spectacle."[19]

Hours before the noon show, about a hundred demonstrators were assembled inside the protest zone established by police barricades. By evening, their number had grown to an estimated one thousand. Noah Richler wrote in the magazine *Punch* of seeing "New York's bizarre religious detritus, men and women on their knees, the barricades for a pew, clutching at rosary beads and muttering Hail Marys."[20] Michael J. Kelly regaled the *Record*'s readers with prose sketches of such exotic personages as Sister Shiva, a self-described "hermit nun"; a Florida woman who had an inflatable alligator, named Big Al, at her side; a former Miss Wyoming beauty queen and holder of a doctorate from Brigham Young University, who was observed "wearing a pink chiffon dress with a white lace collar"; and an outspoken piano repairman who belonged to the group Jews for Jesus.[21] Reporters also could not ignore the American Society for the Defense of Tradition, Family, and Property. The group capped its bicoastal *Last Temptation* appearances with a flourish, its members wearing red capes and toting medieval-style banners outside the Ziegfeld.

The public display of intense religious emotion is always an arresting spectacle. But when it happens in places like midtown Manhattan and Century City in Los Angeles, it can seem to bystanders—and especially to the media—like the eruption of a cultural pathology. The impulse to fix the image of Protestant fundamentalism far outside the pale of the modern world, notes the historian Susan Harding, harkens all the way back to the Scopes Trial of 1925.[22] This fundamentalist "other," in all its colorful, anachronistic, dogmatic, even psychologically unhinged manifestations, became a major motif in reportage of *Last Temptation* openings throughout America—a practice that had the effect, whether justified or not, of stigmatizing the protesters and obscuring deeper understandings of why they objected to the film.

Ziegfeld moviegoers had to endure a wait of two to three hours to get inside. They were greeted at the box office with a sign—"For your safety, patrons seeing 'The Last Temptation of Christ' may be subject to search"—as agents opened bags and purses and used hand-held magnetometers for detecting metal objects. Jay Cocks and his wife, Verna Bloom, were among those admitted to the first showing in the 1,141-seat theater. Although Cocks often accompanied Martin Scorsese to the New York openings of his films, this time it was deemed too dangerous. Tom Pollock had called Scorsese earlier in the week and advised him not to go to the Ziegfeld because the demonstrators would know what he looked like.[23] (A few days later Willem Dafoe walked unrecognized through a crowd of *Last Temptation* demonstrators while taking his son to an afternoon matinee of a Disney film; they were shadowed by two bodyguards, who accompanied him in public for a period of about three weeks.)[24] A twenty-six-minute delay in the start of the film did not dampen the audience's nervous anticipation. When Scorsese's name came up in the opening titles, they stood and gave the screen a thunderous ovation. Paul Schrader, Michael Ballhaus, and Peter Gabriel were also applauded loudly when their names appeared in the credits. After leaving the Ziegfeld, Cocks found a phone booth by a subway on 57th Street and called his friend. "I was near tears," he recalled. "I said to Marty, 'You wouldn't believe the audience.' And he was flabbergasted."[25]

Chicago's opening day began with Plitt Theaters, the wholly-owned subsidiary of Cineplex Odeon, seeking a Cook County Circuit Court injunction against any picketing within five hundred feet of the Biograph Theater.[26] But the courts closed for the day before action could be taken on the petition. Meanwhile, the advance person, Kevin Sites, repeatedly called the alderman of the 43rd ward to request a large and influential police presence at the theater. Sites even thought to remind the alderman's office of the twentieth anniversary of the 1968 Democratic National Convention, a reference to the hordes of Vietnam War protesters who rioted and fought police for several nights in the streets of downtown Chicago.

The Chicago Police Department did show up in sufficient numbers and used wooden barricades and police tape to establish a protest area measuring seventy-five by ten yards in close proximity to the box office. It was so close, in fact, that the Plitt management's fears of customer intimidation were at least partially realized. Moviegoers were subjected to on-the-spot conversion attempts; as one woman told the *Chicago Tribune*, "When you get to the ticket booth, they really put it to you. . . . I was met within three minutes by a

Muslim, a Catholic and other people."[27] The first screening did not proceed without incident. Dust in the Dolby sound equipment (which many of the protesters claimed was put there by God's hand) pushed back the start times for other showings by a half hour. Shortly afterward, a bomb threat was called in to the mayor's office because the theater staff was too preoccupied to answer their phones. Four Intercon agents and several of the police officers conducted a search of the premises between the afternoon screenings. But, like the other bomb threats that day, it was determined to be a hoax.

With each showing of *Last Temptation,* the crowd grew in size and energy. In a memo he faxed to Dennis Walto, Kevin Sites tracked the "hard numbers" and shifting, heterogeneous character of protest activity: "1:00 PM—sold out; 150 protesters (Greek Orthodox Archdiocese). 4:00 PM—sold out; 300–350 protesters (Greeks, the Christian Connection). 7:00 PM—sold out; 500–550 protesters (Greeks, Christian Connection, the Ad Hoc Christian Committee). 10:00 PM—sold out; 650–700 protesters (All above plus free-lance and anti-religion counter-demonstrators)."[28] "It was not always the same crowd," confirmed the journalist Hiawatha Bray, writing for the *Sunday Journal* of Wheaton, Illinois. "When I arrived, just before 6 P.M., the Orthodox Jewish picketers were already gone. The protest was now dominated by Greek Orthodox priests and laity. They circled within the limits posted by the police barricades, bearing crosses and icons and singing in their native tongue. Just down the street, the Islamic Circle of North America passed out leaflets reading, 'Leave Jesus alone. He has suffered too much.' A team of Catholic antiabortion activists checked in soon after my arrival. Hours later, theatergoers were serenaded with Spanish hymns from dozens of Mexican believers."[29]

At one point, a member of the American Nazi Party surfaced in the crowd holding a sign, "Paid for with Jewish Money." As Kevin Sites related in his memo to Walto, the intruder's contribution was not taken kindly by the other protesters: "The Nazi infiltrator was surrounded as he spewed his hateful message to eager cameras. One enterprising protester from the main group quickly drew up a sign, complete with pointing arrow, stating, "He's a NAZI," and held it over his head. [Two of the protest leaders] bade their followers to leave the Nazi alone and concentrate their protest against the movie."[30]

Counterdemonstrators also turned out in the hot, muggy night, needling the protesters and appropriating the anti-*Temptation* discourse for their own purposes. One group, standing across North Lincoln Avenue from the demonstrators, carried signs that read, "Jesus was a fake," and "God Can't." Later in the evening, some of the people standing in line for tickets decided to parody the scene with their own makeshift signs: "Boycott Tucker," and "Tucker Is a Lie."[31] (The film *Tucker* also happened to be premiering at the Biograph that night.)

Despite the bomb threats, the heavy security presence, and occasionally unruly behavior by demonstrators, the premiere of *The Last Temptation of Christ* was a resounding success. The movie shattered house records for paid admissions and gross receipts in New York, Chicago, and Los Angeles. Overall, it did $401,211 in business on the opening weekend, a per-screen average of $44,579. "It's a phenomenal gross average per screen," a spokesman for Exhibitor Relations Company was quoted in the *Wall Street Journal*. "There's no picture to compare it to."[32] (But for the sake of comparison, Twentieth Century Fox's *Young Guns* opened that weekend in wide release as the top film at the national box office, grossing an average of $5,055 per screen.)

The opening weekend's box-office performance seemed to confirm that the massive publicity generated by the summer's controversy would be a net positive for the movie; according to the *Hollywood Reporter*'s industry analyst, Martin Grove, "the fundamentalist Christian pickets . . . appeared to have worked to the advantage of Universal. What the pickets did . . . was to focus intense media coverage on the film's opening."[33] Importantly, Universal hoped that the orderly openings and relatively mild disruptions to theater operations would lessen the concerns of exhibitors who had not yet made up their minds about playing the picture.

The movie's debut was hardly cause for celebration among most of the activists who fought to stop its release. Tim Penland contended that Universal erred seriously in its decision to make *Last Temptation,* but he also admitted, "It has to be a decisive victory for Universal. . . . The appeal to stop it failed. What we did created at least $10 million in free publicity." Such sentiments foreshadowed a period of self-examination in the coming months, as religious leaders discussed and debated their roles in the battle over the movie, whether they had dealt with it wisely, and how it would affect future relationships with the secular media.

Others, like Bill Bright, looked for a silver lining, hoping—as in the adage of turning lemons into lemonade—that the film would stimulate conversations about the biblical Christ. Still others refused to admit defeat. In fact, as the Reverend Donald Wildmon and others saw it, the time to lay down their swords had not yet come. "The more the Christian community sees this thing, the angrier they will get," predicted Wildmon the day after the film's release. Intent on applying more torque to this anger, Wildmon announced on August

16 that the American Family Association would seek to buy ad time on more than a thousand radio stations to renew its call for a boycott of MCA's business interests and any theater showing the film.

Just a month later, Wildmon and other religious leaders recognized a need to readjust tactics. "People are going to see [*The Last Temptation of Christ*]," acknowledged Larry Braidfoot, counsel for the Southern Baptist Convention's Christian Life Commission. "So we have to try something else."[34] That "something else" was a boycott of the video edition of *E.T.—The Extraterrestrial*, which MCA Home Video planned to release on October 27. Steven Spielberg's beloved film, however, was a far less obvious target for boycotters than the fully demonized Scorsese film. A huge promotional momentum was already propelling *E.T.* into the home video marketplace—as of September 15, preorders surpassed 10 million units, more than twice the previous record holder, Disney's *Cinderella*. "We have nothing against *E.T.*," said Larry Poland gamely. "We just want to express our hurt and anger. We know [MCA] is counting heavily on revenues from *E.T.* That's the place to hurt them."[35]

It remained an open question whether the calls for national boycotts would accomplish anything. But evangelical Christians at the local level still felt the sting of *Last Temptation,* and they were loath to let more salt be rubbed into those wounds. And many of them, believing the moral purity of their communities was at stake, began mobilizing to confront it head-on.

LAST TEMPTATION's strong opening lifted Universal's hopes, but this elation was tempered by the knowledge that those results had been achieved in safe havens. The studio now had to start broadening the movie beyond a few culturally sophisticated cities. It soon became evident that Tom Pollock and the studio's distribution team would not hurry this process.

During the second weekend, only nine more markets were added: Vancouver, Phoenix, Tucson, Philadelphia, Detroit, Santa Ana (California), San Diego, and—in an attempt to gingerly test the movie's acceptability in the South—Houston and Austin. Twenty new locations were selected for the third weekend, and thirty-two were added the third weekend. It was not until September 20—nearly six weeks after opening weekend—that the number of screens showing *Last Temptation* topped one hundred. (In contrast, MGM/United Artists' film *Betrayed* also had a platformed roll-out during the same time frame as *Last Temptation,* but within three weeks it was on 1,100 screens.) Moreover, the theaters playing *Last Temptation* "had to be in upscale neighborhoods, have easy security and be available for a long run,"[36] as the *New*

York Times' Aljean Harmetz summarized the studio's thinking. These stipulations meant that the film was often not booked in the suburban multiplexes where Universal films normally played, but rather in smaller "four-plexes" and "six-plexes" as well as single-screen art houses.

Decisions to play *Last Temptation* were held close to the vest until the last moment. Trailers were seldom shown (usually only in Cineplex Odeon theaters), TV spots did not air (although local newscasts ran clips from the electronic press kit), and newspaper ads usually appeared on, or at most two days before, the day of release. The overriding purpose of these deviations from normal practice, as a Universal field operations executive put it, was "to give the minimal amount of time to announce [the film] to not only the public, but more importantly to the protesters . . . because these theaters became such a focal point of the protests, and they really in some cases became quite interfered with, just in the ability of somebody to go out and see the movie, period."[37] Even the staffs at Universal's eight field offices, which had responsibility for coordinating the publicity and promotions within their territories, were not given advance notice of release decisions. Again, the field operations executive: "The field reps could honestly get on the phone and tell the reporters or the critics—many of whom they had obviously done business with on a regular basis—that they didn't know."[38]

Whereas marketing executives at other studios had earlier admired the astuteness of Universal's public relations campaign, they now questioned the studio's exceedingly cautious approach in releasing *Last Temptation*. Universal seemed intent on missing a window of opportunity for exploiting the public's interest in the much-discussed picture. Asked by Aljean Harmetz to respond, Tom Pollock said, "I'd like to introduce those who are criticizing us for not taking advantage of the controversy to those who have accused us of causing the controversy. Our goal is to have the picture open in the top 50 markets within four weeks."[39]

In addition to broadening the film's geographic reach, the second weekend was important because for the first time *Last Temptation* would be opening in several non–Cineplex Odeon theaters. AMC was the first chain to take the plunge.[40] Sonny Gourley, AMC's chief film buyer, saw the film at an exhibitor screening in Pennsylvania on Tuesday, August 16. "A film like this, I wanted to make sure I had seen it first," Gourley told a UPI reporter. "I liked the picture very much as fiction. I can understand some people will be a bit offended, but I didn't feel the movie was that offensive."[41]

Santa Ana's MainPlace Mall posed more serious challenges than the other AMC venues that weekend. Santa Ana is situated in the heart of Orange County, the scene of citizen resistance to the Kazantzakis novel twenty-five years earlier, and still—despite the influx of Asian and Hispanic immigrants—a stronghold of political and religious conservatism. As soon as AMC's decision to play the movie was made public, John Stewart of KKLA radio, fresh from his triumphant organizing of the August 12 Universal City march, began urging listeners to converge on the Orange County theater for "a further demonstration of the offense of this film."[42]

Complicating matters for the Santa Ana opening was the theater's location on the third floor of the enclosed mall. Thanks to a 1979 state supreme court decision, California was one of several states permitting "expressive activity" by members of the public—such as petitioning, leafleting, and political speech—at privately owned shopping centers. Thus, in California a shopping mall can issue permits for "free speech" activities. It can set reasonable limits on time, place, and manner, but it cannot prohibit an activity. "It's one of those many laws that people don't know," said a *Last Temptation* advance person. "So . . . we had to first educate theater owners, especially if they're in malls, that these people have the right to be here. So long as they're not keeping somebody from coming into your store, or coming in to watch a film . . . as long as they're not impeding traffic."[43]

MainPlace's retail tenants dreaded the prospect of large numbers of protesters storming their mall and encamping at the theater for a noisy demonstration. To allay these concerns, on Thursday the mall's management met with religious leaders to work out a solution. They jointly agreed that the demonstrators would stay in the parking lot, away from the mall entrance.

Early the next afternoon, a crowd estimated by police at six hundred (and estimated by the protesters at a thousand)—many of them veterans of the Universal City and Century City protests—swarmed around the mall entrance. The security force, which was tripled from four to twelve for the occasion, got ready to defend MainPlace. "But after they all began marching toward the entrance," said the mall's general manager, "we felt it wouldn't be in our best interest to block them from the mall, so we compromised."[44] Security officers unlocked the doors and hundreds of Christians were off on a brief, spirited march. Singing choruses of "The Battle Hymn of the Republic," they walked into the nearly empty mall and went up the escalators to the AMC 6. In a gesture of conciliation, AMC allowed half a dozen protesters inside the theater's lobby to pass out leaflets and display their signs. It was the only time this happened during *Last Temptation*'s release. Most of the demonstrators exited after ten minutes, but security officers sparred briefly with a few stragglers who insisted on soliciting signed statements of support for the theater boycott from mall merchants. Emotions continued to run high in the community when, a few days later, Bob Emmers of the *Orange County Register* wrote an op-ed column characterizing the protesters as "a bunch of holier-than-thou twits" and critiquing their alleged censorious ways.[45] More than six hundred readers responded by canceling their subscriptions—the largest such reaction in the newspaper's history. Chastened by the outpouring of ire over his opinion, Emmers apologized for the "name calling" and the *Register*'s editorial page editor ran an article expressing his own personal support for the demonstrators' cause.

Universal executives watched the Texas openings closely. Arguably the most socially progressive cities in the state, Houston and Austin would be leading indicators of the kind of reception the film might face when it ventured deeper into the South. Approximately one hundred protesters were on hand for the film's debut at Houston's Spectrum, a Cineplex Odeon theater. A local controversy swirled briefly around a Harris County deputy constable

Protesters going up an escalator to the MainPlace Mall theater, Santa Ana, California, August 19, 1988. (Courtesy of the *Orange County Register*)

who forbade his precinct's officers to work as off-duty security guards at the Spectrum during *Last Temptation*'s run. It was one of the first instances of a city official or a private company denying services to a theater showing *Last Temptation*—but there would be more.

The American Family Association targeted Austin for a special effort. The film was booked into the Village, a north Austin venue owned by the San Antonio–based Presidio chain, a subsidiary of Norman Lear's Act III company. Lear, of course, was the public face of People for the American Way and the archnemesis of the Reverend Donald Wildmon. AFA's state director, Mark Weaver, attended a preview screening at the Village with more than two dozen Austin religious leaders and emerged to pronounce the film "worse than I thought it would be. . . . It is pure fantasy."[46] Weaver's effort helped produce an impressive opening-day turnout of about five hundred Christians.[47] Confined to a section of the parking lot some distance from the theater, they waved Bibles in the air, sang praise and worship songs, held up signs reading, "Don't Mess with Jesus," "Say No to the Last Temptation," and "Honk If You Love Jesus Christ"—which many passing motorists obligingly did—and traded barbs with an ad hoc group calling itself the Citizens against Restrictive Stupidity.[48] Untainted by bomb threats or any serious altercations, the Houston and Austin openings suggested that the film was ready to move into southern markets.

The box-office gross for *Last Temptation*'s second weekend totaled $476,263 at all eighteen locations.[49] The per-screen average of $26,459 represented a drop-off from the previous week that was due to smaller capacities at the nine new theaters and an expected decline in tickets sold at the original nine, but the film was still performing well at this stage of the roll-out. On Monday, August 22, Universal got a boost on the exhibitor front: Loews Theaters, the last remaining holdout among the major chains, announced it would play *Last Temptation* in "appropriate" venues. Just the previous week, it appeared likely that Loews, the nation's fifth-largest exhibitor, with more than six hundred screens, would follow the example of General Cinema and pass on the picture altogether; however, enormous pressure brought to bear on the chain by Universal led to a negotiated settlement of release patterns, play dates, and theater locations.[50] The timely decision afforded Universal the chance to play the film at one or more of the Loews theaters in Boston, an important market for specialty films and one that had been difficult to crack, owing to General Cinema's control of many of Boston's best locations.

Also on August 22, Universal's marketing executives received the results of an exit poll of *Last Temptation* viewers, conducted by Grace Marketing

Research.[51] The report, based on a survey of Saturday night moviegoers in Seattle, Minneapolis, and San Francisco, offered the first systematic look into how moviegoers perceived the film. Of 1,540 respondents who filled out questionnaires, 940 (61 percent) cited the "controversy" as a reason for attending the movie, compared to 37 percent who attended for "the story," 26 percent for "religious themes," and 24 percent for "the director." (These data generally agreed with anecdotal reports indicating that many moviegoers were seeing the film to "stand up" for freedom of artistic expression, or because local opposition groups had said that they shouldn't go.) The percentage saying they would "definitely recommend" *Last Temptation*—a measure of potential word-of-mouth promotion—was 38 percent, which was at the low end of the normal range for all movies tested. Almost half of the respondents said their own religiosity was unaffected by the movie, and another one-third said the movie had a positive influence on their religiosity—although a comparatively large percentage of these viewers, 36 percent, did not identify themselves as "a religious person." (Only 58 people, about 4 percent of the sample, said they were offended in a religious sense by the movie.) Religious moviegoers were not only more likely than the nonreligious to claim a positive effect on their faith from seeing *Last Temptation* (41 versus 22 percent), but also more likely to find the movie offensive (5 versus 2 percent). Overall, the poll results were favorable for Universal and cast doubt on the opponents' claim that seeing the film would shake or damage moviegoers' religious faith; but for whatever reason, the studio saw fit not to publicize the findings.

By the third weekend, the story line that dominated the summer's headlines—the titanic struggle between a Hollywood studio and a bloc of angry religious leaders—had played out, and other events, especially the fall presidential election contest, were filling the void. Some TV evangelists, such as John Ankerberg and D. James Kennedy, continued to inveigh against *Last Temptation,* and their ministries produced videos and books charging the film with a false, unbiblical portrayal of Christ. But the high-profile figures who rode the controversy hardest, like Wildmon, Falwell, and Dobson, were moving on to other issues. Even the Reverend Hymers, whose anti-Semitic-tinged stunts proved so irresistible to the media, left this chapter of his career behind. With no mysteries, rumors, or outrageous actions to drive the story, the collective judgment of the networks, newsmagazines, and agenda-setting newspapers such as the *New York Times* and *Washington Post* was that the controversy was over.

The controversy, however, did not die when the national media turned off their coverage. It simply morphed into a new phase. The film was going into the heartland, the regional urban centers and small cities of "flyover country." As it expanded onto forty-eight screens by August 30, eighty-one screens by September 7, and ninety-four screens on September 13, people realized that *The Last Temptation of Christ* was coming.

The fall of 1988 witnessed conflicts in every part of the United States. Each of these episodes had its own story line, influenced by the degree of cultural conservatism in a community; the energy, ingenuity, and organizational talents of protest leaders; the type of theater booking the film; and in some cases the disposition of theater managers, politicians, and city or county officials for bending to (or resisting) pressures from the warring groups. Not every venue came under attack. When the film opened in North Miami Beach, only a dozen Christian protesters showed up in the fifteen parking spaces set aside for them; four weeks later, the film was still doing strong business at the AMC Marina 8, pulling in $4,400 for the weekend. Similarly, *Last Temptation* was extraordinarily popular during its two-month-long run at Milwaukee's Downer Theater, the cumulative total of more than 20,000 moviegoers breaking the house record. College towns with a history of social tolerance—Palo Alto, California; Urbana, Illinois; Madison, Wisconsin—also largely escaped the antagonism that greeted the film elsewhere. But if the studio took heart from the relative tranquility of these openings, the movie's third weekend in release augured the difficulties that lay ahead.

The evening before the August 26 opening in Salt Lake City, a print of the film arrived at the Cineplex Odeon Centre Theater. The Church of Jesus Christ of Latter Day Saints had earlier issued an official condemnation of *Last Temptation,* advising Mormons to "shun those things that detract from the dignity and spirit of [Jesus Christ's] divine mission."[52] Thinking it was better to err on the side of caution, Scott Levenson, Universal's advance person assigned to work with the Centre Theater staff, recommended to the manager that he bring on a private security detail that night. The theater manager balked; he wasn't sure he could get authorization for that from the Cineplex Odeon head office. Tonight will be fine, Levenson recalled him saying—after the opening, they would put on all-night security.[53]

Levenson reported back to his field director, Dennis Walto, in Los Angeles. "They don't want to put on twenty-four-hour coverage. I've argued with them and basically it's a moot point."

"You did your job," Walto said. "You made your recommendation. It's their money. You're there to give a professional recommendation."

"Listen, I can't hire security people by myself, can I?"

"No. There's nothing we can do. Make sure there's some sort of a patrolling of the theater, you know, on an hourly basis. Make friends with some cops. See what they'll do to help us out."[54]

The next morning the manager walked into the theater and found the screen slashed from top to bottom in two places, with shorter horizontal cuts flapping open—each of the damaged areas resembling a cross. The print of *Last Temptation* was also missing from the projection booth. A backup print was rushed from Denver, and the screen was hurriedly sewn up. By early afternoon, a custodian discovered the missing film in the theater's basement, stripped from its reels and lying in a pile of celluloid on the floor.[55] There was no sign of forced entry. The police surmised that the attacks occurred between 1:00 and 11:00 A.M. by a vandal who had hidden in the theater Thursday night until the employees left. Only the day's first showing was canceled. But beginning that evening, and continuing for the rest of *Last Temptation*'s run, the Centre Theater had round-the-clock surveillance of the premises.

Also on August 26, the deep South played host to the film for the first time. "Sneaking into town like a thief in the night," reported the *Atlanta Constitution,* Universal announced late Tuesday that *The Last Temptation of Christ* would open on two screens in a Cineplex Odeon theater at the Phipps Plaza mall, in the affluent Buckhead neighborhood.[56] According to the newspaper, not even Julie Erickson, a publicist in Universal's Atlanta office, had yet received confirmation of the booking. Resentment of MCA/Universal had been stoked for weeks by the Reverend Richard Lee, pastor of Rehoboth Baptist Church in Tucker, Georgia, who frequently spoke out against the film and collected tens of thousands of signatures of concerned Georgians on petition forms. Now he and two other men—a local businessman, Ray Allen, and Ted Baehr, publisher of *Movieguide*—began coordinating plans and pulling together resources for a full weekend of rallies. They had no shortage of supporters willing to pitch in: a group called Concerned Christians took out a full-page ad in the *Atlanta Constitution,* urging a boycott of the blasphemous movie; another group, Take a Stand for Christ, pledged to send a hundred "soul-savers" to Phipps Plaza with copies of the Gospel of St. John.[57] Religious leaders committed themselves to witness for Christ at the opening—including a Gwinnett County minister who was prepared to go to jail, if necessary, "to stand up for my God."[58]

The rally on Friday evening attracted a hymn-singing crowd of about 250, including some Operation Rescue volunteers, "taking a break from sit-ins at abortion clinics," reported the *Atlanta Journal,* and the entertainer Pat Boone, who was in Atlanta for a religious concert at the amusement park Six Flags over Georgia. Boone hopped on top of a flatbed truck that was parked near the mall's entrance and used by the protesters as a stage. Taking a microphone in hand, he told the crowd that MCA's chairman, Lew Wasserman, did not "know" Jesus. "You can't make a movie about someone you don't know," he said.[59]

Most of the theaters playing *Last Temptation* saw sharp drop-offs in the number of protesters after opening night, but not in Atlanta. On Sunday a crowd reported by the media of about one thousand (and estimated by Universal's advance team at two thousand or more), marched up and down Peachtree Street, then massed at Phipps Plaza for two hours of singing, praying, waving placards—"Lead Us Not into Temptation," "Read the Real Story," "Boycott This Movie Because It Ain't Groovy"—and listening to speeches. The mall was noticeably solicitous of their needs, supplying the protesters with portable toilets and power for their sound truck. With the theater's blessing, a member of the advance team even let the evangelist John Ankerberg and his film crew briefly into the lobby to shoot part of his anti-*Temptation* television show. Said John Toohey: "[He] wanted to get his B roll. That's really all he wanted. . . . He just wanted to do a stand-up while people were going into the theater."[60]

The climax of the rally came when Ted Baehr mounted the flatbed truck to deliver an impassioned speech. Baehr, the *Atlanta Constitution* reported, "drew loud, sustained cheers when he blamed the news media for allegedly portraying the movie's opponents as religious fanatics bent on 'censorship.'" Spotting a nearby cameraman for an Atlanta station, Baehr wheeled around and looked directly into the lens, shouting: "Stop portraying us as fundamentalist fanatics! I'm a believing Christian; I believe in Jesus Christ!" In another development that day, the archbishop of Atlanta, Eugene A. Marino, lent his tacit support to the opposition by asking local Catholics to observe a day of prayer and fasting on Friday, September 2; he encouraged anyone who refrained from seeing the film to donate five dollars, the price of a movie ticket, to a charity.[61]

Ted Baehr's outburst and the archbishop's gentler approach reflected in their separate ways a struggle on the part of Christians—both those who actively protested the movie and those who didn't—to reclaim their dignity.

It wasn't just the film's transgressions or the "fundamentalist" label hung on them by the media that they found insulting. They also fought the idea that Christians were potentially dangerous people. As one Canadian said about the guards' search of carry-in items at theater entrances: "The search implies that good friends of mine, who might be opposed to parts of the film, are fanatical and violent. It reflects badly on the religious community."[62]

The overwhelming majority of Christians opposing the film did not pose any danger. The reason they went off on a protest mission to theaters showing *Last Temptation*—probably the only time most of them had ever participated in a protest—was simple: they wanted politely and respectfully to unburden themselves of their feelings on this dark day in the life of the community. A large number of them "were just wounded," said Laura Quinn, one of the advance people, who spent many hours observing the protesters at close range. "[They] just seemed to talk about Jesus Christ as a member of their family, their closest friend. In very personal terms. . . . And they came out to express their hurt, is the only way I can describe it."[63] They sang together, chanted, prayed, held hands, or just stood silently. Communal moments like these, notes James M. Jasper in *The Art of Moral Protest*, are "the one moment when a large group can attain a certain coordination and unity, can silence the small groups talking among themselves, can concentrate the attention of all."[64] One of the biggest demonstrations in this style of witnessing at a *Last Temptation* opening took place in Pittsburgh, where a crowd estimated at between 3,500 and 4,000 people holding candles marched peacefully to the Kings Court Theater.[65]

Nevertheless, there were Christians who took a more direct, aggressive approach. One member of the advance team characterized this type of protester as "very loud and obnoxious and completely unconcerned about any other person's view."[66] Some accosted people on their way to buy a ticket, telling them that they were putting their souls in danger—"you know, taking them by the arm and trying to warn them against the film. Being very, very confrontational."[67] These interventions rarely worked; only one advance person cited a case of someone deciding against buying a ticket after an encounter with a protester. Other protesters did not even try to persuade anyone. Instead, provocation by any means—by starting arguments, shouting epithets, pushing religious literature on them, spitting on moviegoers and advance people—was their modus operandi. Elizabeth Stevenson saw some of the harshest behavior in Columbus, Ohio, where a crowd pressed in close to the ticket window and patrons. "They weren't really using foul language like a longshoreman would, but [they were] just as insulting and just as damning to these poor people who were just going to a movie. . . . [One woman] had a baby in a stroller and she would look them in the eye and just yell at them until her voice was hoarse."[68]

Occasionally, rivalries between denominational groups flared up, threatening to spin out of control. In Philadelphia, two religious groups—a group of Baptists and some Catholics from New Jersey—nearly came to blows; as the advance person described the scene, "there was rock throwing . . . between these groups because the singing was interrupting the praying, and the praying was out of sync with the singing. And we actually had to establish two separate protest areas so they wouldn't *brawl*."[69] More often, the more "fringe" or "flamboyant" groups were given space by the rest of the protesters, who did not want to be associated with them.

Some protesters did try, or considered trying, various means of hindering the ability of theaters showing *Last Temptation* to do business. Most of these acts of subversion consisted of relatively harmless mischief, from dousing the box office with holy water, to using a small mirror to reflect sunlight into the eyes of ticket sellers, to hurling eggs and paint balls and water balloons, to climbing up to the theater marquee and mixing up the letters of the *Last Temptation* movie title. In some instances, blocking access to the theater itself was the objective. In Rochester, New York, the Citizens for a Decent Community formed a human ring of about 250 people in the front of the theater; however, they left an opening for moviegoers to pass through. An opposition group in North Carolina developed a plan, reported in the *Charlotte Observer,* of having protesters get in line to buy tickets, decline to buy one, and then recycle back through the line in order to prevent legitimate moviegoers from seeing it.[70] And for a time, a statewide Virginia Christian organization reportedly advocated acts of civil disobedience, "if necessary," at a Richmond theater where the movie was scheduled. But few of these plans to block a theater's ingress and egress routes got further than the talking stage.

Personal injury, of course, was the threat of greatest concern. *Last Temptation,* said one advance person, functioned as a "magnet" for deranged people or others whose motives for creating disorder had only an opportunistic relationship to the movie. If an individual's behavior or physical appearance was self-evidently aberrant, the police usually took steps to keep him or her away from the theater. Bag searches and magnetometer scans also yielded a large number of potential weapons, mostly knives, at the front door. It was the possibility of large-scale attacks, however, that loomed ever-present in the thinking and defensive procedures of police, theater security, and the advance team. The danger was recognized early on. In August, before the film had its national premiere, an empty theater in Pine Bluff, Arkansas, was set afire by a *Last Temptation* protester, presumably as a warning to the Commonwealth Theaters chain.[71] More than two hundred bomb threats were reported during the movie's North American run. Only one of them represented an immediate threat situation. On October 5, in Mishawaka, Indiana (near South Bend), a maintenance worker went onto the roof of the Cineplex Odeon Town and Country theater, where *Last Temptation* was playing, and found two explosive devices. "One was a gasoline-type device in a gallon jug with some type of accelerant," said a corporal in the South Bend police bomb squad. "The other was an 8-ounce glass coffee jar filled with smokeless powder."[72] The devices were outfitted with "firecracker-type fuses" for igniting the bombs.[73]

The most violent incident targeting a theater showing *Last Temptation* occurred in the last week of October in Ithaca, New York. An unemployed forty-nine-year-old man, who identified himself as an evangelical Christian, rammed his converted school bus through the lobby of Fall Creek Pictures at 6:12 A.M. on October 25, causing extensive damage to the interior. The theater was empty that Tuesday morning and no one but the driver was injured. Afterward, a coalition of local ministers issued a statement deploring the incident: "Such actions are often intended as defending Christ, yet they defame him. This is an unacceptable way to express opposition."[74]

Universal's advance team handled the many contingencies of the *Last Temptation* openings in a coolly professional manner, using the protest containment techniques they had learned on the campaign trail. After noticing that the Christians lacked adequate skills for conducting a mass protest, some of the advance people turned their attention to other problems. As one of them said, "The concept of picket captains and the use of bullhorns and sound trucks, and, you know, any kind of juice to it [were lacking]. . . . And so fairly early on, I recognized that the pickets weren't going to be my [major] problem."[75] A few of the advance people, especially those who had staged demonstrations themselves, felt mildly disoriented in their new task. "I'm an organizer by training," said Scott Levenson, "so one of the weird things that I experienced was that moment when I was driving in my car and I realized for the first time in my life that I was attempting to *break up* pickets rather than expand them."[76] Similarly, Elizabeth Stevenson, whose experience included organizing civil disobedience events, recalled being "totally through the mirror on the organizing aspect of it. . . . Here we were on the other side, trying to say, 'Well, these people need to follow the same rules as we do.'"[77]

A major difference between opening *The Last Temptation of Christ* and creating a campaign event, other than the difference in level of hostility, was the importance of including protest leaders in the planning for the movie's opening weekend—sometimes to the extent of actually *inviting* protesters to stage their event in an area conveniently located near the theater. John Toohey believed this was one of the most valuable services he performed. "It was important to give them that focal point locally, right in their community, that they could sit down across the table and talk to. They could hurl invectives at you. They could attempt to save your soul. They could do whatever they wanted to. But you were a human being they could talk to. And you could make decisions. And you could sit with them and say, 'Okay, you want to protest this movie—let's figure out how you can protest this movie safely, to insure your safety, to insure that this movie is going to open up. Because, you know, folks, it *is* going to open up. So let's work it out . . .'"[78]

The theater managers didn't always understand why the advance people were so accommodating. But Universal's representatives told them that it was better that way—that giving the protesters the sense that their speech rights would be not only honored, but in fact protected, was just "Conflict Resolution 101," as one of them put it. There was also a security consideration: by positioning the protest zones close to the theater, they would know at a glance where the protesters were at all times and what they were doing. There was one more reason for reserving a place for the protesters near the theater, a reason the advance people did not always disclose to the theater staff: they wanted to help the local media get their pictures.

When the movie arrived in town, the full gamut of the press assembled on the front lines of the "circus": affiliate news crews with microwave vans, local and regional newspapers, radio reporters, even journalists from the college campuses. As advance team member, Noel Boxer, described a typical scene, the media "were out on the sidewalks, on the pavement, and they wanted to get shots of the protesters, and they wanted to get feedback from patrons coming out after they had seen the film."[79] Opening-night scenes of unpredictable conflict were in fact crucial to the film's publicity. The saga of the provocative Christ movie, said Josh Baran, was "a reporter's dream story . . . it's the clash of worlds and cultures. The media love this and they're going to drive it for you. They're going to publicize your movie . . . and make this story as big as they possibly can."[80]

The advance people helped the media capture the kind of visuals that would serve the interests of both. It was a matter of summoning the skills and knowledge they used for styling campaign events: how to arrange crowds, how to identify backdrops with the preferred symbolic meaning, where to put the press to get the best camera angle on the action—according to what the advance person perceived to be the media's news judgment. As Steve Rabinowitz explained, these considerations translated easily to the *Last Temptation* openings:

> You know, it's staging protesters with signs in proximity to, let's say, the marquee or the moviegoers or the facade of the theater. And then, just in case the photographer's blind, you casually mention that, Gee, you know, it looks like from over there, it all kind of "lines up," to use the photographer's term. And then, of course, sometimes a local law enforcement [officer] gives you the license to restrict the access that the photographers and the media have. And so, you know, as luck would have it, we would designate an area for them that again lines up with the picture that we were after. This is the kind of thing we routinely do in campaigns. You know—you can take pictures from anywhere you want, as long as it's *right over there*—which, as luck would have it, is exactly the picture we were hoping you would take. But it's a good picture.[81]

The advance people didn't have to be told to do this. Many of them did it just because it was implicit in the job description, and all the elements were readily available: the media, the protesters, the moviegoers, and, of course, the "candidate" itself—the movie. "Once we had a protest area established," Rob Johnson recalled, "I absolutely positioned the press with sight lines in mind. Whether it was into the theater or into a marquee or not, [that was] determined on the site. . . . I generally tried to put the protesters in between the media and my theater, so that the protesters were foregrounded and the theater or the marquee were background. And early on, when we were getting these big groups, you also wanted to be able to give them a shot that showed sort of the enormity of the crowd—expand the lines."[82] For Craig Livingstone, setting up the scene became an almost "automatic" ritual: "It got to the point where I would go to a theater and I'd know exactly where to put the protesters so that the still photographers could lens through the woman with her blue habit on, with her rosary in her hand . . . kneeling and praying. And he'd be able to lens through her and all that right up to the marquee of *Last Temptation*. . . . And, you know, the media would come and take their click-click-clicks, the protesters would be there while they're taking their click-click-clicks, and everybody would go away and the people would come in and see their movie."[83]

Not all the advance people adopted this practice. One of them considered it a big coup to ensure that the theater *not* get into a shot of the protesters, "because I didn't want people who might be interested in going to see the film to get an impression that there are protesters they've got to walk through."[84] Most members of the advance team, however, saw that media images of open opposition in front of theaters had the effect of creating excitement and boosting attendance, at least for the short term, and if the protesters ever realized how counterproductive their activities actually were, their diminished protests could hasten the film's departure from theaters. It was a short leap from this logic to another level of manipulation; or, as one of the advance people said, "Some of us took all of this to mean a license to really work this in a way that we knew how. To *make sure* the media coverage was there. . . . It was not unlike the kind of creative thinking that, let's say, has graced a campaign or two in our respective pasts."[85]

Crisis propagation was definitely not in their job description, but as the movie's opposition began to wane, at least a couple of the *Last Temptation* operatives engaged in off-the-books, freelance tactics aimed at generating a more robust protest presence. Arriving in a new city, they would go to the phone book to find the major churches, ministries, and evangelical organizations, as well as groups such as the ACLU and the pro-choice organization NARAL that would be able to identify their ideological foes in the community. They also got in touch with local police and coordinated with any officers who specialized in gathering intelligence on radical groups. With this information in hand, they would call the people judged most likely to be angry about the film and—as one of the advance people described the conversation—"try to get them going a little bit. . . . You know, 'What are we going to do about this? This is outrageous. This is a blasphemy.'"[86] After expressing this "anonymous outrage," as he put it, they inquired as to just exactly what the person on the other end of the line was going to do about it. If the response they received indicated that a protest was in fact going to happen at a specific time, the next step was to call the press "and make sure they knew about it."[87]

The studio had no knowledge of this activity, nor would it probably have condoned the activity if it had. But after weeks of managing crises as they unfolded, the advance people got a sense of *how* they unfolded—and the sort of selective interventions that would initiate or amplify the cycle of protest and press coverage. "By the end, we just got a little bit too cocky probably," said Dennis Walto—"or too good at it."[88]

"Is any publicity bad publicity when it comes to a movie?" Walto asked rhetorically. "The more a film gets put out in print, or the more people talk about it, the better it is for the movie and the more people are going to go and judge for themselves. . . . And ultimately—and this is the fine line—whether those situations are authentic or created, *in the end they're real.* Because that situation is unfolding and it's happening, and you'd better have the right precautions in line."[89]

AS *LAST TEMPTATION* dropped under the national media radar, its opponents began trying other methods to stop, or slow down, the film's release— or, in some cases, to blunt its effect. Some religious groups latched on to the idea of running alternative films about Christ just before, or simultaneously with, Scorsese's film. Miami's Grove Art Cinema was the first to try this gambit, booking the Genesis Project's 1979 film, *Jesus,* for a week's run in mid-August; Chicago's WCFC-TV, a Christian station, also aired *Jesus* three times in late August. The motive for playing this film seemed to be less about competing with *Last Temptation* for audiences, or even displacing it with holier imagery, but rather more about Christians wanting to do something more positive than protesting in front of theaters.

Members of the community, both private and governmental, sometimes came to the aid of the anti-*Temptation* forces. Several companies in Orlando— including a direct-mail company, a helicopter charter service, and an engineering consulting firm—severed their business relationships with Universal Studios Florida because of *Last Temptation.* Some newspapers, such as the *Deseret News* (Salt Lake City) and the *Birmingham (Ala.) News,* refused to accept advertising for the movie; after the *Birmingham News'* ad director called Eddie Marks, a vice president for Consolidated Theaters, to inform him of the decision, Marks said of their conversation: "They were mighty nice to tell me but I asked if they were writing about it [the controversy] in the newspaper. He said 'yes,' and I told him I thought that was a double-standard."[90] The theaters themselves were vulnerable to actions focusing on their property insurance or compliance with safety codes. On the afternoon of the film's opening in St. Louis, surrounded by a restless crowd of seven hundred protesters, the city fire marshal's office conducted a surprise inspection of the Avalon Theater, causing it to shut down until a few minor code violations could be resolved. A St. Louis alderman proudly acknowledged that his was one of the calls made to the fire marshal alleging fire hazards at the Avalon.[91]

The police officers charged with keeping order around the theaters harbored views of their own about the propriety of what they were doing. "They're professional to the T," said Dennis Walto about the police generally, "but when it comes to the benefit of the doubt, they would likely give it to a protester, or at least sympathize with them. But if [the protester] breaks the law, they're going to arrest them."[92] During *Last Temptation*'s opening in Jacksonville, the Universal advance person came face to face with the flexible judgment of law enforcement. She and the police department had earlier worked out an agreement for keeping protesters about thirty feet from the moviegoers. But at a crucial moment on opening night, when protesters started moving out of their designated area and approaching the people standing in the ticket line, she turned to the squad leader for help in clearing the path. "And [he] looked at me and sort of shrugged his shoulders, and turned his back and walked away. It was clear that he had made his call. He looked at some of the prominent ministers that had turned up, and said, 'This is not worth it to me.' . . . And from that point on, we really had to do Jacksonville without any police support, and it was really very challenging and somewhat dangerous."[93]

The movie also got caught up in the political winds of the moment. Wayne Dowdy, the Democratic candidate for an open U.S. Senate seat in Mississippi, announced that he was sending a campaign donation of $1,000 back to its source—MCA's chairman, Lew Wasserman. "Because of Wayne's religious beliefs, we didn't want it to be perceived that he endorsed the film," explained his campaign manager.[94] Some state officeholders shared their opinions of the film with little or no prompting. Alabama's Governor Guy Hunt let it be known that "our nation does not need films which persecute those who believe in the values upon which this nation was built." Asked his opinion of the film in a radio interview, Governor Mario Cuomo of New York said, "The idea of profaning the Christ figure by showing him to be as human as the rest of us and leering at a woman and desiring her sexually is something that I find offensive to good taste."[95] Neither governor had seen the film.

Most of the political action, however, took place locally. In jurisdictions across the South—including St. Bernard and Kenner parishes (near New Orleans); Chatham County, Georgia (Savannah); Montgomery and Birmingham, Alabama; and Dallas—elected officials approved resolutions urging theaters to refuse the film or advising people not to patronize any theater showing *Last Temptation*. A few other cities, such as Mobile, tried but failed to pass a resolution. A farcical instance of intervention occurred in Dallas, the last remaining city to operate its own movie classification board. When the

Dallas City Council voted 10–0 to condemn *Last Temptation*, it referred the matter to the classification board, which neither reviewed films for religious content nor judged films that already bore an MPAA rating of R. "We have no authority to prevent it from being shown, and we have no authority to condemn a movie," said the board's vice chairman.[96] Nevertheless, the board bowed to the council's will and screened *Last Temptation*, duly giving it an "unsuitable" rating. The board took no further action on the film. Five years later, the city council abolished the board.[97]

The last temptation of all, at least in the temporal realm of the protesters, was outright censorship. The technical meaning of the term did not apply to anything that had yet happened to *Last Temptation*.[98] The city or county resolutions were symbolic gestures and did not carry the force of law (although, by purporting to convey the sense of the community, the resolutions did exert informal pressure on theater owners). The citizen actions aimed at convincing theaters of the need to turn down the film were also not, strictly speaking, censorship. None of them did what the Supreme Court has consistently ruled to be the illegal act of censorship: prior restraint of free speech by a governmental body. Moreover, blasphemy ceased being a prosecutable offense in the United States after Pennsylvania's blasphemy statute was ruled unconstitutional in a 1971 case.[99] Yet the edifice of constitutional law did not deter the county commissioners of Escambia County, Florida, from banning *The Last Temptation of Christ*.

Situated in the Florida Panhandle, at the west end of the two-hundred-mile-long stretch of white sand beaches known as the Redneck Riviera, Escambia County has more in common with rural Alabama and Georgia than with the rest of Florida. If anything, its religious culture is more conservative than that of the surrounding region; by one estimate, about 30 percent of the population of Pensacola, the seat of Escambia County, was fundamentalist in the late 1980s.[100] Pensacola was also infamous as the South's epicenter for anti-abortion violence; three abortion clinics were bombed on Christmas morning, 1984, and in the mid-1990s two local physicians who performed abortions were shot dead. To say that Pensacola was not friendly territory for Scorsese's film was clearly an understatement.

So when the Plitt Theaters chain announced that the movie would open at its Plaza 3 location in Pensacola on September 9, a group calling itself Citizens against Pornography and other local Christians began lobbying for a ban.[101] The county's board of commissioners called an emergency meeting. Phillip Waltrip—the only commissioner up for reelection that fall—introduced the ordinance that would prohibit the showing of *The Last Temptation of Christ* anywhere in Escambia County. In his account of the September 8 hearing, the First Amendment scholar Leonard Levy wrote that "several citizens, none of whom had seen the film, demanded that its showing be prohibited. One woman was convinced that 'a majority of Americans considered the movie to be blasphemous.' Other witnesses gave similar testimony." Only one of the commissioners, Muriel Wagner, resisted the tide of opinion running in favor of banning it. Wagner, wrote Levy, "cautioned that a ban would merely play into the hands of the movie's producer by making people more curious to see it."[102] But on a vote of 4–1, the board approved the ordinance. It carried a misdemeanor penalty of a $500 fine or a jail term of sixty days, or both, for anyone—including Cineplex Odeon, owner of the Plitt Theaters—violating the ban.

Universal immediately called attorneys at the Holland and Knight law firm in Tampa, who worked on the case during the night and boarded an early morning flight to Pensacola. With the help of an ACLU attorney in Pensacola, who was solicited to appear as a "friend of the court," the legal team planned to seek a preliminary injunction from the U.S. District Court judge to stop enforcement of the new law. Meanwhile, Josh Baran got word that county sheriffs were on their way to the theater to seize the film. He told Dennis Walto to tell the advance person, John Toohey, to protect the print at all costs. Toohey had already picked up the film upon his arrival at the airport. He still had it in his possession when he checked into his hotel. As a precaution until the legal problem was settled, Toohey moved across the street—the print of *Last Temptation* tucked under his arm—and checked into another hotel under a different name.

On the morning of September 9, Toohey looked out his window and saw sheriff's cars pulling up to his original hotel, where he still had a room in his own name. Fearing that the film was in imminent danger, Toohey called Walto; "My instructions," Toohey recalled, "were to load up the film, drive it across county lines, hole up there, and wait for the security folks to hit, and also for the lawyers to hit."[103] He stashed the film in the trunk of a taxicab and headed across the causeway to Santa Rosa County. Safely out of the reach of Escambia County law enforcement, Toohey set up shop at a restaurant near the beach, calling Walto every thirty minutes and passing the time shooting pool with his cabdriver.

Dennis Walto had his hands full trying to manage the crisis from California. He fielded calls from Sally Van Slyke, who was impatiently asking where

the film was. "I was saying, 'Don't worry, we have it.' And Sally said, '*Who* has
it?' And I said, 'Well, the advance person has it.' 'Where is he?' 'He's, you
know, at a restaurant waiting for instructions as to what to do.' So that was
fairly precarious."[104]

Later that morning, the U.S. district judge, Roger Vinson, issued a restraining order on enforcement of the county's ban, calling it a "classic case of
prior restraint" and an obvious violation of the First Amendment.[105] The only
censorship action on a motion picture in decades was halted less than twenty-
four hours after it took effect. Toohey delivered the film to a security agent,
who took it to the Plaza 3 Theaters. Only the first showing was missed; a dozen
well-behaved protesters turned out for the 4:00 P.M. screening.

Years later, Dennis Walto reflected on the wisdom of using an advance
person to keep a disputed film out of the hands of law enforcement: "The
thing is, for our role there, had [Toohey] been discovered with that film, that
would have been a big problem."[106] The authorities' questions, he said, would
have come fast and furious—" 'Who are you?' 'Who's paying *you*?' 'Who *are*
these advance people?' . . . First of all, he would have been immediately identified and noticed and, you know, arrested. And that would have been *really*
cute—these invisible people suddenly being put under arrest." Being exposed
like that would certainly have been a prime example of "bad advance," but
the fact that he wasn't caught, Walto said with a laugh, "almost makes it good
advance."

By the weekend of September 23, *Last Temptation* had played on 105 screens
and tallied close to $5.6 million in gross receipts. In most major markets the
film was finishing its run. Universal was now getting ready to open it wider in
the South, going into markets—such as New Orleans; Charlotte, North Carolina; Columbia, South Carolina; and Knoxville, Memphis, and Chattanooga,
Tennessee—where anti-*Temptation* fervor was still in full swing. To the Chattanooga televangelist John Ankerberg, the studio seemed to be gratuitously
aggressive in pushing the movie into conservative southern communities.
Christians, he said, "just couldn't believe that a company that was actually
trying to make money . . . would offend the public, specifically in places like
Chattanooga. I mean, New York is one thing, but why bring it down to Chattanooga? . . . I have no understanding of how they picked theaters and cities,
because it seemed like they were just making customers angry when they
didn't have to do it."[107]

Universal's executives did believe that the movie would fare well in certain
southern markets and intended to use Cineplex Odeon's theaters in the region

to full advantage. But there was also some truth to the notion that the studio wanted to make a point by releasing the film in the fiercest hotbeds of opposition. At one point Tom Pollock told Fred Mound that he wanted to play *Last Temptation* in Tupelo, Mississippi, where the AFA had its headquarters. Mound responded that they had too much going on to pursue something that was clearly impossible. Pollock, said Mound, "would come up with these things every once in a while, just to spite somebody . . . and when you sit and talk to him for a while, he'd cool down and say, 'All right, all right, I hear what you're saying.' "[108] Universal settled instead for Memphis, some 125 miles from Tupelo, booking it into the Fare 4 Theater, an art house operated by Ambarish Keshani. Keshani, an immigrant from Bombay, was unapologetic about bringing the film to Memphis. "I'm not against any religious beliefs. I'm running a theater business and I show a commercially viable product," he told a reporter. "This is one of the most in-demand films around the country and that's the reason I have decided to show it for those people who want to see it and can make up their own choice."[109]

As the movie filtered down to smaller cities in the South, religious and civic groups in this traditionally gracious region prepared to give it an inhospitable reception. When Cineplex Odeon announced that the film would open at Chattanooga's Eastgate Mall on Friday, September 23, few in the city welcomed it—with the notable exception of the *Chattanooga Times,* which editorialized, "If opponents of *The Last Temptation* succeeded in [suppressing] its showing here or in other cities—it would have a chilling effect on artistic expression in general and would represent an erosion of freedom in this land of the free."[110] In the days leading up to the film's debut, Chattanooga's other daily, the *Chattanooga News–Free Press,* ran articles sympathetic to the opponents' point of view, and both the Eastgate Merchants Association and the mall's management company, Osborne Enterprises, publicly voiced objections to the showing. But there was nothing they could do about it; the theater's lease prohibited only X-rated movies. The mall's management and the police closely studied the Phipps Plaza opening in Atlanta. They saw that the provision of a space to protest, along with adequate separation of the protest area from the mall entrance, seemed to have the effect of tamping down confrontations. Accordingly, Eastgate suspended its no-solicitation policy (in some cities, such as Chattanooga, protesting on private property can be considered a form of solicitation) and made plans for a 7,500-square-foot designated protest area in the parking lot.[111]

On Sunday afternoon, following days of organizing by dozens of Chattanooga-area ministers, a crowd estimated at four thousand gathered in the mall parking lot—the largest number to assemble outside a theater showing *Last Temptation*. Laura Quinn, the only advance person assigned to the Chattanooga opening, felt overwhelmed by the task of trying to manage the scene. She got little help from the theater manager, who, she recalled, was "very, very nervous and worried, and afraid to open his mail. . . . He was holed up in his office the whole time. I think he was physically afraid. He was worried about being bombed."[112] John Ankerberg, one of the leaders at the Atlanta protest, vigorously worked the hometown crowd. Earlier in the week he had told a group of reporters that Universal released Scorsese's film just to "make a few exploitative dollars of Jesus in the sack with Mary Magdalene";[113] now members of his ministry busily hawked protest kits, which included a video critical of *Last Temptation* and a pamphlet enumerating the film's falsehoods. "At that point," said Quinn, who had logged four openings, "I had the impression that this had developed into a real cottage industry."[114] Among the other persons of prominence to visit the Eastgate Mall protest area were members of the Lookout Mountain Knights of the Ku Klux Klan. Wearing camouflage fatigues, boots, and T-shirts bearing the Lookout Mountain Knights insignia, they carried religious flags and mixed easily with the other protesters. "The local media all knew them by name," Quinn recalled. "Ministers knew them, greeted them warmly, and thanked them for coming."[115]

If it took a corporate decision by Cineplex Odeon to force *Last Temptation* into the Chattanooga market, the movie's opening in Montgomery, Alabama, came about largely through the persistence of one person: Martin McCaffery, director of the city's nonprofit independent theater, the Capri Theatre. At the time Montgomery was in the position, not unique in smaller markets, of having all its commercial theaters owned by one company, Carmike Cinema. When Carmike refused *Last Temptation*, the Capri became the only possible outlet in the city. McCaffery was highly motivated to play *Last Temptation*. By the third week of July, he was telling the *Alabama Journal*, "If the movie is released, we'd be more than pleased to show it."[116] He even wrote to Martin Scorsese shortly after Carmike's decision. Explaining the local hostility toward the film, McCaffery told Scorsese, "I have no problem with the controversy, and have received many calls of support. The problem is Universal. Several films Universal has distributed they have refused to release in the South, outside of token screenings in Atlanta. I am writing you with the hope you can insure Universal makes the film available at least before the video release."[117]

The Capri Theater director needed help even more than he realized, as one obstacle after another was thrown in his path. On August 16 the Montgomery City Council, responding to a lobbying effort by several ministers, voted 7–0, with two abstentions, on a resolution encouraging local theaters not to show *Last Temptation*.[118] A week later the theater's insurance company, Alfa Insurance, announced that it would not renew the Capri Theater's policy in October, citing possible vandalism if the theater proceeded with its plans to show *Last Temptation*.[119] That same week the president of Moffitt Theaters Corporation, owner of the building that the Capri Theatre occupied, wrote to his fellow directors on the theater's board objecting to the showing of *Last Temptation*. (He claimed to be writing in his role as a board member, not as landlord.) The Capri's bid to show the film was further undermined when Montgomery's daily newspapers, the jointly owned *Montgomery Advertiser* and *Alabama Journal,* tersely informed McCaffery that they would not accept advertising for *Last Temptation*. No reasons were given. While he was being buffeted by these developments, McCaffery had difficulty coming to terms with Universal, which wanted the film booked for a minimum of one month. Finally, on October 31, McCaffery told the local media that he had arranged to bring *The Last Temptation of Christ* to Montgomery, its only Alabama showing, for a two-week run in January.

Two weeks before the film's debut, Alabama Governor Guy Hunt appeared as the featured speaker at a "Stand Up for Jesus Rally," a jamboree of gospel singing and religious testimonials. Tying *Last Temptation* to a host of societal ills, including alcohol and pornography, Governor Hunt told the overflow crowd at a Montgomery high school auditorium, "I think it's time [for] people who disagree with it to speak out. That's what our society is all about."[120] The rally defused the theater protests that months before had seemed inevitable; only a handful of picketers stood quietly outside the theater on opening night, January 20. When *Last Temptation* ended its run on February 2, more than 2,200 people had come through the Capri's doors to see the film, easily breaking the house record. Martin McCaffery acknowledged that the controversy helped drive up attendance. "Many people came from out of state. . . . A good number of people came out to show support for an organization that showed it," he told the *Montgomery Advertiser*—one of the newspapers that shunned the theater's request for advertising. "They said thank you for bringing it . . . thank you for having the courage to bring it."[121]

In markets where most or all of the screens were controlled by exhibitors that pledged not to show the film, or that didn't have the fortitude to buck the opposition of religious groups, it took a determined manager like McCaffery to get *Last Temptation* shown. And when Universal chose to make it a priority, it could often get the film exhibited, albeit by unconventional means. In Santa Barbara, where Tom Pollock lived, Universal overcame a total market shutout by booking the film into an independent theater that doubled on Sundays as a fundamentalist Christian church. As *Daily Variety* reported the extraordinary situation, "Long lines of ticket-buying patrons had to file past protesters bearing placards that read 'Blasphemy!' and 'Revenge Is His' to sit in the same seats that would be occupied on Sunday by churchgoers of the Vineyard Christian Fellowship, whose pastor had advised [them] not to see the film."[122]

But local conditions often conspired against the film. In a number of large and medium-size markets—including Cincinnati, Louisville, Tulsa, Little Rock, Oklahoma City, Birmingham, Jackson, Orlando, and Nashville—*The Last Temptation of Christ* was never shown in commercial release. In some smaller markets, such as Charleston, West Virginia; Fargo, North Dakota; Coeur d'Alene, Idaho; and Allentown, Pennsylvania, theater owners prudently waited until 1989 to introduce it. In dozens of other markets, no theater dared to play *Last Temptation*.[123]

Probably the textbook case of how to block the film was enacted in Lexington, Kentucky—an action so effective that anti-*Temptation* groups in other cities called its leaders for advice on how to mount their own boycotts. It started when a Baptist layperson, Kathy Cale, heard the James Dobson broadcast on July 11 and decided to heed his call. She began a citywide campaign by circulating petitions among many of Lexington's churches; a local Christian radio station, WJMM-FM, lent vital support by replaying the Dobson show numerous times and serving as a collection point for the petitions.[124] Their efforts helped turn Christians against the film in this largely conservative city. Ministers spoke approvingly of the boycott from the pulpit and people lined up after church services to sign petitions. By mid-August, more than 20,000 signatures had been collected. Cale wrote "a stern letter" to Frank Weldon, a vice president of Loews Theaters, which controlled every privately owned screen in Lexington after buying USA Cinemas only months earlier.[125] (A nonprofit independent theater, the Kentucky Theater, was undergoing renovations after a fire had closed it down.) She mailed all the signatures to Weldon and warned him of the Christians' determination to boycott his circuit's theaters if it played the film in Lexington. Within days, Cale and her associates received word from Loews that it would not be shown.

Lexington showed what it took to create a perfect storm of opposition: an indefatigable organizer, a conservative religious culture ripe for taking action, and only one exhibitor "pressure point" to lean on. Two years later, *The Last Temptation of Christ* was shown at the University of Kentucky; otherwise it has never been screened publicly in Lexington.

BY THE END of November, *The Last Temptation of Christ* was showing on only 23 screens and getting near the end of its North American run. Cumulatively, the movie had been on nearly 130 screens since it opened in August and grossed $8,165,112.[126] Except for a few flashpoints—such as Lawrence, Kansas, where approximately two hundred people turned out to demonstrate—the film no longer attracted much protest. The last of the advance people left in October, some of them to work in the waning days of the Dukakis campaign. Not long afterward, Dennis Walto closed up the field crisis desk and went on a vacation in the Caribbean.

The controversy was now well into its denouement. Some of those who risked capital or reputation in the *Last Temptation* affair felt they needed to give an accounting for their actions and write a proper finish to the narrative arc of their involvement. The efficacy of the boycott against MCA was one of the issues up for scrutiny. The consensus view of stock analysts was that the boycott had no discernible effect, with the possible exception of a temporary dip at the Universal Studio Tours. "The demographic profile of the people most offended [by the film]," one of them observed, "is not the same as [the demographic profile of MCA's customers]."[127] In December a spot-check in Orange County, California, of some of the boycott targets—the *E.T.* video release, Spencer Gifts, the Universal Studio Tours, and other MCA businesses—revealed that none of their sales had suffered. Some of the protest leaders remained optimistic. "Any time now," said Paul Crouch of the Trinity Broadcasting Network, "serious financial problems will begin to surface in all of the companies having anything to do with this blasphemous film."[128] By early 1989 even dead-enders like Crouch were silent or noncommittal about what the boycotts had achieved.

The opponents believed they had a better case to make with respect to the film's financial outcome. Numerous articles in Christian magazines and newsletters, as well as Larry Poland's book, *The Last Temptation of Hollywood*, made much of the alleged "bath" Universal took on the film.[129] The American Family Association was the first to make this claim in a press release on November 1: "MCA/Universal has suffered a humiliating financial loss—$10–

13,000,000—because of a successful boycott. About 1% of the more than 13,000 theaters in the country have shown the movie. Thus far, MCA/Universal has been able to recoup less than $4,000,000 of their approximate $15–17,000,000 investment."[130] The small number of theaters showing *Last Temptation* was thus interpreted by the AFA to be a result of successful Christian activism. Other opponents who closely followed the film's revenues and expenditures were in rough agreement with the AFA's numbers. After adding up all the collateral damage caused by the controversy, Larry Poland estimated that MCA's losses were even greater: "What they lost in terms of goodwill and in Universal Studio's bookings and people who won't rent Universal videos and all that—it's inestimable. What they lost in sheer productivity, because whenever you get 25,000 people marching outside your offices, that shuts you down. Then they got 120,000 letters a day, and so many phone calls. The phone lines were tied up for almost six weeks. . . . You can't shut down a multibillion dollar corporation for six weeks without an incredible amount of direct and indirect costs. It was a very expensive decision to make [the film]."[131]

From the studio's perspective, *Last Temptation*'s balance sheet looked quite different. The deal for the film had been structured to reduce the studio's exposure to risk, and many of the normal marketing expenditures, especially television advertising, were held to a minimum. The studio did incur high expenses, however, which it shared with Cineplex Odeon, for theater security and the field crisis team. As Sally Van Slyke said, once the film went into theaters, "there was just a lot of cash that went out the door."[132] According to Tom Pollock, *Last Temptation* turned a small profit: "At the end of the day, the last time I looked at the books, [Universal] made about $700,000 on the movie." Cineplex Odeon, he said, "lost money on their books a little bit. We made money on ours. But I wanted to make sure that I had an exhibitor, even *that* one who was already closely related to us, behind the movie. . . . But the amounts of money we're talking about are, in Hollywood terms, minuscule. A million dollars breakeven is an accountant's term on a movie."[133] By early fall of 1988 the studio was also beginning to see a revenue stream from *Last Temptation*'s overseas sales, and it looked forward to more earnings in the next year or two from videocassette sales.

What was beyond dispute was the largesse the controversy delivered to a variety of parachurch organizations. "Almost all of the anti–'Last Temptation' efforts involve fund-raising," observed *Daily Variety*'s Amy Dawes—ranging from the Jerry Falwell's *Last Temptation* "Battle Plan" kit for $30 and Campus

Crusade for Christ's price tag of $39.95 for its *Jesus* film on video, to solicitations for money from the American Family Association, Concerned Women for America, and other groups.[134] Many of the organizations, sensing an opportunity to prime their fund-raising pumps, jumped into the *Last Temptation* fray in late July and early August—just in time for a quick windfall. The American Family Association probably benefited the most from the controversy: it reported an income of $3.2 million for 1988, an increase of more than 30 percent over the year before. Most observers attributed the sharp rise to its multipronged *Last Temptation* campaign. Considerably more important to the AFA's long-range interests were the 70,000 new members it gained from the campaign; "they'll probably be around a long time," Wildmon said hopefully in *Daily Variety*.[135]

As 1988 drew to a close, Christians were discussing whether they should have fought the film so vigorously. *The Last Temptation of Christ,* along with the incidents at abortion clinics that year, raised the question of whether protests—and, specifically, what kinds of protest—should be employed by Christians to achieve their goals. The answer, said Harold B. Smith in the October 1988 issue of *Christianity Today,* differed according to the goal: "If the goal of protests against *The Last Temptation* was to discourage people from seeing the movie, it failed. . . . On the other hand, if the goals of the protest were to increase public awareness of the importance of Christ's divinity to American Christians, the protest was a rousing success. How many sermons were preached on just that subject last month? How else could we have gotten *Time* and *Newsweek* to acknowledge so effectively the importance of that question?"[136] John Stewart agreed, going so far as to congratulate Scorsese for "[giving] us a chance to have a dialogue, this public dialogue."[137] Some activists thought that standing up to MCA/Universal had an empowering effect. The people who showed up to march at Universal City, said Rich Buhler, "felt wonderful that they were able to do something to respond to what they believed to be the demonic part of Hollywood."[138] According to Larry Poland, the film enabled many industry professionals to bring their spiritual lives into the open for the first time. "It was a decision point for every Christian," Poland said. "And so every person had a decision to make [about] whether he was going to defend his Lord or hide. And some hid, but most were kind of nudged into the public, into public confession, probably to their friends, associates, coworkers."[139]

Many of those who deplored MCA/Universal's behavior, however, thought the Christians didn't behave much better. According to this view, Christian protesters made a series of glaring mistakes in judgment—the offer to buy the film, the anti-Semitic outbursts, the insistent demands for theaters to refuse the film; and perhaps the most misbegotten of them all, Tim Penland's "bridge-building" venture. At worst, these tactics projected an attitude of disdain for the freedom of audiences to choose what they wish to see. At best, the opponents were guilty of overreaching. The boycott threats, in particular, were seen as a disaster. The whole idea of boycotts, said the producer Ken Wales, an evangelical who spoke out against the film, "perpetuated the confrontational spirit" between Christians and Hollywood.[140]

For Universal, the controversy was a test of wills that it never asked for. It put great stress on the company's relationships with exhibitors, the religious community, and much of the public. But the studio also gained credit in the film community for its staunch defense of the movie and Martin Scorsese. As Sid Sheinberg said, "To a certain degree, I think it made us heroic. . . . Look, we could have done what others have done. We could have taken this picture and given it to, you know, Hodunk Distribution Company or something, and taken our name off of it, and made the best of a difficult situation. But that's not MCA's style. Once we got into this game, we were going to do it the right way. And I think we did. I'm proud of the way we handled it."[141]

In the end, Universal's triumph consisted in the normally routine achievements of getting the film made, released, and shown. With *The Last Temptation of Christ*, though, nothing was ever routine. Those were actually remarkable feats for the film that no one wanted to touch.

10

Scorched Earth Blues

A T A JULY 29, 1988, press conference at Venice's Hotel de Ville, the director of the Venice Film Festival, Guglielmo Biraghi, announced that *The Last Temptation of Christ* had been selected for an out-of-competition slot on the evening of September 7. Bringing *Last Temptation* to Venice was a coup for Biraghi since it guaranteed enormous publicity for a festival that often played in the shadow of Cannes. Martin Scorsese himself thought the venue was the right one for the film's international debut. "I felt that the iconography of the film, the look of the film, have very strong ties to Italy and Italian cinema," said Scorsese. "So I thought that was the best place [to present it]. I would just meet and deal with the world press there."[1]

Any notion that the film's worldwide reception would be less troublesome than its American experience was dispelled almost immediately after the press conference. A Catholic organization, Ente dello Spettacolo, called the film's inclusion in the festival program a "disconcerting decision,"[2] and the Roman Catholic diocese of Venice urged festival officials to reconsider, adding, "We pray the city will be spared a useless laceration of its social fabric."[3] But these voices faded under the glare of attention trained on the Italian director Franco Zeffirelli. In an interview first reported by an Italian news agency, then quoted by National Public Radio's correspondent in Rome, Zeffirelli assailed *Last Temptation* as "truly horrible and completely deranged," and he threatened to pull his own entry, *Young Toscanini,* if Scorsese's film remained on the program.[4] Zeffirelli's fit of pique turned more ill-tempered when, in the same interview, he declared *Last Temptation* a product of "that Jewish cultural scum of Los Angeles which is always spoiling for a chance to attack the Christian world."[5]

Whether he actually feared that his picture would be "contaminated" by *Last Temptation,* as he claimed publicly, or whether his animus sprang, as some suspected, from professional jealousy, Zeffirelli's statements struck a raw nerve.[6] After the first twenty-four-hour news cycle spread the story around the globe, he began backing away from his charges—but only a short distance. Zeffirelli denied saying the anti-Semitic slur attributed to him, but he continued to lash out at *Last Temptation*—"a terrible film, vulgar and obscene, offending the most important personage in the history of mankind"[7]—and blasted Lew Wasserman as "a merchant on the lookout for dollars, and not certainly of quality films that respect precise universal values."[8] Just what those "precise universal values" were, he didn't say. Meanwhile, Zeffirelli purchased a full page in *Variety* and *Hollywood Reporter* for an open letter to Tom Pollock, in which he called himself "a loyal friend and outspoken supporter of the Jewish community throughout the world," and he expressed his "most fervent wish that this preposterous melodrama of fabrications, accusations, and recriminations will soon be 'gone with the wind.'"[9] The brouhaha cooled somewhat when Zeffirelli accepted a compromise worked out by festival planners. They moved the screening of *Young Toscanini* to September 5, presumably giving his film enough of a buffer to keep it from being "contaminated" by *Last Temptation*.

On the eve of the festival's opening, the frenzy of publicity surrounding *The Last Temptation of Christ* was again on the upswing. A "sacrilege" complaint had been filed against the film by a Milan lawyer and awaited review by a Venice magistrate. If the action did go forward, said Paolo Portoghesi, president of the Biennale di Venezia, of which the Venice Film Festival is a part, an appeal would immediately be brought to Italy's Tribunal of Liberty, the high court empowered to deal with censorship issues. The brinksmanship ended on September 3 when a panel of judges, after screening the film along with members of the Italian press corps, decided to postpone a decision on the case—thereby allowing the film to be shown.[10] The reaction of the Roman Catholic Church to *Last Temptation* was surprisingly muted. The Italian Bishops' Conference deemed the film "unacceptable and morally offensive," advising only that Catholics show their displeasure with silence.[11] But rumors circulated that religious groups were making plans for noisy demonstrations in St. Mark's Square. The prospect of pitched battles between protesters and the police brought a record contingent of some two thousand members of the press to the festival. Into this electric atmosphere came Martin Scorsese, Willem Dafoe, Barbara Hershey, Harvey Keitel, Tom Pollock, Sally Van Slyke, and others in their entourage, protected by about ten bodyguards.

On the afternoon of September 7, Scorsese and the actors filed into an auditorium at the Palace of Cinema for a press conference. The scene verged on pandemonium. Many of the journalists stood and shouted questions in Italian, while others gave brief emotional speeches about the film and religious liberty. After a while, a semblance of order was achieved. Wearing a white suit and open-collared shirt, Scorsese answered questions about the film one sentence at a time, waiting for his words to be translated before speaking the next sentence. During the translations, he stared at the ceiling or shut his eyes, concentrating. He had said all this before, in many places and to many people. But with an international audience in front of him, it was more important than ever to be precise about what he meant to say. His approach to Jesus, he said, "is an act of faith. It is not a film for or made by us in an exploitative manner or made for desecration. There is no doubt this film is not based on the Gospels. It is based on a novel. And it being based in this novel, the approach to Jesus that Kazantzakis took in the novel, the approach to Jesus, has Jesus as it is in the Gospel: fully divine, fully human, in one entity."[12]

Only about seventy protesters gathered in St. Mark's Square before the screening.[13] The evening's presentation went off without incident, and for the rest of the weekend, more screenings were added to accommodate all the members of the press and other festival attendees who wanted to see it. Despite some negative critical notices—one review in *La Republica,* Italy's largest circulation newspaper, called it "a crude film, full of violence, without subtlety or refinement, which will not last"[14]—*Last Temptation* had a highly successful run in Italy, opening on October 7 in Rome, Milan, Turin, Naples, and Bologna, and eventually grossing more than $4 million. Of all the countries that allowed the picture to be shown, only Spain—another solidly Roman Catholic nation—had as large a box-office result.

After Venice, the film's international distributor, United International Pictures (UIP) got ready to move *Last Temptation* into the foreign markets. Created in 1981 as a joint venture of MCA/Universal, Paramount, and MGM, UIP operated offices in forty-five countries with a staff of nine hundred. The joint ownership system allowed UIP to reduce the expenses paid by each of the partnering studios for making sure its films successfully negotiated a complicated global patchwork of trade regulations, licensing rules, local and regional exhibitors, marketing vehicles, and language differences. The cost of operating this infrastructure was more than offset by the overseas revenues generated by UIP's movies—especially in Europe. The appetite for American films had grown significantly since the 1960s, when the majority of the films shown in Western Europe were produced by European companies. By the mid-1990s, European producers' share of their own market had shrunk to only 20 percent, and the share of box-office revenues accounted for by U.S. movies averaged more than 70 percent.[15] The South American and Asian territories were also developing a taste for Hollywood stars and production values, a taste that foreign investors aimed to serve better by ramping up the construction of multiscreen cinemas.

The Last Temptation of Christ was just one of several dozen films UIP put into its global distribution system that year, but it rapidly proved to be the most difficult project in the company's history. As UIP's chief executive officer at the time, Michael Williams-Jones, observed, "There have always been films made that have invoked comment, particularly when they have a political or a religious affiliation. In terms of the outrage and the anger and the spleen that was vented, I've never experienced this in my career. . . . It was a unique and rather stressful period for everyone associated with the film. And it's a situation which frankly shocked and dismayed me personally, because it showed how much bigotry there still is out there in the world."[16]

Great Britain was the first country outside North America to introduce *Last Temptation.* In mid-August, UIP submitted the film to the British Board of Film Classification (BBFC). A nonstatutory body similar in some respects to the MPAA, the BBFC awards national ratings "certificates" to theatrical films. Unlike the MPAA, the British board can act as a censor, demanding cuts in films that may promote undesirable behaviors or violate existing legislation—such as the country's archaic blasphemy law. (Originating in seventeenth-century common law, the law evolved as a recourse for protecting the Church of England, and Anglicans generally, from vilification of their religious sensibilities.)[17] As news of the controversy carried across the Atlantic, Mary Whitehouse, whose National Viewers and Listeners Association had fought against sexuality in the media and the arts for more than two decades, began lobbying for the blasphemy law to be invoked against *Last Temptation.* She was Britain's version of Donald Wildmon—a woman who adopted the mantle of self-appointed guardian of the public morality. Credited as the plaintiff in the *Gay News* decision of 1979, which resulted in the United Kingdom's last conviction for blasphemy (for a poem that described homosexual acts with the dead body of Christ), Whitehouse retained a unique credibility on this kind of threat.

James Ferman, the director of the BBFC, had *Last Temptation* screened four times internally for legal experts.[18] Ferman also invited a delegation of twenty-eight church officials to view it with the full twenty-two-member board. The BBFC's statement of August 25 called the film "plainly sincere and the atmosphere reverent" and allowed *Last Temptation* to be shown uncut with an "18 certificate" (no one under eighteen admitted).[19] The film was still subject to the separate judgments of town councils, however, any one of which has the ability to ban a film locally. Although the councils generally follow the lead of the BBFC's opinion, approximately thirty local authorities demanded to see *Last Temptation* in advance—"a completely unusual event in itself," recalled Williams-Jones.[20] Of those, three councils eventually banned the film: Truro, Baksha, and Swansea in Wales. All three bans were appealed and upheld in court.

Following the BBFC's decision, Mary Whitehouse put out the word to her supporters to commence a telephone campaign against the film. The Anglican Church did not take an official position on the movie, but the bishop of Peterborough, who was among the clergy invited to the BBFC's Soho Square offices for the screening, told the press that he found *Last Temptation* "sadistic and obsessed with blood." "It left me feeling unclean," he thought to add.[21] The archbishop of Canterbury, Robert A. K. Runcie, and the head of the Catholic Church in England, Cardinal Basil Hume, both advocated a boycott of the film, although some conservative voices urged a calmer approach. In an editorial the *Daily Telegraph* dismissed the dire warnings of church officials, saying of Christianity, "It is not emphatically a faith so shallow as to be put at risk by the frivolity of Hollywood."[22] The London Transport Authority apparently thought otherwise. Posters advertising the film were prohibited in the city's London Underground tube network. When it came out that no one had complained about the posters, which did not feature any imagery from the film, a spokesman said, "It doesn't matter that we have had no complaints. It is very clear this film is going to offend religious groups because church leaders like Cardinal Hume have urged Christians not to see it. Our job is to protect passengers."[23]

In the days leading up to the September 9 premiere, UIP's headquarters in the Hammersmith section of London received numerous bomb threats. Given the history of IRA–related terrorism in London, bombing had to be taken as a realistic proposition. The first three floors of the building were "plasticized"—the windows sealed with a plastic material to minimize injury from flying shards of glass. Michael Williams-Jones, UIP's French general manager, Danny Goldman, and other staff members also received personal threats, which prompted the company to hire security details for its London and Paris offices. After a bomb destroyed the entrance to UIP's Paris offices in late September, Williams-Jones's car was swept for several weeks and he had twenty-four-hour bodyguard protection for the duration of *Last Temptation*'s worldwide openings that fall. Stricter controls than even those in the United States were imposed on the prints of the film. Guards were assigned to the prints at the theaters where the film played, and when a print shipped from one theater to the next, it traveled under escort and carried a security code that was checked from the point of origin all the way through to destination.

Martin Scorsese arrived in London directly from the Venice Film Festival and held court for the British press on the afternoon of the film's debut at the Leeds Cinema. Asked about the local authorities who were going to screen *Last Temptation,* Scorsese gave due deference to the British system: "I don't think you want a 12-year old seeing it and thinking it is an accurate account of the life of Jesus. The gospels are the truth and this film is a parable on that."[24] At one point in the press conference, a short, balding religious official wearing a cross around his neck stood up. Scorsese was sure that he was going to be on the receiving end of a diatribe. The man said that at first he was against the picture, against everything it stood for, but after going to see it, he changed his mind. *Last Temptation,* he said, was a "very profound spiritual poem."[25] He objected only to the depiction of Christ as a white, blue-eyed, blond-haired icon, saying that many people in the world would find this portrayal offensive. Scorsese explained his reasons for the casting choice, but it was the man's first remark that stayed with him. Said Scorsese, "That saved everything for me, because he had been against it, and he saw it."[26]

The September 9 openings of *Last Temptation* drew several dozen religious protesters to the two Cannon theater locations, but a larger group, about one hundred demonstrators, turned out for the evening showings at the West End Plaza. A group of nuns from the Evangelical Sisterhood of Mary clustered around the theater entrance, passing out leaflets that urged a boycott. One of the nuns approached UIP's head of marketing, Ken Green, on the sidewalk and rebuked him: "You would have publicized Auschwitz."[27] It was, said Michael Williams-Jones, "an astonishing reference."[28] Overall, the disruptions during the London openings were minor and the film played to capacity crowds for the first three days. UIP began preparing for a forty-print release of *Last Temptation* across England and Ireland by September 23.[29]

France loomed as the next major market for opening the film. Here the possibility of violence and the destruction of theaters was not just one of many scenarios. UIP's Paris staffers recognized early on that crisis conditions had already materialized in cities across the nation. The first sign of trouble came in August, when the neo-fascist federation General Alliance against Racism and for the Respect of French and Christian Identity (AGRIF) vowed that it would not hesitate "to infringe the law to jeopardize and prevent the release of such a blasphemous and sacrilegious film."[30] AGRIF's leader, Bernard Antony, also announced, as the *New York Times* reported, that "it would be an honor to go to jail to prevent such impiety and 'anti-Christian racism' from being purveyed in France."[31] A far-right Catholic splinter group of Jean-Marie Le Pen's National Front, which had suffered a political setback in the National Assembly elections just two months earlier, AGRIF was committed to restoring religious and cultural purity to France. Staunchly antiabortionist, many of AGRIF's members were organizing that fall to oppose the introduction of the controversial so-called morning-after pill, RU-486. But they were far less restrained than the National Front in how they pursued their aims. For them, the law of man could be trespassed if God's law was violated or the good name of his Son desecrated. So, when Cardinal Jean-Marie Lustiger of Paris and Cardinal Albert Decourtray of Lyon both criticized *The Last Temptation of Christ* in early September, they helped give a patina of approval to covert plans by shadowy groups of religious terrorists to make the film's exhibition so dangerous that no one would want to go to see it.[32]

The fundamentalists started their fight with multiple legal proceedings before the release of the film. UIP enjoyed the firm support of the French national authorities, in particular the minister of Culture, Jack Lang, who delivered an "all-audience visa" for *Last Temptation*. Local authorities in France, like those in the United Kingdom, have the right to overrule the federal position, however, and prevent the release of specific films in their jurisdictions. In the case of *Last Temptation,* three towns—Arcachon, Salon-de-Provence, and Aix-en-Provence—banned the film. Michael Williams-Jones personally directed the French administration of UIP to take the fight to the local mayoral jurisdictions, pursuing legal actions to press for the principle of freedom of expression. "It did not result in the banning being lifted," said Williams-Jones, "but it was a point that we intended taking."[33] In a separate proceeding, religious opponents demanded that an elaborate disclaimer, one that would explicitly dissociate the movie from the Gospels, be affixed to the beginning of *Last Temptation*.[34] It was upheld at first, but UIP and Universal won on final appeal in the Supreme Court. UIP's French lawyers confirmed that never in their experience had so much pressure been aroused on an issue relating to the media or entertainment in France.[35]

Amid an avalanche of threatening mailings, faxes, and telephone calls to theater owners, and with police officers placed on guard in front of theaters,

The Last Temptation of Christ opened on Wednesday, September 28, in Paris and other French cities. Multiple bomb threats were received at all the Parisian theaters, including the Gaumont Convention, the Pagoda, the Britannia, L'Escurial, and the UGC Odéon. That night, violent demonstrations were held outside three of the Paris theaters. The biggest of them, involving an estimated two thousand protesters, moved against the UGC Odéon theater in the Latin Quarter, smashing windows and lobbing tear-gas canisters at the entrance; later, a group of masked, hooded protesters returned, hurling Molotov cocktails and injuring eight of the policemen who were guarding the theater. At another theater, two religious groups staged quieter rallies, although, as *Daily Variety* noted, they "still managed to beat up the Agence France-Presse religion writer."[36]

The situation degraded over the weekend. In theaters across the country, protesters ripped up and poured acid on seats in theaters, tore movie screens, ransacked foyers and lobbies, threatened employees with physical injury, and called in threats that led to dozens of theaters being evacuated. The front of Paris's L'Escurial theater was completely destroyed by fire. In Marseilles and Lyon, Catholic extremists fired tear gas into theater lobbies and set off stink bombs in the auditoriums, forcing the patrons out into the street, where they were pelted with eggs and pummeled. In Avignon, four moviegoers broke into the projection booth, ripped the film from its reels, and destroyed it. In the town of Besançon, a firebomb ignited a blaze that caused extensive damage to the theater.

With 89,604 paid admissions in seventy-five theaters, *Last Temptation* did respectable business during its first week—but the widely publicized violence took its toll.[37] Going into the second week of release, five of the Paris theaters pulled the film and admissions in other theaters began dropping precipitously. Security was stepped up at theater entrances; the guards confiscated penknives, tear gas canisters, and other weapons from some of the moviegoers. Still, the film's adversaries were able to increase their attacks. The second weekend brought new rounds of bomb alerts, gas explosions, and stink and chemical bombs set off in theaters. In certain cases, multiplexes were collectively stink-bombed, resulting in not only *Last Temptation*'s closing down, but also the evacuation of audiences seeing other movies at the theaters. Exhibitors got more nervous by the day. Even when they were not evacuating theaters or calling for police sweeps, the acrid smell of the stink bombs lingered for days, driving away customers. The staff of many theaters, supported by trade unions, started refusing to work under the dangerous labor conditions.

Because of these labor pressures, a number of suburban and provincial houses closed down. UIP and Culture Minister Jack Lang issued public statements, trying to bring calm to the fragile situation.

The waves of violence climaxed on October 22, when a fire started shortly after midnight in the basement of the Cinéma Saint-Michel in Paris, where *Last Temptation* played on two screens. According to *Variety,* "Unidentified youths allegedly ripped out a seat, doused it with gasoline and lit it, then threw it in the stairway leading down to another basement screen showing Mike Figgis' 'Stormy Monday.' "[38] The Left Bank theater was quickly consumed in flames. Fire engines and ambulances raced to the scene, taking thirteen people suffering from inhalation of toxic fumes to hospitals. One of them, a British woman, was in critical condition for two days. It took more than an hour to put the fire out. The conflagration left the Saint-Michel—one of only two remaining houses in Paris playing *Last Temptation* at that stage—totally destroyed.

Visiting the charred site the next day, Jack Lang said, "Freedom of speech is threatened and we must not be intimidated by such acts."[39] Cardinal Jean-Marie Lustiger, who earlier decried the film without having seen it, now condemned as un-Christian those who chose pitiless aggression as the way to express their feelings. "When you commit violence," the cardinal said, "it is Christ himself you are attacking."[40] On October 24 approximately one thousand people, many of them trade unionists and film industry professionals, gathered outside the Saint-Michel to demonstrate against the perpetrators of violence. Within two days French police raids netted forty suspects in the arson attacks on several theaters. One of the Parisian leaders of the ultraright Catholics' campaign against *Last Temptation* was unrepentant, however. Father Philippe Laguérie told *Le Monde* that "Scorsese's blasphemous and ignominious film" should be blamed for any violence committed at theaters.[41]

The French press rallied behind UIP and the local exhibitors. The attacks on *Last Temptation,* said Michael Williams-Jones, "became a platform for the whole issue of freedom of expression. . . . The French, in spite of many of their actions to the contrary, uphold that notion very close to their hearts."[42] Nevertheless, the Saint-Michel fire took the wind out of the exhibitors' determination to fight the reactionaries. By the end of October, the picture was showing in only a few theaters, and those that did insist on playing it—most prominently, the Gaumont Champs-Elysées, for a thirteen-week run—did so with a huge presence of police surveillance. The film to which UIP once expected to sell as many as a half million tickets in France ended up selling

The Cinéma Saint-Michel in Paris was destroyed by fire in October 1988.
(Nicolas Jose/Sipa)

approximately one-third that number. "The opponents of the film have largely won," a UIP representative admitted to the *New York Times* after the Saint-Michel incident. "They have massacred the film's success and they have scared the public."[43]

On most of the European continent UIP did not encounter opposition on a scale approaching that of France. The film opened in Finland on September 23 and the next weekend in Sweden to strong reviews. But it took a court ruling in Amsterdam against the blasphemy lawsuit filed by a fundamentalist group, the Stop the Film Foundation, to pave the way for *Last Temptation*'s late September opening in the Netherlands.[44] In West Germany, Catholic associations waged a sturdy campaign of protest letters and petitions on theaters and government officials. "I receive hundreds of letters every day calling for the film to be banned. Too many of these letters are full of terrifying hatred," said the minister of education and the arts in the state of North Rhine-Westphalia.[45] In reaction to the protest, two-thirds of the 150 theaters intending to show *Last Temptation* canceled their bookings. But the German film classification board awarded it an "especially outstanding" designation (qualifying it for tax benefits at West German theaters), and with a significant burst of media attention, the film opened on November 10 in what *Variety* called a "low-key 50-print release," accompanied by only scattered, peaceful demonstrations.[46]

That same month, Ireland's film censor, Sheamus Smith, after deliberating on the matter for more than a month, passed *Last Temptation* for exhibition with an "over 18" certificate—with the provisos (designed to placate the Irish Catholic groups opposing it) that Scorsese's disclaimer that the film was based on a novel, not the Gospels, be posted outside the theater, and that no one be allowed to enter the theater after the film had started.[47]

Through the fall of 1988 and into early 1989, a number of countries in UIP's sales territories blocked the film. Some countries, like India, never permitted *Last Temptation* to get to the point of being banned because of a lack of cooperation from the exhibitor community. In others, official decisions on banning the film hinged on a variety of factors: the country's censorship laws and the government's willingness to apply them to mainstream films; the influence of religious bodies in cultural and government affairs; the national disposition to modernity and freedom of thought and art; and—in many cases—the political climate of the moment. The first government entity to use the blunt tool of censorship was the Australian state of Queensland. Australia's Film Censorship Board initially gave the film an "R" rating, and later amended its classification to "M" (suitable for those fifteen and older), citing the film's "reverent, sincere and frequently moving account of aspects of the life and crucifixion of Jesus, providing original and meaningful insights into the Christian faith."[48] But in a model similar to England's, each state has the right to rule on films separately from the national board. Although many of the country's moral reform groups called for the film to be banned—among them the "Festival of Light" Christian movement and the Australian Family Association, a Down Under knockoff of Donald Wildmon's AFA—only conservative Queensland acted on their recommendations. "It's the ultimate case of bureaucracy telling the public what they can or can't see," UIP's manager, Mark Gailey, told *Variety*.[49] The film opened on October 13 throughout Australia—sans Queensland—to large audiences and prayer vigils held by evangelical and Catholic groups outside theaters.

Official bans of *Last Temptation* swiftly followed in Lebanon, Malaysia, the Philippines, and Singapore. Singapore's Controller of Undesirable Publications went so far as to invoke a ban on the Kazantzakis novel, which had theretofore been available in bookstores and libraries.[50] Papua New Guinea might not have been high on UIP's list of markets, but the South Pacific island group's chief censor banned *Last Temptation* anyway, offering by way of explanation: "We must remember how much store is traditionally set by Papua New Guineans on dreams and hallucinations and also how many people say, 'I saw it on the movies, it must be true.'"[51] In South Africa, where the Dutch Reformed Church still exerted influence on the government's cultural policies, a censorship committee viewed the film in October and rejected it.[52]

Last Temptation tested the limits of tolerance even in such democracies as Israel and Greece. Cognizant of the country's unique status as spiritual center to three of the world's great religions, Israeli authorities trod carefully when it came to artistic renderings of religious figures. A clause in the country's Censorship Board regulations prohibiting the release of irreligious films had been invoked just once—in 1977, when the board heeded the complaints of local Christians and banned *The Passover Plot*, a film that disputed the Gospel accounts of Jesus' crucifixion. When opposition to *Last Temptation* began surfacing in Israel in August 1988, UIP's Rachel Surkis expressed confidence that it would not suffer the same fate as *The Passover Plot*. "I cannot imagine that it will not pass the censors," she told *Variety*. But the influence of evangelical Christians and "messianic" Jews in Israel had grown substantially during the 1980s, and to them the idea of *Last Temptation* being shown in Holy Land theaters was unconscionable. In mid-October twenty-one members of the board went into an unusually lengthy closed session after a special screening. They emerged to announce a majority vote to ban *Last Temptation* in Israel. Surkis immediately said that UIP would seek a repeal of the board's decision.

Greece was another democracy that prized its civil liberties. When the Greek Orthodox Church demanded a ban of *Last Temptation* in late August, calling it "horrifyingly vulgar," the government refused on grounds that it had no such authority.[53] The film was requested by UIP to be screened by a committee that forms part of the internal Greek government office that applies age classifications to films. It was approved for adults sixteen and older. But opinions about the film in that country, where the Church once sought the excommunication of Nikos Kazantzakis, remained sharply divided. When *Last Temptation* opened in Athens on October 13, about two thousand angry demonstrators gathered at Athens University, then marched through the streets toward the Opera Cinema. Greek riot police took up positions in front of the theater, shooting tear gas at the approaching mob. With an Orthodox priest crying, "Inside, inside," hundreds of protesters fought their way through the cordon. They burst into the theater while the day's first screening was in progress. Shouting "Down with anti-Christians" and "Orthodoxy or death," they ripped up seats, slashed the screen, and, finally, destroyed the projection equipment. A smaller band of enraged protesters then broke away and headed to the Embassy Cinema, about a mile away. At the Embassy, they used a large wooden cross to knock down posters advertising the film and forced their way into the theater during the middle of a showing of *Last Temptation*. Again they slashed the movie screen.[54] Despite the opening-day rampages, the film did remarkable business in its first five weeks, selling 165,000 tickets at multiple theaters in Athens, although, *Variety* noted, "exibs outside the city got cold feet and never opened the pic."[55]

Meanwhile, eight Orthodox Christian organizations jointly launched a petition to force *Last Temptation* out of the theaters. Claiming that the film violated a clause in the Greek constitution forbidding the display of works of art that "offend the public decency," the groups took their case to an Athenian high court.[56] On November 15 the court issued an injunction on screenings of *The Last Temptation of Christ* everywhere in Greece, on penalty of $700 for each violation. Once the order was put into effect, the same church organizations brought a civil case against the Greek manager of UIP and six Athens exhibitors; after a hearing lasting six hours, the presiding judge dismissed the charges. The film remains banned in Greece.

By late 1988 the furor had moved on to the Spanish-speaking countries of the Western Hemisphere. Over a period of five months, the film was officially banned in Argentina, Chile, Colombia, the Dominican Republic, Mexico, Panama, Peru, and Trinidad. The combination of powerful censorship boards and the strong influence of Roman Catholicism at all levels of society made it difficult for the film to penetrate Latin America. (As if that wasn't enough, there was the rough justice of the region's politics to contend with; a right-wing paramilitary group in Colombia threatened to assassinate the communications minister if he approved the film.)[57] UIP did manage to introduce *Last Temptation* in Uruguay, Ecuador, and Brazil in low-profile premieres, although it could not avoid being victimized by the usual run of political difficulties. For example, on November 18, under considerable pressure from Catholic authorities, the mayor of São Paulo suspended showings of the film at all eight locations just one day after its release, allegedly for "inadequate conditions of the toilets" and other safety issues.[58]

With the passage of time, several countries that originally banned *Last Temptation* reversed their court rulings or censorship board decisions, or simply allowed the film to be shown after a liberalization of their cultural policies. Israel was the first to reconsider its earlier position. In March 1989 the Israeli

Supreme Court heard an appeal from MCA/Universal and its Israeli distributor, Golan Globus, that sought to overturn the decision issued in October 1988
(and reaffirmed on November 7) by the Israeli Censorship Board. In June the
high court voted unanimously to overrule the ban. The only justification for
limiting freedom of religious expression, the court wrote in its decision, occurs
"if a religion is insulted in a severe and extreme way, and it is not enough for
the film to give free rise to possible objections or even revulsion"—conditions
that, the court decided, did not exist in Israel with *Last Temptation*.[59] After the
verdict, UIP announced that screenings would begin in Tel Aviv on June 23.

Other countries were more ambivalent about allowing the film on their
sovereign soil. South Africa's chief censor, Brian Coetzee, temporarily suspended the ban on *Last Temptation* to allow for a special screening at a Johan-
nesburg film festival in late October 1992, with Paul Schrader in attendance.
Coetzee's ruling elicited "howls of outrage from fundamentalist Christians,"
according to *Variety*.[60] The decision was hastily reversed, then rereversed.
Finally, a South African court halted the screening just minutes before it was
due to begin—"Whereupon I just told the audience the movie," recalled
Schrader with a laugh. "And, like, 'Well, it starts out, he has a migraine. . . .'
It's all I could do."[61] South Africa lifted the ban in 1998; even then, hundreds of
vituperative letters and phone calls hailed down on the Film and Publications
Board.[62]

The film had a similarly checkered history in Chile, perhaps the most culturally conservative country in Latin America. On November 11, 1996, after
nearly eight years of censorship, Chile's Film Classification Board voted to
reclassify *Last Temptation* as suitable for adult audiences. Three days later a
court of appeals suspended the board's decision after hearing an appeal by a
conservative group allied with the Catholic Church, El Porvenir de Chile
("Chile's Future").[63] Chile's major newspapers followed the case in front-page
stories, and the issue of whether to admit Scorsese's film became widely
regarded as a litmus test for the prospect of ending film censorship in Chile.
The Supreme Court upheld the ban in June 1997, and subsequently several
Chileans were arrested for trying to organize a public screening—an action
criticized by human rights organizations.[64] Ultimately, in early 2001, Chile's
ban on *Last Temptation* was rescinded.

During the 1990s the major lines of attack on *The Last Temptation of Christ*
shifted to the broadcast and cable television systems that wanted to air it.
Some of the toughest resistance occurred in the recently liberated nations of

Eastern Europe, where Orthodox and Roman Catholics and other Christian-backed organizations tried to stop televised showings in Poland (1993), the Czech Republic (1994), Hungary (1994), and Russia (1997–98). In May 1995 several thousand Israeli demonstrators marched on the offices of a Haifa cable TV company, but it went ahead with its planned showing of *Last Temptation*.[65] After protests forced the BBC to abandon plans to broadcast *Last Temptation* in 1991, Britain's Channel 4 screened it in 1995, generating almost 6,000 complaints to Channel 4 and 1,554 complaints to the United Kingdom's Independent Television Commission—still the record holder for "most complained about" broadcast on a non-BBC television channel.[66]

By the first decade of the twenty-first century, broadcasts of the film—which were relatively rare in any case—did not prompt much more than isolated complaints. The last country to open *The Last Temptation of Christ* theatrically was Mexico. After banning it for fifteen years, the Mexican government gave UIP approval in late 2003 to distribute the film. In March 2004 *Last Temptation* premiered on seventy screens just one week ahead of the release of Mel Gibson's blockbuster, *The Passion of the Christ*. *Variety* reported of the opening night, with no sign of irony, "Screenings of 'Temptation' were packed on Friday night; many ticket buyers seemed to have confused it with the Gibson film."[67]

BY THE END of 1988 *The Last Temptation of Christ* was playing in fewer than a dozen theaters in the United States. At this stage a studio is already planning for the next release "windows" in a film's life cycle: first, the home video window, which in the late 1980s started some six months after a film exited from theaters; and three or more months later came presentations of the film on pay-cable. But two trade press stories laid bare MCA/Universal's nervousness about any future commercial exploitations of the controversial film. In a December 13 story in *Variety*, Cineplex Odeon's garrulous CEO, Garth Drabinsky, was quoted as saying that *Last Temptation* would be reissued in spring of 1989 to take advantage of anticipated Academy Award and Golden Globe nominations and critics' top-ten lists for 1988. Drabinsky opined loftily, "We've never chosen to back down in matters that we believe firmly are exemplary in the spirit of an enlightened democracy." He envisioned a wide rerelease of *Last Temptation*—not a thousand-theater release, but "a much more expanded pattern than was initially the case."[68]

Several days later the studio's fury with Drabinsky's remarks was on full view. An unidentified Universal source told the *Hollywood Reporter* that "the studio's top management did subsequently have conversations with Drabinsky to let him know its displeasure with his statements."[69] Not only did Drabinsky speak without authorization from MCA/Universal, but the paper's "Universal source" made it clear that studio officials never discussed the matter with him, nor had they any intention of reissuing *Last Temptation.*

As it turned out, the film did land on numerous critics' year-end lists; according to a poll of one hundred film critics' lists, *Last Temptation* ranked sixth in the number of top-ten mentions—behind *The Thin Blue Line, Bull Durham, Who Framed Roger Rabbit?, A World Apart,* and *Rain Man*—in what was considered a highly competitive year for quality pictures.[70] The film yielded a Golden Globe best-actress nomination for Barbara Hershey and a best-director Oscar nomination for Scorsese—the third of his career. (Some, however, believed that the best-director honor was given at least as much in recognition of Universal's and Scorsese's hard-fought battles as for the merits of the film.) Still, it was difficult to imagine any circumstances that would have caused Universal to put itself through another contentious round of theatrical openings.

Another mid-December article in *Daily Variety* underscored the studio's sensitivity about the film's video release. According to one story, "MCA Weighing Its Options on 'Temptation' HV Release," the studio was investigating the idea of selling the videocassette rights to another distributor, rather than release the film through MCA Home Video. Although the inquiries were apparently no more than that—testing the waters just in case it did decide to offer the film—the story reflected MCA's unease. *Variety*'s Tom Bierbaum observed, " 'The Last Temptation of Christ' will represent an unprecedented test of the vidstore community's willingness to handle controversial material. With the possible exception of X-rated fare, the vid industry has probably never handled a title that has as much potential for stirring up community ire."[71]

Finally, in late April 1989 MCA Home Video discreetly let the word out that *The Last Temptation of Christ* would be released as a videocassette on June 28, at a list price of $89.95. The announcement was buried at the end of a press release touting a number of other Universal films; even Oliver Stone's *Talk Radio,* which grossed only $3.5 million, was mentioned ahead of Scorsese's film. Paradoxically, the low-key approach itself drew media attention. On the eve of its release, the *Los Angeles Times* noted, "The supposedly quietest release ever of a major movie on videocassette is taking place this weekend as MCA Home Video slips 'The Last Temptation of Christ' into stores—minus any promotion or advertising."[72] Tom Pollock was later to take issue with this characterization. "[The *Last Temptation* video] was released with normal publicity," he said. "What it *wasn't* released with is any special sales campaign."[73] Nevertheless, in sharp contrast to most studio films, video chains were not given discounts for selling *Last Temptation* or required to publicize it in their mailers. MCA Home Video distributors did not assign sales targets for the video and did nothing to promote it—no co-op advertising money, no point-of-purchase sales, no posters or standees for store display.

Arguably, MCA/Universal had valid reasons for downplaying *Last Temptation.* Several national chains, as well as multitudes of "mom and pop" stores, already reported receiving petitions and phone calls from church groups asking them not to stock the film and threatening boycotts if they did. It became apparent that some organizations, among them the American Family Association, had alerted their constituents to expect the video to surface soon. Campus Crusade for Christ's Don Beehler predicted a "grassroots" rebellion of Christians against the video version, especially in communities where the film had not played the year before. "People will just go to their local video stores and ask them not to stock it. . . . They'll threaten to take their business elsewhere," Beehler said about these concerned Christians.[74] Some rental outlets and supermarket video concessions did decide that this one title was not worth the aggravation or the loss of even a small number of loyal customers. But many video chain executives bridled at the implied intimidation. "I eat controversy for lunch," said Gary Messenger, the head of the North American Video chain, based in Durham, North Carolina; "I might order more copies because of the controversy."[75] Allan Caplan, head of the Applause chain, thought the film deserved to be stocked on its own merits: "The movie was nominated for an Oscar. . . . It's a legitimate movie, not some C-picture. People may not agree with its point of view, but it's still a movie that some people want to see. Why shouldn't the people who want to see it be able to see it?"[76] Other video chains, looking at the issue strictly as a business proposition, expected the video to be in high demand, especially among those who hadn't had the opportunity to see it in theaters the first time around.

Then, in early May, the other, much larger shoe dropped: the country's biggest video chain, Blockbuster, announced it would not carry *Last Temptation* in any of its 343 company-owned locations, and would advise its 387 franchisees also to pass on it.[77] MCA/Universal had seen this coming for weeks. Tom Pollock spoke personally to Blockbuster's CEO, Wayne Huizenga, and used the same argument he'd tried on theater owners. "Please don't do that,"

Pollock recalled saying. "Just say that you won't play it in any store that you feel it would offend community standards. . . . But if you have a store, you know, in the middle of a college town or Seattle, Washington, or where they don't care so much—'Nope, we're not going to do it.' Why? 'It's controversial. We don't want to do anything controversial. . . . This is a place where you come to escape controversy.' So, that really pissed me off."[78]

The decision by Blockbuster—which constituted approximately 25 percent of the U.S. video market—was significant and, according to Pollock, the major reason for sending the video out without "a special marketing push," as he put it. Blockbuster's refusal also factored into MCA's decision to ship a relatively low 50,000 units to wholesalers. Although Pollock attributed Blockbuster's stance on *Last Temptation* to an internal calculation of the costs of controversy, it also evidently became part of the chain's family-friendly brand. Blockbuster accepted nearly all R-rated fare, including films featuring "hard action" and "soft-core porn." But it drew the line at sexually explicit titles, a corporate policy extended to all NC-17 films when that rating was introduced in 1990, as well as a smaller group of titles—of which *Last Temptation* was the most prominent example—that the company felt violated standards of public morality.

During its first week in stores, *Last Temptation* rented at a brisk pace. At some locations it exceeded projections, even if, as one store manager put it, MCA handled *Last Temptation* "like a leper colony release."[79] The one regional exception to the videotape's strong rental results was the South, where, one executive said, it was treated like "a film nobody heard of."[80] The *Arkansas Democrat-Gazette* conducted a survey of Little Rock video store owners and found some of them "laying so low on 'The Last Temptation of Christ' they look like 'sail cats.'" Several managers forthrightly placed it alongside other new releases. Others were more cautious. An owner of nine Little Rock stores told the *Democrat-Gazette* that only two of his locations would make it available, and then only if customers asked for it.[81]

Until the Criterion laserdisk version appeared in 1998 (followed shortly afterward by the DVD format), the videocassette lived a fugitive existence in retail outlets. Paul Schrader recalled seeing it in his local Blockbuster store in Westchester County, New York. "So I go up to the manager, and I said, 'I really want to commend you for your courage in stocking this film, because I know that a lot of chains won't stock it.' Then I went back the next week and it was gone."[82] In 1991 Martin Scorsese received a Golden Plate Award from the Academy of Achievement, an organization that brings young people from around the world into contact with "eminent achievers." After his opening remarks at a symposium, a student asked how he felt about *Last Temptation* and its availability in video stores. Scorsese responded that Blockbuster did not want to show it. He recalled saying to the gathering, "They don't want to show it because basically they didn't want any trouble, didn't want their windows broken or anything."[83] At that moment, a hush fell over the audience. The moderator explained to Scorsese that the reaction he heard was due to the fact that Blockbuster's Wayne Huizenga was also one of the Academy's honorees that year. Scorsese later had a long, cordial talk with Huizenga, who confessed that he liked *The Last Temptation of Christ*. Huizenga, said Scorsese, told him that his company's snubbing of the movie was the last time he would have someone under him make a decision like that. Blockbuster, however, persisted in its unwritten policy regarding the film.

The next furor in 1989 arose over the showings of *Last Temptation* on the Cinemax premium cable channel in October. Cinemax quietly scheduled the film in a late-night slot and did not mention the title in its publicity materials. Again, the film's opponents encouraged people to take action if the local exhibitor—this time, the cable operator—did not refuse the movie. "Whack 'em with a three-month cutoff," the Reverend Donald Wildmon advised. And what if canceling one's cable subscription was too great a sacrifice for most consumers? Wildmon responded, "Sure, you'll have withdrawal symptoms, but you'll get used to it. Why, we didn't even have the TV on all last night. We worked in the yard."[84]

As the October 2 premiere date approached, East Arkansas Cablevision in Jonesboro became the first company to accede to local pressures and show a blank screen instead of the movie. Soon cable companies in other communities—including Bethlehem, Lehighton, and Wilkes-Barre, Pennsylvania; Texarkana, Texas; and all of Multimedia's systems in Kansas, Illinois, Oklahoma, and North Carolina—followed suit, even though their contracts with Home Box Office, the parent company of Cinemax, stipulated that the channel's entire schedule had to be carried. The blackouts were not suffered gladly in all the localities. Service Electrical Cable TV in Pennsylvania reinstated the film's showings after receiving 140 subscriber calls complaining about the first night's blackout. "We even had a call from a minister who wanted it shown," the company's president told the *Philadelphia Inquirer*. "He said he told his congregation to watch it as a teaching aid."[85]

In little more than a year, *The Last Temptation of Christ* had survived the denunciations of preachers and politicians, mountains of mail delivered to

Universal City, death threats to executives, demonstrations attended by thousands of citizens, and assaults on theaters and moviegoers. Now it was being shown on television inside American homes. It was not yet ready to become a widely valued text about Jesus or the spiritual meaning of Christianity—and it probably never will be. But surely something of a milestone was quietly reached when the cable network Bravo announced four Easter-season showings of *Last Temptation* for April 2000. No calls or letters of protest were reported.

Epilogue

THE WEEK THAT *The Last Temptation of Christ* opened, Paul
Schrader visited Martin Scorsese's office, just around the corner
from his own office. He found the director in an agitated state. "Marty was
bitching and moaning about all of this controversy. And I said, 'Marty, we
wanted to make a controversial film. We have now *made* a controversial film.'
He said, 'I know, I know, but I didn't think it would be *this* controversial.'"[1]

Controversies rarely go according to plan—if there *is* a plan. Unfortunately
for Martin Scorsese, the *Last Temptation* furor only rarely touched on the
spiritual issues that motivated him to make the picture. He undoubtedly never
thought in the first, quiet stirring of his film's conception that it would one
day become a pretext for attacking "non-Christian" corporate executives, or
that it would become a pawn in the religious right's disagreements with Hollywood, the People for the American Way, and other liberal groups. But *The
Last Temptation of Christ* illustrated the general principle that a film—or any
other work of art—becomes ensnared in other people's interests and agendas
the further it moves down the path toward a full-blown controversy. The
irruption of a controversy opens up opportunities for individuals and groups
to reaffirm or reclaim their own identities, to signal their allegiance to a cause,
and, most important of all, to urgently speak their hearts and minds. Even as
Scorsese raced to finish the film itself, *Last Temptation* was almost literally held
hostage by groups claiming to protect the public from what it contained.

The *Last Temptation* crisis—like most controversies—occurred at a seam
in the transition from one ideological regime to another. The late 1980s was
one of those historical moments of gathered tension. And this made the struggle over the film as much a political battle as a religious one. As Gustav Niebuhr, the religion writer for the *Atlanta Journal,* perceptively noted in August
1988, the protest reflected "a growing self-image on the part of evangelical
Christians, who see themselves as a distinct minority group forced to battle
for its rights in a society often indifferent and occasionally downright hostile
to Christian interests. . . . Gradually, some protest leaders are coming to see
an opportunity in the reaction to the movie, in that Christians may achieve
the unity of voice and vision that other minority groups have had."[2]

The campaign waged against MCA/Universal did have a uniting effect, and
it enabled many activist groups to bounce back from their financial doldrums.

But this controversy involved more than just one film, one set of issues, or one media company. *The Last Temptation of Christ* got swept up into a larger narrative that pitted cultural traditionalists against modernists—a conflict with very high stakes for the freedoms of expression and religion in predominantly secular societies. Within weeks of the film's release in the United States, the global implications of this conflict were made suddenly, frighteningly clear.

On September 26, 1988, a novel written by Salman Rushdie, *The Satanic Verses,* was published in the United Kingdom. A finalist for the prestigious Booker Award and winner of the Whitbread Prize for the best novel of 1988, *The Satanic Verses* was a fantastical political and religious allegory, embodying, as *Time*'s book reviewer wrote, "both an *Arabian Nights* narrative enchantment and a vast rumination on history, on the clash of cultures and individuals, and on the beliefs that people cherish for comfort and salvation."[3] But this same novel was immediately condemned as blasphemous by Muslims, owing to its irreverent reimagining of an episode in the life of the prophet Mohammed. In the ensuing weeks, nearly every country with a substantial population of Muslims banned *The Satanic Verses.* The worldwide controversy culminated on February 13, 1989, with riots in Islamabad in which five people were killed by Pakistani police. The next day Iran's spiritual leader, Ayatollah Khomeini, issued a fatwa—a decree based on Islamic law—calling on Muslims everywhere to actively seek the death of Salman Rushdie and his publishers. As the author went into hiding, Hashemi Rafsanjani, speaker of the Iranian Majlis, excoriated the novel as an "insult to Islamic sanctities" that was "worse than an officially declared war."[4]

Coming so soon after *Last Temptation*'s international release, the Rushdie affair was seen by Western observers as a similar, albeit more extreme, case of religious intolerance. If the ayatollah's death sentence was a state-sponsored act of retribution for an author's having crossed a sacrosanct boundary, the *Last Temptation* controversy was "sponsored" by a coalition of evangelical clergy who also had punishment in mind. Even the Reverend Wildmon saw "very definite similarities on the front end," including the failure of both Scorsese and Rushdie "to take into consideration the deeply felt religious convictions of the people affected."[5] Statements like Wildmon's reveal a major fault line in controversies involving religion and art: religious conservatives typically argue that it is a responsibility of artists to be sensitive to the beliefs of people of faith; but to the modernist ear, this deference to "sensitivity" can sound like an appeal for limiting the expressive rights of artists. Both controversies were also widely viewed as symptoms of a newly resurgent global fundamentalism in the world—a fundamentalism that did not hesitate to assert itself against the excesses of modernity. (Interestingly, the Iranian government showed its solidarity with Christians' angst when it ordered the withdrawal of the only Iranian film in the Istanbul Film Festival in May 1989 because *Last Temptation* was being screened.)[6]

Meanwhile in 1988, another controversy in the art world broke to the surface and forged an unlikely alliance with *Last Temptation.* Andres Serrano, a thirty-eight-year-old New York artist, won a $15,000 award to exhibit his work in the Awards in the Visual Arts, jointly funded by the Rockefeller Foundation, the Equitable (Life Insurance) Foundation, and the National Endowment for the Arts. One of the pieces he selected was a photograph titled "Piss Christ," which depicted a crucifix suspended in an amber medium—the artist's own urine. "Piss Christ," according to Steven Dubin in his book *Arresting Images,* was intended as a commentary on the profanation of religion—and of Christ specifically—in contemporary society.[7] "[Serrano] was born in the Christian faith, he feels very much a part of that," said the owner of the New York gallery that handled Serrano's art. "He has deep religious feelings, but he does not express them exactly the way every other guy does."[8]

The latter half of that remark, it turned out, was one of the year's great understatements. Serrano's work had finished its touring exhibition three months earlier when the Reverend Donald Wildmon took notice of "Piss Christ" in early April 1989. Wildmon proceeded to publicize Serrano's work as an outrageous example of antireligious art funded at the taxpayers' expense, and he called for the firing of the personnel at the National Endowment for the Arts who had approved it. The scandal of "Piss Christ"—joined by an NEA–funded exhibit of homoerotic photographs by Robert Mapplethorpe titled The Perfect Moment—quickly caught the attention of the U.S. Senate. In a speech on the Senate floor about the controversy, Senator Jesse Helms of North Carolina declared, "I do not know Mr. Andres Serrano, and I hope I never meet him. Because he is not an artist, he is a jerk. . . . And he is taunting the American people."[9] Other works funded by the NEA came under critical scrutiny, but it was the Mapplethorpe and Serrano photos that prompted members of the U.S. Senate, under the vigorous leadership of Senator Helms, to consider new legislation for the Endowment—including guidelines forbidding the use of federal funds for "obscene or indecent materials or materials denigrating a particular religion."[10]

Conservative critics began to assail the NEA and the art projects it funded, and the columnist Patrick J. Buchanan emerged as one of the chief ideologues and propagandists. In his May 22, 1989, column in the *Washington Times,* Buchanan drew links between the Serrano exhibit, a museum exhibit in Chicago where patrons were asked to walk over the American flag, and *The Last Temptation of Christ.* Warning his readers about the "downhill slide of American culture [gathering] momentum," Buchanan quoted the conservative art critic James Cooper at length, including Cooper's line criticizing Washington's leaders for pursuing battles against adversaries on foreign soil "while failing to realize the war is also raging on the battlefield of the arts within our own borders."[11]

This was one of the first times the "war" metaphor had been used in reference to disputes about the nation's culture. As the issue of rap music lyrics grew heated in 1989—especially with the release of 2 Live Crew's controversial album, *As Nasty as They Wanna Be,* accelerating pressure on the major record companies to adopt a uniform warning label—and the AFA pressed its campaigns against advertisers sponsoring violent and indecent TV programs, the idea of a permanent, warring split over the purposes and effects of popular culture began to take hold. The conservatives' polemic gained traction with an influential article published in the April 30, 1990, issue of *National Review.* In "The Culture War," Henry J. Hyde, a Republican congressman from Illinois, outlined the complaint against uncivil art. In Hyde's view, there was no doubt about the meaning of the Mapplethorpe and Serrano scandals: "For the Great Arts Controversy demonstrated that America is, in truth, involved in a *Kulturkampf*—a culture war, a war between cultures and a war about the very meaning of 'culture.'" By *culture war* Hyde meant "the struggle between those who believe that the norms of 'bourgeois morality' (which is drawn in the main from classic Jewish and Christian morality) should form the ethical basis of our common life, and those who are determined that these norms will be replaced with a radical and thoroughgoing moral relativism. . . . That is the division in our house." This division could go on unabated, he suggested, leaving the wreckage of American polity in its wake, unless the public agreed on an understanding of art that rejected "self-indulgent self-expression."[12]

In what turned out to be a trial run of his famous 1992 speech to the Republican National Convention, Pat Buchanan responded to Hyde's critique in his April 22 column: "There is method in this madness. The flag defiled, pictures desecrating symbols of Christ, use of kids as sex objects, these are designed not to challenge and stimulate, but to insult and inflame. Given that 90 percent of Americans are revolted, what kind of politics is it? Answer: it is not politics. It is war, cultural war, religious war."[13]

It was an idea whose time had come. The culture war became a powerful lens that brought a wide-ranging set of issues into sharp ideological focus: the "sanctity of life" issues of abortion, euthanasia, and eventually stem cell research; the preservation of traditional marriage; the codification of English as the national language; the display of religious artifacts in public places; the teaching of creationism (and, later, intelligent design) in public schools; revisionist interpretations of history in textbooks and museums; and, of course, indecency and liberal bias in the media. Indeed, James Dobson told *Focus on the Family* readers in 1991, "Nothing short of a great Civil War of Values rages today throughout North America."[14] On one side of this civil war stand the religious conservatives—evangelical Protestants, orthodox Jews, and pre–Vatican II Catholics—who believe the common culture should be governed by values derived from the Judeo-Christian ethical tradition. On the other side are cultural modernists, who generally stand for religious pluralism, the rights of minorities and women, and the full application of scientific rationality in social life. The gulf separating the assumptions of the groups is huge, if not unbridgeable. As S. J. D. Green wrote, the commitment of religious traditionalists to absolute principles arising from their holy texts locks them "into conflict with the liberal belief that the truth arises from a process of continual rational argument, and with the doctrine that 'the good life' can only be achieved through that degree of discretion which permits the greatest possible experimental diversity in the conduct of human affairs."[15]

The Last Temptation of Christ symbolized this "experimental diversity" in the media more pointedly than almost any case from the late 1980s. In his seminal 1991 study, *Culture Wars,* James Davison Hunter chose the *Last Temptation* controversy as the best example of how culture war rhetoric and tactics played out in the film industry.[16] And in Michael Medved's 1992 best seller, *Hollywood vs. America* (a book that attracted its own share of criticism from Hollywood and liberal intellectuals), Scorsese's film exemplified the movie industry's alleged vendetta against people of faith.[17] With each new confrontation in the 1990s—from Oliver Stone's *Natural Born Killers,* Kevin Smith's *Dogma,* and the Miramax film *Priest* to the television series *NYPD Blue, Nothing Sacred,* and *Ellen*—comparisons with *Last Temptation* were often made. The polarization of views peaked with a speech given by Senator Robert Dole on May 31, 1995, in which he decried Hollywood's "nightmares of depravity," and two years later, with a boycott campaign by the Southern Baptist Convention against the Walt Disney Company. Dole's speech at a Los Angeles Republican fund-raiser was widely regarded as a bid to align himself with his party's social conservative wing during his run-up to the 1996 presidential campaign. He did not focus on the issue again in the campaign. The Southern Baptist boycott, announced mainly in protest of Disney's gay-friendly policies at its theme parks, failed to have an economic effect on the company. It was quietly withdrawn in 2005.

Occasionally the culture wars cool off, as they did in the months following the September 11, 2001, terrorist attacks. But inevitably the heat turns up again when conditions are right for new conflicts to claim the public's attention. In the first decade of the twenty-first century, *The Last Temptation of Christ* persists in the collective memory as a tipping point in the conflicts on art and popular culture. For the first time, large numbers of people spoke out against a media product they considered disrespectful of their values—a film they regarded as worse than pornography. For the first time, a media corporation fought to have its product released amid economic and political pressures. And the controversy provided a round of "basic training" for a generation of activists who felt that the media—in particular, the screen media of film, television, the Internet, and video games—needed to be brought back in conformance with traditional moral codes. The *Last Temptation* episode, and others similar to it, indirectly helped spur the growth of parallel cultures in the United States—cultural traditionalists and modernists—the members of each embracing a different vision of the good life and expressing their differences in the way they vote, buy products, raise their children, worship (or not), and engage with media and popular culture. Because these differences are so stark and pervasive, and because each side perceives the stakes of "losing" to be so high, the prospects for the culture wars ending soon are not bright.[18]

For most people, particularly those whose lives were not affected in any meaningful way by it, the *Last Temptation* controversy left no trace—or else lost its singularity by merging with a string of other events that shared certain characteristic forms or topics. But for those working at MCA/Universal in the late 1980s, as well as those who found themselves set against or allied with the film industry, the incident became a signpost of collective memory replete with legendary stories and moral lessons. In Hollywood the legacy of *The Last Temptation of Christ* became something quite different from the heroic icon to which the Director's Guild and other industry professionals paid homage in the summer of 1988. The film took on an almost totemic status as the type of project that should *not* be pursued, except with the greatest caution. Sean Daniel recalled his perceptions of this widely circulated lesson: "I think the experience for . . . the other studios, watching another media company come under siege because it financed and chose to distribute a movie like this, probably was an alarm bell, if you will, for any company thinking about venturing into something similar. It served notice that this level of controversy—real, manipulated, stirred up, however you want [to characterize it]—this level of controversy and overwhelming events could occur [again]."[19] In the months after *Last Temptation*'s release, a chilling effect set in for projects that skirted dangerously close to sensitive issues, particularly ones that risked the displeasure of powerful religious institutions. In January 1989, for example, CBS and Twentieth Century Fox were considering separate projects based on the recent bombing deaths of two devout Mormons; the *Washington Post* reported, "A source close to the film project said 'The Last Temptation of Christ' tempest caused 20th Century Fox to look very, very carefully at 'A Gathering of Saints' to determine the effects of a Mormon-inspired boycott."[20] When the studios did approve nonmainstream projects, they were overly cautious in the execution. *Do the Right Thing* (1989), *The Handmaid's Tale* (1990), and *Basic Instinct* (1992) were all deemed sufficiently controversial that Josh Baran was hired to deploy field crisis teams for the openings, although none of the protests turned out to be remotely as large or contentious as those against *Last Temptation*.

By the mid-1990s, the studios were ready to explore religious subjects again. Financed by Disney's Miramax division, Antonia Bird's 1995 film *Priest* was a serious drama about the ethical dilemmas faced by a homosexual Catholic priest. Even before the film was seen, Cardinal John O'Connor and the Catholic League for Religious and Civil Rights, led by its outspoken president, William A. Donohue, aggressively attacked *Priest* for its purported hostility toward Catholics. Miramax compounded the insult by announcing that *Priest* would open nationally on Good Friday. The choice of Good Friday, according to Mark Gill, who was then president of marketing, was supposed to capitalize on the increased media coverage given to religious issues during the Passover and Easter celebrations. "Opening the movie right on the day was clearly a mistake and was offensive to a lot of people," Gill admitted, and Miramax moved the opening to an earlier date.[21] Nevertheless, the donnybrook resulted in a burst of news coverage for the $1.7 million picture.

Three years later, DreamWorks' Jeffrey Katzenberg directed a large-scale (and widely publicized) consultation with Jewish and Christian scholars and religious leaders about *Prince of Egypt*, its animated film about the young Moses. According to one industry source, Katzenberg's experience with *The Last Temptation of Christ* taught him the value of this form of consultation, although Katzenberg himself denied that *Last Temptation* had anything to do with the decision to vet *Prince of Egypt* so thoroughly with religious experts.[22]

Not unlike Scorsese's, the director Kevin Smith's youthful encounter with Roman Catholicism formed the subtext for his 1999 film, *Dogma*.[23] The Catholic League's use of an early script as the basis for its complaints about *Dogma* took the parallel with *Last Temptation* even further. Unlike MCA, however, the Walt Disney Company, still smarting from its unpleasant experience with *Priest*, sold the film to the Weinstein brothers, who turned around and sold the distribution rights to Lions Gate. Condemnations hurled at the film by the Catholic League, the Southern Baptist Convention, the AFA, and other groups unintentionally helped *Dogma* gross a respectable $18 million in its first two weeks on 1,300 screens nationwide. Overall, however, the late 1990s were a dismal period for convention-challenging films; David Cronenberg's *Crash*, Todd Solondz's *Happiness*, and Adrian Lyne's adaptation of *Lolita* all had problems finding a U.S. distributor.

By the time of Mel Gibson's *The Passion of the Christ* (2004) and Ron Howard's adaptation of Dan Brown's best seller, *The Da Vinci Code* (2006), religious-themed films had advanced beyond publicity strategies aimed at baiting the devout. The Internet in particular provided marketers with new options for engaging movie audiences—or, in the case of certain controversial movies, co-opting their objections. Simultaneously, moral advocacy groups—many of them recognizing the impracticality of mounting boycotts or theater protests in an age of 3,000-screen releases—began backing away from the strident attacks of the past.

The phenomenally successful *Passion of the Christ* was a reverse image of *Last Temptation* in almost every respect. Mel Gibson's orthodox rendering of Christ's final days, embellished with long, graphic scenes of torture and suffering, appealed to a vast audience of believers who had rejected Scorsese's film fifteen years earlier. Moreover, these moviegoers were largely unconcerned about allegations of the film's anti-Semitic content. Unlike Universal in its effort to get top Christian leaders on board with *Last Temptation*, Icon Productions employed at least a half dozen PR shops for an unprecedented outreach to church groups, evangelists, community leaders, sports figures, entertainers—all in an attempt to unite the disparate groups and denominations around the film's core message, "Christ died for our sins."[24] Gibson took the film to mega-churches and Christian media outlets and made himself available for questions and conversations. The film's Web site served as a node for the film's virtual community, offering such features as a sanitized trailer (for the

R-rated film); consumer items like *Passion of the Christ* jewelry, mugs, lapel pins, and leather Bible cases; ticket purchases; and blogs about the film. Even Josh Baran was impressed with *Passion*'s PR campaign. Interviewed on CNN, he said, "This is probably the most extensive grassroots marketing campaign I've ever seen. . . . They're using the film to evangelize, to actually try to convert people to Christianity. So this to them is not a film. This is a major campaign to get more souls for Christ."[25]

On the surface, *The Da Vinci Code* had much in common with *Last Temptation.* Both films were based on novels that did not suffer institutional religion gladly. *The Da Vinci Code*'s theme of a deception existing deep inside a Catholic sect, to say nothing of the proposition that Christ escaped death on the cross and enjoyed a married life in the South of France with Mary Magdalene, did not endear the film to critics like the Catholic League's president, William Donohue. But there the similarities ended. Donohue decided not to gear up his acolytes for an offensive against the film. "First of all, it's a useless exercise," he was quoted as saying in the *New Yorker.* "The movie's going to be a box-office extravaganza the first weekend or two. After that, if it's a good movie it'll continue; if not, it'll fail."[26] Whereas most Americans were unfamiliar with the Kazantzakis novel, *The Da Vinci Code*'s heresies were hardly revelatory, as more than 25,000,000 books had been sold by the time the film came out. And unlike Universal, with its defensive crisis control strategy, Sony Pictures proactively "engaged" with Christians' curiosity about *The Da Vinci Code* by creating a Web site forum for scholarly essays and discussions (some of them critical of the film). Catholics also learned they could do more good by actually accommodating the presence of the film. Although a Vatican official criticized the film's "calumnies, offenses and historical and theological errors" and advocated a boycott of the film,[27] far more Catholic parishes perceived *The Da Vinci Code* as a conversion opportunity and organized hundreds of study groups to deconstruct the film's claims and mysteries.

At the same time that *The Last Temptation of Christ* became a justification for practicing divisive cultural politics, it had a different effect on many Christians in the entertainment field. Although the Christian community had become quite successful in the 1980s at creating their own media outlets and products, there was a sense that they had also created "their own ghetto," as the columnist Cal Thomas aptly put it. "Out of this experience with 'The Last Temptation of Christ,'" Thomas wrote with prescience in 1988, "ought to emerge some leadership that is committed to producing films that will expound the values held by Christians and a strategy developed for thrusting them . . . into the general marketplace of ideas."[28] In early 1989, after the controversy subsided, two televangelists—D. James Kennedy and Paul Crouch—announced plans to go into film production; both men cited *Last Temptation* as the impetus for their aspirations of making more inspirational movies. Of the two, only the Crouch enterprise lasted over the long term, mainly through its later permutation, Gener8Xion Entertainment, which produced *The Omega Code* (1999), among other movies. A new breed of filmmakers has prospered since the mid-1990s, however, making limited-release and straight-to-DVD films that expound Christian values.[29]

Last Temptation also played a role in the evolving attitudes toward religion in Hollywood. Many advocacy groups concluded that the confrontational stand they took against MCA/Universal not only failed to achieve their goals, it also reinforced stereotypes of Christians as dogmatic, censorious fundamentalists. Though groups such as the AFA, the Catholic League, and Morality in Media continued to take an adversarial stance toward studios and networks, other faith-based groups adopted a more conciliatory and pragmatic relationship with the industry. "It was the furor over . . . 'The Last Temptation of Christ,'" wrote the *Los Angeles Times'* John Dart in 1997, "that many say gave rise to the rapprochement."[30] Among the most visible signs of change were the host of entertainment ministries and networking organizations mushrooming in southern California, and the awards events held by such groups as Catholics in Media and Ted Baehr's Christian Film and Television Commission to recognize Hollywood for its responsible, uplifting fare. For its part, the entertainment industry began to take the Christian community more seriously as both a market and a source of material for its projects. By the mid-1990s the "embryonic new movement" of openness to religion, as Michael Medved termed it, was widely noticed and, for the most part, welcomed.[31] Christian characters began to be written into television series, most notably the CBS series *Touched by an Angel,* and studios produced films that put forward spiritual themes in a positive light, such as *Dead Man Walking, Michael, Braveheart,* and *The Chronicles of Narnia: The Lion, the Witch, and the Wardrobe.* More than any other film, *The Passion of the Christ* made film executives aware of the enormous potential of the religion-oriented market—despite the opinions of some that *Passion* was an anomaly, not a model for tapping that market.[32] Although media content considered by religious critics to violate deeply held values is still produced in great abundance, new coalitions and relationships in the film and television industries now temper the climate in which *Last Temptation* was introduced in 1988.

Twenty years after its release, *The Last Temptation of Christ* remains not only a bête noire of cultural conservatives, but a mainstay of "top ten" and "top twenty" lists of the most controversial motion pictures in American history. A metric for evaluating the magnitude of controversies does not exist, but if one considers some of the most pertinent evidence—the amount of news coverage generated about the film; the extreme polarization of opinion about the film in print and broadcast outlets; the numerous theaters that turned down bookings of *Last Temptation;* the volume of protesting mail and phone calls; the tens of thousands of people who publicly protested and marched in opposition to the film in the United States;[33] the number of countries that officially banned it (thirteen); and the damage sustained at movie theaters overseas—there is little doubt that the picture would occupy one of the top rungs of any list, if not the topmost.

But to those who are profoundly moved by Scorsese's film, this history of opposition can be a distraction at best, and at worst a distortion of the film's genuine religiosity. In her 1996 essay, "The Last Temptation Reconsidered," Carol Iannone wrote: "The fact that *The Last Temptation of Christ* has become shorthand for cultural degradation ought to disturb anyone who wants to preserve art's power to engage the moral imagination. If cultural conservatism is not to produce a backlash against itself, we must distinguish between seriously attempted efforts within the legitimate bounds of artistic creativity and ad hoc throwaways like *Piss Christ.*"[34]

Arguably, it is now possible to make that distinction. *The Last Temptation of Christ* is no longer captive to the agendas or polemical discourses of either the political left or right. Scorsese's *Last Temptation* can now be seen as a vibrant film of an extraordinary—and still elusive—figure. It is, according to Garry Wills, writing just two months after the film opened in New York, Scorsese's attempt "to rethink the transcendence of suffering."[35] The film remains alive for Tom Pollock, who wrote in an e-mail message in 2007, "I am extremely proud of the movie Marty made. I think it *is* the movie he wanted to make. . . . For me, it remains highly emotional that Jesus would *choose* to die for everyone else's sins."[36] And to Carol Ianonne the film can be understood as "the effort of an ordinary man to understand Christ's sacrifice from the inside and to experience it as his own. In order to speak to modern man, arriving so late in the ages of belief, Jesus must be made to bear the infirmities of our age—the doubt, the angst, the fear and trembling, the existential dread, and yes, even the sexual obsessiveness."[37] This is in fact not much different from how Peter Bien theorized about the novel's protagonist: a Jesus who must "love and embrace his own demonic depths: the hatred and violence within him"[38]—before he can move forward and become the Son of God.

Nikos Kazantzakis' fiction is only one extrapolation from the Gospels. As these excerpts show, however, it was powerful enough to spark prolific meanings. The willingness to tolerate differences in the way *others* read, view, and listen to a story—even the holiest of stories—is ultimately what the controversy was about. This small, ambitious film had to be staunchly defended for many reasons, not all of them particularly noble. The major reason, however, was not anticipated when *The Last Temptation of Christ* went into production, and it had nothing to do with the version of Jesus Christ that Martin Scorsese and Paul Schrader inherited from Kazantzakis. As the studio and its allies only gradually discovered, their mission was defending not just this film, but all the possible interpretations the film might produce in the audience—and by extension, all the possible interpretations for every film made in Hollywood in the future; otherwise, they would be forced someday to bend to an outside demand for orthodoxy. As Scorsese said succinctly in October 1988, "I think we have to accept a wide range of interpretations of Jesus to survive, and it would be crazy not to."[39]

Notes

Prologue

1. *Last Temptation of Christ* (video) (San Bernardino, Calif.: Arrowhead Productions International, 1988).
2. Scott Fagerstrom, "'Last Temptation' Draws a Crowd," *Orange County Register,* August 12, 1988, 1.
3. Interview with John Stewart. (See Author Interviews at the back of this volume for dates of all interviews cited in the notes.)
4. Ibid.
5. Donald Wildmon and Randall Nulton, *Don Wildmon: The Man the Networks Love to Hate* (Wilmore, Ky.: Bristol Books, 1989).
6. Fagerstrom, "'Last Temptation' Draws a Crowd," 12.
7. Michael Hirsley, "L.A. Christians Protest Movie," *Chicago Tribune,* August 12, 1988, sec. 2, 5.
8. *Last Temptation of Christ* (video).
9. Ibid.
10. Hirsley, "L.A. Christians Protest Movie."
11. Interview with Fred Mound.
12. Interview with Sean Daniel.
13. Interview with John Polwrek.
14. Interview with Sally Van Slyke; Aljean Harmetz, "7,500 Picket Universal over Movie about Jesus," *New York Times,* August 12, 1988, C4.
15. Interview with Josh Baran.
16. Goodwin Berquist and James Greenwood, "Protest against Racism: 'The Birth of a Nation' in Ohio," *Journal of the University Film Association* 26, no. 3 (1974): 39–44.
17. This account of the conversation between Harmetz and Baran is based on interviews with Baran.
18. Interview with John Dart.
19. By comparison, the largest African American demonstrations against *Birth of a Nation* in 1915 were estimated by contemporary newspapers at 5,000 in Boston and 3,000 in Philadelphia. See Berquist and Greenwood, "Protest against Racism."
20. Interview with Polwrek.

21. Interview with Tom Pollock.

22. Interview with Polwrek.

23. Interview with Sidney J. Sheinberg.

24. Interview with Pollock.

25. Interview with Baran.

26. The account of this incident and the conversations he had are based on interviews with Pollock.

27. *NBC Nightly News*, August 11, 1988.

28. Aljean Harmetz, "How Studio Maneuvered 'Temptation' into Hit," *New York Times*, August 24, 1988, C15.

29. Andy Wickstrom, "Discreet 'Temptation,'" *The Record* (Bergen, N.J.), May 26, 1989, 29.

Chapter 1

1. Theodore Ziolkowski, *Fictional Transfigurations of Jesus* (Princeton, N.J.: Princeton University Press, 1972), 16.

2. Salman Rushdie, "Is Nothing Sacred?" *Granta* 31 (1990): 102–3.

3. Lewis A. Richard, "Christianity in the Novels of Kazantzakis," *Western Humanities Review* 21, no. 1 (1967): 52.

4. Nikos Kazantzakis, *The Saviors of God: Spiritual Exercises,* trans. Kimon Friar (New York: Simon and Schuster, 1960), 106.

5. Peter Bien, *Chronology,* www.historical-museum.gr/kazantzakis/chronology.html (September 9, 2000).

6. Nikos Kazantzakis, *The Last Temptation of Christ,* trans. P. A. Bien (New York: Simon and Schuster, 1960), 51.

7. Peter Bien, *Tempted by Happiness: Kazantzakis' Post-Christian Christ* (Wallingford, Pa.: Pendle Hill Publications, 1984), 12.

8. The notion that Judas Iscariot might not have been the treacherous figure of legend certainly did not originate with Kazantzakis. According to New Testament scholars, certain ambiguities and discrepancies in the four Gospels' references to Judas suggest that there might have been more to his relationship with Jesus and the other disciples. See Karen Armstrong, "The Observer Profile: No More Mr. Bad Guy," *Observer,* March 30, 1997, 20; Larry B. Stammer, "New Look at Ancient Betrayer," *Los Angeles Times,* April 21, 2000, A1. According to analysis of the recently discovered Gospel of Judas, a Coptic Egyptian translation of a second-century text, alternative characterizations of Judas similar to the

one proposed in *The Last Temptation of Christ* were apparently held by
Gnostics in Christianity's early years.

9. Kazantzakis, *The Last Temptation of Christ,* 476.

10. Ibid., 496.

11. In off-the-record comments to the *New York Times,* Vatican sources said
that the censure would apply to all future editions and versions of the
book. "Vatican Forbids Novel," *New York Times,* April 29, 1954, 129.

12. Michael Antonakes, "Christ, Kazantzakis, and Controversy in Greece,"
in *God's Struggler: Religion in the Writings of Nikos Kazantzakis,* ed. Darren J. N. Middleton and Peter Bien (Macon, Ga.: Mercer University
Press, 1996), 28–31.

13. Wade Clark Roof, *A Generation of Seekers: The Spiritual Journeys of the
Baby Boom Generation* (New York: HarperCollins, 1993), 54–58.

14. Henry Madden, "On the Firing Line in a Bad Climate," *ALA Bulletin* 59
(1965): 33.

15. Everett T. Moore, "A City in Torment over Kazantzakis," *ALA Bulletin*
57 (1963): 305.

16. "Book Ban Attempted in California," *Christian Century,* December 26,
1962, 1576–77.

17. Clara E. Breed, *Turning the Pages: San Diego Public Library History, 1882–
1982* (San Diego: Friends of the San Diego Public Library, 1983); Everett
T. Moore, "The Intellectual Freedom Saga in California: The Experience
of Four Decades," *California Librarian* (October 1974): 48–57.

18. Mildred Jane Williams, "An Analysis of the Causes and Effects of the
Controversy and Censorship of Nikos Kazantzakis' *The Last Temptation
of Christ* in Selected Public Libraries Cited in Periodical Literature on
the Subject" (M.A. thesis, University of North Carolina at Chapel Hill,
1967).

19. Lisa McGirr, *Suburban Warriors: The Origins of the New American Right*
(Princeton, N.J.: Princeton University Press, 2001).

20. Harold Keen, "Miss Breed's Not for Burning," *San Diego & Point Magazine,* March 1962, 70; "Library Books under Political Attack," *Publishers
Weekly,* November 30, 1964, 39.

21. McGirr, *Suburban Warriors,* 226–27.

22. Williams, "An Analysis of the Causes and Effects," 21–22.

23. "'Adults Only' Label Applied to Novel by Library Trustees," *Bakersfield
Californian,* January 22, 1963, 1.

24. Patt Morrison, "Brave Heart in a Book Battle," *Los Angeles Times,* October 2, 1996, B5.

25. Blanche Collins, "Ordeal at Long Beach," *Library Journal* 90 (June 1, 1965): 2486; "Library Books under Political Attack."

26. Madden, "On the Firing Line in a Bad Climate."

27. Williams, "An Analysis of the Causes and Effects," 9.

28. Moore, "A City in Torment over Kazantzakis."

29. Quoted in Williams, "An Analysis of the Causes and Effects," 26.

30. "California Right-Wing Front Groups Attack Book Selection in Libraries," *Library Journal* 89 (December 15, 1964): 4874.

31. A. H. Weiler, "Judas as Hero?" *New York Times,* February 21, 1971, 2.

32. Ibid.; "Lumet Plans Filming of 'Temptation of Christ,'" *Variety,* February 19, 1971.

33. Pat Broeske, "Scorsese Ends Long Quest to Film Kazantzakis' Novel," *Los Angeles Times,* August 12, 1988, part VI, 1.

34. David Thompson and Ian Christie, ed., *Scorsese on Scorsese* (London: Faber and Faber, 1989), 36; Martin Scorsese, interview by Karen Stetler, March 29, 1997, Criterion Collection laserdisc release of *The Last Temptation of Christ* (New York: Voyager, 2000).

35. Scorsese interview by Stetler, 1.

36. Lee Lourdeaux discusses this analogical resemblance in his volume, *Italian and Irish Filmmakers in America: Ford, Capra, Coppola, and Scorsese* (Philadelphia: Temple University Press, 1990).

37. Mary Pat Kelly, *Martin Scorsese: A Journey* (New York: Thunder's Mouth Press, 1991), 67.

38. Interview with Barbara Hershey.

39. Steve Oney, "The Forces That Fired 'Last Temptation,'" *Washington Post,* August 14, 1988, G1, G6; Scorsese interview by Stetler, 2.

40. Interview with Martin Scorsese.

41. Thompson and Christie, *Scorsese on Scorsese,* 117.

42. Richard Corliss, ". . . And Blood," *Film Comment,* October 1988, 36.

43. Martin Scorsese, "Sacred Images," *Civilization,* February/March 1998, 70.

44. Martin Scorsese, "In the Streets," in *Once a Catholic,* ed. Peter Occhoigrosso (Boston: Houghton Mifflin, 1987), 91.

45. "New York City—Little Italy" (travelogue originally published in 1924), www.oldandsold.com/articles06/new-york-city-60.shtml.

46. Corliss, ". . . And Blood," 40.

47. Scorsese, "In the Streets," 91.

48. Ibid.," 92.

49. Bruce Buursma, "Catholic Board Drops 'Condemned' Film Rating," *Chicago Tribune*, January 4, 1982, sec. 1, 3.

50. Quoted in Ellen Draper, "'Controversy Has Probably Destroyed Forever the Context': *The Miracle* and Movie Censorship in America in the Fifties," *Velvet Light Trap* (Spring 1990): 72.

51. Scorsese, "In the Streets," 99–100.

52. Ibid., 100.

53. Mark Singer, "The Man Who Forgets Nothing," *New Yorker*, March 27, 2000, 95.

54. Interview with Scorsese.

55. Thompson and Christie, *Scorsese on Scorsese*, 133.

56. Scorsese, interview by Stetler, 2.

57. W. Barnes Tatum, *Jesus at the Movies: A Guide to the First Hundred Years* (Santa Rosa, Calif.: Polebridge Press, 1997), 104.

58. Thompson and Christie, *Scorsese on Scorsese*, 136.

59. Ted Mahar, "In the Eye of the Storm of 'Temptation.'" *Sunday Oregonian* (Portland), August 28, 1988, B1.

60. Kelly, *Martin Scorsese: A Journey*, 169.

61. Ann Hornaday, "'Owl Creek Bridge': A Vast Span," *Washington Post*, August 22, 2004, N3.

62. Interview with Scorsese.

63. Corliss, ". . . And Blood," 38.

64. Interview with Scorsese.

65. Helen Kazantzaki to Harry J. Ufland, June 29, 1976. (Photocopy in the author's possession.)

66. Harry J. Ufland to Howard Hausman, August 25, 1976. (Photocopy in the author's possession.)

67. Julia Cameron, "Devoted to Betrayal: Irwin Winkler," *American Film*, October 1989, 52, 50.

68. Harry Ufland to Howard Hausman, August 25, 1976; Howard Hausman to Harry Ufland, September 15, 1976. (Photocopy in the author's possession.)

69. Peter Grossman to Irwin Winkler, March 24, 1977. (Photocopy in the author's possession.)

70. Peter Grossman to Howard Hausman, August 4, 1977. (Photocopy in the author's possession.)

71. Howard Hausman to Peter Grossman, August 18, 1977. (Photocopy in the author's possession.)

72. Patroclos Stavrou to Peter Grossman, November 1, 1977. (Photocopy in the author's possession.)

73. Peter Grossman to Patroclos Stavrou, November 17, 1977. (Photocopy in the author's possession.)

74. Helen Kazantzakis, *Nikos Kazantzakis,* trans. Amy Mims (New York: Simon and Schuster, 1968), 505–6.

75. Helen Kazantzakis to Peter Grossman, December 1, 1977. (Photocopy in the author's possession.)

76. Steven Bach, *Final Cut* (New York: William Morrow, 1985).

77. Interview with Scorsese.

78. Howard Hausman to Harry Ufland, April 1, 1980. (Photocopy in the author's possession.)

79. Paul Schrader, "Collaborations: Paul Schrader on Martin Scorsese," *New Yorker,* March 21, 1994, 124.

80. When he was ten years old, Schrader set about recopying the entire Bible in his basement while the other kids were outside. He made it only to the end of Genesis. Nevertheless, he retained a remarkable grasp of the New Testament, and he continued to follow theological and historical scholarship of Jesus throughout his adult life.

81. Kevin Jackson, ed., *Schrader on Schrader* (London: Faber and Faber, 1990).

82. Quotes from the Christian Reformed Church's weekly publication, the *Banner;* cited in William D. Romanowski, "John Calvin Meets the Creature from the Black Lagoon: The Dutch Reformed Church and the Movies, 1928–1966," *Christian Scholar's Review* 25 (1995): 51.

83. Screenplay Writer Loanout Agreement Re: "The Last Temptation of Christ," Chartoff-Winkler Productions, October 1, 1981. (Photocopy in the author's possession.)

84. Paul Schrader, e-mail message to author, April 21, 2003.

85. Interview with Paul Schrader.

86. Ibid.

87. Kenneth L. Woodward with Loren Jenkins, "Dissidents in Danger," *Newsweek,* December 31, 1979, 70.

88. Marjorie Hyer, "Questioning by Vatican of Theologian Protested," *Washington Post,* December 14, 1979, B14.

89. Quoted in John L. Allen Jr., "Chair Will Not Have Famed Theologian's Name—Edward Schillebeeckx," *National Catholic Reporter,* June 30, 2000, 12.
90. Kelly, *Martin Scorsese: A Journey,* 169.
91. Peter Bien, "Nikos Kazantzakis's Novels on Film," *Journal of Modern Greek Studies* 18 (2000): 161–69.
92. Interview with Schrader.
93. Gene Siskel, "Playing with Ire: Writer/Director Schrader Pushes the Limits," *Chicago Tribune,* September 11, 1988.
94. Kelly, *Martin Scorsese: A Journey,* 170.
95. Universal Studios, "The Making of *The Last Temptation of Christ*" (press kit, 1988).
96. Interview with Schrader.
97. The Scripture passages usually cited in this regard are: "For we do not have a high priest who is unable to sympathize with our weaknesses, but we have one who has been tempted in every way, just as we are—yet without sin" (Hebrews 4:15, New International Version); "For surely it is not angels he helps, but Abraham's descendents. For this reason he had to be made like his brothers in every way, in order that he might become a merciful and faithful high priest in service to God, and that he might make atonement for the sins of the people. Because he himself suffered when he was tempted, he is able to help those who are being tempted" (Hebrews 2:16–18, New International Version).
98. Bien, "Nikos Kazantzakis's Novels on Film," 166.
99. Scorsese also learned in his research that the Galilean Aramaic spoken by Jesus and his disciples probably had a heavy regional accent, not unlike southern Appalachian speech in the United States, that was denigrated by the rabbis of the period. See, for example, Geza Vermes, *Jesus the Jew: A Historian's Reading of the Gospels* (Philadelphia: Fortress Press, 1973), 52–54.
100. Jackson, *Schrader on Schrader,* 136.

Chapter 2

1. Kim Masters, "A Mouse Divided," *Vanity Fair,* November 1994, 206.
2. Dawn Steel, *They Can Kill You but They Can't Eat You* (New York: Pocket Books, 1993), 122.
3. Ibid., 121.

4. Oney, "The Forces That Fired 'Last Temptation'"; interview with Irwin Winkler.

5. Interview with Winkler.

6. Justin Wyatt, *High Concept: Movies and Marketing in Hollywood* (Austin: University of Texas Press, 1994).

7. J. Hoberman, "1975–1985: Ten Years That Shook the World," *American Film,* June 1985, 36.

8. Tony Schwartz, "Hollywood's Hottest Stars," *New York,* July 30, 1984, 27.

9. Michael D. Eisner, with Tony Schwartz, *Work in Progress* (New York: Random House, 1998), 56.

10. Ibid.

11. Steve Jenkins, "From the Pit of Hell," *Monthly Film Bulletin* 55 (December 1988): 353.

12. Interview with Jeffrey Katzenberg.

13. Interview with David Kirkpatrick.

14. Interview with Katzenberg.

15. Interview with Martin Scorsese; Scorsese interview by Stetler; Oney, "The Forces That Fired 'Last Temptation,'" G6.

16. Interview with Scorsese.

17. Oney, "The Forces That Fired 'Last Temptation,'" G6. The agreement among Chartoff-Winkler Productions, Martin Scorsese Productions, and Paramount Pictures was signed on October 6, 1982.

18. Barth David Schwartz, *Pasolini Requiem* (New York: Pantheon Books, 1992), 426.

19. Army Archerd, "Just for Variety," *Variety,* February 16, 1983.

20. "DeNiro to Play Christ in Movie," *Rolling Stone,* March 18, 1982, 38.

21. "Scorsese Scouts Locations in Israel for 'Temptation' Film," *Hollywood Reporter,* February 8, 1983.

22. Jay Carr, "At 50, De Niro Makes Time to Move behind the Camera," *Boston Globe*, September 26, 1993, A9.

23. Kelly, *Martin Scorsese: A Journey,* 171.

24. Interview with Scorsese.

25. Ibid.

26. Ibid.

27. Scorsese interview by Stetler, 40.

28. Martin Scorsese, "Sacred Images," *Civilization,* February/March 1998, 68.

29. Scorsese interview by Stetler, 22.

30. Interview with Jay Cocks.

31. Corliss, ". . . And Blood," 38.
32. Ibid. Cocks and Scorsese removed most of the profanity in Schrader's draft because they thought that any cursing by the apostles would sound ludicrous to a contemporary audience; interview with Cocks.
33. Interview with Cocks.
34. Mary Pat Kelly, "Jesus Gets the Beat: An Interview with Martin Scorsese," *Commonweal,* September 9, 1988, 469.
35. Paul Schrader, "The Last Temptation of Christ" (screenplay), November 23, 1983, 59–60.
36. Interview with Scorsese.
37. Interview with Cis Corman.
38. Ibid.
39. Kelly, *Martin Scorsese: A Journey,* 172; Scorsese interview by Stetler.
40. Thomas DePietro, "Scorsese: Making Jesus Contemporary," *Christianity and Crisis* 48, no. 14 (October 1988): 343.
41. Interview with Harry Dean Stanton.
42. Scorsese interview by Stetler, 39.
43. Interview with Corman.
44. Matt Wells, "Is This the Real Face of Jesus? BBC Creates Icon for 21st Century Using Computer Images from 1st Century Skulls," *Guardian,* March 27, 2001, 3.
45. Ian Wilson, *Jesus: The Evidence* (Washington, D.C.: Regnery, 2000).
46. Jaroslav Pelikan, *Jesus through the Centuries: His Place in the History of Culture* (New York: Harper and Row, 1987), 92–93.
47. Philip Kerr, "Heavenly Creatures," *New Statesman,* April 21, 2003, www.newstatesman.com/200304210033.
48. Interview with Scorsese.
49. Scorsese interview by Stetler, 48.
50. Frank Swertlow, "Holy Smoke," *Los Angeles Herald-Examiner,* December 6, 1983, A2.
51. Interview with Kirkpatrick.
52. Interview with Scorsese.
53. Ibid.
54. Interview with Mary Pat Kelly.
55. Interview with Scorsese.
56. Ellen Lampert, "The Last Temptation of Christ," *Theatre Crafts,* October 1988, 69.
57. Interview with Winkler.

58. Hal Polaire to Pat Gideon, May 25, 1983.

59. Jenkins, "From the Pit of Hell," 353.

60. Ibid.

61. Interview with Winkler.

62. Interview with Scorsese.

63. The breakup of Chartoff-Winkler Productions, which Winkler attributed to creative differences (see Julia Cameron, "Devoted to Betrayal: Irwin Winkler," *American Film,* October 1989, 53), was effected in 1985, although the two producers would continue to produce *Rocky* sequels through 1990.

64. Interview with Winkler.

65. Scorsese interview by Stetler, 10.

66. Interview with Scorsese.

67. Oney, "The Forces That Fired 'Last Temptation,'" G6; interview with Scorsese; Scorsese interview by Stetler, 10.

68. Cameron, "Devoted to Betrayal," 52.

69. Interview with Scorsese.

70. Harry Ufland, "Conversation HU/Katzenberg," October 14, 1983 (notes on a conversation; photocopy in the author's possession).

71. "Resurrected," *Los Angeles Times,* October 19, 1983.

72. Michael London, "Paramount Decides to Resist 'Temptation,'" *Los Angeles Times,* January 6, 1984, part IV, 10.

73. A detailed account of this transformation, and the first year of his activism, is provided in Wildmon and Nulton, *Don Wildmon,* 26–42.

74. Quoted in Christopher M. Finan and Anne F. Castro, *The Rev. Donald E. Wildmon's Crusade for Censorship, 1977–1992,* www.mediacoalition.org/reports/wildmon.html (February 24, 2008).

75. Monroe Friedman, *Consumer Boycotts: Effecting Change through the Marketplace and the Media* (New York: Routledge, 1999), 167.

76. "Film to Have Jesus Fighting against Being Accepted as the Messiah," *N.F.D. Informer,* March 1983, 11.

77. Michael Clancy and Dolores Tropiano, "Dave Marquis Leaving KPNX for Sacramento," *Arizona Republic,* August 15, 1993, A28.

78. The letter was reproduced in its entirety in the article ". . . And the Devil Throws Down His," *National Decency Reporter* 20, no. 6 (November–December 1983): 2.

79. Quoted in Oney, "The Forces That Fired 'Last Temptation,'" G6.

80. Interview with Kirkpatrick.

81. Oney, "The Forces That Fired 'Last Temptation,' " G6.

82. Through early 1984, at least one group, the Citizens for Decency through Law, continued to monitor the moribund production. In its January–February 1984 newsletter, the CDL urged readers to keep the pressure on: "If anyone cares whether this film about sexual perversions and Christ is an offensive idea, express your opinion to Director Martin Scorsese, Last Temptation Office, Paramount Studios, 5555 Melrose Avenue, Los Angeles, California, 90038 (213–468–5000)." "Last Temptation of Christ Film in Trouble, Not Dead," *National Decency Reporter,* January–February 1984, 2.

83. Oney, "The Forces That Fired 'Last Temptation,' " G6.

84. A sampling of approximately one hundred letters was transferred to Gulf + Western's spokesperson, Jon Gould, attached to a memorandum dated December 20, 1983, with copies to Barry Diller, Michael Eisner, and Art Barron (Paramount's chief financial officer), who subsequently copied them for Harry Ufland. Photocopies of the letters are in the author's possession.

85. Art Levine, "Raging Messiah: A Sneak Preview of Scorsese's New Bio-Pic," *Mother Jones,* August 1983, 38.

86. "CBS, Time Help Promote Vicious, Sick Anti-Christian Article," *N.F.D. Informer,* September 1983, 4–5. *Time* and CBS were advertisers in the August issue of *Mother Jones.*

87. Kathryn Harris, "Hassanein Will Quit UA Chain, Sources Report," *Los Angeles Times,* March 6, 1987, part 4, 3.

88. Ibid.

89. Interview with Jon Avnet.

90. Interview with Kirkpatrick.

91. Kim Masters, *Keys to the Kingdom* (New York: William Morrow, 2000); Eisner with Schwartz, *Work in Progress;* George Mair, *The Barry Diller Story* (New York: John Wiley and Sons, 1997).

92. Eisner with Schwartz, *Work in Progress,* 111–12.

93. Interview with Kirkpatrick.

94. A second seminar was planned for New York, but it never happened.

95. Interviews with Kirkpatrick and Kelly. Mary Pat Kelly would convene meetings with the actors playing the apostles at her house, to edify them on the Gospels, the early Christian communities, and Kazantzakis' own interpretation. One afternoon two workers from a furniture company came to deliver a bed while a meeting was in progress. After the workers

left, Kelly was called by the furniture store manager, who wanted know if she was running a religious cult from her living room.

96. Interview with Kelly.

97. John L. McKenzie, "The Social Character of Inspiration," *Catholic Biblical Quarterly,* April 1962, 115–24.

98. Rosemary Radford Reuther, *Sexism and God-Talk* (Boston: Beacon Press, 1983), 135.

99. Interview with Kelly.

100. Interview with Kirkpatrick.

101. Interview with Scorsese.

102. Steel, *They Can Kill You,* 177.

103. The following account of this meeting derives from these sources: Jenkins, "From the Pit of Hell," 353; Kelly, *Martin Scorsese: A Journey,* 178–79; Oney, "The Forces That Fired 'Last Temptation,'" G6; interview with Scorsese.

104. Interview with Kirkpatrick.

105. Interview with Avnet.

106. A studio puts a film into "turnaround" when it decides not to proceed with development, whereupon the producers usually try to set it up with another financier and repay the original studio for its expenditure.

107. Interview with Scorsese.

108. Frank Swertlow, "No Temptation," *Los Angeles Herald-Examiner,* December 7, 1983, A2.

109. Interview with Avnet.

110. Ibid.

111. Jon Avnet to Jeffrey Katzenberg, December 19, 1983. KEM is a brand name for a flatbed 35mm film editing table.

112. Ibid.

113. Interview with Avnet.

114. Pat Broeske, "Scorsese Ends Long Quest to Film Kazantzakis' Novel," *Los Angeles Times,* August 12, 1988, Calendar, sec. 6, 1.

115. Interview with Avnet.

116. Interview with Scorsese.

117. Interview with Avnet.

118. Scorsese interview by Stetler, 11.

119. Interview with Scorsese.

120. Interview with Avnet.

121. "Breakdown of Costs" (undated document; photocopy in the author's possession).

122. Interview with Avnet.

123. Interviews with Avnet and Kirkpatrick.

124. Michael London, "Paramount Decides to Resist 'Temptation,'" *Los Angeles Times,* January 6, 1984, part IV, 1, 10.

125. Interview with Kelly. While he was in London, Quinn called Paramount to verify for the police that he was in fact who he said he was; shortly afterward, his agent contacted him with the news about the film's cancellation.

126. Rena Kleiman, "Par Rug-Pull over 'Temptation' Final; Production on Hold," *Hollywood Reporter,* January 6, 1984, 4; London, "Paramount Decides to Resist 'Temptation,'" 1.

127. Harry Ufland to Joe Roth, memorandum, January 3, 1984. (Photocopy in the author's possession.)

128. London, "Paramount Decides to Resist 'Temptation,'" 10.

129. Jenkins, "From the Pit of Hell," 353.

130. Kleiman, "Par Rug-Pull over 'Temptation' Final"; London, "Paramount Decides to Resist 'Temptation.'"

131. David Puttnam to Harry Ufland, telex, December 30, 1983. (Photocopy in the author's possession.)

132. London, "Paramount Decides to Resist 'Temptation,'" 10. A Paramount executive confirmed that Cannon was not offered *Last Temptation.*

133. Interview with Kelly.

134. Jon Avnet to Hal Polaire, telex, January 13, 1984. (Photocopy in the author's possession.)

135. Harry Ufland file notes, February 1, 2, 1984. (Photocopy in the author's possession.)

136. Interview with Scorsese.

137. Scorsese, "In the Streets," 101.

138. Interview with Scorsese.

139. Ibid.

140. Gary Arnold, "Having the Right Stuff Wasn't Enough," *Washington Post,* January 1, 1984, F1.

141. The term *last straw* in referring to these events came from a well-placed Hollywood journalist, who asked for anonymity. See also Jenkins, "From the Pit of Hell," 353.

142. Interview with Avnet.

143. Interview with Schrader.

144. Interview with Kirkpatrick.

145. "Protest Letters Prompt Paramount to Drop a Movie about Christ," *Christianity Today*, February 17, 1984, 46.

146. Wildmon and Nulton, *Don Wildmon*, 194.

Chapter 3

1. Kelly, *Martin Scorsese: A Journey*, 183.

2. Anthony D'Alessandro, "A Director's Journey," *Variety*, December 9–15, 2002.

3. Chris Hodenfield, "'You've Got to Love Something Enough to Kill It': The Art of Noncompromise," *American Film*, March 1989, 49.

4. Ibid.

5. "Playboy Interview: Martin Scorsese," *Playboy*, April 1991, 62.

6. Thompson and Christie, *Scorsese on Scorsese*, 97.

7. Ibid., 97.

8. Nigel Andrews, "Dynamic Dreamer," *Financial Times*, May 31, 1986, sec. 1, 15.

9. Esther B. Fein, "Martin Scorsese: The Film Director as a Local Alien," *New York Times*, September 29, 1985, sec. 2, 1.

10. "Scorsese on Sale," *Esquire*, April 1985, 213.

11. Ted Mahar, "In the Eye of the Storm of 'Temptation' Scorsese," *Sunday Oregonian* (Portland), August 28, 1988, B1.

12. "Breakdown of Costs" (undated document; photocopy in author's possession).

13. Luke Ford, "Producer Harry J. Ufland" (undated interview), www .lukeford.net/profiles/profiles/harry_ufland.htm (November 15, 2002).

14. Kelly, *Martin Scorsese: A Journey*, 180.

15. Ford, "Producer Harry J. Ufland."

16. George Rush and Joanna Molloy, "Scorsese Benefit: For He's Such a Jolly Goodfella," *Daily News*, February 26, 1996, 14.

17. Interview with Martin Scorsese.

18. Kelly, *Martin Scorsese: A Journey*, 179.

19. Interview with Scorsese.

20. Ford, "Producer Harry J. Ufland"; Kelly, *Martin Scorsese: A Journey*, 180.

21. Ford, "Producer Harry J. Ufland."

22. Ibid.

23. "Temptation Two," *Los Angeles Times,* January 27, 1984, part VI.

24. "Temptation Resurrected," *Los Angeles Herald-Examiner,* January 24, 1984.

25. Denis O'Brien to Harry Ufland, telegram, April 26, 1984. (Photocopy in author's possession.)

26. Ray Stark to Harry Ufland, December 4, 1984. (Photocopy in author's possession.)

27. [Sender's name withheld] to Harry Ufland, October 5, 1984. (Photocopy in author's possession.)

28. Harry Ufland's notes of conversation with Jeffrey Katzenberg, September 15, 1984. (Photocopy in author's possession.)

29. File memo, Harry Ufland's notes of conversation with Helene Hahn of Paramount, October 15, 1984. Agreement between Paramount Pictures Corporation and Martin Scorsese Productions, Jon Avnet Company, and Ufland Roth Productions, October 31, 1984. (Photocopy in author's possession.)

30. Lenny Borger, "France Promises 300G to Scorsese Pic," *Daily Variety,* November 29, 1984, 2.

31. "The Greatest Story Never Made?" *Stills,* April 1985, 13.

32. Ibid.

33. Lenny Borger, "'Temptation of Christ' Pic Delayed as French Protest," *Variety,* March 20, 1985.

34. Ibid.

35. E. J. Dionne Jr., "Godard Has a Bad Day in Cannes . . . and Tries to Withdraw 'Hail Mary' in Italy," *New York Times,* May 11, 1985, sec. 1, 13.

36. Caryn James, "Paul Schrader Talks of 'Last Temptation' and His New Film," *New York Times,* September 1, 1988, sec. 3, 19.

37. William Morris Agency to Harry Ufland, telex, June 17, 1985.

38. Gene Siskel, "Playing with Ire: Writer/Director Schrader Pushes the Limits," *Chicago Tribune,* September 11, 1988, 6.

39. Thompson and Christie, *Scorsese on Scorsese,* 94.

40. Frixos Constantine to Jay Julien, telex, September 11, 1985. (Photocopy in author's possession.) In light of the history of the Kazantzakis novel in Greece, it is worth noting that Prime Minister George Papandreous told Constantine that they "shouldn't worry about any reaction from the church, or any other organization, as the government of Greece would be behind the film."

41. Pam to Harry Ufland, file memo, December 12, 1986. (Photocopy in author's possession.)

42. Richard Zimbert to John Daly, September 11, 1986. (Photocopy in author's possession.)

43. "Year-Old Ufland/Roth Productions in Development on Some 12 Pics," *Variety*, May 23, 1984.

44. Interview with Perry Katz.

45. David Ehrenstein, *The Scorsese Picture: The Art and Life of Martin Scorsese* (New York: Birch Lane Press, 1992), 18.

46. Interview with Jon Avnet.

47. Michael Cieply, "Hollywood Star: An Agent Dominates Film and TV Studios with Package Deals," *Wall Street Journal*, December 19, 1986, 1.

48. Charles Schreger, "CAA: Packaging of an Agency," *Los Angeles Times*, April 23, 1979, part IV, 13, 16.

49. L. J. Davis, "Hollywood's Most Secret Agent," *New York Times Magazine*, July 9, 1989, 54.

50. Janice Castro, "Pocketful of Stars," *Time*, February 13, 1989, 58–59; Michael Cieply, "Inside *the* Agency," *Los Angeles Times*, July 2, 1989, Calendar, C6–7, 23, 29–30.

51. Janice Castro, "The Ultimate Mogul," *Time*, April 19, 1993, 58.

52. Connie Bruck, *When Hollywood Had a King* (New York: Random House, 2003).

53. Schreger, "CAA," 13.

54. Cieply, "Inside *the* Agency."

55. Ibid., 7.

56. In its September 1988 issue, *Spy* magazine divulged CAA's complete client list in the categories of directors, writers, actors, performers, and composers. "Ten Percent of Everything Everybody Makes," *Spy*, September 1988, 50, 52.

57. Interview with Scorsese.

58. Interview with Michael Ovitz.

59. Mark Singer, "The Man Who Forgets Nothing," *New Yorker*, March 27, 2000, 94.

60. Interview with Scorsese.

61. Karen Stabiner, "Barefoot Boy with Cheek," *Gentlemen's Quarterly*, March 1988, 283.

62. Tom Pollock, e-mail to the author, December 30, 2007.

63. Jonathan Kirsch, "Clout! California's Most Powerful Lawyers—And How They Run Your Life," *California Magazine,* December 1981, 85–92, 162–69. Aljean Harmetz, "Now Lawyers Are Hollywood Superstars," *New York Times,* January 11, 1987, sec. 3, 1, 4.
64. Stabiner, "Barefoot Boy with Cheek," 282.
65. Aaron Latham, "M.C.A.'s Bad Cop Shoots from the Hip," *Manhattan, Inc.,* July 1988, 80.
66. Interview with Sally Van Slyke.
67. Stabiner, "Barefoot Boy with Cheek," 354.
68. Michael Cieply, "Universal's Pollock Focuses on Finances, Relationships," *Los Angeles Times,* October 5, 1988, 6.
69. Latham, "M.C.A.'s Bad Cop," 80.
70. Aljean Harmetz, "Universal Pictures Aide Resigns under Pressure," *New York Times*, September 17, 1986, C20.
71. Kathryn Harris, "Pollock to Head Motion Picture Group at M.C.A.," *Los Angeles Times,* September 19, 1986, sec. IV, 1.
72. "Attorney Pollock Takes Case to M.C.A.," *Variety,* September 24, 1986, 3.
73. Ibid., 33.
74. Harris, "Pollock to Head Motion Picture Group," 1.
75. Interview with Sidney Sheinberg.
76. Cieply, "Inside *the* Agency," 23.
77. Interview with Ovitz.
78. Interview with Tom Pollock.
79. Ibid.
80. Sally Van Slyke remembers Pollock telling her that the comparative religion course was the only college course in which he received a failing grade. "No kidding, buddy," she reports her reply.
81. Interview with Pollock.
82. Ibid.
83. Kelly, *Martin Scorsese: A Journey,* 202.
84. Interview with Sean Daniel.
85. Ibid.
86. Interview with Katz.
87. Interview with Daniel.
88. Interview with Pollock.
89. Interview with Scorsese.
90. Jack Mathews, *The Battle of Brazil* (New York: Applause, 1998).

91. Michael Cieply, "MCA's No. 2 Tower of Power," *Los Angeles Times,* August 12, 1987, sec. VI, 4.

92. Interview with Scorsese.

93. Barbara De Fina worked on *The King of Comedy* as the post-production supervisor and went on to produce *The Color of Money.* She and Scorsese were married February 8, 1985.

94. Interview with Scorsese.

95. Interview with Barbara De Fina.

96. Ibid.

97. Scorsese's next feature film after *Last Temptation* and his "Life Lessons" part of the *New York Stories* trilogy, *Wise Guys* was released as *Goodfellas* in 1990.

98. *Cape Fear* was originally put into development with Steven Spielberg directing, and Scorsese planned to direct *Schindler's List* from Steve Zailian's script adaptation of the Thomas Keneally historical novel. In 1990 the two directors began to experience reservations about making their respective films, and agreed to trade projects. Janet Maslin, "Martin Scorsese Ventures Back to *Cape Fear,*" *New York Times,* November 10, 1991, sec. 2, 13.

99. Interview with Pollock.

100. Interview with Sheinberg.

101. Laura Landro, "The Movie Moguls Reel Off One More Tale of Big Bucks," *Wall Street Journal,* February 24, 1988, sec. 1, 30.

102. Kelly, *Martin Scorsese: A Journey,* 202.

103. Hassanein announced his resignation in March 1987, three months after Tele-Communications, Inc., purchased 55 percent of the Naify family's stock in UAC and effectively took control of the company. Kathryn Harris, "Hassanein Will Quit UA Chain, Sources Report," *Los Angeles Times,* March 6, 1987.

104. Interview with Ovitz.

105. Lawrence Zehr, "Screen Giant: Garth Drabinsky Jars Movie-House Industry, Sets New Standards," *Wall Street Journal,* March 16, 1987, 1.

106. Lisa Gubernick, "Movie Madness," *Forbes,* February 8, 1988, 37.

107. Richard Trainor, "Let's Get Vertical," *American Film,* June 1988, 44.

108. Zehr, "Screen Giant," 16.

109. K. J. Lathan and Suzane Ayscough, "The Last Emperor," *Film Comment,* January–February 1990, 45.

110. Garth Drabinsky, *Closer to the Sun* (Toronto: McClelland and Stewart, 1995), 330.
111. Interview with an anonymous source.
112. Kelly, *Martin Scorsese: A Journey*, 202.
113. Interview with Pollock.
114. Interview with Scorsese.
115. "Attorney Pollock Takes Case to M.C.A.," 3.
116. "Playboy Interview: Martin Scorsese," 66.
117. Thompson and Christie, *Scorsese on Scorsese*, 123.
118. Kevin Lally, "Producer De Fina Discusses *Last Temptation* Controversy," *Film Journal,* September/October 1988, 10.

Chapter 4

1. Interview with Willem Dafoe.
2. Interview with Cis Corman.
3. John Lyttle, "Calling for the Leading Lady's Man," *Independent* (London), April 15, 1994, 22.
4. Kelly, *Martin Scorsese: A Journey,* 203.
5. Lori J. Smith, "Willem Dafoe," *American Film,* October 1988, 52.
6. Interview with Dafoe.
7. "Paul Sorvino Regretfully Told Martin Scorsese . . . ," *Daily Variety,* October 8, 1987.
8. Lou Lumenick, "Kathy Baker's an Expert at Working from Scratch," *Record* (Bergen, N.J.), August 14, 1988, E1.
9. Thompson and Christie, *Scorsese on Scorsese*, 126.
10. Scorsese interview by Stetler, 41.
11. Interview with Martin Scorsese.
12. Ibid.
13. Interview with Tom Pollock.
14. Ibid.
15. Universal City Studios, "The Making of *The Last Temptation of Christ*" (press kit, 1988).
16. Interview with Joe Reidy.
17. Ibid.
18. Scorsese interview by Stetler, 20.
19. Interview with Reidy.
20. Interview with Scorsese.

21. Interview with Reidy.

22. Interview with Dafoe.

23. Martin Scorsese, e-mail to the author, January 20, 2002.

24. Alona Wartofsky, "Dark Side of the Actor: Harvey Keitel, Plumbing the Depths of the Soul," *Washington Post,* September 13, 1995, B1.

25. "Living in Communion: An Interview with Father Thomas Hopko," *Parabola,* August 1987, 51.

26. D. M. Dooling, "This Word Forgiveness," *Parabola,* August 1987, 6.

27. Paul Tillich, "To Whom Much Was Forgiven," *Parabola,* August 1987, 40.

28. Interview with Dafoe.

29. Smith, "Willem Dafoe"; interview with Dafoe.

30. Interview with Dafoe.

31. Ibid.

32. Universal, "The Making of *The Last Temptation of Christ.*"

33. Interview with Reidy.

34. Interview with Scorsese.

35. Tom McDonough, "Traveling Light," *American Film,* December 1987, 48.

36. Michael Goldman, "Fade to Black: Michael Ballhaus, Cinematographer," *Millimeter,* October 2000, available as "Michael Ballhaus, Cinematographer" at http://digitalcontentproducer.com/mag/video_michael_ballhaus_cinematographer/.

37. Scorsese interview by Stetler, 27.

38. Interview with Reidy; Kelly, *Martin Scorsese: A Journey,* 209. While they were shooting in Meknes one night, the main generator went down. To salvage the evening's shoot, they tied into the main power line, which risked popping the city's electricity.

39. Scorsese interview by Stetler, 30–31.

40. Interview with Reidy.

41. Kelly, *Martin Scorsese: A Journey,* 208.

42. Interview with Thelma Schoonmaker.

43. Interview with Reidy.

44. Ibid.

45. Interview with Schoonmaker.

46. Ibid.; Stephen Pizzello, "Thelma Schoonmaker: Assembling Art with Marty," *American Cinematographer,* October 1993, 45–50.

47. According to Schoonmaker, the actors did not usually see the video play-backs because Scorsese did not want "a committee sort of deciding whether it's good or not." Interview with Schoonmaker.

48. Ibid.

49. Scorsese interview by Stetler, 38.

50. Interview with Reidy.

51. Mark Kram, "Ladies and Gentlemen, the Next Brando," *Esquire,* January 1989, 78–85; Scorsese interview by Stetler, 47.

52. V. Tzaferis, "Crucifixion: The Archaeological Evidence," *Biblical Archaeology Review,* January–February 1985, 44–53.

53. Scorsese interview by Stetler, 48.

54. Kelly, *Martin Scorsese: A Journey,* 228.

55. Janet Maslin, "Pinewood Dialogue with Martin Scorsese" (interview), November 9, 2002, Pinewood Dialogues Online, Museum of the Moving Image, http:pinewood.movingimage.us/.

56. Gavin Smith, "Street Smart," *Film Comment,* May–June 1998, 71.

57. Interview with Scorsese.

58. Scorsese interview by Stetler, 49.

59. Ibid.

60. Maslin, "Pinewood Dialogue with Martin Scorsese."

61. Interview with Reidy.

62. Interview with Scorsese.

63. Interview with Schoonmaker; Scorsese interview by Stetler, 24.

64. Interview with Schoonmaker.

65. Interview with Jay Cocks.

66. Interview with Scorsese.

67. Interview with Dafoe.

68. Interview with De Fina.

69. Interviews with Scorsese, De Fina, and Reidy.

70. Interview with Scorsese.

71. Ibid.

72. "Marilyn Beck," *Long Beach Press-Telegram,* July 17, 1987.

73. "Scorsese's 'Christ' Underway Shortly," *Variety,* September 30, 1987.

74. "'Passion' Flowers," *Los Angeles Herald-Examiner,* September 19, 1987.

75. Kathy O'Malley and Hanke Gratteau, "Political Shorts," *Chicago Tribune,* November 15, 1987.

76. Interview with Roger Armstrong.

77. Interview with Perry Katz.

78. Interview with Sally Van Slyke.
79. Ibid.
80. Ibid.
81. Wildmon and Nulton, *Don Wildmon*, 194.

Chapter 5

1. Clyde Wilcox, "Premillennialists at the Millennium: Some Reflections on the Christian Right in the Twenty-first Century," *Sociology of Religion* 55 (1994): 246.
2. Quentin L. Schultze, "The Invisible Medium: Evangelical Radio," in *American Evangelicals and the Mass Media,* ed. Quentin L. Schultze (Grand Rapids, Mich.: Zondervan, 1990).
3. John W. Kennedy, "Mixing Politics and Piety," *Christianity Today,* August 15, 1994, 43.
4. Interview with Tom Pollock.
5. *PR Newswire,* November 25, 1987; Jack Mathews, "Universal Set to Make 'Freedom' a S. Africa Event," *Los Angeles Times,* December 3, 1987, sec. VI, 7.
6. In early 1988 the South African government began to signal its unwillingness to allow UIP to distribute *Cry Freedom* uncensored. In July the film was banned just hours after it opened in theaters; the government cited dangers to public safety. "UIP to Begin Screening 'Cry Freedom' throughout South Africa," *PR Newswire,* January 26, 1988; " 'Cry Freedom' Film Banned on Opening Day in S. Africa," *Orange County Register,* July 29, 1988, A14.
7. Mathews, "Universal Set to Make 'Freedom' a S. Africa Event."
8. Interview with Pollock.
9. Deidre Sullivan, "Targeting Souls," *American Demographics,* October 1991, 42–57.
10. Aljean Harmetz, "Sometimes a Movie Makes a Studio Proud," *New York Times,* February 6, 1982, sec. 1, 11.
11. Tim Penland, "What's All the Fuss? It's Only a Movie" (lecture, Hillsdale College, Hillsdale, Mich., March 8, 1992); Tom Minnery, "*Chariots of Fire* Hits the Heights," *Christianity Today,* March 19, 1982, 34–35.
12. Penland, "What's All the Fuss? It's Only a Movie."
13. Ibid.
14. Larry Poland, *The Last Temptation of Hollywood* (Highland, Calif.: Mastermedia International, 1988), 14.

15. Ibid., 15.
16. Interview with Pollock.
17. Ibid.
18. Poland, *The Last Temptation of Hollywood,* 17.
19. Donald Wildmon to John Dart, July 25, 1988.
20. Poland, *The Last Temptation of Hollywood,* 18.
21. Interview with Fred Mound.
22. Interview with Thelma Schoonmaker.
23. Interview with Barbara De Fina.
24. Poland, *The Last Temptation of Hollywood,* 37–38.
25. Interview with Roger Armstrong.
26. Josh Baran, *365 Nirvana.* (London: Element, 2003), xii.
27. Interview with Susan Rothbaum.
28. For a detailed description of the process of withdrawal from religious cults, see Susan Rothbaum, "Between Two Worlds: Issues of Separation and Identity after Leaving a Religious Community," in *Falling from the Faith: Causes and Consequences of Religious Apostasy,* ed. David G. Bromley (Newbury Park, Calif.: Sage, 1988).
29. Interview with Rothbaum.
30. Patricia Loverock, "'The Day After': How to Promote a Nuclear War," *On Location,* March 1984, 170–71.
31. Harry F. Walters, "TV's Nuclear Nightmare," *Newsweek,* November 21, 1983.
32. Loverock, "'The Day After.'"
33. Tom Shales, "'The Day After' Approaches," *Washington Post,* October 11, 1983, C1.
34. Interview with Rothbaum.
35. Simon Houpt, "Pass the Popcorn, Save the World," *Globe and Mail* (Canada), May 29, 2003.
36. In 1990 Josh Baran and Associates was sold to the public relations firm Edelman Worldwide, where he continued in issues-oriented PR as an executive vice president until 1995. For the next two years Baran served as director of communications for Microsoft. Since 1997 he has operated primarily out of New York City, serving in executive positions for Tommy Boy Records and Fenton Communications.
37. Interview with Josh Baran.
38. Ibid.
39. Ibid.

40. Ibid.

41. Ibid.

42. Ibid.

43. Ted Baehr, "Can NRB Influence Hollywood?" *Religious Broadcasting,* February 1988, 77.

44. An informal poll taken by Penland registered 95 percent awareness of *The Last Temptation of Christ* among the NRB conventioneers. Michael Hirsley, "Film on Christ Has Clergy Wary," *Chicago Tribune,* May 20, 1988, Chicagoland sec., 7.

45. Interview with Baran.

46. Poland, *The Last Temptation of Hollywood,* 30.

47. Ibid., 31.

48. Universal Studios, "Universal Pictures Clarifies Its Position Concerning 'The Last Temptation of Christ'" (press release), June 17, 1988.

49. Steve Rabey, "Producer Tries to Dim Fears over Movie," *Christianity Today,* March 4, 1988, 43.

50. Poland, *The Last Temptation of Hollywood,* 37.

51. The interviews conducted for this book did not resolve the question of whether Universal officials thought the two consultants' work would compete with each other.

52. Larry Sandler, "Rumor of Film on Jesus Is False; Outcry Isn't," *Chicago Tribune,* March 9, 1981, sec. 4, 5.

53. Trevor Beeson, "Outcry over Pornographic Film on Jesus," *Christian Century,* October 27, 1976, 934–36; "Protests Fail to Halt Planned Film on Jesus' Sex Life," April 1976, publication unknown.

54. Beeson, "Outcry over Pornographic Film on Jesus," 934.

55. Stan Hastey, "'Sex Life of Jesus' Film Not Produced," *Baptist Press,* February 13, 1978, 30.

56. Typically feverish lines from letters protesting the Jesus sex film read: "We must not allow this perverted world to drag Our Lord through the dirt. . . . Such a movie would be blasphemous and would be an outrage and contrary to the truth"; "Gay Jesus Film," *Urban Legends Reference Pages,* www.snopes2.com/inboxer/petition/gayjesus.htm (December 22, 2000). Sandler, "Rumor of Film on Jesus Is False."

57. An example of this type of confusion is this sentence from a late 1983 letter protesting Paramount's involvement with *Last Temptation:* "Other countries have put a stop to this film and I hope and pray it will also be stopped in the U.S.A."

58. Interview with Rich Buhler.

59. Rich Buhler, "Scientists Discover Hell in Siberia," *Christianity Today,* October 1990, 28–29.

60. Interview with Buhler.

61. John Stewart, *Holy War: An Inside Account of the Battle for PTL* (Enid, Okla.: Fireside, 1987).

62. Interview with John Stewart.

63. John Stewart, *God in the Chaos* (Eugene, Ore.: Harvest House, 1991), 113.

64. Interview with Sally Van Slyke.

65. Pat Broeske, "'Last Temptation': Is It Already Bearing Its Cross?" *Los Angeles Times,* April 17, 1988, 21.

66. Ibid.

67. "'Temptation' Stirring Up Controversy," *Atlanta Journal,* April 22, 1988, B4.

68. Poland, *The Last Temptation of Hollywood,* 35–36.

69. The line is taken from the Kazantzakis novel.

70. Poland, *The Last Temptation of Hollywood,* 34.

71. Broeske, "'Last Temptation': Is It Already Bearing Its Cross?" 21.

72. Poland, *The Last Temptation of Hollywood,* 33.

73. Hirsley, "Film on Christ Has Clergy Wary."

74. Interview with Baran.

75. Quoted in William Cash, "PR as the Driven Snow," *Independent,* April 19, 1998, 3.

76. Interview with Baran.

77. Ibid.

78. Interviews with Baran and Rothbaum.

79. Interview with Rothbaum.

80. Ibid.

81. Susan Rothbaum, "IX—Differences between the Book and the Film," in "*The Last Temptation of Christ*—Positioning Points" (undated), 24. (Photocopy in author's possession.)

82. Interview with Rothbaum.

83. Rothbaum, "Overview—The Central Argument," in "*The Last Temptation of Christ*—Positioning Points," 1.

84. Rothbaum, "VI—Why 'Sacrilege' and 'Blasphemy' Are Not Grounds for Limiting Free Expression," in "*The Last Temptation of Christ*—Positioning Points," 17.

85. Rothbaum, "VII—The Film Industry's Affirmative Responsibility to Support Freedom of Expression," in "*The Last Temptation of Christ*—Positioning Points," 22.

86. Poland, *The Last Temptation of Hollywood*, 39–40.

87. Former representatives of Universal have said that a specific date for the screening was not promised to Wildmon or the other religious leaders who were invited.

88. Interview with Ted Baehr.

89. Poland, *The Last Temptation of Hollywood*, 48; Wildmon and Nulton, *Don Wildmon*, 197.

90. Poland, *The Last Temptation of Hollywood*, 48.

91. Wildmon and Nulton, *Don Wildmon*, 200.

92. Interview with Van Slyke.

93. Mahar, "In the Eye of the Storm of 'Temptation' Scorsese," *Sunday Oregonian* (Portland), August 28, 1988, B1.

94. Interview with Pollock.

95. Interview with Schoonmaker.

96. Interview with Sidney Sheinberg. The former MCA president described his response to the movie and its critics this way: "The people who are really into this subject can really wax very intellectually about *The Last Temptation of Christ*. I don't count myself among them. I'm not competent to do that. You know, the people that admire Marty Scorsese—and I guess he thought of being a priest—this is not a light, frivolous subject to them. This is very heavy stuff with great religious consequences. And they consider it extremely pro-religious. As I said, I would neither affirm nor defend or justify or even comment on that, other than to say that it's a very serious work. And I think that's what the people on the other side probably didn't ever quite give it."

97. Jenelle Riley, "Director's Cuts," *BPI Entertainment News Wire*, February 5, 2003.

98. Interviews with Pollock and Mound.

99. Interview with David Sameth.

100. Interview with Baran.

101. Interview with Sameth.

102. Interview with a former Universal executive (not for attribution).

103. Interview with Van Slyke.

104. Interview with Mound.

105. Pollock made an interesting comparison of this situation to other occupational dilemmas involving media content: "I don't think it is any more or less unprofessional than when you see a film filled with violence. You don't like violence, you may think that violence is morally wrong, but you do your job anyway. It's the business you're in. Unless it crosses some line. I wouldn't expect, you know, if it was pornography [that] people would work on it. But I don't think that's what [*The Last Temptation of Christ*] was." Interview with Pollock.

106. Interviews with Mound and Pollock.

107. Interview with Pollock.

108. Interview with Baran.

109. Interview with Armstrong.

110. Poland, *The Last Temptation of Hollywood,* 50–52, 52–55; John Dart (religion reporter for the *Los Angeles Times*), undated reporter's notes. (Photocopy in author's possession.)

111. Josh Baran admitted that this was the practical, though not intentional, effect of Penland's work: "He did provide a certain service in a sense if you look at it from a cynical point of view. He kept the Christian right from attacking the film for about two months, or three months. Because he did a certain job in the sense that he went to them and said, Don't attack it." Interview with Baran.

112. Universal Studios, "Universal Pictures Clarifies Its Position."

113. Poland, *The Last Temptation of Hollywood,* 49.

114. Dart, reporter's notes.

115. Universal Studios, "Universal Pictures Clarifies Its Position."

116. Penland Productions, "Re: 'The Last Temptation of Christ,' a Universal Pictures Release" (news release), June 14, 1988.

117. Universal Studios, "Universal Pictures Clarifies Its Position."

118. Dart, reporter's notes.

119. Interview with Pollock.

120. Interview with Katz.

Chapter 6

1. Philip J. Hilts, "Short-Term Forecast 'Pretty Grim' for Drought-Stricken Midwest," *Washington Post,* June 21, 1988, A3.

2. Howard LaFranchi, "Deep Doubts about Bush Surface among GOP Conservatives," *Christian Science Monitor,* June 13, 1988, 3.

3. Bill Peterson, "Bush Blasts Dukakis over Prison Program," *Washington Post,* June 19, 1988, A4.
4. Robert Reinhold, "Scene 14 of Writers Guild Strike: Tough Times in Hollywood," *New York Times,* June 12, 1988, sec. 1, 24.
5. John Dart, "Church Leaders Upset at Delay in Film Screening," *Los Angeles Times,* June 18, 1988, sec. II, 1.
6. Donald E. Wildmon to John Dart, July 25, 1988.
7. Ibid.
8. Interview with anonymous source.
9. Larry W. Poland to the Mastermedia readership, July 6, 1988.
10. Poland, *The Last Temptation of Hollywood,* 62.
11. They were characterized as such by Larry Poland in various contexts, including Steve Cooper, "Religious Leaders Assail Movie Depicting Christ," *(San Bernardino County) Sun,* July 12, 1988.
12. Poland, *The Last Temptation of Hollywood,* 67.
13. Tim Stafford, "His Father's Son: The Drive behind James Dobson, Jr.," *Christianity Today,* April 22, 1988, 16–22.
14. John W. Kennedy, "Mixing Politics and Piety," *Christianity Today,* August 15, 1994, 42–46.
15. Stafford, "His Father's Son," 18.
16. " 'The Last Temptation of Christ' Film," *Focus on the Family* (radio broadcast), BR 838, July 11, 1988. Subsequent quotes are from this source.
17. Interview with Roger Armstrong.
18. Interview with Jack Valenti.
19. Michael Morris, "Fundamentalists Fight 'Last Temptation,' " *National Catholic Reporter,* July 29, 1988, 17.
20. " 'Last Temptation of Christ' Assaults Christians," *Morality in Media, Inc. Newsletter,* September/October 1988, 2.
21. Ibid.
22. Interview with Sally Van Slyke.
23. Morris, "Fundamentalists Fight 'Last Temptation,' " 17.
24. Interview with Susan Rothbaum.
25. Cynthia B. Astle, "Views Agree Film Could Be Shocking," *National Christian Reporter,* August 5, 1988, 1.
26. Morris, "Fundamentalists Fight 'Last Temptation,' " 17. Scorsese's remarks are reconstructed from interviews with Rothbaum, Fore, Bergstrom, and Thompson, and from Morris, "Fundamentalists Fight 'Last Temptation.' "

27. John Dart, "Some Clerics See No Evil in 'Temptation,'" *Los Angeles Times,* July 14, 1988, sec. VI, 11.

28. Aljean Harmetz, "New Scorsese Film Shown to Religious Leaders," *New York Times,* July 14, 1988, C30.

29. "61 Clerics X-Rate New Film on Christ," *Washington Post,* July 16, 1988, B14.

30. Interview with Robert Thompson.

31. Interview with Josh Baran.

32. Interview with Van Slyke.

33. Ibid.

34. Interview with Rothbaum.

35. Morris, "Fundamentalists Fight 'Last Temptation.'"

36. Interview with Tom Pollock.

37. Interview with Van Slyke.

38. Interview with Martin Scorsese.

39. "61 Clerics X-Rate New Film on Christ."

40. Interview with Van Slyke.

41. Conversation reconstructed from interviews with Van Slyke.

42. See Poland, *The Last Temptation of Hollywood,* 59–61.

43. Interview with Larry Poland.

44. Interview with anonymous source.

45. Interview with Pollock.

46. Howard Rosenberg, "Small Screen Takes on the Big Issues—Again," *Los Angeles Times,* September 17, 1987.

47. Thomas Rosenstiel and Stephen Braun, "Entertainment, Media Leaders' Power Cited," *Los Angeles Times,* September 16, 1987, part 1, 1.

48. Poland, *The Last Temptation of Hollywood,* 80–81.

49. Claudia Eller, "Uni Stands behind 'Last Temptation' Despite Controversy," *Hollywood Reporter,* July 13, 1988, 21.

50. "61 Clerics X-Rate New Film on Christ."

51. Eller, "Uni Stands behind 'Last Temptation' Despite Controversy."

52. Aljean Harmetz, "Ministers Vow Boycott over Scorsese Film on Jesus," *New York Times,* July 13, 1988, C15.

53. Eller, "Uni Stands behind 'Last Temptation' Despite Controversy."

54. Cooper, "Religious Leaders Assail Movie Depicting Christ."

55. Eller, "Uni Stands behind 'Last Temptation' Despite Controversy."

56. Larry Poland wrote that Wildmon's absence "wasn't a big problem for us because we had determined that it would be best to have this be a

'Southern California coalition.' We also knew that Wildmon had played to extremely mixed reviews even among the more responsible members of the press community." Poland, *The Last Temptation of Hollywood,* 78.

57. "Christians Threaten Uni Tour Boycott over 'Temptation,'" *Hollywood Reporter,* July 15, 1988, 36.

58. Poland, *The Last Temptation of Hollywood,* 116.

59. Ibid.

60. Ibid., 117.

61. John Dart, "The Making of *Jesus,*" *Christian Century,* June 6–13, 2001, 26–31.

62. Jesus Project, "Tonight, the Eyes of the World Will Be on Jesus" (undated promotional piece).

63. Interview with Rich Buhler.

64. Bill Bright, "New Life 2000: Claiming a Billion New Christians by the Year 2000," *Religious Broadcasting,* February 1988, 32.

65. John Dart, "Campus Crusade's Bill Bright Dies," *Christian Century,* August 9, 2003, 13.

66. In a letter to the *Los Angeles Times*' John Dart, thanking the reporter for his "very fair and balanced" story on *Last Temptation,* Campus Crusade's communications director, Don Beehler, discussed the importance of the Jesus film to the ministry. "We know from experience what a powerful impact a motion picture on the life of Christ can have on people. If [*The Last Temptation of Christ*] is released and portrays Jesus as a confused and immoral man, I believe it will do great harm to the cause of Christ." Don Beehler to John Dart, June 20, 1988.

67. Quoted in Poland, *The Last Temptation of Hollywood,* 122. According to Poland, Campus Crusade's communications director, Don Beehler, drafted the letter "on behalf of Bill Bright" and incorporated "input" from Tim Penland, Bright, and others.

68. Interview with anonymous source.

69. Interview with Pollock.

70. Interview with Armstrong.

71. Interviews with Baran and Rothbaum.

72. Interview with Rothbaum.

73. Open letter from Universal Pictures to Bill Bright, *Hollywood Reporter,* July 21, 1988.

74. Interviews with Baran and Van Slyke.

75. Interview with A. D. Murphy.

76. Interview with Pollock.

77. Interview with Valenti.

78. This meeting is reconstructed from interviews with Van Slyke, Pollock, Baran, and Rothbaum.

79. Interview with Van Slyke.

80. Interview with Rothbaum.

81. Interview with Baran.

82. Cynthia Gorney, "The 'Temptation' Furor," *Washington Post,* July 22, 1988, D1.

83. Interview with Armstrong.

84. "Scorsese Pic Center of a Holy War," *Variety,* July 27, 1988, 26.

85. Interview with Coleman Luck.

86. Interview with Buhler.

87. Interview with Rothbaum.

88. Dan Martin, "Southern Baptists Concerned over Film," *Baptist Press,* July 15, 1988, 1.

89. Dan Martin, "Vines Urges Americans Not to See 'Temptation,'" *Baptist Press,* July 19, 1988, 3.

90. "Publicist Quits Film Project," *Christianity Today,* July 15, 1988, 51.

91. Craig Modderno, "Theaters May Shun 'Temptation,'" *Los Angeles Times,* July 15, 1988, part IV, 8.

92. Ibid.

93. Interview with an anonymous source.

94. Michael Fleming, Karen Freitfeld, and Susan Mulcahy, "Inside New York," *Newsday,* July 19, 1988, 6.

95. Interview with anonymous source.

96. Interviews with Simon Kornblit, William Soady, Armstrong, and Baran.

97. Interview with Baran.

98. Interview with Jay Cocks.

99. Interview with Scorsese.

100. Kazantzakis, *The Last Temptation of Christ,* 1.

101. Interview with Scorsese.

Chapter 7

1. Amy Dawes, "Christian Groups Blast Universal over 'Christ' Pic," *Variety,* July 20, 1988, 1.

2. Ibid., 8.

3. Charisse Jones, "Baptists Picket Studio over 'Christ' Movie," *Los Angeles Herald-Examiner,* July 17, 1988, A3.

4. Leo Noonan, "The Temptation of R. L. Hymers," *Jewish Journal,* July 29–August 4, 1988, 6.

5. Jonathan D. Sarna, "Jewish-Christian Hostility in the United States: Perceptions from a Jewish Point of View," in *Uncivil Religion,* ed. Robert N. Bellah and Frederick E. Greenspahn (New York: Crossroad, 1987), 10.

6. R. L. Hymers Jr., "Valiant Protest against the Film 'The Last Temptation of Christ'" (B.F.T. no. 1623; pamphlet published by the Fundamentalist Baptist Temple, 1988).

7. Four days later, at Hymers's invitation, Rubin attended Sunday service at the fundamentalists' downtown church to try to reach a rapprochement. When Rubin told the congregants that they owed the Jewish community an apology, Hymers abruptly cut him off and signaled his parishioners to start singing hymns. Openly frustrated, Rubin told a *Los Angeles Times* reporter on his way out of the church, "We're dealing with a crazy man here." Marita Hernandez, "Effort to Ease Disagreement over 'Temptation' Film Ends in Rancor," *Los Angeles Times,* July 25, 1988, 6.

8. Noonan, "The Temptation of R. L. Hymers."

9. Aljean Harmetz, "Film on Christ Brings Out Pickets, and Archbishop Predicts Censure," *New York Times,* July 21, 1988, C19.

10. National Conference of Christians and Jews, "Statement by Robert M. Jones, Executive Director, Southern California Region, NCCJ" (press release), July 21, 1988. (Photocopy in author's possession.)

11. B'Nai B'rith International, "B'Nai B'rith Hits Anti-Semitic Tone of Attacks on Film" (press release), July 20, 1988. (Photocopy in author's possession.)

12. American Jewish Congress, "AJ Congress Condemns Falwell Statement for Leading to Anti-Semitism" (press release), July 20, 1988. (Photocopy in author's possession.)

13. David Ferrell, "Hymers' Fight—He Sees Sin All around Him," *Los Angeles Times,* August 12, 1988, part 1, 3; Noonan, "The Temptation of R. L. Hymers."

14. "Film Protester Seen as Anti-Semitic," *Newsday,* August 13, 1988, 12.

15. Interview with Larry Poland.

16. John Dart, "2 Step Back from Film Protest over Anti-Jewish Tone," *Los Angeles Times,* July 23, 1988, part II, 1.

17. Ibid.

18. Ibid.

19. Harmetz, "Film on Christ Brings Out Pickets."

20. "MCA Seeks to Intimidate Wildmon with Possible Lawsuit," *AFA Journal*, September 1988, 22.

21. Leonard Dinnerstein, *Anti-Semitism in America* (New York: Oxford University Press, 1994).

22. Neal Gabler, *An Empire of Their Own: How the Jews Invented Hollywood* (New York: Crown, 1988).

23. Neal Gabler, "Jews, Blacks and Trouble in Hollywood," *New York Times*, September 2, 1990, sec. 2, 7.

24. Interview with Tom Pollock.

25. Ibid.

26. Office of Public Affairs, Archdiocese of Los Angeles, "Archbishop Mahony on 'The Last Temptation of Christ'" (press advisory), July 20, 1988.

27. Donald Wildmon, "This Controversy Goes to Heart of Religion," *USA Today*, July 25, 1988, 8A.

28. Jonathan H. Wilson, "Movie on Christ Has Power to Leave Wrong Impression," *Los Angeles Herald-Examiner*, July 30, 1988, F5.

29. In this context, impurity implies a view of the human condition as inherently corrupted, or "sinful." For a classic anthropological work on the role of purity in religious ritual, see Mary Douglas, *Purity and Danger* (London: Routledge, 1966).

30. William F. Buckley Jr., "Be Loyal to Your God—Don't See the Movie," *Washington Post*, August 16, 1988, A15.

31. Mark Silk, "Renowned Theologian to Head Emory Interdisciplinary Seminar," *Atlanta Constitution*, September 21, 1988, A1.

32. Maurice Ogden, "An Invitation to More Than Ever Love Christ," *Los Angeles Times*, August 11, 1988, sec. II, 7.

33. Patrick J. Buchanan, "Is It Art or Sleaze?" *Harrisonburg (Va.) Daily News-Record*, July 27, 1988, 6.

34. Ibid.

35. Ibid.

36. Ibid.

37. Ibid.

38. Lisa Goff, Lewis Lazare, and David Snyder, "Speaking Out in Favor of 'Temptation,'" *Crain's Chicago Business*, August 15, 1988, 8.

39. Michael Hirsley, "Churchmen at Odds over 'Temptation,'" *Chicago Tribune,* July 17, 1988, sec. 1, 21.
40. Interview with Robert Thompson.
41. Ibid.
42. Ibid.
43. Ibid.
44. Only one of Baran's projects included a conversation about *Last Temptation* among Bergstrom, Thompson, and Rabbi Alexander Schindler, videotaped in a suite at Chicago's Fairmont Hotel and intended for promotional use later in the campaign. It never aired on television, however. Interview with Thompson.
45. Interview with Pollock.
46. In a report submitted to the People for the American Way, Bergstrom recorded his activities in support of *The Last Temptation of Christ:*

   July 13: *Los Angeles Times* interview
   July 16: *Milwaukee Sentinel* interview
   July 16: KABC (Los Angeles) radio talk show appearance
   July 16: *New York Times* interview
   July 16: Conversation with Paul Budline (PAW referral)
   July 18: Conversation with Dwight Silverman (PAW referral)
   July 19: KFI (Los Angeles) radio talk show appearance
   July 20: *Fort Worth Times* interview
   July 25: WOAI (San Antonio) radio talk show appearance
   July 25: KDKA (Pittsburgh) radio talk show appearance
   July 25: *Los Angeles Times* interview
   July 27: WJR (Providence, R.I.) television show appearance
   July 28: *Fort Lauderdale News* interview
   July 29: *Time* interview
   July 31: Videotaping in Chicago with Robert Thompson and Alexander Schindler
   July (no date): *People* interview
   July (no date): Italian magazine interview
   July (no date): WUWM (Milwaukee) radio show interview
   July (no date): WEZW (Milwaukee) radio show interview
   July (no date): Meeting with four members of the *Milwaukee Sentinel* staff
   August 1: *Memphis Commercial* interview
   August 3: *Palm Beach Post* interview

August 4: *Nightline* (ABC) interview and taping

August 4: *San Francisco Chronicle* interview

August 5: Alex Ben Block, *Show Biz News,* interview

August 5: WXRL (Richmond, Virginia) radio show interview

August 5: ABC Radio interview

August 5: *Newsweek* interview

August 5: Canadian News Network interview

August 6: *New England Lutheran* interview

August 6: *Cape Cod Times* (Massachusetts) interview

August 7: KDEN (Denver) radio talk show appearance

August 7: Trinity Lutheran Church preaching and adult forum

August 10: *The Late Show* (Fox) television appearance

August 10: *Seattle Times* interview

August 12: WXYZ (Detroit) *Kelly and Co.* television appearance

August 12: WXYT (Detroit) radio talk show interview

August 16: *The Oprah Winfrey Show* (Chicago) television appearance.

47. Interview with Charles Bergstrom.

48. Ibid.

49. Interview with Roger Armstrong.

50. Interview with Dan Slusser.

51. Interview with Pollock.

52. Interview with Armstrong.

53. Few, if any, calls to the 777–1000 number were put through to the individuals requested. Universal's production and management operations did not suffer major disruptions, since most business calls from the outside went through direct lines. Barbara De Fina said that she once forgot the extension of the person she was trying to reach. "I called the main number and had somehow been directed to the *Last Temptation* sort of hotline, which I thought was, like, *wow.*"

54. Interview with Slusser.

55. Interview with Sally Van Slyke.

56. Interview with Armstrong.

57. Interview with Slusser.

58. Pamela Lansden, "Take One," *People,* August 15, 1988, 33.

59. Interview with Slusser.

60. Later that year, one of the guards assigned to the producer's building during the *Last Temptation* period was shot and killed at one of the

studio gates by a former mental patient who was trying to get to the television star Michael Landon.

61. Interviews with Perry Katz and John Polwrek.
62. Interview with Fred Mound.
63. Interview with Jim Fredrick.
64. Interview with Sid Sheinberg.
65. Ibid.
66. Harvey J. McGeorge II and Christine C. Ketcham, "Protection of Senior Executives," *World Affairs* (Winter 1983–84): 277–83.
67. Interview with Slusser.
68. Interview with Van Slyke.
69. Interview with Slusser.
70. Interview with Van Slyke.
71. Interview with Pollock.
72. Interview with Poland.
73. Interview with Slusser.
74. No one interviewed for this book could cite an instance of any MCA employee being dismissed or disciplined as a result of activity in support of the protest.
75. Interview with Armstrong.
76. Ibid.
77. Interview with Josh Baran.
78. Interview with Katz.
79. Interview with Van Slyke.
80. Interview with Katz.
81. Interview with Catherine Leach.
82. Interview with Pollock.
83. Interview with David Sameth.
84. Interview with Van Slyke.
85. Interview with Fredrick.
86. Ibid.
87. Interview with Baran.
88. Ibid.
89. Interview with Richard Ostling.
90. "What TIME Readers Said in '88; Issues of God and Man Dominated the Year's Mailbag," *Time*, February 20, 1989, 13.
91. Interview with Susan Lyne.
92. Interview with Steve Oney.

93. Interview with Van Slyke.
94. Interview with Pollock.
95. Stewart, *God in the Chaos,* 116–18.
96. Anne Thompson, "Furor about 'Last Temptation' Overshadows the Film," *Orange County Register,* August 14, 1988.
97. Interview with Mound.
98. Interview with Katz.
99. Interview with Van Slyke.
100. Interview with Mound.
101. Interview with Pollock.
102. Interview with Thelma Schoonmaker.
103. Interview with Martin Scorsese.
104. Interview with Schoonmaker.
105. Interview with Scorsese.
106. Scorsese interview by Stetler, 43.
107. Jon Pareles, "The Ethnic 'Passion' of Peter Gabriel," *Premiere,* February 1990, 102.
108. Interview with Scorsese.
109. Christopher Grove, "Enduring Partnerships," *Daily Variety,* May 31, 2002, Special Section 2, B1.
110. Interview with Schoonmaker.
111. Hal Hinson, "Scorsese, Master of the Rage," *Washington Post,* November 24, 1991, G1.

Chapter 8

1. Aljean Harmetz, "Scorsese 'Temptation' Gets Early Release," *New York Times,* August 5, 1988, 13.
2. Universal Studios, press release, August 4, 1988.
3. Pat Broeske, "Universal Moves Up Release Day of Film 'Last Temptation,'" *Los Angeles Times,* August 5, 1988, sec. II, 1.
4. Interview with Susan Lyne.
5. Interview with Sally Van Slyke.
6. Broeske, "Universal Moves Up Release Day," 3.
7. Ibid., 1.
8. Mike Trout, Vice President of Broadcasting, Focus on the Family, to Station Manager, August 5, 1988.
9. Broeske, "Universal Moves Up Release Day," 3.

10. Tom Seppy, "Falwell Calls on U.S. to Resist 'Temptation,' Boycott MCA," *Louisville Courier-Journal*, August 6, 1988, 6A.

11. Scott Fagerstrom and Valerie Takahama, "'Last Temptation' to Debut Next Week," *Orange County Register*, August 5, 1988, A12.

12. Broeske, "Universal Moves Up Release Day," 3.

13. Todd Putnam and Timothy Muck, "Wielding the Boycott Weapon for Social Change," *Business and Society Review* 78, no. 2 (1991): 5–8.

14. Studies conducted in the late 1980s and early 1990s suggested that both boycott participation and the actual effect of most boycotts on product sales are usually minimal. Proprietary research and public polls reported that less than 2 percent of the general population had ever boycotted a single product, or considered a boycott of products in response to objectionable television programming to be an action that they would personally engage in. Jenny Pfalzgraf, "Boycott Phobia: Separating Fact from Fiction," *American Advertising* 10, no. 2 (Summer 1994): 18–20.

15. Friedman, *Consumer Boycotts*.

16. Clarence Matthews, "Louisville Churches Join National Protest over Film Portrayal of Jesus," *Louisville Courier-Journal*, July 21, 1988, 1B.

17. "'Last Temptation' Draws Record Number of Callers," *Orlando Sentinel*, August 2, 1988, A9.

18. A week later the resolution was ruled invalid when it was revealed that the abstaining commissioner owned shares in a mutual fund that included a small amount of MCA stock and thus had a financial conflict of interest. "City's Vote Condemning Film about Christ Ruled Invalid," *Miami Herald*, August 3, 1988.

19. Michel Lafferty, "Titusville Condemns Christ Movie; Onlookers Cheer Non-Binding Vote," *Orlando Sentinel*, August 10, 1988, B1.

20. Claudia Eller, "'Last Temptation' to Bow Exclusively through Cineplex," *Hollywood Reporter*, August 9, 1988, 1.

21. "Southern Chains Likely to Reject Film on Jesus," *The Record* (Bergen, N.J.), August 1, 1988, A8.

22. "Three Local Movie Chains Likely to Pass on 'Temptation,'" UPI, August 11, 1988.

23. "'Temptation' Movie Unlikely to Get Wide Play in West Virginia," UPI, August 11, 1988.

24. Doug Grow, "Theaters Make Dafoe's Hometown Resist 'Temptation,'" *Orange County Register*, August 18, 1988, K3.

25. William P. Barrett, "A Wal-Mart for the Movies," *Forbes,* August 22, 1988.
26. Interview with Fred Mound.
27. Interview with anonymous source.
28. Interview with Jack Valenti.
29. Interview with Tom Pollock.
30. Valerie Takahama and Scott Fagerstrom, "OC Theater Chain Rejects 'Last Temptation,'" *Orange County Register,* August 6, 1988, A1.
31. Ibid., A1, A21.
32. Claudia Eller, "'Temptation's' Fate Rests with Filmgoers as Uni Ups Release," *Hollywood Reporter,* August 5, 1988, 44.
33. Interview with confidential source.
34. Interview with Mound.
35. Interview with anonymous source.
36. Claudia Eller, "Blair Withholds Judgment on 'Christ' until UACI Screening," *Hollywood Reporter,* August 4, 1988, 8.
37. Interview with Mound.
38. Ibid.
39. Ibid.
40. Claudia Eller, "GCC Resists 'Temptation'; Others Withhold Judgment," *Hollywood Reporter,* August 11, 1988, 1.
41. Interview with Mound.
42. Ibid.
43. Interview with Josh Baran.
44. James Risen and Judy L. Thomas, *Wrath of Angels: The American Abortion War* (New York: Basic Books, 1998).
45. Ibid.
46. "Minister Says 'Christ' Could Incite Violence," *San Diego Union-Tribune,* August 8, 1988, D6.
47. Interview with Dennis Walto.
48. Amy Dawes et al., ". . . Nail 'Christ' & Universal," *Variety,* August 10, 1988, 18. Though Hymers staged the most vivid demonstration, he was not the only one envisioning problems at theaters. A few days later, in San Antonio, Texas, a group of preachers spoke to a rally of several hundred people, calling on them to initiate a boycott of the Santikos Theatres chain if it showed *Last Temptation.* One of the preachers, the Reverend Gerald Ripley, reportedly told the crowd, "I will pray for and expect malfunctions of the equipment used to screen this film. I will

pray for and expect inexplicable breaks, tears, and scratches on the film itself." "About 300 Texans . . . ," UPI, August 12, 1988.

49. "The Flick of Violence," *Time,* March 19, 1979, www.time.com/time/magazine/article/0,9171,947013,00.html?promoid = googlep (February 29, 2008).

50. Clifford May, "On L.I., Fights Follow a Film on Rap Music," *New York Times,* November 6, 1985, B1, B2.

51. "Calif. Man Killed in Shooting at Site Screening 'Colors,'" *Variety,* May 4, 1988, 12.

52. Interview with Walto.

53. Interview with anonymous source.

54. Interview with Mound.

55. Ibid.

56. Interview with Pollock.

57. Interview with Baran.

58. Ibid.

59. Interview with Robin Schepper.

60. Interview with Walto.

61. Interview with Steve Rabinowitz.

62. Interview with Walto.

63. Interview with Laura Quinn.

64. Interview with Kevin Sites.

65. Interview with Rabinowitz.

66. Interview with Walto.

67. Interview with Schepper.

68. Walto, e-mail message to author, February 20, 1998.

69. Interview with Rabinowitz.

70. Interview with Elizabeth Stevenson.

71. Interview with Schepper.

72. Interview with Walto.

73. Ibid.

74. Interview with John Toohey.

75. Interview with Quinn.

76. Interview with Schepper.

77. Ibid.

78. Interview with Toohey.

79. Interview with Charles Sweeney.

80. Interview with Walto.

81. Interview with Rob Johnson.

82. Steve Pond, "The Siege at Universal," *Washington Post,* August 12, 1988, B7.

83. Interview with Roger Armstrong.

84. Joseph Gelmis, "One Man's Passion Play," *Newsday,* August 11, 1988, part II, 4.

85. Dan Martin, "Controversial Film Released; SBC Leaders to Get Screening," *Baptist Press,* August 5, 1988, 1.

86. Martin, "Controversial Film Released; SBC Leaders to Get Screening," 1.

87. Kathy Palen, "Baptists React to Screening of 'Last Temptation' Film," *Baptist Press,* August 16, 1988, 2.

88. "Last Temptation," AP wire copy, August 9, 1988.

89. Michael Hirsley, "Bishop's Call: Shun 'Last Temptation,'" *Chicago Tribune,* August 10, 1988, sec. 1, 12.

90. "Archdiocese of Detroit Statement on the Film," *PR Newswire,* August 19, 1988.

91. Jorge Casusco and Charles Mount, "Protesters, Fans Flock to 'Last Temptation,'" *Chicago Tribune,* August 13, 1988, sec. 1, 2.

92. "Last Temptation," AP wire copy.

93. Greek Orthodox Archdiocese of North and South America, "The Last Temptation of Christ" (news release), August 3, 1988.

94. Rosaries for Peace, "Statement of Mother Teresa of Calcutta on 'The Last Temptation of Christ'" (news release), August 9, 1988.

95. Interview with Martin Scorsese.

96. Ibid.

97. "'Last Temptation' Controversy," *Nightline* (ABC News), August 9, 1988; transcript produced by Journal Graphics, Inc.

98. Interview with Scorsese.

99. Duane Byrge, review of *The Last Temptation of Christ, Hollywood Reporter,* August 8, 1988, 8.

100. Hal Hinson, "The Imperfect Power of 'Temptation,'" *Washington Post,* August 12, 1988, B2.

101. Janet Maslin, "'Last Temptation,' Scorsese's View of Jesus' Sacrifice," *New York Times,* August 12, 1988, C1.

102. Amy Dawes et al., ". . . Nail Christ."

103. By comparison, the paperback edition's cumulative sales from 1966 to 1988 were about 150,000 copies. Deirdre Donahue, "A Renewed 'Temptation' for Readers," *USA Today,* August 19, 1988, D1.

104. Amy Dawes, "Solons Join 'Temptation' Fray," *Daily Variety*, August 11, 1988, 11.

105. Ibid.

106. Others claimed that a reciprocal influence also occurred, that the studio gained substantially in audience interest for the film from the opposition's show of force.

107. Stewart, *God in the Chaos*, 122.

108. "Last Temptation of Christ" (video) (San Bernardino, Calif.: Arrowhead Productions International, 1988).

109. The backstory to Steve Gooden's performance at the August 11 rally, including the role of John Stewart in helping Gooden arrive at the decision to give up his MCA contract, is provided in Valerie Takahama, "Pact with God Came First," *Orange County Register*, August 18, 1988, K1, 3.

110. Interview with Shana Weiss.

111. "'Temptation' Film Opens Amid Massive Protests," *St. Paul Pioneer Press*, August 13, 1988, 4A.

112. Annette Haddad, "Domestic News," UPI, August 12, 1988.

113. George Landau, "Protesters Aiming to Stop Movie," *St. Louis Post-Dispatch*, August 13, 1988, 6A.

114. "Orlando Gets Protesters but Not Film," *Orlando Sentinel*, August 13, 1988, D1.

115. Marjorie Williams, "Falwell and the Faithful," *Washington Post*, August 13, 1988, C1.

116. Interview with Glen Gumpel.

117. Interview with Charles Warn.

118. Ibid.

119. Ibid.

120. Charles Fleming, "Top Directors Lash Out against 'Thought Police,'" *Los Angeles Herald-Examiner*, August 13, 1988, B1.

121. Andrea King, "Directors Defend 'Temptation' as Protests Surround Opening," *Hollywood Reporter*, August 15, 1988, 17.

122. Fleming, "Top Directors Lash Out."

123. Jim Robbins and Amy Dawes, "Brouhaha Hurls 'Christ' to Record Biz," *Daily Variety*, August 17, 1988, 5.

124. King, "Directors Defend 'Temptation.'"

125. Robbins and Dawes, "Brouhaha."

126. Fleming, "Top Directors Lash Out."

Chapter 9

1. Paul Bilodeau, "Sell-Out Crowds See Christ Film as Protesters Pray for Them," *Toronto Star*, August 13, 1988, A9.
2. Interview with Laura Quinn.
3. John Dart and Russell Chandler, "Full Theaters, Protests Greet 'Temptation,'" *Los Angeles Times*, August 13, 1988, sec. I, 29.
4. Interview with Robin Schepper.
5. Ron Smith, "Demonstrators Say Film Debases Christ," *St. Paul Pioneer Press*, August 13, 1988, 1A, 4A.
6. Interview with Rob Johnson.
7. Jim Robbins and Amy Dawes, "Brouhaha Hurls 'Christ' to Record," *Variety*, August 17, 1988, 20; UPI, August 13, 1988.
8. Interview with Elizabeth Stevenson.
9. Interview with Dennis Walto.
10. Ryan P. Murphy, "Temptation Opens to Protest, Praise," *Miami Herald*, August 13, 1988, 1A.
11. Laura Sessions Stepp, "Long Lines for 'Last Temptation'; Police, Tight Security Mark Film's Opening," *Washington Post*, August 13, 1988, C1.
12. Murphy, "Temptation Opens to Protest, Praise," 20A.
13. Interview with Perry Katz.
14. Ibid.
15. Ibid.
16. Dart and Chandler, "Full Theaters, Protests Greet 'Temptation.'"
17. Ibid.
18. Interview with Steve Barr.
19. Interview with Craig Livingstone.
20. Noah Richler, "Wanna See the Movie or Wanna Protest?" *Punch*, September 2, 1988, 26.
21. Michael J. Kelly, "Ire for Last Temptation," *Record* (Bergen, N.J.), August 14, 1988, A3.
22. Susan Harding, "Representing Fundamentalism: The Problem of the Repugnant Cultural Other," *Social Research* 58, no. 2 (Summer 1991): 373–93.
23. Interviews with Martin Scorsese and Jay Cocks.
24. Interview with Willem Dafoe.
25. Interview with Cocks.
26. Jorge Casuso and Charles Mount, "Protesters, Fans Flock to 'Last Temptation,'" *Chicago Tribune*, August 13, 1988, sec. I, 2.

27. Ibid., 1–2.
28. Kevin Sites, "L.T.O.C. Opening Night" (faxed memo), August 13, 1988.
29. Hiawatha Bray, "Taking Scorsese's Jesus Personally," *Wheaton (Ill.) Sunday Journal*, August 14, 1988; reprinted at www.surfinthespirit.com/entertainment/scorsese.html (July 25, 2005).
30. Sites, "L.T.O.C. Opening Night."
31. Ibid.
32. "Scorsese 'Last Temptation' Drew Big Weekend Crowd," *Wall Street Journal*, August 16, 1988, 35.
33. Martin A. Grove, "Controversy Fuels Boxoffice Success of 'Last Temptation,'" *Hollywood Reporter*, August 16, 1988, 1.
34. Dennis Hunt, "Fundamentalists Urge 'E.T.' Video Boycott; Pre-Orders Set Record," *Los Angeles Times*, September 16, 1988, 4.
35. Ibid.
36. Harmetz, "How Studio Maneuvered 'Temptation' into Hit," C15.
37. Interview with John Polwrek.
38. Ibid.
39. Harmetz, "How Studio Maneuvered 'Temptation' into Hit."
40. Amy Dawes, "AMC Chain to Play 'Last Temptation,'" *Hollywood Reporter*, August 17, 1988, 1.
41. "Controversial Film on Christ Coming to Detroit," UPI (regional news), August 17, 1988.
42. Scott Fagerstrom and Valerie Takahama, "'Last Temptation' to Make OC Debut at Santa Ana Theater," *Orange County Register*, August 17, 1988, A1.
43. Interview with Barr.
44. Erin Kelly, "'Temptation' Protesters March inside MainPlace," *Orange County Register*, August 20, 1988, 20.
45. M. L. Stein, "Readers React," *Editor & Publisher*, September 10, 1988, 15.
46. Terrence Stutz and Julie Mason, "Film on Jesus Draws Pickets in Texas Cities," *Dallas Morning News*, August 20, 1988, A1.
47. UPI wire story (dateline, Austin, Tex.), August 19, 1988.
48. Stutz and Mason, "Film on Jesus Draws Pickets in Texas Cities."
49. Amy Dawes, Jim Robbins, and Robert H. Brown, "Loews Giveth and Carmike Taketh Away," *Variety*, August 24, 1988, 28.
50. Claudia Eller, "Loews Will Yield to 'Temptation,'" *Hollywood Reporter*, August 23, 1988, 1.

51. All data from Grace Market Research, Inc., "Universal Pictures—'The Last Temptation of Christ' Saturday Night Survey—August 20, 1988."

52. "Utah Paper Will Not Take Ads for Movie," *Editor & Publisher,* September 10, 1988, 15.

53. Interview with Scott Levenson.

54. Dialogue reconstructed from interviews with Levenson and Walto.

55. Dan Harrie, "'Temptation' Utah Premier Foiled by Burglary, Vandalism," UPI, August 26, 1988; Claudia Eller, "Vandals Strike Salt Lake City Theater Showing 'Temptation,'" *Hollywood Reporter,* August 29, 1988, 3, 23.

56. Steve Dollar, "Controversial 'Last Temptation' Set to Open in Atlanta Friday," *Atlanta Constitution,* August 24, 1988, D1.

57. Gustav Niebuhr, "100 'Soul-Savers' to Greet 'Last Temptation' Viewers," *Atlanta Constitution,* August 26, 1988, A17.

58. Hollis R. Towns, "Clergy Assail Movie on Christ," *Atlanta Journal,* August 25, 1988, J2.

59. Gustav Niebuhr and Gayle White, "Atlanta Debut of Film Draws 250 Protesters," *Atlanta Journal,* August 27, 1988, A1.

60. Interview with John Toohey.

61. Gustav Niebuhr, "Protest on 'Last Temptation' Draws 1,000," *Atlanta Constitution,* August 29, 1988, A11.

62. "Temptation Moviegoers Searched in Edmonton," *Toronto Star,* August 29, 1988, C8.

63. Interview with Quinn.

64. James M. Jasper, *The Art of Moral Protest* (Chicago: University of Chicago Press, 1997), 193.

65. "Thousands March to Protest 'Temptation' Film," UPI, August 28, 1988.

66. Interview with Steve Rabinowitz.

67. Interview with Quinn.

68. Interview with Stevenson.

69. Interview with Quinn.

70. "Letters Protesting 'Last Temptation' Flood N.C. Theaters," *Charlotte Observer,* August 14, 1988, 4D.

71. John Quinn, "K.C. Gets Share of Protesters as Pic Plays One Site," *Variety,* October 5, 1988, 23.

72. "Bombs Found at Theater Playing Protested Film," *Chicago Tribune,* October 7, 1988, 3.

73. UPI wire story (dateline, Mishawaka, Ind.), October 5, 1988.

74. "Man Drives Bus into Theater Playing 'Last Temptation,'" UPI, October 25, 1988.

75. Interview with Levenson.

76. Ibid.

77. Interview with Stevenson.

78. Interview with Toohey.

79. Interview with Noel Boxer.

80. Interview with Josh Baran.

81. Interview with Rabinowitz.

82. Interview with Johnson.

83. Interview with Livingstone.

84. Interview with Levenson.

85. Interview with confidential source.

86. Ibid.

87. Ibid.

88. Interview with Walto.

89. Ibid.

90. Debra Gersh, "Birmingham News Refuses 'Last Temptation' Ads," *Editor & Publisher,* August 20, 1988, 13.

91. Terry J. Hughes, "700 Protest 'Temptation,'" *St. Louis Post-Dispatch,* September 24, 1988, 1, 4; Victor Volland, "Aboussie Claims Credit for Effort to Close Theater," *St. Louis Post-Dispatch,* September 25, 1988, C1, 4.

92. Interview with Walto.

93. Interview with anonymous source.

94. "Dowdy Returns $1,000 Donation, Prepares for Campaign Swing," UPI, September 6, 1988.

95. "Film 'Offensive' to Cuomo," *New York Times,* August 14, 1988, I36.

96. James Ragland, "Latest Job Puzzles Film Panel," *Dallas Morning News,* August 26, 1988, A21.

97. For a history of the Dallas movie classification board, see Brian O'Leary, "Local Government Regulation of the Movies: The Dallas System, 1966–93," *Journal of Film and Video* 48, no. 3 (1996): 46–57.

98. In August 1988 an evangelical Christian group, Renaissance Canada, called *Last Temptation* "hate propaganda" and appealed to the Canadian federal government to stop it from being exhibited. No legal action was taken. "The Last Temptation of Christ: A Chronology," *Toronto Star,* July 2, 1989.

99. Levy, *Blasphemy;* Robert C. Post, "Cultural Heterogeneity and Law: Pornography, Blasphemy, and the First Amendment," *California Law Review* 76 (1988): 297–335.

100. Pensacola earned a place of prominence on the national fundamentalist map later, in the mid-1990s, when the Brownsville Assembly of God church began playing host to the longest-running revival in the country, drawing thousands of devout Christians nightly from every part of the United States and the world.

101. "Judge Overturns Ban on Film," *New York Times,* September 11, 1988, I34.

102. Levy, *Blasphemy,* 532.

103. Interview with Toohey.

104. Interview with Walto.

105. Levy, *Blasphemy,* 532.

106. Interview with Walto.

107. Interview with John Ankerberg.

108. Interview with Fred Mound.

109. "Controversial Film Will Be Shown in Memphis," UPI, September 15, 1988.

110. "'Temptation' Comes to Chattanooga," *Chattanooga Times,* September 23, 1988, A8.

111. Randy Arnold, "Televangelist Will Protest 'Temptation,'" *Chattanooga Times,* September 23, 1988, B1.

112. Interview with Quinn.

113. Jeffrey M. Fleming, "Ministers Voice Opposition to 'Last Temptation' Film," *Chattanooga News-Free Press,* September 22, 1988, A2.

114. Interview with Quinn.

115. Ibid.

116. John Jackson, "Churches Start Petitions against Showing Film," *Alabama Journal,* July 22, 1988.

117. Martin McCaffery to Martin Scorsese, August 5, 1988. (Original at Auburn Montgomery Library [Archives and Special Collections]).

118. Lori Allen Dendy, "Montgomery Council Resists 'Temptation,'" *Montgomery Advertiser,* August 17, 1988, 1A, 12A.

119. John Jackson, "Movie Could Cost Capri Its Insurance," *Alabama Journal,* August 25, 1988, 1, 6.

120. Rhonda Pines, "Local Political Leaders Attend Religious Rally," *Montgomery Advertiser,* January 7, 1989, 2A.

121. Rhonda Pines, "'Last Temptation' Sets Capri Theatre Record," *Montgomery Advertiser,* February 8, 1989.

122. Ann Van Der Veer, "Santa Barbara Venue for 'Last' Doubles as Church," *Daily Variety,* September 28, 1988, 9.

123. One of the communities that succeeded in keeping the film out was Paul Schrader's hometown of Grand Rapids, Michigan. Recalled Schrader, "My father did not care for motion pictures. . . . And he didn't care for what I did for a living. So, out of the blue, I started getting phone calls from him. And he's sort of interested in this *Last Temptation* movie. And he wants to know how many theaters it's opening in, and when it's opening. And by the third time he calls—now this is a man who probably had never even seen any of my films—I said, 'Dad, are you by any chance involved in the opposition to this film?'" Schrader paused, laughing at the memory from fourteen years earlier—"And he said, 'Yes, but only locally.'" Interview with Paul Schrader.

124. Rick Bailey, "Film about Jesus Sparks Local Outrage," *Lexington Herald-Leader,* July 23, 1988, B2.

125. Rick Bailey, "Protests Block Film; 'Last Temptation of Christ' Not Coming to Lexington," *Lexington Herald-Leader,* August 12, 1988, A1.

126. "The Last Temptation of Christ," *Box Office Grosses* (Baseline FT, Inc., n.d.).

127. Michael Stremfel, "Takeover Talk, Not 'Temptation' Fuels MCA Price Increase," *Los Angeles Business Journal,* August 22, 1988, sec. 1, 16.

128. Nicole Brodeur, "'Last Temptation' Boycott Isn't Rubbing Off on 'E.T.': County Church Protests Not Affecting Sales of Home Video," *Orange County Register,* December 10, 1988, E26.

129. Frank York, "'The Last Temptation' Is a Box Office Flop," *Focus on the Family Citizen,* November 1988, 1–2.

130. American Family Association, "For Immediate Release" (press release), November 1, 1988.

131. Interview with Larry Poland.

132. Interview with Sally Van Slyke.

133. Interview with Tom Pollock.

134. Amy Dawes, "Christian Groups Reaping Monetary Fruits from 'Last,'" *Daily Variety,* September 7, 1988, 8.

135. Ibid.

136. Harold B. Smith, "Holy Indignation," *Christianity Today,* October 21, 1988, 15.

137. Interview with John Stewart.

138. Interview with Rich Buhler.

139. Interview with Poland.

140. Ken Sidey, "Last Temptation Boycott Gets Mixed Reviews," *Christianity Today*, April 21, 1989, 37.

141. Interview with Sid Sheinberg.

Chapter 10

1. Interview with Martin Scorsese.

2. Hank Werba, "Inclusion of 'Christ' at Venice Protested," *Daily Variety*, August 1, 1988, 19.

3. Amy Dawes et al., "'Last Temptation' Touches Off Protests among European Groups," *Variety*, August 24, 1988, 5.

4. "Zeffirelli Protests 'Temptation of Christ,'" *New York Times*, August 3, 1988, sec. III, 22.

5. Ibid.

6. "Fest Chief Expects Little Commotion over 'Temptation,'" *Variety*, August 24, 1988, 42.

7. Jim Robbins, "'Last Temptation' War Rages On; Exhibs Pressured, Italy Quakes," *Variety*, August 3, 1988, 6.

8. Claudia Eller, "'Temptation' Fate Rests with Filmgoers as Uni Ups Release," *Hollywood Reporter*, August 5, 1988, 44.

9. Franco Zeffirelli, open letter to Tom Pollock, *Hollywood Reporter*, August 5, 1988, 24.

10. In December 1989, Martin Scorsese and the Venice Biennale Festival were cleared of all charges of religious contempt, blasphemy, and obscenity. People Column, *St. Louis Post-Dispatch*, December 10, 1989, 4A.

11. Clyde Haberman, "Scorsese's 'Last Temptation' Creates Furor at Venice Festival," *New York Times*, September 8, 1988, C17.

12. "Transcript of Last Temptation of Christ—Venice Press Conference 1988," Cappa Productions. (Photocopy in author's possession.)

13. "Venice Festival Screens Scorsese's 'Last Temptation,'" *Los Angeles Times*, September 9, 1988, part VI, 4.

14. Ibid.

15. Colin Hoskins, Stuart McFadyen, and Adam Finn, *Global Television and Film: An Introduction to the Economics of the Business* (New York: Oxford University Press, 1997), 62–63.

16. Interview with Michael Williams-Jones.

17. Peter Cumper, "Religious Human Rights in the United Kingdom," *Emory International Law Review* 10 (Spring 1996).

18. Interview with Williams-Jones.

19. "British Censors Refuse to Cut 'Temptation,'" *New York Times*, August 27, 1988, I14.

20. Interview with Williams-Jones.

21. Paul Mungo, "U.K. Film Board Oks Uncut Exhib'n of 'Last Temptation,'" *Hollywood Reporter*, August 29, 1988, 3.

22. "Boycott of Film on Jesus Given Runcie Backing," *Los Angeles Times*, September 3, 1988, part I, 10.

23. "London Cool to 'Temptation,'" *New York Times*, September 10, 1988, sec. 1, 16.

24. Andrew Billen, "Director Defends Film about Jesus," *Times* (London), September 10, 1988, 36.

25. Don Groves, "British Audiences Flock to 'Temptation' Boxoffice," *Daily Variety*, September 12, 1988, 2.

26. Interview with Scorsese.

27. Interview with Williams-Jones.

28. Ibid.

29. Groves, "British Audiences Flock."

30. Interview with Williams-Jones.

31. James M. Markham, "Religious War Ignites Anew in France," *New York Times*, November 9, 1988, A6.

32. The cardinals also said that they had no intention to "attack the freedom of artistic creation, nor censor anyone's thoughts, nor judge the intentions of the novelist or the filmmaker." "Temptation Protests Continue; Vandals Damage H'Wood House," *Variety*, September 7, 1988, 49.

33. Interview with Williams-Jones.

34. Bethany Haye, "'Christ' Opens throughout Paris amid Much To-Do," *Hollywood Reporter* (Weekly International Edition), October 4, 1988, I-1.

35. Interview with Williams-Jones.

36. Farah Nayeri, "'Last' Tangle in Paris as Scorsese Pic Bows," *Daily Variety*, September 30, 1988, 34.

37. Farah Nayeri, "Paris Sites Drop Film after Protester Assaults," *Variety*, October 19, 1988, 481.

38. "Fire at Paris 'Temptation' Site Leaves Theater Gutted, 13 Hurt," *Variety*, October 26, 1988, 10.

39. Ibid.

40. Ibid.

41. Simon Haydon, "Forty Right-Wingers Arrested after Scorsese Film Fire," *Reuter Library Report,* October 25, 1988.

42. Interview with Williams-Jones.

43. Steven Greenhouse, "Police Suspect Arson in Fire at Paris Theater," *New York Times,* October 25, 1988, sec. III, 21.

44. "Dutch Court Rules against 'Last' Ban," *Hollywood Reporter,* September 23, 1988, 3.

45. Kevin Liffey, "'Hate-Filled' Letters Greet Christ Film in Germany," *Reuter Library Report,* November 10, 1988.

46. "'Christ' Rates a German Tax Cut after Getting 'Outstanding' Grade," *Variety,* November 2, 1988, 8; "No Big Incidents as 'Temptation' Opens at 50 W. German Screens," *Variety,* November 16, 1988, 7.

47. "'Over 18' Rating Given to 'Christ' in Ireland," *Variety,* November 16, 1988, 7.

48. "'Temptation' Bows Down Under as UIP Lifts Secrecy," *Variety,* October 12, 1988, 3.

49. Ibid.

50. Ruth Youngblood, "Censors Blasted for Outlawing 'Last Temptation,'" UPI wire story, n.d.

51. John Voland, "Morning Report," *Los Angeles Times,* October 20, 1988, part 6, 2.

52. "South Africa Bans Controversial Film on Christ," *Reuter Library Report,* October 25, 1988.

53. "'Temptation' Ban Sought in Greece," *Chicago Tribune,* August 23, 1988, sec. 1, 5.

54. "'Temptation' Protest Leads to Slashing of Athens Screens," *Variety,* October 19, 1988, 481; Ralph Joseph, "Crowds Rampage at Screening of 'Last Temptation,'" UPI, October 13, 1988.

55. "'Temptation' Banned for Now in Greece," *Variety,* November 30, 1988, 6.

56. Ibid.

57. "Colombian Body Prohibits 'Temptation' amid Threats," *Variety,* January 18–24, 1989, 19.

58. Nelson Hoineff, "São Paulo Release of 'Temptation' Is Delayed under Fire," *Variety,* November 23, 1988, 10.

59. Itour Gelbitz, "Israeli High Court Strikes Down Ban on 'Temptation,'" *Hollywood Reporter*, June 16, 1989, 53.

60. Bryan Pearson, "At Last Minute, S. Africa Bars 'Temptation' Again," *Variety*, November 2, 1988, 73.

61. Interview with Paul Schrader.

62. Michael Morris, "Film Provides a Test of Tolerance," *Africa News*, November 2, 1998.

63. U.S. Department of State, "Chile Country Report on Human Rights Practices for 1996," January 30, 1997, http://64.233.167.104/search?q=cache:_EY96gd8qEEJ:www.chipsites.com/derechos/images/usreport.rtf+1997+%22Department+of+State%22+%22Chile+Country+Report+on+Human+Rights+Practices%22&hl=en&ct=clnk&cd=3&gl=us.

64. "Nation Waits for Last Word on Last Temptation," *Santiago Times*, January 31, 2001.

65. "Christians in Uproar over Jesus Film," *APS Diplomat Recorder*, May 6, 1995.

66. Andr Paine, "Temptation of Christ Tops TV Complaints," *Evening Standard* (London), December 18, 2003, A23.

67. Ken Bensinger, "Scorsese's 'Christ' at Last," *Variety*, March 17, 2004.

68. Will Tusher, "U, Cineplex Plan Reissue of 'Temptation' for 1989," *Daily Variety*, December 13, 1988, 2.

69. "Uni Resists 'Temptation' Re-Issue," *Hollywood Reporter*, December 21, 1988, 26.

70. Pat McGilligan and Mark Rowland, "Film Critics' Poll Rating the 1988 Films," *Washington Post*, January 8, 1989, G1.

71. Tom Bierbaum, "MCA Weighs Options on 'Temptation' Homevideo," *Daily Variety*, December 16, 1988, 1.

72. Terry Atkinson, "Quiet Release of Controversial 'Last Temptation of Christ,'" *Los Angeles Times*, June 30, 1989, 25.

73. Interview with Tom Pollock.

74. Dennis Hunt, "'Temptation' Video to Rekindle Fundamentalist Ire?" *Los Angeles Times*, June 2, 1989, part VI, 13.

75. Bierbaum, "MCA Weighs Options on 'Temptation' Homevideo," 45.

76. Hunt, "'Temptation' Video to Rekindle Fundamentalist Ire?"

77. According to one estimate, approximately 80 percent of Blockbuster's franchise stores went along with the ban on the *Last Temptation* video

when it was released. Tom Bierbaum, "'Temptation' Yields Brisk Biz in Vid Debut," *Variety*, July 5, 1989, 1.

78. Interview with Pollock.

79. "Video Dealers Say Little about 'Temptation,'" *Arkansas Democrat-Gazette*, June 24, 1989.

80. Bierbaum, "'Temptation' Yields Brisk Biz in Vid Debut," 1.

81. "Video Dealers Say Little about 'Temptation.'"

82. Interview with Schrader.

83. Interview with Scorsese.

84. David Braaten, "3-Month Boycott of Pay TV Protests 'Last Temptation,'" *Washington Times*, October 6, 1989, A4.

85. "'Last Temptation' Back after Cable Blackout," *Philadelphia Inquirer*, October 7, 1989, D8.

Epilogue

1. Interview with Paul Schrader.

2. Gustav Niebuhr, "Holy War against Hollywood: Offending Film Provides Evangelicals with a New Rallying Point and Self-Image," *Atlanta Journal*, August 7, 1988, C1.

3. Paul Gray, "An Explosive Reaction," *Time*, February 13, 1989, 82.

4. Rafsanjani quoted in Lisa Appignanesi and Sara Maitland, eds., *The Rushdie File* (Syracuse, N.Y.: Syracuse University Press, 1990), 69.

5. Michael Hirsley, "'Verses' Furor Looks Familiar," *Chicago Tribune*, February 24, 1989, Chicagoland sec., 8.

6. Barbara G. Baker, "Christians and Muslims Unite to Oppose The Last Temptation," *Christianity Today*, May 12, 1989, 57.

7. Steven C. Dubin, *Arresting Images: Impolitic Art and Uncivil Actions* (New York: Routledge, 1992).

8. Ron Harrist, "Group: Government Supports Bigotry with Art Exhibit," Associated Press, April 25, 1989.

9. "Debate in Senate over the NEA, Statements by Sen. Alfonse D'Amato and Sen. Jesse Helms, with Letter of Protest to NEA's Hugh Southern, May 18, 1989," in *Culture Wars*, ed. Richard Bolton (New York: New Press, 1992), 30.

10. Bolton, *Culture Wars*, 346.

11. Patrick Buchanan, "Losing the War for American's Culture?" in *Culture Wars*, ed. Richard Bolton, 33.

12. Henry J. Hyde, "The Culture War," *National Review*, April 30, 1990, 25, 27.

13. Patrick J. Buchanan, "American Arts Radicals Declare War on Public," *Sunday Oregonian* (Portland), April 22, 1990, K4. He apparently had an advance copy of Hyde's article, as his column appeared a week before the *National Review* issue appeared.

14. Dobson quoted in John S. Detweiler, "The Religious Right's Battle Plan in the 'Civil War of Values,'" *Public Relations Review* 18 (1992): 247–55.

15. S. J. D. Green, "Beyond *The Satanic Verses:* Conservative Religion & the Liberal Society," *Encounter* 74 (1990): 12–20.

16. James Davison Hunter, *Culture Wars: The Struggle to Define America.* (New York: Basic Books, 1991).

17. Michael Medved, *Hollywood vs. America: Popular Culture and the War on Traditional Values* (New York: HarperPerennial, 1992).

18. Just as the culture wars seem to wax and wane, so also do prognostications of their future course. A prime example is a recent article by the political commentator E. J. Dionne, who wrote in March 2008, "We are at the beginning of a new era in which large, secular problems related to war and peace, economics and the United States' standing in the world will displace culture and religion as the electorate's central concerns." E. J. Dionne, "Culture Wars? How 2004," *RealClearPolitics*, March 11, 2008, www.realclearpolitics.com/articles/2008/03/reclaiming_faith_and_politics.html.

19. Interview with Sean Daniel.

20. Peter H. Brown, "Tales Told Out of Church: The Rumblings over 'Mormon Murders,'" *Washington Post*, January 22, 1989, G1.

21. Interview with Mark Gill.

22. Interviews with a confidential source and with Jeffrey Katzenberg.

23. Scorsese reportedly told Harvey Weinstein to tell Smith to get ready for the worst year of his life—"because I lost a year of my life after *The Last Temptation of Christ.* I didn't go out for a year and when I did, I had bodyguards." Siobhan Synnot, "Cross Purposes," *Scotsman*, December 18, 1999, 20.

24. Anita Chabria, "Passion Campaign Aims to Overcome Christian Rifts," *PR Week*, March 8, 2004, 1.

25. Paul Zahn Now (transcript), aired February 11, 2004, http://transcripts.cnn.com/TRANSCRIPTS/0402/11/pzn.00.html.

26. Peter J. Boyer, "Hollywood Heresy," *New Yorker*, May 22, 2006, 38.

27. Ian Fisher, "Vatican Official Urges Boycott of 'Da Vinci' Film," *New York Times*, April 29, 2006, B8.

28. Cal Thomas, "Cursing Darkness Sells Devil's Product," *Los Angeles Times*, August 12, 1988, sec. II, 7.

29. Scott Spencer, "Lights! Camera! Rapture!" *New Yorker*, September 10, 2001, 105–9.

30. John Dart, "Seeing a New Spirit in Hollywood," *Los Angeles Times*, April 1, 1997, A16.

31. Michael Medved, "Hollywood Makes Room for Religion," *American Enterprise*, March–April 1995, 59–64.

32. Sharon Waxman, "Hollywood Rethinking Films of Faith after 'Passion,'" *New York Times*, March 15, 2004, E1.

33. An average of 200 protesters appeared at each of the 140 screens showing *Last Temptation* in 1988. At least another 30,000 people assembled at various demonstrations held at Universal City and other places around the country.

34. Carol Iannone, "The Last Temptation Reconsidered," *First Things*, February 1996, 50.

35. Garry Wills, "Jesus in the Mean Streets," *New York Review of Books*, October 13, 1988, 10.

36. Tom Pollock, e-mail to author, December 30, 2007.

37. Iannone, "The Last Temptation Reconsidered," 52.

38. Peter A. Bien, *Tempted by Happiness: Kazantzakis' Post-Christian Christ* (Wallingford, Pa.: Pendle Hill, 1984), 13.

39. Thomas DePietro, "Scorsese: Making Jesus Contemporary," *Christianity and Crisis*, October 10, 1988, 344.

Selected Bibliography

Ammerman, Nancy. "North American Protestant Fundamentalism." In *Fundamentalisms Observed,* edited by Martin E. Marty and R. Scott Appleby. Chicago: University of Chicago Press, 1994.

Ankerberg, John, and John Weldon. *The Facts on "The Last Temptation of Christ": The True Story behind the Controversial Film.* Eugene, Ore.: Harvest House Publishers, 1988.

Antonakes, Michael. "Christ, Kazantzakis, and Controversy in Greece." In *God's Struggler: Religion in the Writings of Nikos Kazantzakis,* edited by Darren J. N. Middleton and Peter Bien. Macon, Ga.: Mercer University Press, 1996.

Appignanesi, Lisa, and Sara Maitland, eds. *The Rushdie File.* Syracuse, N.Y.: Syracuse University Press, 1990.

Babington, Bruce, and Peter Williams Evans. *Biblical Epics: Sacred Narratives in the Cinema.* Manchester, U.K.: Manchester University Press, 1993.

Bien, Peter. *Kazantzakis: Politics of the Spirit.* Princeton, N.J.: Princeton University Press, 1989.

———. *Nikos Kazantzakis.* New York: Columbia University Press, 1972.

———. "Nikos Kazantzakis's Novels on Film." *Journal of Modern Greek Studies* 18, no. 1 (2000): 161–69.

———. *Tempted by Happiness: Kazantzakis' Post-Christian Christ.* Wallingford, Pa.: Pendle Hill Publications, 1984.

Bird, Brian. "Film Protesters Vow Long War on Universal." *Christianity Today,* September 16, 1988, 41–42.

Black, Gregory D. *Hollywood Censored.* Cambridge: Cambridge University Press, 1994.

Blake, Richard A. "An Autopsy on 'Temptation.'" *America,* March 4, 1989, 199–201.

Bloom, Harold. *The American Religion: The Emergence of the Post-Christian Nation.* New York: Simon and Schuster, 1992.

Braudy, Leo. "The Sacraments of Genre: Coppola, DePalma, Scorsese." In *Native Informants,* by Leo Braudy. New York: Oxford University Press, 1991.

Bronski, Michael. "Reel Politick." *Zeta,* November 1988, 74–77.

Bruck, Connie. *When Hollywood Had a King: The Reign of Lew Wasserman, Who Leveraged Talent into Power and Influence.* New York: Random House, 2003.

Buchanan, Patrick J. "Is It Art or Sleaze?" *Harrisonburg (Va.) Daily News-Record,* July 27, 1988, 6.

Christon, Lawrence. "'Temptation': Protest and the Pain Beneath." *Los Angeles Times,* August 21, 1988, Calendar.

Cieply, Michael. "Inside *the* Agency." *Los Angeles Times,* July 2, 1989, Calendar, sec. C.

———. "MCA's No. 2 Tower of Power." *Los Angeles Times,* August 12, 1987, sec. VI.

Cook, Pam. "The Last Temptation of Christ." *Monthly Film Bulletin* 55 (1988): 287–88.

Corliss, Richard. "Body . . ." *Film Comment,* October 1988, 34, 42–43.

———. ". . . And Blood." *Film Comment,* October 1988, 36–42.

Couvares, Francis G., ed. *Movie Censorship and American Culture.* Washington, D.C.: Smithsonian Institution Press, 1996.

Dart, John. "Portrayals of Christ Tempt Controversy." *Los Angeles Times,* July 30, 1988, sec. I.

Davis, L. J. "Hollywood's Most Secret Agent." *New York Times Magazine,* July 9, 1989, 24–27, 51–54, 74–75.

DePietro, Thomas. "Scorsese: Making Jesus Contemporary." *Christianity and Crisis* 48, no. 14 (1988): 342–44.

Diamond, Sara. *Not by Politics Alone: The Enduring Influence of the Christian Right.* New York: Guilford Press, 2000.

Dinnerstein, Leonard. *Anti-Semitism in America.* New York: Oxford University Press, 1994.

Douglas, Mary. *Purity and Danger.* London: Routledge, 1966.

Drabinsky, Garth. *Closer to the Sun.* Toronto: McClelland and Stewart, 1995.

Draper, Ellen. "'Controversy Has Probably Destroyed Forever the Context': The Miracle and Movie Censorship in America in the Fifties." *Velvet Light Trap* 25 (1990): 69–79.

Driver, Tom F. "Jesus: God, Man, and Movie." *Christianity and Crisis* 48 (1988): 338–41.

Dubin, Steven C. *Arresting Images: Impolitic Art and Uncivil Actions.* London: Routledge, 1992.

Durant, Will, and Ariel Durant. "Nikos Kazantzakis." In *Interpretations of Life: A Survey of Contemporary Literature.* New York: Simon and Schuster, 1970.

Ehrenstein, David. *The Scorsese Picture: The Art and Life of Martin Scorsese.* New York: Birch Lane Press, 1992.

Fine, Gary Alan. "Among Those Dark Satanic Mills: Rumors of Kooks, Cults, and Corporations." *Southern Folklore* 47 (1990): 133–46.

Friedman, Monroe. *Consumer Boycotts: Effecting Change through the Marketplace and the Media.* New York: Routledge, 1999.

Gabler, Neal. *An Empire of Their Own: How the Jews Invented Hollywood.* New York: Crown, 1988.

Gomery, Douglas. "Thinking about Motion Picture Exhibition." *Velvet Light Trap* 25 (1990): 4–11.

Greeley, Andrew. "Blasphemy or Artistry?" *New York Times,* August 14, 1988, sec. 2.

Green, S. J. D. "Beyond *The Satanic Verses:* Conservative Religion & the Liberal Society." *Encounter* 74 (1990): 12–20.

Harding, Susan. "Representing Fundamentalism: The Problem of the Repugnant Cultural Other." *Social Research* 58, no. 2 (Summer 1991): 373–93.

Harmetz, Aljean. "How Studio Maneuvered 'Temptation' into a Hit." *New York Times,* August 24, 1988, sec. 3.

Himmelstein, Jerome L. *To the Right: The Transformation of American Conservatism.* Berkeley: University of California Press, 1990.

Hodenfield, Chris. "'You've Got to Love Something Enough to Kill It': The Art of Noncompromise." *American Film,* March 1989, 46–51.

Hoskins, Colin, Stuart McFadyen, and Adam Finn. *Global Television and Film: An Introduction to the Economics of the Business.* New York: Oxford University Press, 1997.

Hougland, James G., Jr., Dwight B. Billings, and James R. Wood. "The Instability of Support for Television Evangelists: Public Reactions during a Period of Embarrassment." *Review of Religious Research* 32 (1990): 56–64.

Hunter, James Davison. *Culture Wars.* New York: Basic Books, 1991.

Hyde, Henry. "The Culture War." *National Review* 42, no. 8 (1990): 25–27.

Iannone, Carol. "From 'Lolita' to 'Piss Christ.'" *Commentary* 89, no. 1 (1990): 52–54.

———. "The Last Temptation Reconsidered." *First Things,* February 1996, 50–54.

Jackson, Kevin, ed. *Schrader on Schrader.* London: Faber and Faber, 1990.

James, Caryn. "Paul Schrader Talks of 'Last Temptation' and His New Film." *New York Times,* September 1, 1988, sec. 3.

Jarvie, Ian. "Suppressing Controversial Films: From *Objective Burma* to Monty Python's *Life of Brian.*" In *Current Research in Film: Audiences, Economics, and Law.* Vol. 1, edited by Bruce A. Austin. Norwood, N.J.: Ablex, 1985.

Jasper, James M. *The Art of Moral Protest.* Chicago: University of Chicago Press, 1997.

Jenkins, Steve. "From the Pit of Hell." *Monthly Film Bulletin* 55 (1988): 352–53.

Kaplan, J. "The Outsider on the Margins." *New York,* March 4, 1996, 32–40, 101.

Kazantzakis, Helen. *Nikos Kazantzakis: A Biography Based on His Letters.* Translated by Amy Mims. New York: Simon and Schuster, 1968.

Kazantzakis, Nikos. *The Last Temptation of Christ.* Translated by Peter A. Bien. New York: Simon and Schuster, 1960.

Kellman, Steven G. "'The Last Temptation of Christ': Blaming the Jews." *Midstream,* December 1988, 33–37.

Kelly, Mary Pat. "Jesus Gets the Beat: An Interview with Martin Scorsese." *Commonweal,* September 9, 1988, 467–69.

———. *Martin Scorsese: A Journey.* New York: Thunder's Mouth Press, 1991.

———. "Scorsese: Last Visitation." *Commonweal,* October 7, 1988, 518–19.

Keyser, Lee. *Martin Scorsese.* New York: Twayne Publishers, 1992.

Lally, Kevin. "Producer De Fina Discusses *Last Temptation* Controversy." *Film Journal,* September/October 1988, 10, 134.

Lampert, Ellen. "The Last Temptation of Christ." *Theatre Crafts,* October 1988, 66–69, 78–80.

Latham, Aaron. "MCA's Bad Cop Shoots from the Hip." *Manhattan, Inc.,* July 1988, 71–83.

Lawton, David. *Blasphemy.* Philadelphia: University of Pennsylvania Press, 1993.

Lefebvre, M. "The Scriptures through Postmodern Strategies: Challenging History." *Canadian Journal of Political and Social Theory* 14, nos. 1–3 (1990): 219–29.

Leo, John. "A Holy Furor." *Time,* August 15, 1988, 34–36.

Levine, Art. "Raging Messiah: A Sneak Preview of Scorsese's New Bio-Pic." *Mother Jones,* August 1983, 36–42.

Levitt, Morton P. *The Cretan Glance: The World and Art of Nikos Kazantzakis.* Columbus: Ohio State University Press, 1980.

Levy, Leonard W. *Blasphemy: Verbal Offense against the Sacred, from Moses to Salman Rushdie.* New York: Alfred A. Knopf, 1993.

Lopate, Phillip. "Fourteen Koans by a Levite on Scorsese's 'The Last Temptation of Christ.'" *Tikkun,* November–December 1988, 74–78.

Lourdeaux, Lee. *Italian and Irish Filmmakers in America: Ford, Capra, Coppola, and Scorsese.* Philadelphia: Temple University Press, 1990.

Loverock, Patricia. "'The Day After': How to Promote a Nuclear War." *On Location,* March 1984, 170–71.

Lutzer, Erwin W. *"The Last Temptation of Christ": Its Deception and What You Should Do about It.* Chicago: Moody Press, 1988.

Lyons, Charles. *The New Censors: Movies and the Culture Wars.* Philadelphia: Temple University Press, 1997.

Mahar, Ted. "In the Eye of the Storm of 'Temptation.'" *Sunday Oregonian* (Portland), August 28, 1988, B1.

Martin, William. *With God on Our Side: The Rise of the Religious Right in America.* New York: Broadway, 1996.

Marty, Martin E. "Literalism vs. Everything Else." *Bible Review* 10, no. 2 (1994): 38–43, 50.

Masters, Kim. "The Careful Strategy of 'Temptation.'" *Washington Post,* August 10, 1988, C1, 16.

McGirr, Lisa. *Suburban Warriors: The Origins of the New American Right.* Princeton, N.J.: Princeton University Press, 2001.

Medved, Michael. *Hollywood vs. America.* New York: HarperCollins, 1992.

Meredith, Lawrence. "The Gospel according to Kazantzakis: How Close Did Scorsese Come?" *Christian Century,* September 14–21, 1988, 799–802.

Middleton, Darren J. N., ed. *Scandalizing Jesus? Kazantzakis's "The Last Temptation of Christ" Fifty Years On.* New York: Continuum, 2005.

Montgomery, Kathryn. *Target: Prime Time: Advocacy Groups and the Struggle over Entertainment Television.* New York: Oxford University Press, 1989.

Noonan, Leo. "The Temptation of R. L. Hymers." *Jewish Journal,* July 29–August 4, 1988, 6.

O'Brien, Tom. "Jesus as Hamlet." *Commonweal,* September 23, 1988, 470–71.

O'Leary, Brian. "Local Government Regulation of the Movies: The Dallas System, 1966–93." *Journal of Film and Video* 48, no. 3 (1996): 46–57.

Oney, Steve. "The Forces That Fired 'Last Temptation.'" *Washington Post,* August 14, 1988, G1, G6.

Ostling, Richard N. "Who Was Jesus?" *Time*, August 15, 1988, 37–42.

Pareles, John. "The Ethnic 'Passion' of Peter Gabriel." *Premiere*, February 1990, 102–3.

Pelikan, Jaroslav. *Jesus through the Centuries: His Place in the History of Culture.* New York: Harper and Row, 1985.

Pizzello, Stephen. "Thelma Schoonmaker: Assembling Art with Marty." *American Cinematographer*, October 1993, 45–50.

Poland, Larry. *The Last Temptation of Hollywood.* Highland, Calif.: Mastermedia International, 1988.

Post, Robert C. "Cultural Heterogeneity and Law: Pornography, Blasphemy, and the First Amendment." *California Law Review* 76 (1988): 297–335.

Risen, James, and Judy L. Thomas. *Wrath of Angels: The American Abortion War.* New York: Basic Books, 1998.

Romanowski, William D. "John Calvin Meets the Creature from the Black Lagoon: The Dutch Reformed Church and the Movies, 1928–1966." *Christian Scholar's Review* 25 (1995): 47–62.

Roof, Wade Clark. *A Generation of Seekers: The Spiritual Journeys of the Baby Boom Generation.* New York: HarperCollins, 1993.

Rothbaum, Susan. "Between Two Worlds: Issues of Separation and Identity after Leaving a Religious Community." In *Falling from the Faith: Causes and Consequences of Religious Apostasy*, edited by David G. Bromley. Newbury Park, Calif.: Sage, 1988.

Rushdie, Salman. "Is Nothing Sacred?" *Granta* 31 (1990): 97–111.

Sarna, Jonathan D. "Jewish-Christian Hostility in the United States: Perceptions from a Jewish Point of View." In *Uncivil Religion*, edited by Robert N. Bellah and Frederick E. Greenspahn. New York: Crossroad, 1987.

Schatz, Thomas. "The New Hollywood." In *Film Theory Goes to the Movies*, edited by Jim Collins, Hilary Radner, and Ava Preachen Collins. New York: Routledge, 1993.

Schrader, Paul. "Collaborations: Paul Schrader on Martin Scorsese." *New Yorker*, March 21, 1994, 124.

Schreger, Charles. "CAA: Packaging of an Agency." *Los Angeles Times*, April 23, 1979, part IV.

Schultze, Quentin J. "The Invisible Medium: Evangelical Radio." In *American Evangelicals and the Mass Media*, edited by Quentin J. Schultze. Grand Rapids, Mich.: Academic Books/Zondervan, 1990.

Schwartz, Tony. "Hollywood's Hottest Stars." *New York*, July 30, 1984, 25–33.

Scorsese, Martin. "In the Streets." In *Once a Catholic*, edited by Peter Occhiogrosso. Boston: Houghton Mifflin, 1987.

Smith, T. W. "Trends: Religious Beliefs and Behaviors and the Televangelist Scandals of 1987–1988." *Public Opinion Quarterly* 56 (1992): 360–80.

Stabiner, Karen. "Barefoot Boy with Cheek." *Gentlemen's Quarterly*, March 1988, 281–83, 354–55.

Stallybrass, Peter, and Allon White. *The Politics and Poetics of Transgression.* Ithaca, N.Y.: Cornell University Press, 1986.

Stewart, John. *God in the Chaos.* Eugene, Ore.: Harvest House Publishers, 1991.

Tatum, W. Barnes. *Jesus at the Movies: A Guide to the First Hundred Years.* Santa Rosa, Calif.: Polebridge Press, 1997.

Thompson, David, and Ian Christie. *Scorsese on Scorsese.* London: Faber and Faber, 1989.

Trainor, Richard. "Let's Get Vertical." *American Film* 13, no. 8 (1988): 43–48.

Victor, Jeffrey S. *Satanic Panic.* Chicago: Open Court, 1993.

Wales, Ken. "Can Anything Good Come Out of Hollywood?" *Christianity Today,* September 21, 1984, 19–25.

Wilcox, Clyde. "Premillennialists at the Millennium: Some Reflections on the Christian Right in the Twenty-first Century." *Sociology of Religion* 55 (1994): 243–61.

Wildmon, Donald, and Randall Nulton. *Don Wildmon: The Man the Networks Love to Hate.* Wilmore, Ky.: Bristol Books, 1989.

Williams, Mildred Jane. "An Analysis of the Causes and Effects of the Controversy and Censorship of Nikos Kazantzakis' *The Last Temptation of Christ* in Selected Public Libraries Cited in Periodical Literature on the Subject." M.A. thesis, University of North Carolina at Chapel Hill, 1967.

Wills, Garry. "Jesus in the Mean Streets." *New York Review of Books,* October 13, 1988, 8–10.

———. *Under God: Religion and American Politics.* New York: Simon and Schuster, 1990.

Wyatt, Justin. *High Concept: Movies and Marketing in Hollywood.* Austin: University of Texas Press, 1994.

York, Frank. "'The Last Temptation' Is a Box Office Flop." *Focus on the Family Citizen,* November 1988, 1–3.

Ziolkowski, Theodore. *Fictional Transfigurations of Jesus.* Princeton, N.J.: Princeton University Press, 1972.

Author Interviews

Ankerberg, John	December 8, 1998
Armstrong, Roger	December 15, 1997
Austin, Ron	July 21, 1999
Avnet, Jon	June 9, 1998
Baehr, Ted	June 28, 1995
Baran, Josh	April 5, 1996; May 10, 1996; June 24, 1997
Barr, Steve	July 25, 2000
Bergstrom, Charles	February 18, 1999
Biskind, Peter	May 15, 1998
Boxer, Noel	June 18, 1997
Buhler, Rich	November 22, 1996
Burnett, Iris	June 26, 1998
Busch, Anita	May 14, 2000
Cocks, Jay	September 14, 2000
Corman, Cis	March 19, 2003
Dafoe, Willem	August 15, 2001
Daniel, Sean	June 10, 1996; November 26, 1996
Dart, John	February 17, 1996
De Fina, Barbara	November 20, 1997; January 9, 1998
Fore, William	April 12, 1999
Fredrick, Jim	February 2, 1999
Gill, Mark	August 20, 1998
Gumpel, Glen	October 5, 1998
Hershey, Barbara	May 29, 2001
Johnson, Rob	August 26, 1998
Katz, Perry	April 10, 2000; June 14, 2000
Katzenberg, Jeffrey	November 24, 2002
Kelly, Mary Pat	July 10, 2000
Kirkpatrick, David	April 12, 2000
Kornblit, Simon	April 18, 1996
Leach, Catherine	August 27, 1998
Levenson, Scott	April 21, 1998
Livingstone, Craig	June 8, 1998
Lond, Harley	May 1997
Luck, Coleman	February 20, 1996
Lyne, Susan	February 10, 1998
Mound, Fred	July 30, 1997
Murphy, A. D.	November 18, 1996

Oney, Steve   August 9, 1998
Ostling, Richard A.   July 15, 1997
Ovitz, Michael   January 18, 2002
Poland, Larry   February 20, 1996; November 15, 1996
Pollock, Tom   May 15, 1997; June 21, 1997; June 20, 2000
Polwrek, John   September 24, 1998
Quinn, Laura   July 1, 1997
Rabinowitz, Steve   June 23, 1997
Reffe, Paige   August 15, 1998
Reidy, Joe   June 17, 2004
Rothbaum, Susan   May 19, 1997; June 18, 1997
Sameth, David   October 1, 1996
Schall, David   February 1996
Schepper, Robin   July 15, 1997
Schoonmaker, Thelma   May 25, 2002
Schrader, Paul   July 1, 2000
Scorsese, Martin   December 18, 2001
Sheinberg, Sidney J.   April 10, 2000; May 19, 2000
Sheldon, Louis   May 16, 1997
Sites, Kevin   March 23, 1997
Slusser, Dan   September 20, 2001
Soady, William   February 16, 1996
Stanton, Harry Dean   April 23, 2001
Stevenson, Elizabeth   February 15, 1998
Stewart, John   November 25, 1996
Sweeney, Charles   June 27, 2000
Thompson, Robert   February 2, 1999
Toohey, John   June 4, 1997; June 6, 1997
Ufland, Harry   April 23, 2001
Valenti, Jack   January 27, 1997
Van Slyke, Sally   March 12, 1996; June 12, 1996; June 17, 1997;
                                     June 23, 1997

Wales, Ken   February 19, 1996
Walto, Dennis   January 6, 1998
Warn, Charles   April 10, 2000
Weiss, Shana   March 4, 1998
Wilde, Allegra   April 28, 1998
Williams-Jones, Michael   August 7, 1997
Winkler, Irwin   August 21, 2003

Index

Page numbers in *italics* refer to illustrations or material contained in their captions.